HANDBOOK OF PERCEPTION

Volume VIII

Perceptual Coding

ADVISORY EDITORIAL BOARD

This is Volume VIII of

HANDBOOK OF PERCEPTION

EDITORS: *Edward C. Carterette and Morton P. Friedman*

Contents of the other books in this series appear at the end of this volume.

HANDBOOK OF PERCEPTION

VOLUME VIII

Perceptual Coding

EDITED BY

Edward C. Carterette and Morton P. Friedman

Department of Psychology
University of California, Los Angeles
Los Angeles, California

ACADEMIC PRESS   New York   San Francisco   London   1978

A Subsidiary of Harcourt Brace Jovanovich, Publishers

ACADEMIC PRESS, INC.
111 Fifth Avenue, New York, New York 10003

United Kingdom Edition published by
ACADEMIC PRESS, INC. (LONDON) LTD.
24/28 Oval Road, London NW1   7DX

Library of Congress Cataloging in Publication Data

Main entry under title:

Perceptual coding.

    (Handbook of perception ; v. 8)
    Bibliography: p.
    Includes index.
    1. Perception. 2. Coding theory. 3. Human
information processing. I. Carterette, Edward C.
II. Friedman, Morton P.
BF311.P362   153.7   78–16753
ISBN 0–12–161908–7 (v. 8)

PRINTED IN THE UNITED STATES OF AMERICA

CONTENTS

PART I. REPRESENTATIONS OF OBJECTS AND VISUAL SPACE

Chapter 1. A Different Kind of Vision: The Compound Eye

G. Adrian Horridge

Chapter 2. Perceptual Development: Object and Space

T. G. R. Bower

Chapter 3.   Transformations on Representations of Objects in Space

Lynn A. Cooper and Roger N. Shepard

Chapter 4.   Perception of Motion

Myron L. Braunstein

Chapter 5.   Color in Contour and Object Perception

Robert M. Boynton

PART II.   REPRESENTATION OF TEMPORAL, AUDITORY, AND HAPTIC SPACES

Chapter 6.   Time and Rhythm Perception

Paul Fraisse

Chapter 7.   Auditory Patterns: Studies in
             the Perception of Structure

   Mari Riess Jones

Chapter 8.   Haptics

   John M. Kennedy

PART III.   INTERACTING PERCEPTUAL SYSTEMS

Chapter 9.   Multimodal Perception

   Lawrence E. Marks

PART IV.   PERCEPTUAL MEMORY CODES

Chapter 10. Sensory Memory Systems

   Robert G. Crowder

Chapter 11. The Relationship between Verbal and Perceptual Codes

Allan Paivio

LIST OF CONTRIBUTORS

Numbers in parentheses indicate the pages on which the authors' contributions begin.

T. G. R. Bower (83), Department of Psychology, University of Edinburgh, Edinburgh, Scotland

Robert M. Boynton (173), Department of Psychology, University of California, San Diego, La Jolla, California 92093

Myron L. Braunstein (147), School of Social Sciences, University of California, Irvine, Irvine, California 92717

Lynn A. Cooper (105), Cornell University, Ithaca, New York 14850

Robert G. Crowder (343), Department of Psychology, Yale University, New Haven, Connecticut 06519

Paul Fraisse (203), Laboratoire de Psychologie Experimentale, Université René Descartes, Paris, France

G. Adrian Horridge (3), Department of Neurobiology, Research School of Biological Sciences, The Australian National University, Canberra, Australia

Mari Riess Jones (255), Department of Psychology, Ohio State University, Columbus, Ohio 43210

John M. Kennedy (289), Scarborough College, University of Toronto, West Hill, Ontario, Canada

Lawrence E. Marks (321), John B. Pierce Foundation Laboratory and Yale University, New Haven, Connecticut 06519

ALLAN PAIVIO (375), Department of Psychology, University of Western Ontario, London, Ontario, Canada N6A 5C2

ROGER N. SHEPARD (105), Department of Psychology, Stanford University, Stanford, California 94305

FOREWORD

The problem of perception is one of understanding the way in which the organism transforms, organizes, and structures information arising from the world in sense data or memory. With this definition of perception in mind, the aims of this treatise are to bring together essential aspects of the very large, diverse, and widely scattered literature on human perception and to give a précis of the state of knowledge in every area of perception. It is aimed at the psychologist in particular and at the natural scientist in general. A given topic is covered in a comprehensive survey in which fundamental facts and concepts are presented and important leads to journals and monographs of the specialized literature are provided. Perception is considered in its broadest sense. Therefore, the work will treat a wide range of experimental and theoretical work.

This ten-volume treatise is divided into two sections. Section One deals with the fundamentals of perceptual systems. It is comprised of six volumes covering (1) historical and philosophical roots of perception, (2) psychophysical judgment and measurement, (3) the biology of perceptual systems, (4) hearing, (5) seeing, and (6) which is divided into two books (A) tasting and smelling and (B) feeling and hurting.

Section Two, comprising four volumes, covers the perceiving organism, taking up the wider view and generally ignoring specialty boundaries. The major areas include (7) language and speech, (8) perceptual coding of space, time, and objects, including sensory memory systems and the relations between verbal and perceptual codes, (9) perceptual processing mechanisms, such as attention, search, selection, pattern recognition, and perceptual learning, (10) perceptual ecology, which considers the perceiving organism in cultural context, and so includes aesthetics, art, music, architecture, cinema, gastronomy, perfumery, and the special perceptual worlds of the blind and of the deaf.

The "Handbook of Perception" should serve as a basic source and reference work for all in the arts or sciences, indeed for all who are interested in human perception.

EDWARD C. CARTERETTE
MORTON P. FRIEDMAN

PREFACE

Any theory is built from what has excited the experimenter, but the nervous system works on what excites the neurons of the next higher order, says G. Adrian Horridge in Chapter 1 where he systematically lays out the details of the compound eye, a different kind of vision.

Insects *do* avoid objects; take off and land successfully; find flowers, prey, and mates; and chase each other. But even the idea that insects see is derived from our knowledge of our own introspective world. And *"to think of a mosaic vision with each ommatidium conveying one coarse grain to a picture of the visual world made up of dots of overlapping fuzzy patches is a complete misrepresentation of the situation* [p. 51]." What has been learned about the seeing of insects from pattern perception, receptor output and projections to higher levels (e.g., lamina ganglion cells) is that the main signal is the moving contrast. "If relative movement across the eye is essential, it follows that *the essential pattern of excitation is in the timing*, as well as in the spatial projection across the optic lobe."

Horridge had particularly wanted his synthesis of the insect visual system to appear in *The Handbook* for two reasons. One was that students of human perception would profit from knowledge of the anatomical, physiological, and behavioral features of the insect visual system and from the analysis of the insect visual mechanisms. The summary of this knowledge is admirably and critically presented. Another reason was to document his belief that it no longer suffices to frame an explanatory theory of the mechanisms of insect vision on the class of data that gave rise to it. A theory must be based on the (four) classes of data arising from the basic methods: inferences from anatomy, electrophysiology of single neurons, accounts of whole-animal behavior, and mathematical analysis of models. Furthermore, Horridge believes that there has been successful analysis only where the system has been cut down to an extremely simple form, and only the direct attack will allow us to see neurons in action or to discover their relevant interactions. What is the direct attack? "It is *the multichannel analysis, step by step through the causative chain of named neurons while the relevant behavior is going on* [p. 78]." If there is a question of whether this method is a practical possibility for analyzing how the bee sees (p. 79), what of analyzing how we see?

The two original, opponent, classic theories of perceptual development are *nativism* and *empiricism*. As Bower reminds us in his Chapter 2, *Perceptual Development: Object and Space*, the first theory in its extreme form gives to a perceptually naïve organism *all* the perceptual capacities of a mature, experienced organism. And again in extreme form empiricism gives to a perceptually naïve organism *none* of the perceptual capacities of a mature experienced organism. It is easy to test these two theories. "They are still influential and indeed, despite their patent absurdity, have adherents even today."

Bower's aim is to select out, from the great variety of problems that have been studied on neonates, the problems of the perceptual constancies and of intersensory coordination in perceptual development. In these problems the oppositions and methods of the two theories are seen. By drawing on recent work on constancies, Bower shows that neither theory is consistent with the data. Just where nativism and empiricism differ most sharply, in intersensory coordination, the available research validates neither. As a third alternative, Bower proposes the *differentiation* theory of perceptual development, "that in development the output of perceptual structures becomes more and more precise, more and more detailed, more and more specific [p. 91]." Bower discusses tests of the differentiation theory and looks to some findings of molecular biology for support.

A significant perceptual interpretation of a stimulus sometimes emerges only after the active completion of additional, optional mental operations of transformations or comparison, or both. This is the position taken by Cooper and Shepard in Chapter 3, *Transformations on Representations of Objects in Space*. Although the notion of such mental transformations goes at least as far back as the British empiricists, such eminences as Helmholtz and Mach discussed these notions, and Galton tackled them empirically but introspectively. The renaissance of chronometric methods in 1960 in cognitive psychology affected the study of mental operations on spatial objects only in the 1970s. The most central theoretical issues are, first, the nature of these transformations, and next, the nature of the internal representations which undergo transformation.

The basic chronometric paradigms and major findings are set out in Section II on rotational transformations while Section III deals with other spatial transformations—of size, translation, sequential rigid motions and structure. Essential recent findings are that "such spatial transformations as expansion or contraction, translation, reflection, rotation, folding, and joining of parts into wholes have been discovered to take times, when carried out purely mentally, that strongly suggest an internal simulation of the corresponding physical processes in the external world [p. 142].'' For Cooper and Shepard these mental processes have a central role not only in problem solving but in mundane perceptual acts of discriminating and identifying.

The everyday perception of motion in three dimensions is almost always combinations of the four categories of rigid motions which Braunstein reviews in Chapter 4, *Perception of Motion*. These are (*a*) rotations in depth, where the axis of rotation is perpendicular to the line of sight, as in a Ferris wheel seen from the front; (*b*) translations in depth, as when an automobile approaches or recedes; (*c*) rotations in the plane, about the line of sight, as in a Ferris wheel seen from the side; (*d*) translations in the plane. The first category is the least familiar but obviously in both (*c*) and (*d*) translation may be in many different planes at once since most objects are three dimensional. Section VI deals with a relatively new area of research, elastic or nonrigid motions such as the bending and stretching of a person walking.

This chapter will serve as an introduction to Braunstein's 1976 monograph, *Depth Perception through Motion*. For a discussion of the egocentric coordinate system and the physical and physiological cues to spatial localization, see Whitman Richards (Chapter 10, Volume 5, this *Handbook*).

Where is color? In the object, in the light, or in the observer? Color perception must be explained in terms of relations among these three domains, says Boynton in his unorthodox Chapter 5, *Color in Contour and Object Perception*. At times provocative, but always clear and scientifically impeccable, Boynton reviews the complexities of surface properties and the paradox of being able to judge the character of the illuminant even though ''we usually do not, in fact, see light.'' We see objects and surfaces that have been rendered visible by the presence of light. It is good to have color vision owing to the importance of surface color in providing information about an absolute property of a surface, a fact exploited by nature and man (Section VI). Contour perception is critical for object perception and though chromatic vision is not usually necessary for perceiving contour, purely chromatic differences can affect contour (Section VII). Boynton's important final topic, color constancy (Section IX), is complex and depends ''upon very many physiological mechanisms and psychological cues.'' An intriguing summary of the ideas of the chapter, the Epilog, consists of direct quotes from leading visual scientists of every age.

Part II of this volume takes up the representation of temporal, auditory, and haptic perception.

For Paul Fraisse (Chapter 6, *Time and Rhythm Perception*) the psychological present is nothing more than the temporal field in which a series of events is rendered present and integrated into a unique perception. The temporal field is a set of stimulations, like the spatial field. "We do not perceive duration or space as such, but only the duration or space of perceptual data, which thus enables us to define the extent of these fields." A temporal field is involved in apprehending as a unit an uninterrupted series of letters or digits, a rhythm, a melody, or a sentence. Of course, the temporal field is limited to about 7 ± 2 perceptible elements or chunks and can be distinguished from memory. The perceived present endures maximally for about 5 sec.

Thus armed, Fraisse proceeds to a thorough survey of the evidence from all the senses on the perception of succession (Section II), of duration (Section III), and of rhythm (Section IV). Fraisse provides a great wealth of experimental detail together with explanatory systems and critiques thereof.

Outstanding examples of Fraisse's temporal field are taken up by Mari Riess Jones in Chapter 9, *Auditory Patterns: Studies in the Perception of Structure.* "Patternness" is central to the problem of structure in temporal sequences such as rhythms. Musical or not, an auditory pattern moves inexorably past. There is no hope of a second look as in vision. Whether a serial structure unfolds quickly or slowly, rhythmic groupings aid the listener: "Rhythmic structures reflect a fundamental and pervasive organizing process that is largely temporal in nature." Riess Jones reviews a variety of ways in which patterns are specified as relations in serial structure, for example, ordered sets, alphabets (a musical scale is an auditory alphabet), and speech.

A quarter of a century ago Lashley's intrigue with serial ordering "suggested to him the existence of an active central mechanism flexibly moving amidst preplanned schemes." Modern theories of central preplanning are laid out by Riess Jones, in three categories, according to whether the listener associates, structures, or detects structure. Auditory pattern perception has recently become more directed by theory with some coherence of topics of research, major ones being evaluation of pattern structure, rate of presentation, and relative timing.

Haptics (Chapter 8) is *not* passive, cutaneous touch, does not take the skin to be studded within points, dots, or spots. In haptics, the skin, muscles, and joints play as an ensemble in touching, contracting, and exploring in the act of obtaining information. As Kennedy emphasizes, haptic touch is a hypothetical sensory system frankly opposed to the hypothetical sensory system of passive, cutaneous touch. The sensory ensemble of haptics embraces the use of tools and cognizing. The environment for haptics may be physical (e.g., surfaces, streams, films) or social (touching or caressing) and the scale of haptic acts can range from micromanipulation to geographical. Haptics entails more than the natural medium of superficial skin and appendages; it also includes intermediate adjuncts like fabric, rubber gloves or, to put it generally, tools. Is haptics a mode of functioning distinct from passive cutaneous touch? Neither evidence from physiological receptors and pathways, nor from perceptual and cognitive processes, clearly reveals haptics as a possible sensory system. Kennedy presents a set of interesting arguments for his conclusion that haptics is that discipline which studies the acquiring of knowledge by contact.

In any case, haptics prepares us for Part III, *Interacting Perceptual Systems* which begins with L. E. Marks's *Multimodal Perception* (Chapter 9). The usual divisions of perception into topics like seeing, hearing, tasting, smelling, and touching are really research categories. Marks feels that multimodal perception has the fundamental role in perception because the sensory systems are continuously, actively, interrelating—"one might even treat multimodal perception as coextensive with virtually all of perception." What features of the environment are perceived through more than one modality? With what precision does each sense perceive? To what extent do different senses provide equivalent data? How are multimodal data collected and integrated? What happens when different senses disagree? These questions set the topics of multimodal perception. In answering them—and there are some fascinating and surprising answers—Marks confines himself to multimodal perception of size, space, and form. (For a fuller treatment of these multimodal topics and others such as synesthesia, see Marks' monograph, *The Unity of the Senses*, 1978).

Almost everyone believes in the existence of sensory memory, that is, some kind of buffer for holding raw sensory data long enough for a perceptual act on it. An example used by Crowder in *Sensory Memory Systems* (Chapter 10) is that perceiving a stop consonant depends on resonance changes taking place over a duration of about 40 msec. The failure to distinguish sensory memory from imagery memory has led to controversies over the demonstration of sensory memory. And the tendency of some to interpret stores as *structures* rather than *functions* led them to fear proliferation of sensory stores. Taking the functional view allows one (and Crowder also) "the further advantages of drawing the general problem of memory back to the general problem of information processing."

Crowder devotes the substantial Section II to detailing the evidence for iconic (visual) and echoic (auditory) sensory storage. Felicitously, the common methods of repetition, continuation, sampling, and masking, allow a combined discussion of the issues and data in research on iconic and echoic sensory storage.

What is it like to fly a glider? Can you find the future General George C. Marshall in his class photograph at the Command and General Staff College? We translate perceptual acts into words or remembered acts into search with great ease. It is the problem of Paivio's Chapter 11, *The Relationship between Verbal and Perceptual Codes* to explicate the nature of the mental codes involved in the perceptual processing of language and real events. Whatever the form of memory substrate postulated, all theorists assume that stimulus pattern and underlying representation are compared. When words are also involved the relation of word to percept must also be represented, a complex problem upon which turn the major questions. Will a single code do? If not, how many will and how are they related? Paivio covers the major views on deep memory coding with "illustrative observations": (*a*) coding is primarily linguistic; (*b*) nonverbal perceptual processes are ascendant; (*c*) verbal–nonverbal distinctions are stored in long-term memory; and (*d*) coding is abstract and amodal.

Part I

Representations of Objects and Visual Space

Chapter 1

A DIFFERENT KIND OF VISION:
THE COMPOUND EYE

G. ADRIAN HORRIDGE

I. INTRODUCTION

In a study of what insects see, and how they do it, we can begin with a study of the receptors. From a knowledge of the way these respond to light, we can infer something of the nature of the signals that they convey. The receptor signals, however, do not tell us what the animal sees, although they indicate how vision is limited and governed by receptor performance. Conversely, we can begin with the animal's behavior when presented with a variety of visual stimuli and infer something about what features of the visual world it can see from the discriminations it is able to make. I propose to take both of these approaches, but each reveals only a partial picture. To discover fully how visual perception works, it would be necessary to carry investigation into the optic lobes by use of the microelectrode, and that is a task that has hardly been initiated.

II. SPLITTING THE VISUAL WORLD INTO ANGLE-LABELED NEURONS

First we must list the receptors and their principle features of physiological significance that limit the nature of the visual excitation that can be processed at any deeper level.

A. The Retina

1. STRUCTURE OF A TYPICAL DIURNAL INSECT RETINA

In day-flying insects, such as the bee, dragonfly, butterfly, and mantis, there are the following components of the retina (see Fig. 1). The facet of the cornea is a convex lens. Below this lies a crystalline cone that is probably optically neutral, acting like the space in a telescope, across which the lens is focused upon the tip of the rhabdom. The cone tip is surrounded by dense, screening pigment cells that absorb oblique rays. Below the cone tip the seven to nine receptor retinula cells form a long pod surrounding the central specialized rhabdom, which is the effective receptor structure (see Fig. 1). The contribution of each receptor cell to the rhabdom is called a *rhabdomere*, which is an organelle formed by microvilli, which in turn contain the visual pigment. The rhabdom as a whole acts as an absorbing light guide. Its microvilli are organelles of the receptor cells, and photons absorbed in the microvilli cause graded depolarizations of the retinula cell membrane. This depolarization is carried electrotonically (without spikes) to the terminals of the receptor axons in the next neuropile, the lamina. To follow the process of reception, the above paragraph should be read in conjunction with a study of Fig. 1. For alternative reviews see Goldsmith and Bernard (1974), Horridge (1975), and Laughlin (1975b).

2. ORIGIN OF RECEPTOR VISUAL FIELDS

Light from a distant point is focused on the distal end of the rhabdom (Fig. 2). It is not focused to a point, even if the lens is perfect, but rather, on account of diffraction, to a small area called the point-spread function,

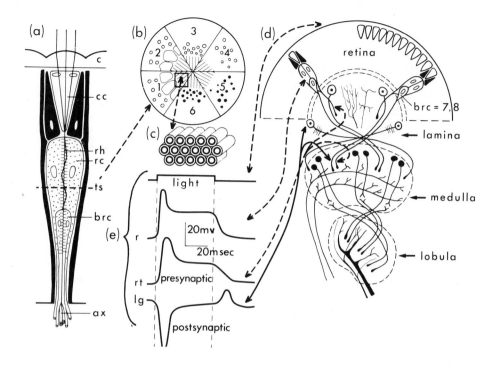

Fig. 1. Basic anatomy of the compound eye of the ant, bee, butterfly, dragonfly, and many other insects (but not flies) that fly by day. (a) Single ommatidium (visual unit). Behind the lens formed by the cornea (c) is a spacing element, the crystalline cone (cc), across which light is focused upon the end of the rhabdom (rh). The retinula cells (rc) and basal retinula cells (brc) each with an axon (ax), form the rhabdom. (b) Section across at the level indicated (ts), with six numbered retinula cells. The light-adapted cells 3 and 6 have mitochondria or pigment grains acting as a light attenuator against the central rhabdom rod. The dark-adapted cells 1, 2, 4 and 5 have the organelles scattered, or spaces of the endoplasmic reticulum against the rhabdom, so improving its light-guide properties. (c) Microtubules, which carry the visual pigment rhodopsin. (d) Schema showing the three neuropiles, lamina, medulla and lobula, behind the eye in horizontal section. Each ommatidium of the retina projects to a corresponding unit of the lamina, with two axons, numbers 7 and 8 bypassing the lamina and connecting directly with the medulla. The arrangement of the cross-over behind the lamina is such that the visual world is projected in serial order upon the medulla. This order is maintained in the medulla and to a lesser extent in the lobula. These deeper neuropiles also contain widely ramifying neurons that must have converted the angular projection into other information. (e) The response potential in the retinula cells (r), in its axon terminal showing *no spikes* (rt), and in the lamina ganglion cell (lg) hyperpolarization and no spikes.

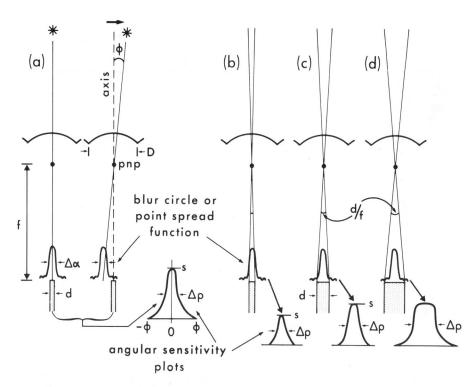

Fig. 2. Origin of visual fields of single receptors. A distant point source is focused by the corneal lens to a blur circle or point-spread function in the focal plane (of width $\Delta\alpha$ at 50% intensity). The end of the rhabdom rod (Fig. 1) lies in this plane and catches light according to its diameter (d) in relation to the blur circle. (a) In the measurement of angular sensitivity, the point source is moved across the visual axis so that the blur circle moves across the receptor. The angle ϕ is measured at the posterior nodal point (pnp) of the lens. The acceptance angle $\Delta\rho$ is defined as the width of the angular sensitivity curve at 50% of the maximum sensitivity (s). (b)–(d) The effect of receptor (rhabdom) diameter (d) on the acceptance angle ($\Delta\rho$). Approximately $\Delta\rho$ is d/f, the angle subtended by the rhabdom diameter at the pnp.

or *blur circle*. When the lens is optically perfect, the blur circle has an angular width at its 50% intensity level of

$$\Delta\alpha = \lambda/D \text{ radians,} \tag{1}$$

where λ is the wavelength and D is the diameter of the aperture. This measure of the blur circle (Snyder, 1977; Horridge, Mimura & Hardie, 1976) is more convenient than the usual measure (i.e., radius of the Airy disk to the first dark ring = 1.22 λ/D) because field widths are also given at the 50% sensitivity level. The larger the facet, the smaller is the blur circle, and therefore the better the possible resolution.

The way in which visual fields of the retinula cells are formed is illustrated in Fig. 2a. When a point source moves across the optical axis of an ommatidium, as is done in the measurement of the size of the receptor field, the blur circle moves across the end of the rhabdom. The visual axis is defined by the direction from which maximum light reaches the rhabdom, the actual amount depending on the ratio of blur-circle area to rhabdom cross-sectional area. As the point source moves away from the axis, the rhabdom cuts off a smaller and less intense segment of the blur circle. By measuring the sensitivity toward a point source over a solid angle around the axis, we plot a bell-shaped angular-sensitivity surface, which is usually drawn in two dimensions, as in Figs. 2 and 4. This is the field of the unit receptor—the retinula cell. The width of 50% sensitivity is usually called the *acceptance angle* $\Delta\rho$ (see Fig. 2). As will be mentioned again in Section IV, the property of invariance at the receptor level means that light of any intensity and angle sums on the receptor linearly, as the integral under the angular sensitivity curve.

When rhabdomeres of individual retinula cells are fused to form a common rhabdom, of which there is one in each ommatidium, these retinula cells share a common field.

A simple way of calculating $\Delta\rho$ is to take it as the angle subtended by the receptor structure, the rhabdom, in the outside world—see Fig. 2 (b–d). Then

$$\Delta\rho = d/f \text{ radians,} \tag{2}$$

where d is the diameter of the rhabdom and f is the distance from rhabdom to the *posterior nodal point* of the lens. The lens is formed by the corneal curvature, together with any other ray-bending inhomogeneity that may be present. Drawing the lines in Fig. 2 through the *posterior nodal point* means that the angle of a ray to the axis inside the eye is the same as the angle of the same ray to the axis outside the eye. This definition of the posterior nodal point avoids complications that arise from the difference in refractive index inside and outside the eye. In a large insect with thick cornea the refracting surface is often on the *inside* of the cornea.

Another important property of an eye, as of a camera, is the F value, which determines the sensitivity toward contrasting objects that are large enough to fill the fields of the individual receptors. By definition

$$F = f/D, \tag{3}$$

with f measured to the posterior nodal point. So that

$$\Delta\rho \simeq d/DF \text{ radians,} \tag{4}$$

where d is the rhabdom diameter, D is the facet aperture, and F is the F value of the lens.

Convenient values for a large diurnal insect are 2 μm for d and 29 μm for D, with F ranging from about 2 in the housefly to about 3 in dragonflies, so that $\Delta\rho$ would be 2° for the fly and 1.33° for the dragonfly. Fields measured experimentally by recording from single receptors, as shown in Fig. 3, show that this simple calculation gives reasonable values. This calculation implies that the field width at 50% sensitivity is independent of the wavelength, which is approximately true, at least for fly retinula cells. However, $\Delta\rho$ is only one arbitrary measure of the field; the shape of the whole angular-sensitivity curve does depend on wavelength, so that narrower stripes could be resolved at shorter wavelengths.

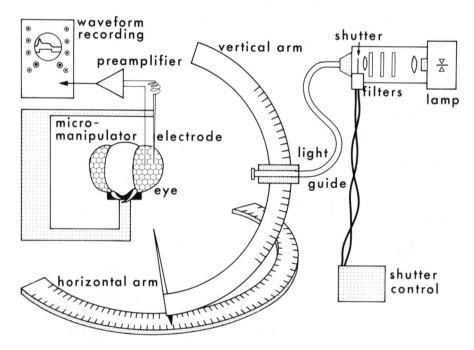

Fig. 3. The method of measuring field sizes of single retinula (receptor) cells. A small source (the end of a quartz light guide) is moved around the eye by a cardan arm that measures to an accuracy of .1° in two coordinates. Flashes of the source at each angle cause responses that are recorded by a microelectrode from a single cell and amplified. Angular sensitivity is the reciprocal of the number of photons required to give a constant response at each angle to the eye. Of all measurements on the eye, the physiological determination of $\Delta\rho$ is the most likely to be unreliable because of defocusing by mechanical deformation, which increases $\Delta\rho$ and reduces sensitivity on axis.

3. MODULATION OF LIGHT IN THE RECEPTOR

Arbitrarily, we take a regular stripe pattern of period $\Delta\theta$ radians subtended at the eye as a representative stimulus for seeing real objects. The angular-sensitivity function of width $\Delta\rho$ at 50% sensitivity, which is measured by moving a point source in front of the eye, can be converted into an expected response toward stripes of regular period $\Delta\theta$ because intensity is linearly additive. Any pattern is a sum of points of light, and for receptors—but not for optic-lobe neurons—the intensity–response curve is independent of the stimulus angle. As the stripes cross the visual field, the summed intensity falling on the single receptor rises and falls (Fig. 4).

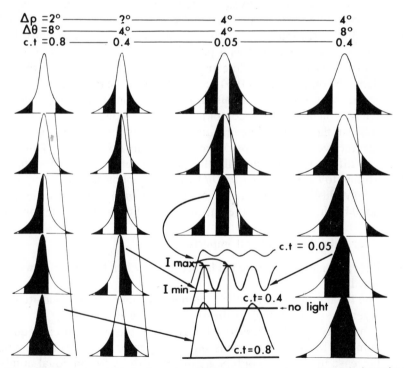

Fig. 4. The way in which the intensity of light in the receptor oscillates in intensity as stripes of different repeat periods ($\Delta\theta$) cross the visual field of acceptance angle $\Delta\rho$. The oscillation of intensity is measured as contrast transfer (ct), which is defined as $(I_{max} - I_{min})$ / $(I_{max} + I_{min})$ where I_{max} and I_{min} are the maximum and minimum intensities as shown in the central inset. The oscillation in intensity is *the only stimulus the receptors receive*. The contrast transfer can be calculated from Eq. (6). When $\Delta\theta = \Delta\rho$ (center column) the contrast transfer falls below .04, which, in bright light, is in the region of the behavioral threshold.

When a black stripe is on axis, the intensity is at a minimum; with a white stripe on axis it is at a maximum. The fluctuation of intensity at the receptor is called *intensity modulation*, and it is, in the ultimate analysis, *the only stimulus* to the visual system. The normalized or relative contrast transfer—*ct*(norm) is:—

$$ct(\text{norm}) = (I_{\max} - I_{\min})/(I_{\max} + I_{\min}), \tag{5}$$

where I is the light at the receptor. If we assume that the angular sensitivity curve is a Gaussian, a useful approximation for *ct*(Norm) from Götz (1964) is:—

$$ct(\text{norm}) = \exp\left[- \frac{\pi^2}{4 \log_e 2} \left(\frac{\Delta\rho}{\Delta\theta}\right)^2 \right] = \exp -3.56 \frac{\Delta\rho^2}{\Delta\theta^2} \tag{6}$$

This equation, however, gives only the relative modulation as a fraction of the maximum modulation that could be caused by stripes sufficiently broad to fill the receptor fields. The actual stimulus to the receptor is an absolute intensity measured as a photon flux.

The sensitivity of a device like an eye or a camera depends on the area of the lens and on the area of the receptor or sensitive particles in the film. For a point source on axis, focused on a receptor of sufficient size, the effective photon flux at the receptor is $I_\rho = I\varepsilon\pi D^2/4$ photons sec^{-1}, where I is the photon flux (parallel beam) μm^{-2}sec^{-1}, ε is the fraction of photons that are effective (say 90% at peak wavelength) and D is the facet diameter.

For a diffuse source that fills the field the effective photon flux is proportional to $I_0 D^2 (d/f)^2 = I_0 d^2 (D/f)^2$, where I_0 photons μm^{-2}sec^{-1} is the diffuse light flux, D is the facet diameter and (d/f) radians is the angle subtended by the receptor in the outside world through the posterior nodal point.

This formula shows several important points:

1. Receptors, and therefore fields, are larger when they have to work in dim light.
2. The focal ratio is f/D, or the F number of a camera, and sensitivity is inversely proportional to the square of the F number.
3. Sensitivity is not necessarily the same in two eyes with an equal F number, because it depends on the receptor cross-sectional area. Increase in eye size confers greater sensitivity for an equal number of receptors.

When the rhabdom is small compared to the width of the blur circle (d/f comparable to $\Delta\alpha$ in Fig. 2) we have a further reduced sensitivity, because not all the light in the blur circle is caught by the receptor. Eyes with high resolution are thus reduced in sensitivity. In the more usual case, d/f is greater than $\Delta\alpha$, so that all the light in the blur circle is caught. In that case the field width $\Delta\rho$ is equal to (d/f) radians, because the width of the blur circle is insignificant.

For the absolute photon flux caused by stripes that fill the field we can now write, after Snyder (1977):

$$I_{max} = .89 \, I_0 \varepsilon D^2 \, \Delta\rho^2 \text{ photons sec}^{-1}, \tag{7}$$

and for any (sinusoidal) stripe period

$$I_{max} = .89 \, I_0 \varepsilon D^2 \, \Delta\rho^2 \exp -3.56 \left(\frac{\Delta\rho}{\Delta\theta}\right)^2 \text{ photons sec}^{-1}. \tag{8}$$

Equations (6)–(8) are strictly for sinusoidal intensity patterns of period $\Delta\theta$, but are approximate for square-edged patterns *near threshold*. From the values of Eq. (8), plotted in Fig. 5, we see quantitatively that for a given facet diameter, large receptors with large fields ($\Delta\rho$ large) do not see such fine stripes as narrow receptors with small fields, but that *large receptors get a stronger absolute stimulus from large stripes*. For any eye, curves like those in Fig. 5 define the relation between object size, receptor-field size, and the actual intensity received at the receptor. The logarithmic plot is helpful, because for *slow movements* across the eye the electrical response follows the light intensity by the relation known as the $V/\log_{10} I$ curve, which is the plot of receptor potential against $\log_{10}$ of the intensity for the static case. For fast movements, the temporal response of the receptor causes responses to high spatial frequencies (fine stripes) to be further attentuated. The main point is that each size of receptor field sees only a limited range of widths. At the upper limit of spatial frequency, stripes that are too narrow are not seen when the modulation does not exceed the noise level at the average light level: Stripes that are too wide saturate by overfilling the field. The possibility of summation of receptor fields becomes important when the animal must see in light that is so dim that even large objects can only be seen by integrating the light emitted over their whole area.

4. Photon Noise

Long ago Wolf (1933) showed, using response to the movement of stripes, that the intensity discrimination of the bee, $\Delta I/I$, which is closely related to $(I_{max} - I_{min})/(I_{max} + I_{min})$, is dependent upon the illumination I. Values of $\Delta I/I$ ranged from 5 at low light levels to .2 in the brightest light he used, and presumably would have been lower in sunlight. The interesting point is that the probable error of $\Delta I/I$ in large numbers of experiments varied with I in the same way (i.e., greater errors at low light levels). The results can be attributed to the uncertainty at lower light levels caused by

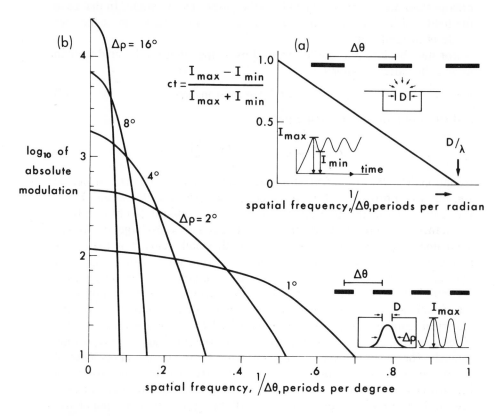

Fig. 5. The modulation of light in a receptor caused by stripes of various widths which pass in front of it. (a) An optical black box accepting light from a 180° field yields a contrast transfer ct (norm) that is almost a straight line relation to the spatial frequency (reciprocal of stripe period $\Delta\theta$). There is an absolute cutoff at D/λ stripe periods per radian. (b) Absolute modulation (I_{max} when $I_{min} = 0$) as a function of spatial frequency for five values of $\Delta\rho$ for a receptor with a Gaussian field (which is not only determined by the aperture D). The curves are calculated from Eq. (8). At increasing spatial frequency (narrower stripes) the response falls off more quickly for receptors with larger fields (larger $\Delta\rho$). At low spatial frequencies, receptors with larger fields are more sensitive (by a factor $\Delta\rho^2$). At high spatial frequencies the receptors with small fields are the only ones that respond at all, and they are relatively insensitive for any width of stripe. A receptor of given value of $\Delta\rho$ performs better than other receptors when $\Delta\rho = \Delta\theta/2$ (i.e., when the field width at 50% is equal to the width of a single stripe).

the random arrival of photons, and they show that a threshold value of ct (norm) must be reached for contrasts to be discriminated against the background of photon noise.

The ratio of the signal to the noise, therefore, not the signal by itself, is the important factor that determines threshold. The origin of the noise in the visual signal is only partially attributable to the random arrival times of the photons. In addition, each photon does not cause an equal response, as observed in the variable heights of the bumps, or miniature potentials, caused by individual photons. One further source of noise— variable numbers of bumps from each captured photon—is not an item, but there is certainly a reduction in the effectiveness of each additional photon as the average photon flux increases (called *light adaptation*) as a result of absorption by screening pigment and reduction in receptor sensitivity.

In so far as these effects are random (at low intensities), a measure of the uncertainty in the signal is proportional to the square root of the intensity. For the purely Poisson process of the random arrival of photons, excluding the other sources of noise, the noise is $N^{\frac{1}{2}}$, where N is the signal measured in numbers of photons. The ratio of signal to noise is therefore $MN/N^{\frac{1}{2}}, = MN^{\frac{1}{2}}$, where M is the modulation and N is the photon flux.

To ensure that the signal is seen above the noise with a bearable proportion of false alarms, we can, in a model, set the maximum absolute modulation from Eq. (8) equal to the noise derived from $N^{\frac{1}{2}}$ and so derive relations between field size and facet diameter for compound appositional eyes that function at different intensity levels (Snyder, 1977). This argument can be continued after the concept of the density of sampling stations, as set by the interommatidial angle, has been introduced.

5. MEASURING INTEROMMATIDIAL ANGLE $\Delta\phi$ BY THE PSEUDOPUPIL

When one examines the eye of some insects with an instrument that accepts only a narrow beam of light, like the human eye (but unlike a typical microscope), one sees a tiny black spot, which is called the *pseudopupil*. The center of the pseudopupil is, in fact, the place on the compound eye that is looking at the observer, and it is the *indicator of the optical axis* (see Fig. 6).

To make a map of the optical axes of the eye, the head of the insect must be fixed so that the pseudopupil can be photographed with a narrow-aperture lens (see Fig. 7). Some dust is blown on the eye to mark individual facets for identification. Pictures are taken at intervals of 10° across the area of the eye. From the set of pictures the facet diameters and

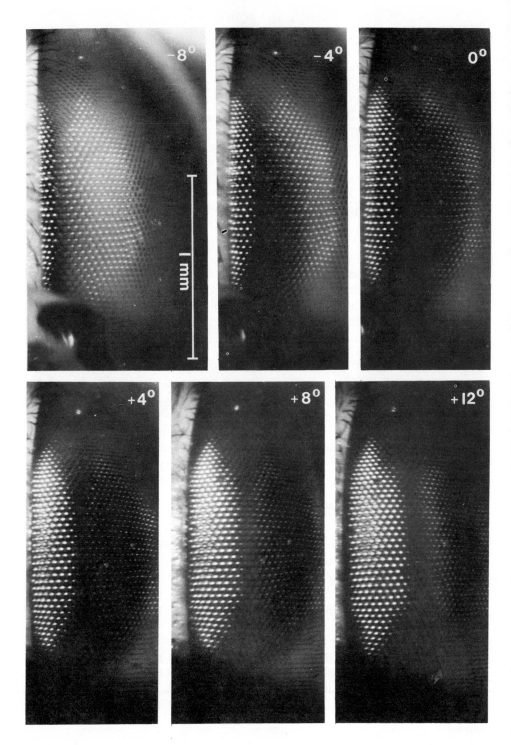

the apparent distances moved by the center of the pseudopupil are measured. From this primary data the radius to the optical center (see Fig. 11) and the interommatidial angle can be calculated for any point on the eye. There is a further problem in making a map of a curved eye on a flat surface. A single photograph naturally gives a projection that is technically orthographic. When a series of photographs along a line are brought together, the simplest solution to the problem is one in which the eye is "rolled out" along the line to make an orthographic projection on the paper on either side of the line (Fig. 8).

B. Compromises in the Design of Compound Eyes

1. SENSITIVITY VERSUS RESOLUTION

At this stage we can consider the first compromise upon which natural selection acts. The compromise lies in the relation between the diameter of the blur circle at 50% intensity, $\Delta\alpha$, and the diameter of the rhabdom on which it falls. The ratio selected depends upon function. When the rhabdom end is very narrow, as shown in Fig. 2(b), it catches only a small fraction of the total light in the blur circle and retains all of the potential resolution—$\Delta\rho$ *cannot be less than* $\Delta\alpha$. When the rhabdom is wide, as shown in Fig. 2(d) it catches all the light from a point source, but at the expense of resolution. The angle subtended by the rhabdom end in the outside world is d/f radians. A compromise for *good resolution is when* $\Delta\alpha = d/f$, as in Fig. 2(b). Sensitivity to a point source on axis is then 50% of the maximum possible and $\Delta\rho$ is nearly $\Delta\alpha$. A different compromise that gives sensitivity of 95% is when $2\Delta\alpha = d/f$ as in Fig. 2(c). The resulting angular-sensitivity function (receptor field) is then twice as wide as the point-spread function (blur circle). Taking into account Eq. (2),

$$\Delta\rho_s \text{ for sensitivity} > \text{resolution}, \qquad 2\Delta\alpha = \Delta\rho_s \qquad (9)$$

and

$$\Delta\rho_r \text{ for resolution} > \text{sensitivity}, \qquad \Delta\alpha = \Delta\rho_r. \qquad (9a)$$

Many insect eyes fall in the range $\Delta\alpha > \Delta\rho > 2\Delta\alpha$ in my experience, but some that function in dim light must, at all costs, increase the field size still further to catch sufficient photons to see at all, even though this means that they see only large objects. The only ways to achieve this in an

Fig. 6. The movement of the pseudopupil in relation to marks on the cornea as the eye is rotated relative to the narrow aperture camera. This is a series from the front of the eye of the wasp *Bembix*, taken at intervals of 4° in the horizontal plane. The center of the fovea at 0° looks straight ahead. Scale = 1 mm.

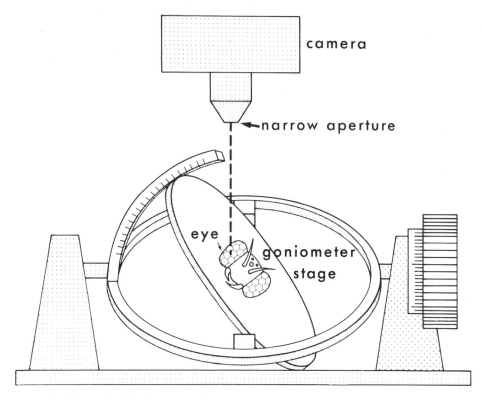

Fig. 7. Insect head fixed upon a goniometer stage so that it can be tilted at any (calibrated) angle under a narrow aperture lens for photomicrography. The interommatidial angle is the angle in the appropriate plane through which the eye must be moved to cause a movement *of the center of the pseudopupil* by one facet. The eye radius is calculated from this angle and the interfacet separation.

appositional eye are to increase the eye size or the receptor diameter still further, as in Fig. 2(d), or to sum the responses of groups of receptors. As shown in Fig. 5(b), where $\Delta\theta = 2\Delta\rho$, in looking for a slightly contrasting object in dim light, the performance is optimum *when the field size of the receptors matches the angular size of the object that is sought.* Larger objects give out more photons, which can be collected in dim light by receptors with larger fields. For evidence of summation of receptor effects at a deeper level, see Fig. 22.

2. THRESHOLD MODULATION

Next we must consider the measured threshold modulation that is required to give a response at all. In the case of insect eyes, one can

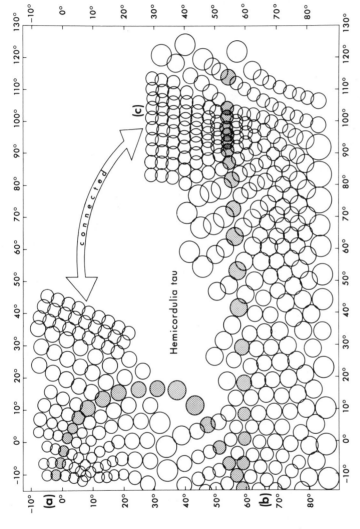

Fig. 8. A map showing the directions of seeing and the best possible resolving power of each ommatidium of the dragonfly *Hemicordulia tau* in angular coordinates. Every fifth facet is mapped. The lines of circles represent the rows of facets. The diameter of each circle is five times the width of the narrowest possible field of view ($5\Delta\alpha$). The distance between centers is five times the interommatidial angle. Therefore the relation between the circles shows the ratio of the resolving power behind each facet to the resolution of the group of facets as a whole in that part of the eye. The separation or overlap of the circles shows the local value of the eye parameter in that $5\Delta\theta/5\Delta\alpha = D\Delta\theta/\Delta\alpha = D\Delta\theta/\lambda$. This is a left eye seen from the front (0°) and side (90°). The zero of the vertical axis is taken as the center of the upwardly looking acute zone. The shaded circles emphasize the differences along two rows of facets that start at the forward-looking acute zone.

choose from a wide range of experimentally determined thresholds that depend on species, ambient intensity, and nature of the test. With regard to an upper limit for bees there are the careful measurements by Labhart (1974) on the ability of the bee to *discriminate* intensities, giving threshold ct(norm) in Eq. (6) of about 10% in bright light. At the other extreme there are careful measurements by Thorson (1966) on the optomotor response of the locust, which place the ct (norm) at threshold at about .3%. More accurate values of $\Delta\rho$ for the locust (Wilson, 1975) increase Thorson's values to at least 3%. Let us calculate the relation between stripe period and field size at threshold. Conveniently, from Eq. (6), *when ct $\simeq$ 2.86% the stripe width $\Delta\theta$ is equal to the field width $\Delta\rho$*. Also, from Eq. (6) and Fig. 5, on account of the $(\Delta\rho/\Delta\theta)^2$ term, the modulation decreases very rapidly with $\Delta\theta$ when $\Delta\theta$ is less than $\Delta\rho$. So we take threshold vision for stripes *in bright light* when

$$\Delta\theta = \Delta\rho. \tag{10}$$

As mentioned earlier, on account of the unpredictability of light intensity due to the random nature of photon arrivals (called *photon noise* or *shot noise*), threshold ct(norm) increases as the ambient intensity is lowered. Suppose that the modulation must be 10% to overcome noise; then the threshold $\Delta\theta$ is increased to only $1.24\Delta\rho$, and when $\Delta\theta = 2\Delta\rho$ the modulation is 41%. In brief, at constant $\Delta\rho$, the threshold $\Delta\theta$ can range up to about $4\Delta\rho$, when ct (norm) $\simeq$ 80%, so

$$\Delta\rho < \Delta\theta < 4\Delta\rho. \tag{11}$$

The reason for the upper limit is that a *single receptor*, even when pushed to the extreme in detecting modulation, gets no additional modulation from objects subtending more than about $4\Delta\rho$, because the receptor field is then filled to 80%. There is therefore extreme selection pressure for larger fields in eyes that operate in dim light, for mechanisms that widen the fields on dark adaptation, and for summation of receptor fields at a deeper level—for which there is some evidence in the fly (see Fig. 22) and strong indications in nocturnal insects.

It is important to note that the considerations of eye design relate to thresholds that may be determined experimentally when the eye is dark–adapted. In sunlight, many insect eyes have a sensitivity that is reduced by attenuation in the optics, and it is often difficult to see what compensating advantage they get in return.

3. Optimum Angle between Ommatidia

Having considered threshold modulation we can now turn to the angle between ommatidia $\Delta\phi$. Seeing by the compound eye is a *sampling of the visual world by an array of light detectors*, each with a narrow field that points in a different direction. The angle between the ommatidia $\Delta\phi$, together with the field width $\Delta\phi$, determines the amount of overlap of the fields. So that the eye as a whole can make full use of the resolution of the individual ommatidia, the separate fields must overlap. We have seen that, with high ambient light, black and white equal stripes passing slowly in front of the eye cause a threshold modulation of light in the receptors in bright light when $\Delta\theta = \Delta\rho$, from Eq. (10). Stripes that can be resolved above the diffraction limit then cause sufficient modulation. In addition, *for the whole eye to see the black and white regions separately there must be an ommatidium directed simultaneously to adjacent black and white areas*. Therefore, where parallel stripes are at right angles to the rows of ommatidia, the spacing of visual axes of the ommatidia will be governed by

$$\Delta\theta = 2\Delta\phi. \tag{12}$$

Most compound eyes, however, have a hexagonal lattice, so that, as pointed out by Snyder and Miller (1977), for stripes of any direction relative to an ommatidial row

$$\Delta\theta = 3^{\frac{1}{2}}\Delta\phi \tag{12a}$$

Actual insect eyes tend to have their facet rows oriented in particular directions in different parts of the eye, presumably in order to make the best use of their resolution in relation to the usual direction of motion of objects across the eye. Therefore, they probably obey Eq. (12) rather than (12a), but the difference is not critical.

The first criterion is that the static eye can reconstruct the pattern before the eye when the pattern can just produce the critical absolute modulation. For bright light we have $\Delta\Theta = \Delta\rho$ for the narrowest stripes visible, so that combining Eqs. (10) and (12) for 3% modulation,

$$\Delta\rho_{\text{bright}} = 2\Delta\phi. \tag{13}$$

This is represented by the overlap of visual fields illustrated in Fig. 9. On the other hand, when 40% modulation is required, from Eq. (11) we take $\Delta\theta = 2\Delta\rho$ so that

$$\Delta\rho_{\text{dim}} = \Delta\phi. \tag{13a}$$

A greater overlap than that implied by these considerations gives more receptors than necessary per unit solid angle of the eye; having less overlap implies that the ability of the eye as a whole to see a pattern is not as good as the resolution that the individual receptors allow.

In the fly type of eye, which is quite different from that in most insects,

G. ADRIAN HORRIDGE

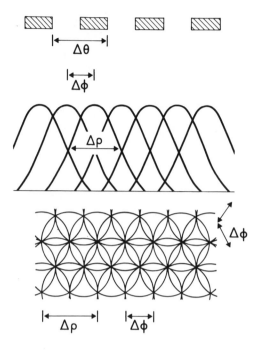

Fig. 9. The maximum overlap for adjacent receptive fields. To receive sufficient modulation from a regular pattern of period $\Delta\theta$, the width of the receptive field at 50% sensitivity must be less than $\Delta\rho = \Delta\theta$. Simultaneously, to separate the adjacent black and white areas, the receptor fields must be spaced not further apart than $\Delta\phi = \Delta\theta/2$. Closer together is unnecessarily fine; wider apart would miss some detail. In fact, my general finding from a large number of eyes is that circles of diameter $\Delta\alpha$, placed in angular coordinates over each facet, approximately *touch*, not overlap to this extent. Overlap as shown here is never found; but it is approached in insects that fly in bright sunlight.

$\Delta\phi$ is about twice $\Delta\rho$, because the receptors have to be separated to avoid optical coupling and therefore also have well-separated axes in angular terms. The fly more than makes up for this in sensitivity by having a summation from six receptors looking out in each direction (Snyder *et al.*, 1977).

An eye adapted to bright light will have a narrow rhabdom, so that $\Delta\rho = \Delta\alpha$, and from Eq. (1) $\Delta\alpha = \lambda/D$. Therefore, from Eqs. (1) and (13)

$$\Delta\rho_{\text{bright}} = \Delta\alpha = \lambda/D = 2\,\Delta\phi \text{ radians}$$

so that

$$D\Delta\phi = .25\ \mu\text{m}, \tag{14}$$

where λ is taken as .5 μm (green light).

Similarly, an eye adapted to light so dim that 40% modulation is required will have a larger receptor, so that, say, $\Delta\rho = 2\Delta\alpha$ and 95% of the photons of the blur circle fall on the receptor area. Then

$$\Delta\rho_{\text{dim}} = 2\Delta a = 2\lambda/D = \Delta\phi \text{ radians}$$

so that

$$D\Delta\phi = 1\ \mu\text{m}. \tag{14a}$$

The maximum spatial frequency resolvable by each lens is D/λ radians^{-1}, and the maximum spatial frequency seen by the system as a whole is $1/(2\Delta\phi)$ radians^{-1}. Therefore $D\Delta\phi/\lambda$ is one half of the ratio of these two resolutions. To map values of $D\Delta\phi$ for a variety of eyes and eye regions, a value has to be given to λ, which is nominally taken as .5 μm. The product $D\Delta\phi$, called the *eye paramter*, is a measure of how much the resolution of each lens is sacrificed to sensitivity by the increases of field size and receptor size that are essential if the eye is to be able to see even large objects at low light intensities.

The eye parameter $D\Delta\phi$ for any eye or eye region depends on the average intensity to which the eye is adapted. The theoretical values of $D\Delta\phi$ as a function of intensity have been worked out by Snyder (1977) and by a different theory, based on optimizing the information flow into the eye, by Snyder, Stavenga, and Laughlin (1977). For methods of mapping the eye parameter see Horridge (1977a, b).

The important practical point is that $D\Delta\phi$, being the product of facet diameter and interommatidial angle, is measurable from outside the eye by the pseudopupil measurement. In most groups of insects, the observed values of $D\Delta\phi$ are quite reasonably related as expected to the ambient intensities at which selection may be considered to act. The observations show that only compound eyes that function in very bright light approach the diffraction limit set by Eq. (1) in their design. All other compound eyes are designed as if the governing limit were the photon noise (Horridge, 1977a, b).

It is remarkable that by the above theory the values of $D\Delta\phi$ can be calculated from the effective light intensity at which the eye acts, because there is little evidence to support the basic premises leading to the criterion of simultaneous sampling in Eq. (12). It can be argued that

1. The specialized and predictable visual behavior of insects does not require universal feature detectors. In fact, exhaustive tests with bees fail to show much reconstruction of an image (see Section III).
2. All behavioral work indicates that the visual system is adapted to the detection of moving objects, not the dissection of static patterns (see Section III).
3. In motion perception, the principle signal is the rate and direction of motion of the modulation across the successive neurons, rather than the spacing of the pattern across the eye. In technical language, the phases of the Fourier components of the pattern are relatively unimportant (see Section V).
4. It is observed that somehow large numbers of ommatidia acting together initiate a response *to the movement of large objects* by as

little as .01$\Delta\phi$, and so $\Delta\rho$ is not tied rigidly to $\Delta\phi$, as is implied by Eq. (13).

5. Observations show that somehow, possibly by repeated eye tremors, integration over a long period, and sensitivity to small modulation, it is possible for many insects to see details less than $\Delta\phi$ (see Section III, Figs. 13 and 20, for example).

6. As shown by optokinetic memory (see Section IV), processing is dependent on the history of the stimulus.

These objections to the assumption behind Eq. (12) to some extent neutralize each other by the following arguments. One response requires the direction of the contrasts, another is specialized for small contrasts, another depends on small movements of large objects, and another on small relative movements of small objects. Therefore the retina must pass the maximum information for subsequent processing in different ways. The objections from the study of motion perception are irrelevant, because measuring velocity is quite different, and much simpler, than sampling a moving pattern as finely as possible in order to pick out some visual cues from it.

Insects that see in dim light, however, are quite different in that their visual fields are large and $\Delta\rho/\Delta\phi$ can reach a value of 10. The functional significance of this large ratio is quite unknown. *In addition*, some insects have other optical systems, so that more than one facet contributes to the receptor field (superposition eyes).

4. Eye Radius and Facet Size

The above quantitative treatment considers the compound eye as an array of individual receptors that all look out in different directions through the posterior nodal points of their lens systems. The larger the eye, the more light it collects, and so the more sensitive it is to some classes of objects (such as edges and points of light). Larger eyes can also have larger lenses, and therefore better resolution by individual ommatidia.

Large compound eyes go together with complex visual behavior for two reasons. First, they confer improved resolution and sensitivity, and more sampling stations, simultaneously. Second, a larger eye allows more room for a deeper, broader fovea, or for several foveas in the same eye. A fovea is defined as a region of reduced $\Delta\phi$, and as the facet diameter is never reduced in it, the fovea is also a place of increased eye radius. The compound eye is flatter at its foveas. The contrast with the vertebrate type of eye is startling.

For any place locally on a compound eye

$$\Delta\phi = D/R \text{ radians,} \tag{15}$$

where R is the local optical radius measured to the point of cross-over of adjacent visual axes in a specified plane. If the eye parameter $D\Delta\phi$ is to remain constant for the different parts of an eye, including the foveas, then facets must be larger in the fovea where $\Delta\phi$ is smaller. A fovea therefore takes up additional space on the eye. In contrast, receptors in the vertebrate eye can be crowded into a fovea with no change in eye radius.

From Eq. (15) and the relation between $D\Delta\phi$ and intensity, it follows that D^2/R is a function of intensity. Therefore, facet diameter (Fig. 10) is proportional to the square root of eye radius for whole homogeneous eyes or, locally in each part of the eyes, with foveas or other gradients of interommatidial angle. For eyes of a given size, dim-light eyes will have larger and fewer facets that bright-light eyes.

The actual eye sizes cannot be predicted without introducing other factors such as head weight, numbers of neurons needed to process the visual information, and the importance of vision in behavior. All one can say is that bigger eyes perform better.

5. THE NUMBER OF FACETS

The number of facets N in a compound eye of any given radius or facet diameter is a straightforward consequence of the above calculations. R is calculated from D, or vice versa. Then, taking the eye as a hemisphere divided into circular facets of diameter D, the number of facets

$$N = 8R^2/D^2 = 8/\Delta\phi^2, \tag{16}$$

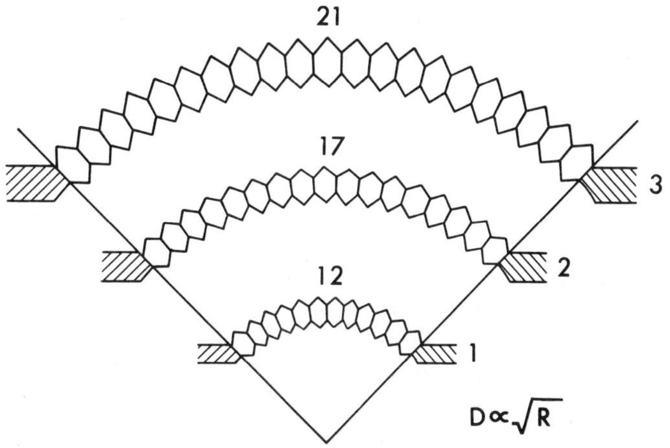

Fig. 10. The relation between facet diameter and eye radius for a given and constant compromise between sensitivity and resolution is given by Eq. (16). Model eyes, drawn to scale, show the effect of eye size on facet size when overlap of fields and threshold modulation is kept constant.

or more accurately, as the facets are hexagonal,

$$N = 4\pi R^2/(3^{\frac{1}{2}}D^2) = 4\pi/(\Delta\rho^2 3^{\frac{1}{2}}).$$ (16a)

Even more briefly,

$$N = 8R/P$$ (17)

where R is measured in microns and P is the eye parameter $D\Delta\phi$, from which we calculate that a homogeneous hemispherical eye of radius 1000 μm and having a P of .5 will have 16,000 facets. The number of facets fixes the number of parallel neural channels that simultaneously process visual information, the size of the optic lobe, and also the complexity of the patterns that the insect can possibly see.

C. Compound Eyes Are Regionally Specialized

The above argument concerns eyes in which the ommatidia, including optics and receptors, are uniform over the whole eye. Eyes of real insects, however, usually have a different radius of curvature and a different facet diameter in different parts of the eye. In fact, the relation between radius and facet size in different parts of the eye tend to follow the relation $D^2 = KR$ from Eq. (14) rather than the relation $D = KR$, which would imply that interommatidial angle is constant. Moreover, in most insect eyes, the radius to the optical center and interommatidial angles differ along different facet rows at any one place on the eye, so that D follows a compromise between these different optical radii. Eyes of insects that see better in one direction or in one plane than another have hardly been studied, although many examples exist. Some dragonflies even have three foveas on each eye. A fovea is defined as *an area of better seeing* by local reduction in $\Delta\phi$ (see Figs. 8 and 11).

A *marked fovea looking directly forward* is found in damselflies, dragonflies, dragonfly larvae, water boatmen, wasps, mantids, some hoverflies. These are all active insects for whom the capture of prey or mate depends on vision in one direction. A less well developed fovea is found at the front of the eye in some butterflies, grasshoppers, flies, mayflies, bees, and probably most insects that fly by day and see food objects such as flowers. Typically, the interommatidial angle is less at the front of the eye than at the side, and less in the vertical than in the horizontal direction when the insect is in its normal posture. This is related to the customary motion of the visual world across the eye—slower at the front, faster at the side of the eye. Running, flying, or dashing at prey must be visual experiences with many features in common between insect and man. To avoid crashing into twigs, for example, a more finely divided sampling of the visual world is required at the front than at the side of the eye.

Fig. 11. The fovea in compound eyes as a region of locally increased eye radius. Part (a) illustrates uniform radius and interommatidial angle; (b) a forward-looking fovea, as in many wasps; (c) a forward-looking and a sideways-looking fovea, as in many large dragonflies; (d) vertebrate eye showing that the effective eye radius (to posterior nodal point) is fixed, in contrast to the compound eye, where receptor size, lens aperture, and eye radius are independent variables; (e) binocular vision in a compound eye. The requirement to increase the number of sampling regions, S_1, S_2, S_3, so that objects can be measured *in depth*, puts a premium on the development of a fovea that looks in the direction of interest.

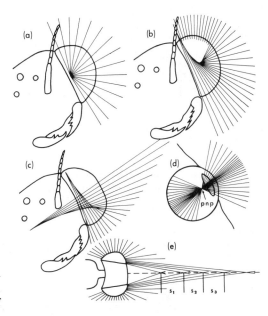

Many insects, including most of the above, have an increased eye radius in the vertical planes along the equatorial line that scans the horizon all around the eye. *A fovea that looks out sideways*, at right angles to the body axes, is found in some dragonflies. Insects that catch prey or a mate against the background of the blue sky have *upward-looking fovea* on each eye. Examples are most dragonflies, some male mayflies, and the owlfly *Ascalaphus*. These eye regions are particularly sensitive to short-wavelength light. The above information is mainly from the author's observations (Horridge 1977a, b).

These insects wear their visual habits on the outside of their eyes. If one picks up an insect with light-colored eyes and examines the eyes by a small lens with the light behind one, one will see the black spot that is the pseudopupil. As the insect is turned in the fingers, one sees the pseudopupil always looking at one's own eye. As one comes to the fovea, usually at the front of the eye, the pseudopupil center suddenly moves more quickly with eye rotation. It also increases in size, as shown in Fig. 12, but pseudopupil *diameter* depends on many complex factors.

Angles measured from pseudopupil centers show that more ommatidia are looking in the direction of the human observer from the fovea region than from any other part of the eye (i.e., $\Delta\phi$ is reduced). With a high-power lens one may also be able to see that in the fovea region the facets are larger. Where this is so the resolution and sensitivity are improved in

that region of the eye: the sensitivity because more light is caught by those facets, the resolution because it is inversely proportional to facet diameter (if the lens is optically perfect). An interesting question is whether the value of $D \Delta \phi$ at the fovea is the same as that elsewhere on the eye, as it should be if all parts of the eye are to be used simultaneously at the same ambient intensity. Another question is how big the fovea can be without taking a disproportionate amount of angular space and surface area of the eye. Presumably, large dragonflies can afford three foveas only because they have relatively enormous eyes.

The anatomy of higher-order neurons and study of behavior in relation to foveas of compound eyes has hardly started. One unique neuron of the fly's third optic neuropile has a projection corresponding to the forward part of the eye that has binocular overlap (Strausfeld, 1976). Almost the only published study of anatomy and behavior relating to a fovea is that on the fly *Syritta* (Collett & Land, 1975).

Insects with a fovea presumably use it to look in a particular direction. They turn their head to gaze in a way that is not found in most animals with compound eyes, and when they do so, an additional factor, *eye tremor*, becomes significant (see Section IV).

III. VISUAL BEHAVIOR

There has been an enormous volume of work on the visual behavior of animals with compound eyes, especially insects, and we suppose that the compound eye provides sufficient information about the visual world to make complicated behavior possible. Splendid examples can be seen in the chasing of one housefly by another in flight, the behavior of a fly on coming in to land, and the avoidance of a swat by a fly. There are numerous elegant examples, some of which are listed later.

The points at issue are: What does the compound eye see, how does the data processing work, and how is the visual behavior limited by having this kind of eye with a neural network behind it? In particular, is the compound eye adapted to reconstruct static pictures, to conserve facet numbers by eye tremor, or to obtain only a few necessary clues as the visual world sweeps across the array of visual axes?

Fig. 12. The eyes of the dragonfly *Orthetrum sabinum* (Drury) from four different angles: (a) the dorsal fovea; (b) the eye seen with the pseudopupil behind the antenna, at 25° ventral to (a); (c) the forward-looking fovea, 36° ventral to (a); (d) the eye seen at 25° lateral to (c). In (a), (b), and (c) the two eyes are seen symmetrically and so the visual axes at the center of the pseudopupil are parallel to the midline of the animal. Note that on the two foveas the pseudopupil is large. At the side of the eye it shows, by its elongated shape, the smaller $\Delta \phi$ in the ventral direction. The facet diameter is greatest on the dorsal fovea where $\Delta \phi$ is smaller, and smallest behind the antenna where $\Delta \phi$ is largest.

A. Examples of Seeing by Compound Eyes

The following examples have been selected for their diversity. Taken together, they confirm the general view that visual behavior patterns are initiated by relatively straightforward mechanisms by which the optic lobes pick out predictable trigger stimuli from the visual world, and that eye movements, both large and small, are important in vision.

1. TURNING TO LOOK

One of the most obvious responses of many insects is that they turn toward and approach a visual stimulus of adaptive significance. Examples are numerous (e.g., chasing a mate, as in the fly or drone bee; chasing a prey, as in dragonfly; turning and stalking a prey, as in tiger beetles, dragonfly larvae, and mantids. Most insects turn to escape either to the brightest or darkest part of their visual world. Comparisons with the tropisms of plants led to extensive early studies of insect orientation. Of particular relevance are the words of Mast (1923): "The turning effect of stimulation of a given region of the retina is obliterated by simultaneous stimulation of the same region of the opposite eye. If the stimulus in one eye is located relatively farther forward than that in the other eye, the former, in order to produce complete inhibition, must be stronger than the latter, if farther backward it must be weaker." From different evidence, this is strikingly similar to the model in Fig. 15(d).

Also from Mast is the finding that when a firefly sees a flash from the opposite sex it *turns in the dark through the correct angle* before making its way on a straight course toward the partner. Attraction in fireflies, however, is not so simple. Although the European firefly *Lamlyris noctiluca* is sensitive to light from visible yellow to ultraviolet, a decoy must be of the correct brightness and size, as well as color (Schwalb, 1960). Two alternative flash systems are common. In the first, the stationary female flashes to attract the male. In the other, the female flashes in response to the spontaneous flashes of the male, who is then attracted to her. The attraction can result in large aggregations and also in synchronous flashing. Specific flash patterns are common, but not much is known about how critical they are. Amazingly, nothing is known about the responses of optic lobe neurons to stimuli at different angles to the eye in ways related to the numerous known tropisms of insects.

2. BUTTERFLY SEES BUTTERFLY

The unexpected cue by which the male white cabbage butterfly, *Pieris*, distinguishes a female from another male is that the male reflects less than 1% of the ultraviolet of sunlight, whereas the female reflects more than 50% from her upper wing surfaces (Lutz, 1924). The human eye sees both males and females as white. We therefore expect ultraviolet receptors in the eyes of white butterflies, perhaps in both sexes. This is an example of a simple trigger cue, of which there are innumerable examples of great diversity. The real problems of understanding how insects see lie elsewhere, not in trigger stimuli that are clearly properties of the *receptors*. The point is that the male does not mistake any ultraviolet patch for a *Pieris* female.

3. THE SUN–COMPASS RESPONSE
OF THE BEE AND ANT

Bees and ants can use the position of the sun in the sky to bring them back home after a foraging trip. Therefore, the animal need not retrace its steps exactly nor remember all the landmarks on the way—but two abilities are essential (Mittelstaedt, 1962). The first is that the average angle to the sun on the outward journey has to be turned through 180° for the return journey. The second is that the preferred angle to the sun must alter with respect to the insect's head in time with the real movement of the sun across the sky, because bee and ant navigation takes account of time. Young bees reared without seeing the sun do not innately take into account the sun's movement (Lindauer, 1969). As a navigating instrument, an eye fixed to the head might be very convenient, in that a preferred direction of orientation could be switched slowly from facet to facet with the passage of time, or quickly by 180° for the return journey. We have as yet, however, no corresponding features in anatomy or recordings of neurons to give a clue as to how the reversal or the diurnal rhythm of adjustment of preferred direction actually takes place.

4. SPONTANEOUS PREFERENCE
FOR VERTICAL EDGES

As has been known for many years, many insects run spontaneously toward the nearest upright contrasting edge when dropped on an open arena. The tendency goes with the habit of living in trees, bushes, or grass. As the stripe period is reduced, the preference of one favorite subject, *Drosophila*, falls to zero at a pattern wavelength of 9.5°, and stripes narrower than this are preferred when horizontal (Wehner, 1975). This observation throws some doubt on Jander's (1971) hypothesis of a vertical-stripe detector in the optic lobe, but possibly eye tremor in the vertical plane is at work enhancing horizontal stripes. A very strange finding in these experiments (Wehner & Wehner von Segesser, 1973) is that *Drosophila* shows no pattern preference at all to vertical and horizontal stripes on ground glass screens when no other light source is in sight. Pattern recognition by *Drosophila* evidently depends upon adequate top light, perhaps acting via the ocelli.

A fly that is suspended by the thorax but otherwise flying normally in a drum with a few vertical marks drawn on the inside spends most of its time flying toward one or other of the vertical marks in sight (Land, 1975). When it turns from one landmark to another, the fly first jerks its head in a sudden deflection and then turns in flight, following its own head movement. Once initiated by the head jerk, the fixation upon one particular vertical stripe can be accounted for by an asymmetry in the optomotor response to the movement of a single edge relative to the eye. Single edges moving forward across the fly's eye are less effective in making the fly turn than they are when moving backward (Geiger, 1974). Therefore, once the stripe is at the front, the fly will tend to stabilize on it (Poggio & Reichardt, 1973) until another jerk of the head takes it toward a different edge.

The preference for edges that are vertical is, therefore, possibly related to a habitual limitation of head oscillations to the horizontal plane, but again these aspects, and deeper neuronal mechanisms, have not been investigated.

5. Branch Patterns Attract Stick Insects

In choosing spontaneously between different patterns, stick insects prefer those with the most black and with most contrasts near to the horizon. Moreover, the stick insect prefers patterns that resemble branches with side twigs at an angle to the main stem (see Fig. 13). The behavior can be attributed to the summed responses of edge detectors that are selectively sensitive to contrasting edges orientated at 30° intervals along the three principal axes joining neighboring ommatidia. At right angles to each angle detector causing attraction is another detector causing inhibition. A curious point, suggesting a possible significance of eye tremor, is that roughening the edges makes them more attractive when horizontal, or when 60° to the horizontal, but not when 30° to the horizontal (Jander & Volk-Heinrichs, 1970). Here is another example of behavioral work that suggests that interneurons with a predetermined trigger response to particular patterns will be found in the optic lobe.

6. Distance Estimation by Jumping Insect

If a locust is made to "walk the plank," when it reaches the end it will stop and wave its head *from side to side*; this is called *peering* (as distinct from eye tremor, which is an angular oscillation). After peering, the locust jumps by an amount that is appropriate for the distance to the nearest convenient landing point. The evidence that the peering is important for distance estimation comes from the fact that the jump is too short or too long when the target is moved as the peering movement is made (Wallace,

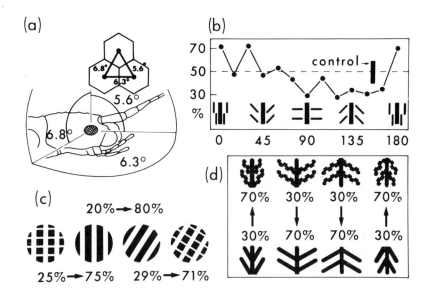

Fig. 13. Visual preference of the stick insect, as shown by its walking toward one pattern rather than another when given a choice: (a) the similar interommatidial angles along the three axes of the eye; (b) the angle of the wide branches greatly influences the choice frequency; (c) the effect of angle of plain stripes and whether they are broken up, showing preference always to the one on the right in each pair; (d) whether dissected branches are preferred depends on their angle. [Modified from Jander & Volk-Heinrichs (1970).]

1959). Estimation of distance by peering can be observed in many different insects, including mantids. The response implies that neurons detect parallax of near objects relative to far ones caused by the lateral motion of the eye, and also explains why insects have not in general developed widely separated eyes for the binocular estimation of distance.

7. PREY RECOGNITION BY DRAGONFLY LARVAE

Long ago Baldus (1926) established that the large-eyed aquatic dragonfly larva triangulates with its two eyes and strikes at a prey that moves exactly in the range of the extensile mouth parts. A target zone at the appropriate distance on the midline presumably lies on the line of sight of a critical group of ommatidia on each eye. In the region of crossover, illustrated in Fig. 11(e), a small contrasting object, light or dark, is more effective when moving in a two-dimensional jiggle than when oscillating in a single plane or regularly. The maximum effectiveness is at a velocity of

2.5 cm s^{-1} across the target zone. Corresponding ommatidia on both eyes are involved in such a way that a flashing signal presented to both eyes simultaneously is less effective than a signal occurring once every second on the two eyes alternately (Etienne, 1969).

This is a favorable preparation for analysis of the discrimination of a small moving target. The effects, inhibitory or otherwise, of neighboring stimuli or background movement could be studied as described for *Velia* in Section IV (Fig. 20). Whether the particular group of ommatidia that are necessarily involved have special optic-lobe connections or responses, has never been examined.

8. THE LANDING RESPONSE

Coming in to land is a common event for every flying insect, and the prompt detection of imminent collision is a vital function of the eye. Most flying insects have a definite landing response, which can be used to discover the visual trigger stimulus (Coggeshall, 1972; Goodman, 1960). The two adequate stimuli are dimming in the visual field (as if entering the shadow of an object) and centrifugal expansion of the visual field. These two adequate stimuli are independent—as shown by the use of rotating spiral patterns, which cause apparent expansion of the visual surroundings but no change in average illumination.

The main finding from the behavioral work is that the detector mechanism for the expanding pattern appears to be similar to the motion-detecting system as used in the optomotor response, but with a different set of connections—so that expansion of the visual world is effective, rather than one-way motion (Perez de Talens & Ferretti, 1975). As in motion detection, the response must be insensitive to contrast reversal and sensitive to velocity, but not to spatial wavelength, as discussed in Section V and illustrated in Figs. 22(d) and 22(e).

Optic lobe neurons that respond to the landing stimulus are known. The type-BF units found in the locust optic lobe by Horridge, Scholes, Shaw, and Tunstall (1965) had 20° fields with inhibitory centers and excitatory surrounds, and did not behave like motion-perception units. *Looming* neurons, such as those in the optic lobe of the moth, respond to the expansion of objects and are closely comparable to those of the locust (Collett, 1972). Possibly centrifugal expansion is abstracted as an invariant trigger stimulus by identifiable optic-lobe neurons, but we await recordings to show that their response characteristics are exactly those that would initiate a landing behavior.

9. MANTID RECOGNIZES AND STRIKES AT A FLY

From the time it hatches, a mantid relies for food on striking at smaller insects with its front pair of legs. It recognizes small contrasting moving objects of a certain size range at a certain distance. This distance naturally depends upon the length of the leg. Present indications are that the changing proportions of the head during growth provide an automatic adaptation to the change in the foreleg length (Maldonado, Rodriguez, & Balderrama, 1974). For the mantid to strike, the prey must be contrasting, moving preferably in a jerky way, and having moving legs and wings. Prey size and distance are independently important, but color and shape are not. In the recognition of prey by mantids, experience plays no part (Rilling, Mittelstaedt, & Roeder, 1959).

The direction of the strike is controlled by the eye in association with the posture of the head on the neck (see Fig. 14). In some species, a large area on the anterolateral part of the eye can guide the strike, so that there must be some kind of central projection of the optical axes of the ommatidia involved in the control of the strike direction (Mittelstaedt, 1962). Estimation of the distance of the target could be achieved either by triangulation between the two eyes (not yet proved *off the midline*) or by changes in parallax caused by peering movements of the head, which are obvious in some mantids. On the other hand, two eyes are essential for the strike. Several mantids that I have examined have a marked fovea looking forward on each eye, but the fovea, as an area of reduced $\Delta\phi$, is not correlated with the eye region essential for the strike (Maldonado & Barros-Pita, 1970). The estimation of distance appears to depend on the density of sampling stations, $1/\Delta\phi$, as shown in Fig. 11(e). Apart from the stalk-eyed flies, mantids are the obvious insects in which to search for disparity detectors. The deimatic display response of some mantid species to particular predatory birds depends only on the size of the image subtended at the eye, and one-eyed mantids show that *they can recognize the bird shapes* that arouse the display. This is one of the few pieces of positive evidence for inherited discrimination toward a particular form by an insect eye (Maldonado, 1970).

10. FLY CHASING FLY

Anyone who has watched flies buzzing round a ceiling lamp will have seen a characteristic interaction between them. As a visual response, this has been analyzed by Land and Collett (1974), who took films from below (see Fig. 15). A fly goes back and forth under the lamp, often in short, straight runs with a tight corner at the end of each run. The flight path is almost always in a horizontal plane, and flies flying separately are stacked at different altitudes.

Interactions take place only between males. If an intruder comes across the flight path occupied by another fly, there is a short flurry with one or two tight loops, and one of the flies breaks away. The chaser fly travels faster than the chased fly and continually turns toward it. The difference

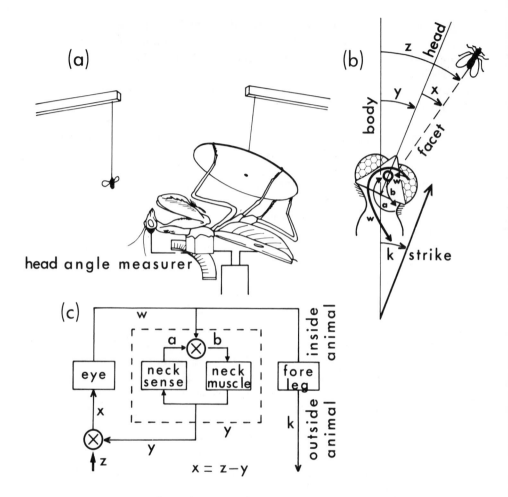

Fig. 14. The strike of a mantid at a fly with its first leg: (a) The mantid hangs upside down for preference. The direction of the fly, the angles of the head and the success of the strike are recorded; (b) the angles of the head, the fly, and the strike relative to the body axis. Only the horizontal plane is considered; (c) the formal diagram of interactions that were finally inferred by Mittelstaedt (1962). The mantid sees the fly and turns its head. The fly still subtends an angle x to the head axis: This angle is converted to the persistent order w which is conveyed to the neck muscles and the foreleg strike center. The angle of the strike k is therefore at a fixed value for each value of w, which in turn is fixed for each value of x. This system implies that the head angle y is a fixed value for each value of w and of x. If so, k would have a preadapted and fixed value for each value of z. This system, however, appears to be inappropriate for many mantids, which have a marked fovea. [Mainly after Mittelstaedt (1962).]

between the direction the chaser is facing and the direction of the chased fly is traveling is the error angle (e_1 in Fig. 15). The analysis of the films shows that, at the prevailing ambient intensity, the rate of turning of the chaser is proportional to the value of the error angle existing 30 msec previously, as a result of the neural delay. The pursued fly is not caught, because it makes sharp turns that are not anticipated, so that the chaser fly takes a longer path. The whole flight path of the chaser fly is predicted by this relatively simple relationship, which implies that the rate of turning is controlled by which ommatidium is looking toward the chased fly.

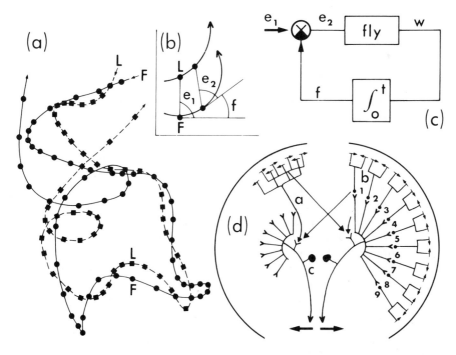

Fig. 15. Fly chasing fly: (a) flight path of leading (L) and following (F) flies in an interaction; (b) the new direction (e_2) of the leading fly, as seen by the following fly, is given by the difference between the angle e_1, which is the old bearing of the leader relative to the follower, and the angle f, which is the turn increment of the follower. The rate of turn (w) of the follower fly is a simple function of the error angle 30 msec previously; (c) The rate of turn (w) by the follower fly is integrated over time to yield the turn increment of the follower fly, which is subtracted from the old direction in a simple feedback loop.

(d) A suggested model that would steer the fly. Neuron a detects velocity in one direction at the front of the eye. Neurons $b1$–9 detect any movement of a small object *at a particular angle*, and signal it *with increasing strength* (1–9) into the neuron c which gathers all the turning tendency, for control of the wings. Neurons which control head turning, as in (d), can be inferred on similar evidence for many insects. [Modified from Land & Collett (1974).]

Model neurons that would perform this task have been suggested (see Fig. 15(d). One neuron, *a*, detects velocity in the front region of the eye. Other neurons (*b* 1–9) pick up any movement in the visual field of a small contrasting object like a fly, but are insensitive to the motion of large fields (see DCMD unit of locust, Fig. 26). The *b* neurons must act with increasing strength in the order of 1–9 to cause increased turning toward small objects at greater angles to the main axis of the fly. Collector neuron *c* transmits the total turning excitation to the wings. Even if these neurons do not exist in this exact form, the search for the equivalent system is much assisted when the man with the electrode knows what to seek and how to recognize it when found.

B. Classical Pattern Recognition in the Bee

1. GENERAL PROPERTIES

A long series of patient observations on the spontaneous preferences of naive bees and discrimination tests with trained bees have isolated four main factors:

1. Patterns evoking the same preference in *spontaneous preference tests* are unlikely to be distinguished, or distinguished only with difficulty, in learning trials.
2. *The figural intensity* of a test pattern is the ratio of the length of edge to the area. Early work, mainly by Hertz (1929–1934), showed that black-and-white patterns differing in figural intensity were readily distinguished by bees, whereas some patterns with similar figural intensity but looking strikingly different to the human eye were poorly or not at all discriminated by bees. Many types of studies suggest that figural intensity is the most important parameter in insect vision.
3. *Figural quality* refers to the type of figure (e.g., *N*-pointed stars, checkerboard, dart board, radial spokes, and parallel stripes). Bees can distinguish between two patterns of the same figural quality when they differ in figural intensity. They can sometimes discriminate patterns of similar figural quality and intensity, especially when angles of edges differ. For example, Schnetter (1968, 1972) showed that a four-pointed star is not distinguished from a six-pointed star, but bees can be taught to distinguish either from a five-pointed star.
4. *Angular orientation* of contours presented *on a vertical surface* is readily recognized by bees (Wehner, 1972a). Even if the test object differs in size or figural intensity from the object the insect has been trained to, it can still be correctly picked out by the angles of its

edges to the vertical. There is spontaneous preference for vertical smooth stripes, as against zigzag stripes or a checkerboard pattern. The spontaneous attraction decreases as the stripes are more inclined. Bees trained to a pattern with edges sloping at 45° will distinguish it from a similar pattern at a different slope. At 45°, the necessary increment is 10°, but for vertical stripes the necessary increment for discrimination is only 4°.

This implies, on any simple theory of pattern-abstracting neurons, that the eye of the bee is held very constant relative to the vertical while the bee is in flight. When measured, this proves to be so (Wehner, 1972a). The direction and extent of head or eye tremor caused by wing oscillations may also be relevant, but is unknown.

2. Quantitative Work on Differences between Patterns

Reducing the contrast between two shapes reduces the ability of the bee to discriminate in the same way that reducing the difference in contour length between two patterns does. The effects are unsymmetrical, in that two shapes are discriminated better if the rewarded one has the higher contrast, and worse if the rewarded one has the lower contrast. Therefore, differences seen by the bee increase with increasing contrast, and the influence of the contrast of the rewarded shape is greater than that of the unrewarded one. This suggests that the bee emphasizes the rewarded shape, as one would suppose, since that is the one it has learned. Only the rewarded shape need be stored in the memory.

When the two shapes (of area F_1 and F_2) to be discriminated by the bee are laid one over the other, if the overlap is G, the two-dimensional cross-correlation coefficient Cruse (1974) reduces to

$$r_{xy} = G\sqrt{F_1 F_2}. \tag{18}$$

The number r_{xy} is zero when the shapes do not coincide at all, and unity when they are identical, thus giving an arbitrary measure of their difference in overlap area. Since on a horizontal surface the bee is free to rotate around the patterns, to calculate r_{xy} calculated for any shape seen by the bee, compared with r_{xy} for the rewarded shape, is a way to handle data on whether the bee will respond positively. But Cruse (1972) also found another measure of overlap to be adequate, namely $(R_1 + R_2)/G$, where R_1 and R_2 are the *nonoverlapping* areas in the two shapes, and G is the area in common, as shown in Fig. 16. This number increases from zero when the shapes are identical, to infinity when they do not overlap at all, and so $\exp -(R_1 + R_2)/G$ was taken as more appropriate, as it ranges from

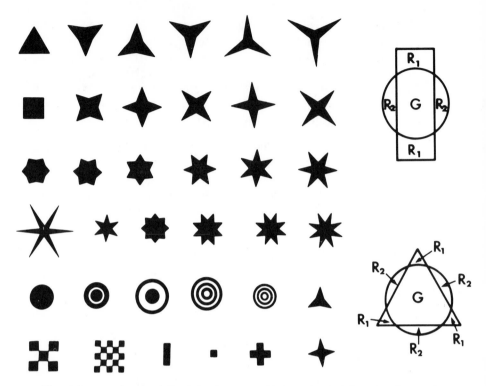

Fig. 16. Patterns for visual discrimination tasks with bees. On the left are the figures with which Cruse (1972) tested Eqs. (18) and (19). Subsequently the agreement with the theory of cross-correlation of shapes was shown with the hexagons and six-pointed stars in the third and fourth lines (Cruse, 1974). On the right it is shown how the area of overlap G and the areas R_1 and R_2 of nonoverlap are defined.

one to zero. Cruse (1972, 1974) also found the lengths of contour edge, K_1 and K_2, for the two figures to be significant, and derived an empirical function in which edges and overlaps were weighted relative to each other:

$$\text{Choice function} = \left[C_2 \log \frac{K_1}{K_2}\right] + \exp - \left[C_1 (R_1 + R_2) \frac{F_1}{G}\right], \quad (19)$$

where C_1 and C_2 are weighting factors, F_1 is the total area of the rewarded shape, R_1 and R_2 are the nonoverlapping areas of the rewarded and unrewarded shapes, and K_1 and K_2 are their lengths of edge.

At present, this is the most sophisticated empirical equation that fits the ability of the bee to discriminate some shapes under some conditions of training. However, the constants are different when a different range of tests is considered. Discriminations between shapes of the same form but different size (Schnetter, 1968) fit only the cross-correlation coefficient, not the empirical formula. Experiments with reverse contrast or with different angles of an edge (Wehner, 1972b) do not fit these relations at all. Moreover, bees seem able to pick out factors such as flat versus pointed tops (Anderson, 1972) or more complex concepts (Mazochin-Porshnyakov, 1969).

It is worth considering how a single equation can predict how much two patterns appear different to a bee. In my opinion, the length of edge and the overlap of area are large factors, because patterns moving across an array of receptors with narrow fields necessarily generate flicker and correlations that depend on edges and areas. Different cues in the patterns must excite different combinations of optic lobe neurons, which necessarily have fields that are adapted to cues in the visual world of the bee. It is unlikely that in a typical scene filled with detail, such as a flower bed that is recognized from different angles, the cues are concerned with overlap of areas or length of edge; and possibly the abstractions *length of edge* and *overlap of area* are products of the artificial flat geometrical patterns with which the experimental bee does its best. We can raise the question (but cannot answer it): To what extent are the fields of the bee's optic-lobe neurons adapted to particular cues that are likely to be encountered? In this regard, see also Section V,C,3 (p. 51).

3. The Ability of Bees to Generalize

We are currently observing a controversy that will result in a clarification of ideas and more thoroughly controlled experiments in this area. In 1969, two papers were published by Mazochin-Porshnyakov, suggesting that bees can form a variety of generalizations. He claimed to show the following:

1. Shape discriminations, as distinct from color contrast, were investigated by training the bees to distinguish a complex triangular pattern from a complex square pattern of about the same figural intensity; this was followed by testing with patterns of the same shapes but different color. The training was then repeated with other color combinations and further tested on yet others. Discrimination of shape persisted, despite the changes in color.

2. Shape discrimination when figural intensity is altered was investigated by training the bees on a solid black triangle and a solid black square, then testing them on the same figures drawn much broken-

up, or training on the latter and then testing on open contour figures. The shape was apparently learned.

3. Shape discrimination, as distinct from orientation or size, was investigated, as well as changes in the relative size of objects. Again, shape as such was learned.

4. Discrimination of whether a pattern was composed of one color or two, irrespective of the colors, was investigated by a flag pattern with four quadrants, like the international signaling flags representing the letters l and u. Training was on a succession of rewarded two-color patterns, as against single-color squares of the same size, and tests showed an ability to pick out a two-color pattern of a color combination that had not appeared in the training.

5. Discrimination of whether a square black spot was outside or inside an irregular closed shape, irrespective of that shape, was the most difficult of the tests for the bee.

6. Finally, it was found that the rate of learning was increased when the bees had had previous training on figures that have some resemblance to those on a new program.

For several reasons, these results were not accepted by workers outside the Soviet Union. First, it was clear that figural intensity could have been the basis of the discriminations. Many workers had repeated the finding of Hertz (1929) that bees do not discriminate a square from a triangle if the figural intensity of the two are matched. Second, repetition of the same tests by Anderson (1972) and by Wehner (1972a, 1975) and his pupils, failed to show generalization.

The stimulus to reinvestigate, however, caused two real advances, and no doubt more will follow. First, Wehner (1972b) showed that bees could be trained to discriminate the inclination angle of edges of patterns— shown in Fig. 17(a) and 17(b)—when rotated by about 10° *if presented on a vertical surface*. It follows that any patterns with net differences of inclination and of a suitable size subtended on the eye could be discriminated. Therefore, bees could have been trained to the clue of sloping edge, and this could wrongly have been interpreted as the abstraction of some more sophisticated general feature. With patterns (a) and (b) in Fig. 17, Wehner (1972b) showed that the bee could pick out the stripe inclined 45° to the left or to the right, even when the contrast was reversed. This shows that the theories of pattern detection based on amount of overlap or cross-correlation cannot be correct.

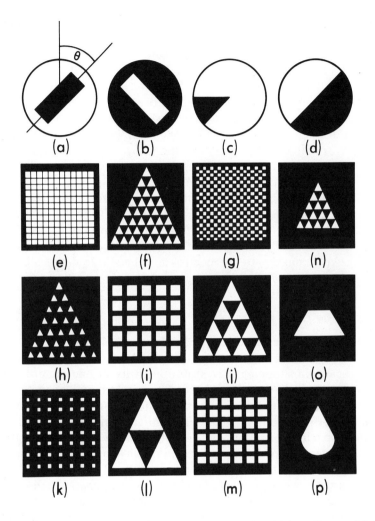

Fig. 17. Patterns for more subtle visual discrimination tasks with bees. Patterns (a)–(d) at different angles were used to demonstrate discrimination of angle of an edge, and generalization of contrast reversal (Wehner, 1972a, 1975). From the series (f) to (m) the bees could discriminate any of the squares from any of the triangles, but could not generalize from one square or triangle to another. For further details see text.

Second, the meaning of *generalization* has been clarified. Some of Mazochin-Porshnyakov's experiments, as modified by Anderson (1972), illustrate this. With the same kind of dissected figures that had been found essential for success in the Soviet work, bees were trained to distinguish a triangular pattern, such as (f) (n) or (h) in Fig. 17, from a similar square pattern. When performing adequately, the bees selected the triangle, even when inverted, in preference to the square. However, the same bees could not distinguish the inverted triangle from the original triangle without further training, and they could not distinguish two triangles, (f) and (n), of the same subunit size but different numbers of units. Therefore, there is no need to introduce the complex idea of generalization.

Going back to the Soviet experiments, we see that at the start of the experiment the spontaneous preferences of the bees for the training patterns should have been determined (for further explanation, see the following text). Secondly, when it is thought that the bee is generalizing between two or more patterns, control tests must also demonstrate that the same bee *can distinguish between the patterns from which it is supposed to generalize.*

4. Training along a Continuum

In training along a continuum, two patterns are selected, such as a plain solid triangle and square, between which bees cannot discriminate even after eight days of training. The figural intensity of one pattern is then increased—that is, to (f) in Fig. 17—and the bees discriminate it very well (Anderson, 1972). The figural intensity is now progressively changed— that is, from (f) to (l) in Fig. 17, until the original triangle and square are reached, when it is found that discrimination is now possible. Clearly the bees have been led to shift from figural intensity to some other clue. By testing these bees with shapes like those in (o) and (p) of Fig. 17, it was found that (p) but not (o) would be treated as a triangle, which suggests that the feature of a pointed apex can indeed be picked out by the bee when its normal cues, such as figural intensity and angle of edge, are not available. Training along a continuum had previously worked only with vertebrates.

5. Spontaneous Preferences

If a bee shows no spontaneous preferences between a pair of unre-warded patterns it will not be able to learn to distinguish between them (Anderson, 1972). This strongly suggests that the experiments do not test the ability to learn a pattern, but rather the ability to notice a difference. If a difference is noticeable (meaning that interneurons in the optic lobe are differently excited), then learning a discrimination is possible. So it may be safe to conclude that inputs of pattern-abstracting neurons are not changed by training; what is altered is the relative attention given to their output.

6. BEES DIFFER

Whether the difference lies in past experience or in their perception equipment is not known, but bees clearly differ in spontaneous preferences for the same pairs of patterns. Individual bees without spontaneous preference between two patterns were unable to learn to discriminate them although other bees learned quite well (Anderson, 1972).

7. PROJECTION OF THE VISUAL WORLD

Bees in flight can be trained to respond to patterns on a vertical surface in such a way that they view the pattern with a particular part of the eye, and in a constant orientation on the eye. With this experimental arrangement, it can be shown that the bee always *fixates* relative to the pattern. The midfrontal visual field is most decisive There is no evidence that patterns learned with one part of the eye can be transferred and recognized by a previously covered part of the eye. Again this suggests that learning is localized in the feature detectors for the rewarded pattern.

8. CONCLUSIONS

Although the study of the visual behavior of the bee has far to go, it is evident to the neurophysiologist that the bottleneck in understanding is at the interneuron level. We have no information of any value on the way in which optic-lobe interneurons make possible behavioral discriminations, or whether learning is localized to individual neurons.

The obvious lesson from the pattern-discrimination studies is that mechanisms must be sought in the nervous system whereby the most obvious attributes of a pattern, such as correlations between different ommatidia, are abstracted by interneurons *while the pattern is moving rapidly across the eye*. The attribute of major importance in the learning experiments, figural intensity, is to a physiologist little more than a measure of the amount of flicker per unit solid angle. Also, in real life, where three dimensional objects are normal, there must be other natural attributes of patterns (notably parallax) besides figural intensity, color, and edge angle, which are the only features at present studied experimentally.

IV. FEATURES OF THE INSECT VISUAL SYSTEM

A number of what one might call "selling points," which are the attractive or at least notable features of the insect visual system, will be dealt with in this section.

A. Anatomical Features

1. ANATOMICAL DETAIL

A pleasant relaxation for the student of nervous systems is to browse through the beautiful illustrations of the fly's optic-lobe neurons published by Strausfeld (1976), or the equally marvelous illustrations in the older work of Cajal and Sanchéz (1915), some of which are reproduced in Bullock and Horridge (1965, pp. 1079–1085). The wealth of detail of the neurons is an anatomical gold mine waiting to be extended by electron-microscopy and exploited by recording from marked neurons.

2. IDENTIFIABLE NEURONS

Working with arthropods brings an important bonus in that every neuron so far studied is unique, identifiable, and constant for all individuals of one species. Some of the neurons are recognizable in other species or even families. One can return again and again to one named neuron and progressively work out its function as a component, as new insights arise.

3. THE SPATIAL PROJECTION

An important generalization for all insects studied is that the array of visual axes of the retinula cells is projected as an ordered array upon the lamina and thence upon the medulla (Fig. 1). A parallel projection of one or two retinula cell axons per ommatidium (three in the bee) runs directly from the retina to the medulla. The lamina and medulla are neuropile regions that are arranged in a regular two-dimensional array of units with a large number of neuron types per unit. The projection of the visual world continues to the next level, the lobula, and from there to the ventral regions of the brain, but beyond that nothing is known. Contralateral projections to the optic lobe of the opposite side are usually whole-eye fields. The part played by different regions of the eye in whole-animal behavior is a topic that has yet to be explored. The use of the fovea is a prime example.

As this spatial projection peters out, it is presumably replaced by an excitation pattern with a different kind of order from which all the relevant correlations between different ommatidia have been abstracted. The only known examples of the new domain are the motion detectors and the (DCMD) unit (q.v. Fig. 26 and p. 68).

4. DISTORTION BY CHANGING EYE CURVATURE

The representation of the visual world into the retina is not necessarily undistorted. In fact, several requirements suggest that a distorted representation is more efficient. For example, most relative motion across the eye is horizontally backward and is relatively slow at the front. Moreover, vision straight ahead and sideways in the horizontal plane is most important in flight, but upward and downward when resting, and therefore more of the eye's surface area is often devoted to these directions. Insect foveas (defined as a region of reduced $\Delta\phi$) are more common than the literature suggests. Many insect eyes have become specialized away from spherical symmetry, some with a gradient of interommatidial angles with one or more foveas, and many with a smaller interommatidial angle that provides higher resolution in a vertical than in horizontal direction along the equator of the eye. They pay a price, however, in that the rest of the eye as a result has poorer resolution. Often the front of the eye has the best resolution, and this is conferred by larger facets, smaller interommatidial angle, greater overlap of fields, and greater local eye radius—in fact a fovea—but this has been neglected in anatomical, behavioral, and physiological work.

5. The Repeated Array

A great advantage of working with any visual system is the two-dimensional array of repeated components, which aids the description from sections, the finding of units by microelectrode probing, and the interpretation of responses (because they arise from a limited number of neuron types).

The disadvantage of the two-dimensional array is illustrated by the complexity of the mathematical analysis which has emerged from one simple interaction, namely, the lateral inhibition in the *Limulus* eye. There, each ommatidium inhibits its near neighbors with an effect that falls off with distance, and also strongly inhibits itself. The outcome of this two-dimensional multiple feedback is difficult to work out quantitatively even for the static linear case with a simple stimulus, and even harder for moving stimuli, complex targets, or nonlinear interactions.

The progress of analysis on the two-dimensional retinal array, however, is taking us toward the recognition of progressively more regional differences. This is already apparent in the study of the variety of insect and crustacean foveas; for example, the specialized region (not a fovea as defined here) for detection of polarized light on the dorsal part of the ant's eye (Duelli, 1975) and the regional differences in spectral sensitivity in dragonflies. There is much old work on tropisms (e.g., Mast, 1923) and the new work of Collett and Land on flies that indicates that visual stimuli from different directions have differing effects in visual behavior. Components that occupy analogous positions in the regular array are then in reality different. This experimental fact alters the whole electrophysiological approach, so that neurons must be named by the angle they represent on the eye.

6. SPREAD OF DENDRITES AND AXON BRANCHES

Neurons of arthropod optic lobes fall into natural classes on the basis of the lateral spread of their branches. Retinula cells and lamina ganglion cells end in club-shaped terminals without (or with very tiny) arborizations. This feature is possibly a consequence of the mode of transmission by electrotonic spread in these fibers, because the closed end enhances the transmission. Many of the small neurons of the medulla have local branches that are not distinguishable as axons or dendrites, others have a spread ranging from a few degrees (in terms of the visual world subtended on the eye) to the whole eye. Because the extents of arborizations indicate where synaptic connections are *possible* and because single neurons can be perfused with dye while they are analyzed physiologically, it is most important to work from the anatomical framework on which all the other data is hung.

B. Physiological Features

1. INVARIANCE IN SENSITIVITY PLOTS AT RECEPTOR LEVEL

Sensitivity of a receptor is defined as the reciprocal of the number of photons (falling on the cornea) to give a constant response. It is an important property of arthropod photoreceptors that when the visual field is plotted as angular sensitivity it is invariant with change in the selected amplitude of the constant response. This is a consequence of the fact that the slope of the graph when response is plotted against intensity is independent of the angle of the stimulus. Similarly, spectral sensitivity cuves are (almost) invariant with reference to intensity because the relation between response and intensity is independent of color. One of the conditions for these relations in the retina is that there is a linear summation of light, with no lateral interaction between receptors (when the electroretinogram is excluded) and no feedback from the optic lobe. When modulation is considered, as in Fig. 4, it is an important feature that the slope of the $V/\log I$ curve is not changed by background light. Invariance requires more conditions than the simple equivalence of photons, which is in fact not a condition.

2. LACK OF INVARIANCE IN SENSITIVITY PLOTS, HIGHER-ORDER CELLS

When we come to the lamina level (Fig. 1), the situation is quite different (Laughlin, 1975a, b). Fields of lamina ganglion cells can still be plotted as the sensitivity to a point source placed at different positions in their visual field. The relation between response and intensity, however, is now dependent on the position of the stimulus in the visual field of the neuron. The only way to plot the visual field is therefore to calculate the sensitivity from the intensity–response curve *at each angle*. A result of this is that the size and shape of the field then depends on the selected amplitude of the constant response. An important consequence is that responses to other stimulus shapes, such as striped patterns, are not readily calculable from a field shape that is measured when the test light is a point source. One source of the nonlinearity in the lamina ganglion cells is the mutual suppression between neighboring cells in the lamina. One effect of this interaction is to narrow the fields of these cells, but the main function of this system probably lies elsewhere, in the amplification of contrasts at moving edges, and the increase in the dynamic range while the amplification of change in intensity is maintained at maximum.

The breakdown of invariance at the level of the second-order cells is a warning that the optic-lobe neurons at any deeper level are also unlikely to have fields that are invariant with intensity. Any lateral interaction between parallel channels is able to generate nonlinearities. One practical consequence is that the field of each identified neuron has to be measured experimentally *over its normal working range*. A theoretical consequence is that the way interneurons abstract pattern cannot be predicted from simple stimuli or from the final behavior.

3. THE TRANSFORMATION AT THE FIRST SYNAPTIC LAYER

Although much remains to be discovered about the physiology of the lamina, a few major generalizations have emerged. Just as the receptors act as a filter for stimuli from the outside world, so the lamina synapses act as the first completely neural transformation. The way they act gives some clues about the later neural processing. The following results are mainly from Laughlin (1975a, b):

1. *Hyperpolarizing responses*. The ganglion cells of the lamina (*lam.*, in Fig. 18) have responses that are hyperpolarizing and without spikes, in response to surprisingly small (<1 mV) depolarizations of the retinula cell axons. There is an initial peak, a plateau, and an off-response to a flash of light. Why the response is hyperpolarizing is not clear, except that the field effects may have an influence on transmission velocity and on adjacent cells. These lamina cells could be a model of nonspiking neurons throughout the insect central nervous system.

2. *High synaptic gain and low noise*. Let us look first in the circle in Fig. 18. Here we have the dark-adapted responses at low light intensities.

The outstanding feature is that the postsynaptic response is about 10 times as large as the presynaptic response, so that the $V/\log I$ curve for the lamina cells rises to maximum over an intensity range of little more than 1 log unit. In effect, it cannot combine high gain with wide range. At the same time, possibly because there is a convergence of six or so retinula cells upon the lamina cells, the lamina cell responses are not much more noisy than the retinula cell responses, because synaptic noise is smoothed, whereas responses are summed.

3. *Off-response*. The lamina cell response always has a *depolarizing* off-response, which with bright background light becomes as large as the hyperpolarizing on-response (Fig. 18). This response may be significant for signaling the passing of trailing edges or leading edges of black objects.

4. *Floating zero*. The lamina cells respond well to transients in the retinula cell depolarizations, but hardly at all to the maintained depolarization of light-adapted retinula cells. In Fig. 18, at a background intensity of 3, the retinula response starts to depolarize near 10 mV (see I_b), whereas all lamina responses take off near resting potential (the zero on mV axis). The effect is to *back off* the standing intensity and amplify the modulation.

5. *Light adaptation*. With increased background intensity the lamina cell responses move to the right in Fig. 18, but the peak response preserves its high gain and narrow range. The effect of light adaptation, however, is to slide the lamina cell responses along the intensity axis. Deeper neurons of the optic lobe are therefore working with responses that are standardized with respect to contrast, rather than to intensity. Possibly the axon labeled *Rec* in Fig. 18 is an inhibitory gain-control loop that brings an influence from the medulla.

6. *Lateral inhibition*. At least in the blowfly and dragonfly, a suppression spreads from neighboring units in the lamina, acting mainly on the plateau response of the lamina cells, but to a lesser extent on the peak response. The effect is to narrow the receptive fields, but care must be exercised in the way these are measured, because the intensity–response curve ($V/\log I$ curve) is not invariant when the angle of the stimulus is changed. As explained above, sensitivity at different angles must be calculated from responses with a series of neutral density filters at each angle.

7. *Summation of color and polarization information*. The larger lamina cells, which are the ones recorded from, have spectral sensitivity curves that suggest that they simply sum the retinula cells of different color types from one ommatidium. This is not true in the fly, where they sum only one color type. In all species, the lamina cells also sum retinula cells with polarized light maxima in different directions, so that this property also is lost in this pathway. As many insects, however, show abundant be-

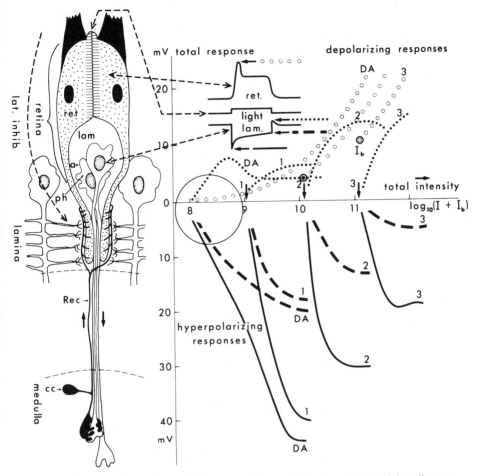

Fig. 18. The transformation at the first synaptic layer, the lamina. On the left is a diagram of the pod of retinula cells and the unit of the 1st synaptic layer, the lamina cartridge, with its projection to the medulla. Retinula cell axons *Ret* (six to eight in number) make synapses with lamina ganglion cells *Lam* (about five in number), which run to the medulla as a bundle. There is an angle-conserving projection back from the medulla (Rec), and some kind of lateral interaction in the lamina (Lat. inhib.). On the right are response curves of *Ret* and *Lam* cells at different states of light adaptation. Responses are shown from the peak of the receptor response (open circles and top oscillograph record in inset), and from the peak of the onset (continuous lines), the plateau (dashed lines) and the off-response (dotted lines) of the *Lam* postsynaptic cells. Absolute values of membrane potential are plotted against total intensity (background intensity plus stimulus intensity). Intensities are given at $\log_{10}(I + I_b)$ in photons $cm^{-2}sec^{-1}$. The three arrows show the intensities of the three alternative background intensities I_b (on axis) in effective 524 nm quantal irradiance. Curves are labeled DA (dark-adapted) or numbered to indicate at which background intensity they were recorded. The recurrent neuron (cc) was described for the fly by Trujillo-Cenóz and Melamed (1970); the physiology is for the dragonfly, redrawn from Laughlin (1975a).

havioral evidence of polarization and color sensitivity, other pathways must carry these modalities.

4. FUNCTION OF THE LAMINA SYNAPSES

When the seven features above are brought together, it is evident that the largest lamina ganglion cells carry a signal which has been selected for the following features: maximum efficiency for conveying flicker and contrast at lowest noise and highest possible gain, angular resolution, and transmission rate. As the lamina cells provide one of the major inward paths of visual excitation, their features strongly suggest what we have already learned from the receptors and from pattern perception, that the *main signal is the moving contrast*. Study of the lamina informs us that the main interangle correlations must be performed deeper in the optic lobe than the lamina.

C. Behavioral Features

1. EYES FIXED TO HEAD

Because both eyes are fixed on the head (and therefore fixed relative to each other) in insects, the recording of relative movement, and of possible effects of it, as shown in Figs. 12, 19, is greatly simplified. Therefore it is astonishing that head movements have hardly been studied at all.

2. RELATIVE MOTION ACROSS THE EYE

Almost all work on vision by compound (or indeed simple) eyes has been done with a freely moving animal. When a bee flies or walks to a target, the visual world sweeps across its eye. The phenomenon in man of an image that fades when stabilized on the retina reminds us that relative movement may be essential for vision.

The concept of memory of the location of a stimulus on the eye is beginning to appear in the works of Wehner (1972a, b, 1975) and his pupils studying form vision in bees. For the first time, in these studies, form vision has been related to the eye region that sees, but relative motion is not eliminated. One series of experiments, however, on optomotor memory in the crab *Carcinus*, shows that a compound eye can make a directional response to a visual stimulus with no relative motion at all. This is described further in the text and illustrated by Fig. 20. In fact, the experimental discriminations often described require little pattern vision at all. Color cues, direction of maximum brightness, direction of movement of contours across the eye, angle of tilt of contours, number of contours, and an effect of the region of the eye stimulated are the only parameters that have so far been investigated in visual discriminations and learning behavior.

This being so, *to think of a mosaic vision with each ommatidium contributing one coarse grain to a picture of the visual world made up of dots or overlapping fuzzy patches is a complete misrepresentation of the situation.* The attraction of this idea is so great that such pictures are still reproduced. Anthropormorphism reigns where it yet can.

3. NARROW FIELDS OF RECEPTORS SET UP FLICKER

The primary signal is the modulation of the intensity at the receptor as a function of pattern period (or spatial frequency). This basic concept, illustrated in Figs. 2, 4, and 5, implies that small objects passing across the eye, and edges of large objects that fill the receptor fields, cause flicker. A complicated visual pattern is therefore represented as a series of flickers in each ommatidium, each series appearing at successive times in successive ommatidia across the eye. We have the reverse of the process of moving the "news flash" across the front of a newspaper building. In the news flash, each vertical row of light bulbs gets power in a certain pattern that is repeated, with a delay, at the next vertical row of bulbs, so that the pattern sweeps across the building. In the compound eye, the pattern of light is the whole message presented all at once. As it sweeps across the eye it generates a sequence of voltages in each receptor. Along the direction of motion the sequence of receptor responses is the same in each receptor, but delayed progressively across the eye. This comparison makes clear the distinction between measuring the motion vector and seeing the picture, and also emphasizes that the resolution applies to moving as well as to static patterns. There is still, however, the open question of whether the processing of parallel channels is necessarily simultaneous in insects.

4. EYE TREMOR

An almost totally neglected area of study is whether eye movements play a part in vision by the compound eye. A variety of behavioral work on resolution of patterns by small compound eyes with relatively few facets suggests that the eyes see patterns that are finer than would be expected from the interommatidial angle. Examples are the stick insect (Jander & Volk-Heinrichs, 1970), several ants (Jander, 1957), and the water bug *Velia* (Meyer, 1974). Earlier work on eyes of larval insects has established that visual integration makes use of scanning movements.

One of the remarkable features of the crab eye, and possibly a main function of the mobile eyecup of the higher crustacea, is the continual eye tremor in the horizontal plane (see Fig. 19). A special phasic muscle keeps the tremor going. There is evidence that this tremor serves to enhance the contrast of vertical edges. Tests for improvement of resolution have not

(a)   **(b)**

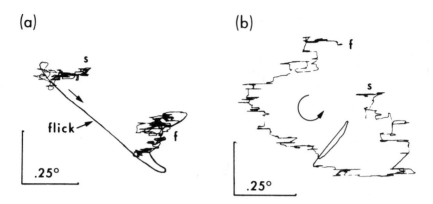

Fig. 19. Eye tremor of the crab *Carcinus*, recorded in two dimensions (note the tremor is predominantly in the horizontal plane): (a) tremor over a period of 40 sec with the eye seeing only a single stationary small light. About halfway through this period, a flick of the eye takes it to a new position, where it stabilizes as before. (b) The light moves in a circle of diameter 2.7° subtended at the eye, starting at the 12 o'clock position and taking 48 sec for the full circle. The eye responds with a movement in a rough circle about .5° in diameter. The sudden flick near the middle of the response was probably caused by a single impulse in a fast-twitch muscle fiber. The response itself is controlled by slow muscle fibers, and the tremor is induced by a special muscle. The amplitude of the tremor, .5°, is greater than the threshold for responding to the change in position of a contrasting object, so that tremor must influence vision. [From Barnes & Horridge (1969).]

been made. As the eye tremor is significant, there is no doubt that the analysis of compound vision will have to take it more seriously, mimicking the tremor in experimental setups, and devising processing mechanisms that are improved by the tremor.

Tremor influences the choice of modulation required in Eq. (11), which decides the separation of receptor fields. In a nutshell, eye tremor means that fewer ommatidia can cover the visual world, but the mean intensity is reduced. Therefore, in an eye, or particularly in a fovea, that tremors, $\Delta\phi$ can be larger than it otherwise would be in relation to $\Delta\rho$, and there is room on the eye for facets of larger diameter.

5. RECEPTOR FIELD SIZE SEEN IN BEHAVIORAL OUTPUT

Three examples show how the limited size of receptor fields, and their spacing on the compound eye, can be identified by appropriate experiments at the behavioral level.

1. *Inhibitory interaction between neighboring fields*. A pretty piece of purely behavioral analysis has led to the uncovering of mutual suppression (not necessarily lateral inhibition, as in *Limulus*) between excitation

units that correspond to facets (Meyer, 1974). The water bug *Velia*, when hungry, dashes toward a moving stimulus, on condition that vibrations on the water surface come from the same direction. Two horizontal rows of ommatidia across the lower middle of the eye are most sensitive to the targets that arouse the response. One stimulus can be systematically varied while the insect is given a choice between it and a standard stimulus. A black disk is optimal when it subtends an angle of 4° at the eye, independent of its distance. When the angle between ommatidial axes becomes as great as 10.3°, we are faced with a problem of how the edges of a small object are sampled. Furthermore, when choosing between radial patterns of different qualities, *Velia* selects a complex silhouette when the figure subtends 3°, and a plain one when it subtends 4°. These details are therefore standardized in the experiments that are discussed in the following text (see Fig. 20).

The contours of inhibition caused by a second black spot, located at different angles to the first black spot, form a pattern corresponding to the interfacet angles (or possibly to the interactions between facets). The peaks of sensitivity mean that visual units correspond to the facets. With reference to Eq. (13) p. 19, note the extreme separation of visual fields. When two visual units are excited simultaneously, the one most excited (and ultimately the one controlling the behavior) suppresses its neighbors and is suppressed by the surrounding visual units, with rapid fall-off with distance, as shown in Fig. 20(b). The whole phenomenon strongly suggests a lateral interaction at the level of the lamina or medulla.

Flicker at 1.6–8 Hz increases the stimulus value but at .4–3 Hz inhibits it, and a light–dark period of 1 : 3 is optimal. Therefore, taking the temporal and spatial properties of various stimuli into account, there may be an effect of the time constant in the lateral interaction, giving a positive or negative response to flicker. Each of these outputs interacts with those of neighboring units.

One of the important lessons from the work on *Velia* is that *early in the study* the optimum stimulus was found to be a black spot subtending an angle of 4° at the eye. Subsequent work with a second black spot revealed the strong lateral interaction. Simple experiments quickly revealed the elements of the situation. From this example we can see that the self-luminous stimuli used by electrophysiologists are not necessarily the ones to which the neurons are sensitive. Finding the functional significance is an important part of the analysis.

2. *The Wechselfolge in motion perception.* A striped drum rotated about an arthropod induces a strong turning tendency, which can be expressed by walking, flight, head turning, or—in crabs—by eyestalk movement. This is called the optomotor response. In the fly, the angles between the visual axes of the retinula cells are very regular and the visual

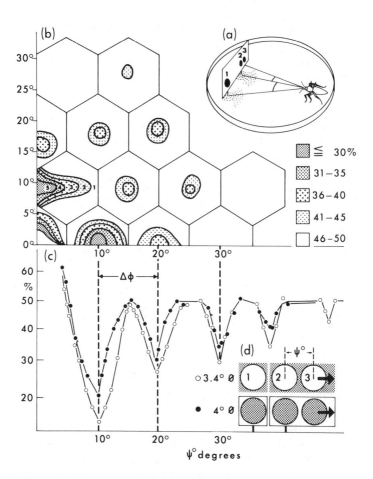

Fig. 20. A lateral interaction in the pond skater *Velia*. (a) The choice of visual targets, Spots 1 and 2, reinforced with water ripple. The interaction is demonstrated by the partial suppression below 50% choice, of the visual response to a small object (Spot 2, representing a prey) by a similar neighboring object (Spot 3), as related to the angular periodicity of the eye. The third spot—see (d)—the one on the extreme right, is moved to the right by the angle $\psi°$ in steps of 1°. The relative choice frequency between Spot 2 and Spot 1 is altered by change in $\psi°$, as plotted in the graph in (c). The ordinate is a choice frequency transformed to a probit which represents the strength of the interaction. (b) The pattern from (c) plotted as contours in two dimensions and superimposed on the hexagonal pattern of the retina. (c) One set of experimental values of stimulus strength plotted against $\psi°$ in the horizontal plane. (d) Key to the arrangement of targets, as in (a). [After Meyer (1974).] The data suggest (i) that the field width $\Delta\rho$ is smaller than the interommatidial angle $\Delta\phi$; (ii) that the *Velia* orients its eyes very accurately with reference to the target; (iii) eye tremor must be significant for the discrimination of such small targets and their angular separations.

fields do not overlap. Therefore stripes of a repeat period that subtends exactly the same angle at the eye as the angle between receptors will not generate a response when moved across the eye, and stripes slightly narrower than this will cause a response in the opposite direction. This is shown at the top left hand corner of Fig. 22(a) where the turning response is negative for stripe periods near 3°.

3. *Zones in optomotor memory*. The optomotor memory paradigm is described below. Basically, it is a response to a movement that is made during a dark period, after which a contrasting edge reappears at a slightly different angle to the eye—see Fig. 23(c), and 25(f).

Working on the crab *Pachygrapsus* with a wide variety of stripes of different widths, Wiersma and Hirsch (1975) found the direction and strength of the optomotor memory to be compatible with the theory that a black–white border projected on the eye induces a memory zone 4° wide on each side of the edge, as illustrated in Fig. 23(e). Presentation of a new stimulus that causes changes within these zones is interpreted as motion. Changes on the black side of the edge (dark-adapted), where the zone is white-sensitive, have more effect than changes in the black-sensitive (light-adapted) zone on the other side of the edge. Of course, these zones do not necessarily lie at the same level as the motion detecting mechanism. The zones could be due to lateral inhibition between any units in the peripheral optic lobe with fields of about 4°, and could be the units of the lamina, as described by Laughlin (1975a, b) and others for insects.

V. ANALYSIS OF VISUAL MECHANISMS

Although any one advance is made by one technique or another, the analysis of a complex system, such as that behind the compound eye, can only be done by bringing together results from a wide variety of techniques. The progressive unfolding of how such a system works carries the most conviction when lines of evidence from different disciplines converge. Data from anatomy, optics, electrophysiology, discrimination learning, innate behaviour patterns, mathematical models, cytochemistry of neural transmitters and so on, must be fitted together as a coherent story that is cross-checked and progressively vindicated in the effort towards deeper understanding.

A. Motion Perception: A Case Study

The most obvious universal feature that is abstracted by the visual system is the direction and angular velocity of motion of the visual world around the eye. In early evolution, possibly, compound eyes multiplied their facet numbers and become geometrically regular under selection pressure for better motion perception.

The ease with which many insects respond in direction and magnitude to the motion of the whole visual field around them has attracted many to the study of motion perception in insects, but the actual mechanisms are not yet known. The first obstacle faced by all investigators in this field is the extensive mathematical analysis that is really a search for appropriate models that agree with the final behavioral output. The second difficulty is that motion abstraction is apparently located in the optic medulla, where the wiring diagram is unknown and where a high proportion of neurons are small.

The third obstacle to finding the actual mechanism is that there is possibly no place where a single electrode could reveal the process of motion detection. Recording from a motion-detecting neuron would be too late in the process, whereas recording from one of the inputs to that neuron would be too early. One would have to record from the motion-detecting neuron and show that when two known neurons are excited there is a response only when the time delay between them matches the previously measured sensitivity to velocity in the appropriate direction. Without this, we have only an inferred model.

In any model of vision, the pattern in the outside world must first be transformed into a pattern of intensity in each receptor. In the case of a regular striped pattern, the motion of the stripes causes an oscillation of intensity in each receptor, as shown in Fig. 4. These intensity fluctuations can be broken down to their sinusoidal components, which are the Fourier components in the time domain of the contrast pattern in the spatial domain. This is a convenient linear representation of the light stimulus. Although the sum of the Fourier components reproduces the stimulus, the effects of the light in the retinula cells, or deeper, are not necessarily the same as the sum of the effects of the Fourier components taken separately. In fact, on account of changes in time constants and lateral interactions as a function of repetition rate and intensity, we know they are not.

1. AUTOCORRELATION

We have to accept that velocity is abstracted in the optic lobe by the correlation of the excitation in one ommatidium with that in a nearby ommatidium delayed or advanced in time (see Fig. 21). The word *correlation* is here used as an ordinary loose figure of speech. To make a more exact mathematical representation, the incoming signal behind one facet is correlated in the mathematical sense with itself at a later time as seen

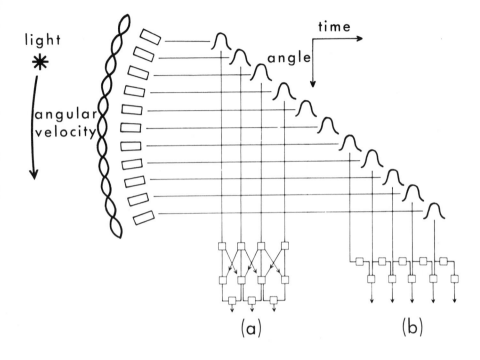

Fig. 21. The basic system for motion detection. Movement of a point source *outside* the eye causes successive flashes through each facet in succession. These are mixed by some system, not necessarily, however, at a single stage. The motion measuring system has been modelled by either correlation from cross-multiplication between neighbors, as shown in (a), or lateral interaction through a delay and then inhibition as, shown in (b). See also Fig. 24.

through the adjacent facet, but delayed in time by an interval τ. If the signal as a function of time is $f(t)$, this autocorrelation is defined as

$$R = \int_{-\infty}^{\infty} f(t) \cdot f(t-\tau) \cdot dt. \tag{20}$$

This implies that there is an exact multiplication of each value of $f(t)$ at time $t = 0$ with the values of $f(t)$ in the adjacent facet. In addition, in order to determine the magnitude of a velocity one must consider all possible delay values τ, because what is sought is the positive or negative value of τ that gives the optimum *amplitude and direction* of the correlation R. (Incidentally, it appears to me more likely that time is built into the velocity-measuring mechanism in a simpler way.)

The model due originally to Reichardt (1957) is a literal application of

Eq.(20) and the convolution integral. The Fourier components of the stimulus are cross-multiplied, taking into account the delay between adjacent channels. All the cross-products are summed algebraically over as large an area of the eye as is desired. The result is the magnitude and direction of the autocorrelation R.

There are three main objections to this way of attacking the problem of motional perception. The first depends on what we mean be explanation and understanding. To say that the system must work by autocorrelation, then set up an exact theory, with numerous unknown parameters, is all very well, but a macroscopic mathematical model does not define the underlying microscopic mathematical models (e.g., in physics the gas laws do not define kinetic theory). If we know the interactions of the components we can go up to the gross laws, but not vice versa. If the excitation from adjacent ommatidia were multiplied *linearly* behind the eye then Eq. (20) would necessarily follow. The converse, however, is not true: If the behavior fits the autocorrelation theory, it does not follow that multiplication between adjacent pathways necessarily occurs.

Second, in testing the autocorrelation theory, certain parameters, such as the response as a function of velocity, the optimum velocity as a function of spatial frequency, and the response as a function of spatial frequency, can be measured. From these results, the constants in the model can be calculated. The objection is that the limiting factors that determine these parameters are not necessarily due to the motion perception mechanism at all, but relate to totally different aspects, such as the mechanical inertia of the motor output, the effect of flicker on arousal or turning tendency, and other intensity effects, such as dark adaptation of receptors.

Third, we cannot ignore that the motion-detecting system has been evolved over a long period of time to give an output that is a good representation of the input over the physiological range, even though the optic lobe components have floating zeros, are highly nonlinear, have variable gain, feedback loops, lateral interaction, logarithmic transformations, and so on. If, over a small dynamic range, the output is a good representation of the input, then it is likely to fit any model that measures the velocity vector, so that any reasonable model would fit.

2. MOTION OF OBJECTS OF DIFFERENT SIZES

In discussing the light input to a single retinula cell, we took stripes of different periods as representative of visual patterns containing objects of all different sizes. Light modulation at the receptor level was plotted against stripe period or the reciprocal of this—the spatial frequency (see Figs. 4 and 5).

In exactly the same way, the response of the whole visual system, taken as any convenient measure of the optomotor response and plotted as a function of the stripe period or spatial frequency, provides a summary of the response of an actual eye to objects of different sizes. At the same time, the predicted response of a hypothetical model of the motion-detecting system may be calculable for this stimulus, so that the model of motion detection can be tested against the actual responses in a mathematically compact way. Most results to date have been plotted in terms of stripe period rather than its reciprocal, spatial frequency (see Fig. 22).

As stripes are progressively narrowed, the response to their motion falls to zero at some value at which the stripes are no longer resolved. This is a poor test of receptor resolution, however, because the slightest irregularity in the stripes can cause a response when the stripes themselves are no longer resolved. Irregularities are equivalent to added components of greater width, and give values of acceptance angle that are too low. As stripes are progressively increased in width, the response increases to a maximum. From Eq. (6), ct (norm) = 80% when the stripe period is four times the acceptance angle. The increase in the response is attributed to the increasing modulation caused in the receptors by stripes of increasing period. In the fly, negative responses (in the opposite direction) are found at intermediate stripe widths, as explained previously.

For the widest stripes, the situation is very instructive. If the motion-detecting system in the optic lobe is designed to measure velocity, it should do so independently of object size. One black–white edge crossing the eye should give the same response, for the same velocity, as many narrower stripes. It is clear, however, that stripes of a period more than four times the acceptance angle will saturate the receptor modulation (Fig. 5). Therefore, if motion detection is only the correlation between receptors that are adjacent or subadjacent on the retina, the response should fall off at large stripe periods (i.e., motion of large objects should be underestimated). In fact, in the fly this fall off at large stripe periods does not occur, as shown in Fig. 22(c), unless most of the eye is covered, leaving only a small region able to see, as in Fig. 22(e). At low light intensities only wide stripes are seen, even in the fly—Fig. 22(a)—and the apparent acceptance angle increases from 1.7° to more than 10°, as shown in Fig. 22(b), once again strongly indicating that motion of large objects across the eye as a whole is detected by a mechanism that correlates flicker between widely separated, as well as between adjacent, ommatidia. Night-flying insects have receptors with acceptance angles of 10° or more, which is their compromise between catching the essential photons and dividing up the visual world into angle labeled neurons.

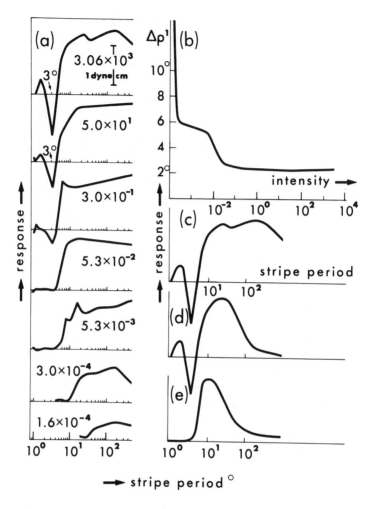

Fig. 22. Turning responses of a flying fly to moving stripes as a function of stripe period. The stripes are wider toward the right side of the abscissa. Part (a) shows that in dim light (lower traces on left, relative intensities shown) only the responses to the widest stripes persist. Part (b) shows the field width $\Delta\rho$ in degrees measured as acceptance angle, which is inferred from the responses in (a), as a function of intensity. The field is constant with $\Delta\rho' = 1.7°$ over a wide range of bright light, but there is a sudden transition in dim light, when the resolution is lost and field widths jump to about 10°, as if a system of combined fields is then revealed. Part (c) shows the smoothed curve for bright light, as in (a). Part (d) illustrates the theoretical curve from the cross-multiplication model of motion perception—Fig. 21(a). Part (e) shows the response of a fly with only a small group of facets not occluded. The responses to broad stripes, and the reversal of the direction near 3° period, have disappeared. Evidence for interaction between well-separated parts of the eye comes from (b) and (e). [From Eckert (1973) with (e) added from personal communication.]

3. Motion at Different Angular Velocities

From an enormous literature one example must suffice.

Locusts have a very sensitive head-rotation response when a striped drum is rotated around them with its axis along the long axis of the animal. Oscillation of the drum at frequencies from .0014 to 6 Hz, with an optimum near .5 Hz, is followed with great precision at amplitudes down to .005°, which is about .005 of the interommatidial angle in this plane (Thorson, 1966). Incidentally, there is, unlike the response for the motion-detecting neurons, a fall-off in response to stripes subtending more than 12° at the eye. Careful analysis has revealed that:

1. Measurements of optomotor responses do not permit one to distinguish between a large number of available models of the mechanism.
2. Failure of the optomotor response at low angular velocity can be interpreted as adaptation of receptors, and attenuation of the response at high velocity as failure of the muscles to respond fast enough.

Furthermore, other considerations show that model building based on behavioral output is misleading with reference to mechanisms or explanations of the optomotor response. The response of the insect visual system, even at the receptor level, to sine wave modulation of the light intensity is not a linear function of modulation frequency, either in the locust (Pinter, 1972) or in the fly (Zettler, 1969), especially when the extensive changes over several orders of magnitude caused by light adaptation are included. The summation of photons as light at the receptor is approximately linear (see Fig. 5), but the summation of responses at deeper levels is clearly not so. As the lateral interactions in the lamina and deeper are certainly nonlinear, the summation of Fourier components of a pattern at lamina level is also unlikely to be independent of the temporal frequency. In short, the response as a function of velocity is not a good indicator of the motion-detecting mechanism, because the experimental results are influenced by additional, highly nonlinear processes that obscure the actual mechanism.

A general principle of many nervous systems is that properties of the outside world that take on different magnitudes become coded into different nerve cells according to magnitude. This is called *range fractionation*, as one form of line labeling, and can be reasonably expected to apply to velocity measurement. In the crab, for example, fast motion across the eye excites high-velocity detectors that eventually feed into fast motor units, whereas slow-velocity detectors feed into slow motor units (Horridge & Burrows, 1968). Therefore, one transfer function that fits the responses of the whole system obscures, rather than elucidates, the separate components that act in parallel.

There is also a doubt whether motion is measured accurately at all in the nervous system, because the precision of the freely moving animal stems from the visual feedback loop with a high gain (Fig. 23d), and intensity differences are compensated by the first synaptic layer.

4. NUMBER OF ESSENTIAL OMMATIDIA

In the fly, the turning tendency as measured behaviorally on a Y-maze globe is measurable when illumination of a single receptor is switched repeatedly to a neighboring receptor (Kirschfeld, 1972). Quite a different result is found with the locust (Kien, 1975), where at least 50 ommatidia must be excited, even with a strong stimulus, before a directional response is observed. This being so, an actual motion stimulus across many ommatidia is essential, and excitation of numerous parallel channels cannot be avoided.

5. DISTINCTION BETWEEN MOTION PERCEPTION AND VISION

If the minimum number of ommatidia is large, it implies only that the signal from each is weak, for the neuron on which they converge must be an averager. The system can only pick out the magnitude and direction of average motion. We know that the visual field usually contains random-sized objects, the actual positions of which are irrelevant to the measurement of motion. Therefore, we might suppose that the motion-measuring system evolved so that the relative angles to the contrasts cannot be detected in the final output. In fact, this is what has been found in the optomotor (Reichardt, 1957) and landing response of the fly (Perez de Talens & Ferretti, 1975), so that Eq. (13) in Section II cannot be based on data from motion perception. The experimental fact that the sine-wave components of a pattern of stripes can be shifted in phase without effect on velocity measurement means that *the motion detectors* of the fly are not making use of its angle-distributed ommatidia to see a pattern of stripes in space; but the fly proves by its other responses that at the same time it sees the directions of contrasts very well.

6. THE OPTOMOTOR MEMORY PARADIGM

If an arthropod is allowed to view a contrasting pattern for a time (called the build-up time), following which the lights go out and the pattern is moved during a dark period of up to 15 min, when reilluminated there is a response that shows that the animal has interpreted the change as movement. The existence of this response shows that the former position of the pattern has persisted in some way in the visual system. Much more is known about optomotor memory in crabs that in insects, but in both groups the optomotor memory stimulus excites the unidirectional motion-detecting neurons of the optic lobe.

The optomotor memory paradigm is a useful tool as follows:

1. It allows the stimulus to be placed at two points or lines on the retina with no stimulus to the intervening ommatidia, so that correlation can be tested as a function of distance between ommatidia (see Fig. 23).
2. The stimulus does not itself move, so that motion detection can be analyzed without motion of the input. Modulation in the receptors is therefore more easily controlled.
3. The durations of the initial stimulus, the dark period, and the second stimulus can be varied. This makes possible the measurement of time constants that could be part of the motion detection mechanism.

Optomotor memory is apparently an incidental consequence of long-time constants in the mechanism of velocity measurement, but there are differences between responses to motion and the equivalent optomotor memory stimulus (same distance moved in same time). For the memory stimulus, never met in nature, there is no reason that the same relations between stimulus and response should be maintained, because the sudden transients introduce additional nonlinearities.

The nature and location of the persistent factor in optomotor memory is not known, but possibly this is one of the most accessible points where long time constants, essential for responses to angular velocities down to .002° sec^{-1}, can be studied in the nervous system.

7. The Model with Asymmetrical Delay

Motion of a contrast across the eye causes excitation in one channel followed at regular intervals by similar excitation in successive channels across the projection in the optic lobe (see Fig. 21). We can argue that if the eye has to measure velocity it has to have an inbuilt measure of time that makes itself felt in the measuring process. A very simple model was suggested by Barlow and Levick (1965) for motion-detecting ganglion cells of the rabbit's retina. The essential feature is a lateral inhibition in one direction with inbuilt delay in the lateral connection—see Fig. 21(b). Responses of a directionally selective locust optic lobe neuron are illustrated in Fig. 25.

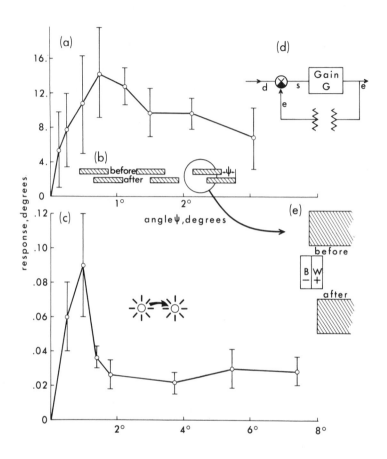

Fig. 23. Optomotor memory. A contrasting object is moved during a brief period of darkness. When the light returns, the insect (or in these cases, the crab) responds to the new situation as if it infers the direction of the movement from the new position in relation to the remembered old position. (a) Responses for drum movements ranging from .125° to 3.125°. The stimulus is to a clamped seeing eye: The response is from the other eye, which is blind but free to move. We therefore have the open loop situation—no visual feedback, see (d)—in which gains measured as (response)/(stimulus) are up to 100. [After Horridge (1966a).] (b) Regular stripes before and after the dark period. (c) Responses to a single light that is switched off and replaced by a similar light at a small angle to the first. Both eyes of the crab are free to see and move (closed visual loop). [After Horridge (1966b).] (d) The effect of the high gain G in all normal activity is to make the optomotor response follow closely the external stimulus because $e = Gs$ and $s = d - e$. Therefore $e/d = G/(1 + G)$ where $d =$ stimulus velocity, $e =$ eye velocity and $s =$ relative velocity across the eye. If G is large, therefore, $e/d \simeq 1$. (e) The theory that a white–black edge induces a black-sensitive (B−) and white-sensitive (W+) zone. Large responses are attributed to changes in one of these zones. [After Wiersma & Hirsch (1975).]

64

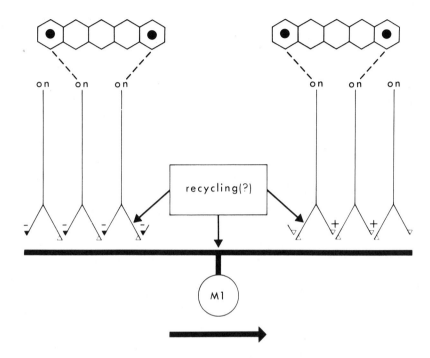

Fig. 24. Summary of the properties of the Ml neuron in the lobula of the locust. In one-way motion detection every ommatidium projects into the motion-detecting network, but the lateral interactions are between every fifth ommatidium. Open triangles represent excitatory synapses; closed triangles are inhibitory. Both of the circuits drawn are to be considered as covering all the input field of the neuron. Compare with M1 in Fig. 27. [After Kien (1975).]

8. Motion-Detecting Neurons

In this section it is essential to keep separate the data relating to the fly and the locust, the only two insects that have been investigated in detail. Locusts have two convenient motion-detecting neurons in the deep optic lobe, one (M1) responsive to forward motion, the other (M2) to backward motion across the eye. The following main findings from Kien (1975) relate to the mechanism of detection of motion of edges.

1. The relation between response and velocity is independent of stripe width, for regular stripes, over a wide range.
2. Using the optomotor memory paradigm as the stimulus makes it possible to present changes in stimulus to particular facets at con-

trolled spacings. The pattern is moved during a short period of darkness and the neurons respond on reillumination, by which time the pattern is in a new position on the retina. The response of the M1 neuron as a function of the spacing of successive presentations shows that the M1 neuron receives numerous inputs from small fields each with a diameter of about 1–5°, and that interactions leading to motion perception occur with a maximum effect between every fifth input along a horizontal row. The inputs are clearly retinula cells, lamina ganglion cells, or other neurons connected only to single ommatidia.

3. The M2 neuron has *in addition* other inputs from fields of 2.5–4° (probably pairs of ommatidia), and here the interaction leading to motion detection is between units separated by six ommatidia.

4. The time course of the lateral interaction can be studied by varying the dark period in the optomotor memory paradigm. For the M1 neuron the excitatory effect decays in about .5 sec (corresponding to a minimum velocity of 20°/sec) but the period for the M2 neuron is up to 2 sec (corresponding to about 5°/sec).

At present, the model of inputs shown in Fig. 24 is the simplest arrangement that is compatible with the single-neuron responses. The optomotor responses of the locust show a remarkable sensitivity, particularly in the vertical plane. With both eyes stimulated, the locust *Schistocerca* detects oscillations down to .01°, but this is certainly the result of summation over both eyes, and local stimulation of selected facets produces no responses.

No doubt there are many other small motion-detecting neurons that have not yet been found with the microelectrode. By the size principle (Davis, 1971), small neurons should be the tonic ones, responsive to a slower range of movement. It is therefore not surprising to find that the range of the largest neurons does not extend to the low velocities of 38°/day observed in the behavioral optomotor response (Thorson, 1966).

Fly optic lobes have large directionally sensitive neurons in the deepest optic neuropile, the lobula plate. By careful adjustment of the position and timing of two small bright stimuli, it is possible to elicit responses that agree with the model in Fig. 24. The preferred direction is first determined, then two small spots of light are arranged along the preferred axis of the neuron and flashed in succession. With the spot sequence in the preferred direction, responses are elicited or enhanced; with the spot succession in the null direction, the expected response to the second flash is occluded. Furthermore, in the preferred direction the excitatory interaction peaks at each 5° of angle and extends to 20° or more. The inhibitory interaction does not spread so far, only about 10° in the null

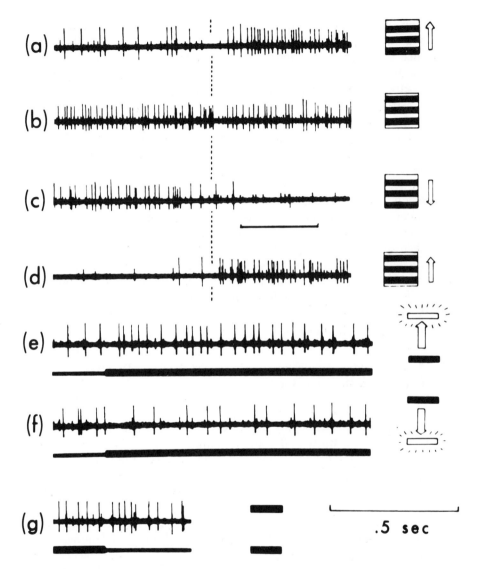

Fig. 25. What one actually observes via the microelectrode is a series of nerve impulses, and the discoveries at this extracellular level come from manipulation of the stimulus, rather than from the character of the responses: (a) Motion in the preferred direction causes a response; (b) Stopping does not necessarily restore the background rate; (c) Motion in the opposite direction suppresses spikes; (d) Return to (a); (e) A single light jumping to a new position simulates motion (phi phenomenon (e), (f)). The response wanes *slowly* although the stimulus is abrupt; (f) The apparent motion in the opposite direction inhibits slightly; (g) Both lights going on together—but otherwise as in (e), (f) cause a small burst. The responses are from a monocular unit with 50° field in the deep optic lobe of the locust, probably as in Fig. 24. [From Horridge *et al.* (1965).]

direction. These experiments (Mimura, 1975) agree with the model that has a unidirectional lateral spread of inhibition, in that an inhibitory influence can indeed be demonstrated. Evidence that there is a mechanism of motion perception acting between nearby ommatidia is obtained by directly stimulating single receptors (Kirschfeld, 1972).

An instructive comparison can be made between neurons recorded at different levels in the cat. When sensitivity is plotted against spatial frequency, the curves for retinal ganglion cells are broad, but fall into several classes covering different parts of the range from .05 to 5 cycles degree^{-1}. For lateral geniculate cells, the curves are more peaked and overlap less. Simple cortical cells, however, have quite narrow spatial frequency ranges, with many different classes (Maffei & Fiorentini, 1973). Moreover, there is evidence that the gain varies with stripe width, which compensates for the greater modulation caused by larger stripes. In the cat, therefore, *spatial frequency becomes progressively more perfectly line-labeled in the ascending pathway*, strongly suggesting that we have a system that improves the means of later classifying the size of the objects subtended at the eye. Although Northrop (1975) describes the method in his extensive review, no spatial frequency spectra have yet appeared for arthropod optic-lobe units.

B. The Descending Contralateral Movement Detector (DCMD): Indicator of Research Trends

One of the most thoroughly described of all identified neurons is that studied by Parry, Burtt and Catton, Satija, Cosens, Palka, Horn and Rowell, O'Shea and others, in the locust. The cell body lies at the base of the optic lobe, the axon descends in the contralateral ventral cord as far as the metathoracic ganglion (see Fig. 26). A very similar but less-studied neuron has its fiber on the ipsilateral side. The neuron identification is reliable; the known outputs are limited to some metathoracic motoneurons that are associated with preparation and release of the jump.

Adequate stimuli are abrupt movements of contrasting objects anywhere in the visual field of one eye, or dimming of a small area. Whole-eye changes of brightness are hardly effective. Sensitivity to movement of a small area in a vertical plane is greatest near the equator (probably due to greater receptor-field overlap); the sensitivity to horizontal movement is greatest behind the head, diminishing linearly to nothing for stimuli that are dead ahead—compare Fig. 15(d).

The most obvious feature of this neuron is its extreme lability. Habituation is detectable at stimulus intervals as great as 19 min, and when pinned

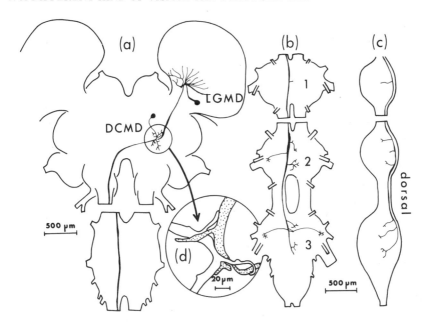

Fig. 26. Topography of the DCMD and LGMD neurons of the locust. (a) The short LGMD forms a synapse with the DCMD in the brain. The DCMD runs from the deep optic lobe in the brain, and down the cord. (b) The DCMD in the three thoracic ganglia of the ventral cord. (c) Lateral view. (d) The synapse from the lobula giant neuron (LGMD), which is a spiking interneuron of the lobula (third optic neuropile). [Modified after O'Shea & Williams (1974).]

down, full responsiveness is not regained by a thoroughly habituated animal for about 1 hr. The habituation process is so local that regional independence can be demonstrated at angles corresponding to a few facets on the eye. Dishabituation cannot be brought about by visual stimuli, but results from a great variety of mechanoreceptor inputs or spontaneous changes in the animal's state of arousal, or by unrestrained activity.

Although there is no clear directional selectivity, there is preference, even on the first presentation, to the rotation of a small striped wheel or to linear movements in one direction, and the evidence is that the DCMD is fed by numerous small-field units that change their relative contributions. All the responses are labile and depend on the history of the stimulation pattern, for example, directional sensitivity depends on the direction of the first presented stimulus (primary effect).

The most interesting feature of this neuron is that in the normal course of the animal's own motion it fails to respond to general motion, but still responds normally (i.e., as if to an isolated stimulus) to the movement of a small contrasting object. Flying or walking is accompanied by an enormous increase in responsiveness. There is no significant difference in the background activity when the animal is stationary and when it is turning passively or actively relative to the visual field. This behavior deserves further analysis, and it illustrates that features that are adapted to complex stimulus situations are not discovered at the first, or even the hundredth, recording of a unit.

All stimuli have simultaneous inhibitory and excitatory effects which sum in such a way that stimulation by complex patterns over large areas inhibits, but small-area stimulation excites. The optimum area of stimulation is also a complex function of stimulus strength. After a small area is dimmed, the unit recovers in .5 sec, but a small moving stimulus on the same spot suppresses it for up to 5 sec. The inhibitory effects of other moving stimuli influence the entire visual field of the unit and are therefore quite different from the local effects of repetition.

The minimal movement of a single contrasting object is small. A moving point source of light excites when rapidly moved about .3°. To a movement at $3°\ sec^{-1}$ the response occurs with a latency of about .1 sec.

The main input to the DCMD must be from retinula cell axons, or cells excited by them directly. The medulla cartridges are the most proximal probable inputs because the habituation is independent in regions down to this small scale, but other inputs must confer the primacy features.

The other main input comes from the motion-detecting system of the optic lobe, which acts in such a way that motion of a small object can be detected even relative to a moving background. My own view is that here we have a clue to the operation of the whole system behind the compound eye: pattern perception takes place on the inescapable background of motion perception by the compound eye, in that the directions are seen, but the background motion is cancelled out.

C. The Search for Invariants

At the initial stages in pattern perception, the activity of the neurons is a direct result of the angle-dependent intensity modulation in the outside world. We know this is true for retinula cells and lamina ganglion cells, but not for some neurons, even of the lamina (Mimura, 1976). At the final stage the activity loses its angle-dependent components and becomes the specific neuron control of the visual behavior.

The question is which invariant properties of the pattern are picked out by the higher-order neurons from the lower-order ones. These invariant

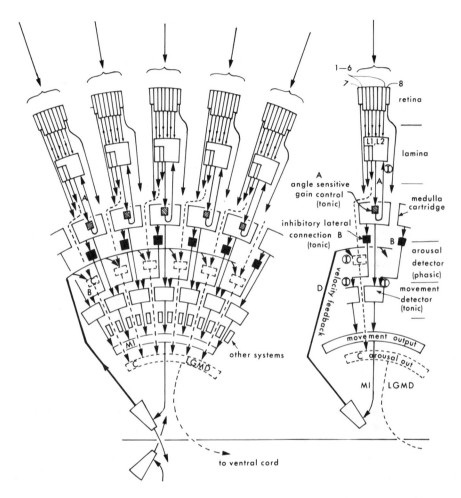

Fig. 27. A system that represents the detection of a small moving contrast without response to a background that is itself moving. On the right is a single unit of the system, lying behind a single ommatidium. On the left, five such units brought together show how the eye, being compound, necessarily has a repeated array of neuronal units, which could correspond to the anatomical cartridges (neuron bundles) of the medulla and lobula (second and third optic neuropiles). 1–6, 7, 8: retinula (receptor) cells. L1, L2: lamina ganglion cells. (A) There is a local gain control in the lamina, to which angle-conserving neurons of the medulla contribute. (B) Lateral interaction by delay and inhibition abstracts one-way movement. (C) Any change in intensity registered on a lamina cartridge excites the arousal system (dashed line). (D) The motion detecting system (M1 feedback) is a gate to the arousal system, so that background movement of whole fields prevents excitation of the LGMD (see Fig. 26).

properties may be found by analyzing responses at any level with a large number of patterns and by searching for which classes of patterns are confused, which are discriminated, spontaneously preferred, or systematically ignored. The responding unit may be a neuron or the whole animal. The best known invariants are flicker, light at a particular angle, regular repetition (which is soon ignored), and linear motion of contrasts across the eye.

1. STRATEGIES FOR BLIND BIOLOGISTS

Let us consider for a moment how we ourselves deal with the mass of objects of the outside world, seen as images in our visual world. We see them with edges as something we could pick up to handle, and we give them names that accentuate their independent existence. Having ourselves this breakdown of the outside world, we naturally wonder whether seeing objects has any meaning for insects. Unfortunately, experiments so far have not suggested anything of the sort.

As another exercise in skin casting, let us consider our own way of thinking about the stimulus–response relationship. We can readily see the response as a *function* of the input. This notion is quickly translatable into the idea that a mathematical function relates the output to the input for each neuron and by extension for the whole animal (i.e., response = f (inputs). The question the researcher directs himself toward is whether the nature of the function f can be worked out from observations on the whole animal and its components. For reasons discussed, because many channels lie in parallel, this is rarely possible with the whole animal, nor with individual components unless the reacting system is so limited that it no longer represents normal activity.

A third way of looking at the problem is to search for neurons that respond specifically to trigger stimuli of obvious adaptive significance, such as the branched twigs in Fig. 13. Having found the stimulus behaviorally, the problem is to find the neuron that is triggered by it, if a unique one exists. Alternatively, having found a neuron by blind recording, the problem is to find what it responds to.

The interaction between microelectrode and behavior studies is well illustrated by the work at Sussex. First anatomical studies were linked with careful characterization of the optic-lobe units of the moth (Collett, 1972 and previously), but behaviorally the moth was not suitable for analysis. Secondly, detailed studies of the tracking behavior of flies (Collett & Land, 1975), which have better-defined behavior in flight, show what kind of stimuli would be required for sorting out the properties of neurons that could be relevant in the optic lobe, and hypothetical neurons are proposed—Fig. 15(d). The next step is to demonstrate them.

2. BEHAVIORAL CUES

Those who study only behavior sometimes argue that, if they can make sufficient tests, they can define the bottlenecks in the nervous system so closely that they may be recognizable as chunks of mechanism that one day might actually be found inside.

One practical but tedious approach, with the visual responses of the bee, described by von Helversen (1972), is to use a series of relatively simple patterns which progressively differ more and more from each other in one way (along a stimulus dimension). A stimulus dimension is taken to be any attribute of the pattern, like length of edge, angle of edge, color of parts, number of corners, or brightness, which is convenient to work with. The responses to each feature are defined quantitatively *in its own separate dimension*. When the bee consistently confuses the quantity in one dimension with a different quantity in another dimension, we assume that we have found some invariant factor that it sees in common between the two patterns. Because there are numerous possible kinds of patterns, we have to work with multidimensional stimulus space, and we have to define stimulus clusters. Within the cluster, different effective stimuli are interpreted similarly by the insect. These stimulus clusters in multidimensional space will be the more significant to the analysis the more there are of them and the closer they are together. Their proximity, as seen along different dimensions, is measured by varying the test patterns and counting the numbers of spontaneous choices of patterns or results of tests where a choice is made by trained animals.

The question is whether we can anticipate what stimuli to use by trying a variety of patterns that contain features that might be relevant to the behavior of the animal. Another way to express this is to say that feature detectors of the nervous system have evolved, and are therefore likely to be matched to commonly recurring features of the outside world that are useful as cues in situations relevant for survival. We would call them "good" cues, and they will be marked by a low threshold.

Certainly, some of these good cues can be found behaviorally (see Section III). The trouble is that the feature detector may be a combination of neurons that are very difficult to find simultaneously when the response to the cue is examined *while in action* by probing with a microelectrode. The more specialized and easily elicited the response, the more hopeful we are that the behavioral invariant will turn out to be the combination of inputs necessary to excite a single higher-order neuron. In most cases examined, however, a hiatus has been reached because many feature detectors excited in parallel act on many motoneurons in parallel, and in examining neurons one at a time it is impossible to say how much each is contributing to what proportion of the response.

The previous paragraph sets out the reason why the understanding of optic-lobe function in pattern recognition has hardly moved off the first square. Some of the rules of the game, and the probable best direction in which to move can be discerned, but we await a research breakthrough that will start real progress. No invariant class of features has yet been found. A lucky strike on the right neurons will quickly lead to rapid advances.

3. The Principle of Necessary Neuronal Complexity

I do not want to inhibit efforts to present simplified visual abstraction mechanisms of the bee, or efforts that reduce behavior to numbers, but one relevant and very damning inference can be made from the great numbers of neurons in parallel in the optic tracts.

Each different interneuron in the tract from the optic lobe to the brain represents a dimension of information from the eye. Each has its frequency code of impulses as a measure of stimulus intensity along this dimension. No two neurons can be alike, or else they would have the same inputs and dendritic pattern. Therefore, we can justifiably ask why these numbers of neurons are necessary if perception can be reduced to a few parameters.

4. Maximum Earliest Information for Simultaneous Processing

Because the maximum information is found in the receptor responses and is reduced at every neural stage thereafter, the best place to extract an invariant is immediately behind the receptors. Therefore, we can expect all the invariants to be extracted simultaneously as far forward as possible in the processing system. In practice, we find one stage of gain control and lateral interaction at the level of the lamina, as discussed previously. Even the lamina, however, is bypassed by one or two receptor axons that run directly to the medulla from each ommatidium. In fact, the histological maps of the second optic neuropile, the medulla (see Strausfeld, 1976), could be interpreted in terms of multidimensional simultaneous processing.

5. Necessity to Examine Every Stage

Unfortunately, it is characteristic of outputs of neurons and of behavior that the animal's repertoire is limited in relation to the number of possible cues available to it. For all the varied intensity distributions of light, photoactivated behavior is a simple movement either toward or away; for all of the relative motions across the retina, the optomotor turning response is limited to plus or minus in three dimensions. Alerting responses are *on* and *off*. Discrimination as a response carries little information about the invariants that have been relied upon for the behavior.

To see what the insect really sees we would like a response on our oscilloscope as rich as that given by a camera, which provides a picture crowded with detail rather like our own introspective view. A camera would be no use in revealing the transform at a lens and silver bromide surface if its best response were a single depolarization pattern, an amount of heat generated, or a weight of silver formed. With something like 10^{200} bits of information per unit integration time potentially carried by a compound eye, even the general principles of the mechanism are not likely to be inferred from an output containing about 10 bits of information. To see what goes on, we have to examine the abstraction of invariants by each identified neuron, as there is not sufficient information in the end product of each stage to allow exclusion of the alternative possible activities of the earlier stages. That is why the characterization of identified neurons has become such a crucial step in the analysis of neural processing.

VI. CONCLUSION

A. What Insects See

The idea that insects see is derived from our knowledge of our own introspective visual world. But, however adaptive the responses are that insects make to visual stimuli, we cannot infer from them the internal representation of visual space that we have ourselves. Taking the bee or dragonfly as examples of visually specialized arthropods, we find that they avoid objects and stabilize themselves visually in flight, recognize prey or flowers, recognize their territory visually, land successfully, respond differently to colors according to the situation, and chase each other. Directional responses show how important it is which facet is stimulated. We have seen, however, that there is hardly any evidence that animals with compound eyes see objects that are stationary relative to the eye, although this may be only because the appropriate tests have never been made. If relative movement across the eye is essential, it follows that *the essential pattern of excitation is in the timing*, as well as in the spatial projection across the optic lobe.

To explain these responses that the insect clearly makes we must, as set out above, find out what all the neurons are doing all along the chain from receptors to effectors *while the behavior is in progress*. This exhaustive process is the only way to find out what goes on. However, we can interpret the question of what insects see, as whether we can find from behavioral experiments alone what aspects of the stimulating situation the insect is able to utilize. By simple discrimination tests we find that bees, for example, see the angle of a contrasting edge relative to a base line or to the vertical. But because the edge sweeps across the retina at every movement, we cannot infer that the bee sees the angle of the edge as such. We have no evidence at all that the bee can extract from the relative movement across the eye the whole medley of angles presented at one time by the natural visual world. So although bees do see angles, we have no evidence that they see *the angles in complex patterns*. After numerous tests we might be able to say what the bee sees in the simple patterns of the tests, but we are hardly justified in saying that the bee can then pick out these features in a more complex natural situation. We form a different picture of what the bee sees with reference to color, because it responds to color according to the context. When attracted to light, it prefers ultraviolet, when seeking nectar it recognizes a cue best in the green region, but it learns most quickly when the cue is blue.

The relation between sight and motion perception can be considered as follows. If the animal stabilizes when flying, walking, or swimming by means of the optomotor response, it clearly makes a response to the amplitude and direction of the environmental relative motion. For this the direction of objects is irrelevant. Vision is more effective however, if the motion-detecting systems control the appropriate movements without entering into the circuits to do with attention, recognition, learning, "turning toward," and navigation, which are the circuits where the direction of the stimulus matters. The feature of the DCMD unit of the locust, which increases our understanding, is that it detects a small local movement while the eye is moving relative to the whole background. Perhaps the study of the optic lobe should be carried out while the optomotor mechanisms are in action, but paying attention only to neurons that do not see the general motion.

B. The Analysis of Insect Visual Mechanisms

What form would explanatory theories of the mechanisms of insect vision take? Up to the present decade, theories have depended on the kind of observation that gave rise to them, but this no longer suffices. We have four basic methods: inferences from anatomy, electrophysiology of single neurons, accounts of whole-animal behavior, and mathematical analysis of models. A theory based on any one class of data, or even on two, is not likely to be relevant to the explanation of the other kind of observation, but this has often been done. In this respect, the mathematical models of whole-animal behavior have been the worst offenders, in that they have tended to ignore the anatomical substrate and the physiological activity of the units of the system, the neurons.

In this decade (note that we can operate only within a historical context), the analysis of other nervous systems has just reached a point where we recognize that the neurons often form numerous repeated *circuits of restricted locality and action*. Examples in the vertebrate retina, spinal cord, cerebellum, and ascending sensory systems will be familiar to many. These circuits consist of a few neurons connected together in a pattern that is repeated in a regular array. They are comparable to integrated transistor circuits in which a number of interacting units form a subsystem that is a repeated component of a larger system. In neuroanatomy, the initial task of naming the neurons is well advanced, and now we face the larger task of function-finding and identifying these unit circuits. Similarly, electrophysiological recording has hitherto been directed at the activity of single neurons, but a consequence of their arrangement in numerous parallel channels is that the responses of a single neuron may have significance only when considered together with the simultaneous responses in many other neurons. So far, the analyses that have proved successful are those where the system is so simple that even dual channel recording is hardly necessary. Also we realize now that feedback loops, together with gross nonlinearities, make the analysis of neuronal circuits very difficult. The only cases successfully analyzed where feedback loops are important are those in which the loop is an external movement of the whole animal or eye, or is a loop that can be readily removed for the analysis. *There has been successful analysis only where the system has been cut down to an extremely simple form.*

The arthropod optic lobe is the example par excellence of numerous circuits of restricted locality and action in parallel, with successive neuropiles of ascending sensory circuits in cascade, and with abstraction by many neurons in parallel leading off at each level. In such a system we must stress again what kinds of explanations we seek—descriptions of what acts on what, or accounts of the optimization by which each neuron field is adapted to its function.

One simplifying factor is that the number of outputs is so reduced that some of those significant in behavior are single neurons. One-way movement in the whole visual field is boiled down to an output that is spikes in a single neuron or a small group of neurons in each optic lobe. So, we find four small classes of neurons covering movement in the four main directions of the visual field. Similarly, a few outputs of the optic lobe that feed into the two DCMD fibers of the ventral cord are sensitive to arousal by any small movement in the visual field—even relative to a moving background—with habituation to repetition, but are sensitive to some kinds of novelty in the signal. With these neurons in the main control line, it then becomes possible to explain the major features of movement perception or arousal, but this straightforward approach omits two complications.

First, where analysis has been pushed a little further there has always turned out to be other, smaller, slower and more subtle pathways in parallel with the main one. In this respect, the search for further, finer, and more subtle pathways in parallel is an open-ended question of how much detail of the behavior is examined. Secondly, the motor centers on which a single interneuron studied acts, and the interneuron itself, have properties that vary with time and with the history of the preparation. Therefore, even with a single transmission line in which every impulse can be recorded, the responses are not necessarily explicable in detail.

Second, the most interesting aspect of finding the function of interneurons is that the electrode does not see the pattern of excitation that is relevant to the next neurons down the line. Any theory is developed from what excited the experimenter, but the nervous system works on what excites the neurons of the next higher order. I wish to point the way forward and therefore stress that, before measurements on any particular neuron have gone too far, it is essential to make some test of the relevance of the responses to the next neurons down the line. This is why the behavior of the whole animal is relevant to the analysis of neuron function.

Finally, just as it is impossible to jump from the anatomy to a physiological interpretation, or directly from the behavioral to the mathematical model, so it is invalid to infer a relationship between the stimulus, the sensory neurons, interneurons at different levels, motoneurons, movements, and whole animal behavior unless the actual step in the causative chain has been demonstrated. For example, different kinds of behavioral responses to colors cannot be attributed, except in a superficial way, to the spectral sensitivity of the receptors. When we know that many lines lie in parallel, but cannot say what is the relative significance of the excitation in each, there is a great temptation merely to describe the input–output relations and suggest the first plausible model that fits. To do this, however, obscures the issue and begs the very question that one is setting out to answer, detracting attention from the direct attack. What is the direct attack? It is *the multichannel analysis, step by step through the causative chain of named neurons while the relevant behavior is going on*. This may sound like an electrophysiologist grinding his own electrode, but no other method of observation allows one to see the neurons in action, or to pick out the relevant interactions between neurons. The question as to whether the behavior can be analyzed becomes a question as to the practical possibility of analyzing the behavior by this method. If the neurons are too small or too numerous, then for more than one step of inference beyond the direct observations their action will forever remain a mystery.

References

Anderson, A. The ability of honeybees to generalize visual stimuli. In R. Wehner (Ed.), *Information processing in the visual systems of arthropods*. Berlin: Springer, 1972.

Baldus, K. Experimentelle Untersuchungen über die Entfernungslokalisation der Libellen (*Aeschna cyanea*). *Zeitschrift für vergleichende Physiologie*, 1926, **3**, 475–505.

Barlow, H. B., & Levick, W. R. The mechanism of directionally selective units in rabbit's retina. *Journal of Physiology*, 1965, **178**, 477–504.

Barnes, W. J. P., & Horridge, G. A. Two dimensional records of the eyecup movements of the crab *Carcinus*. *Journal of Experimental Biology*, 1969, **50**, 673–682.

Bullock, T. H., & Horridge, G. A. *Structure and function in the nervous systems of invertebrates*. San Francisco: Freeman, 1965.

Cajal, S. R., & Sanchez, S. D. Contribución al conocimento de los centros nerviosos de los insectos. Parte 1. Retina y centros opticos. *Trabajos del Laboratorio de Investigaciones biológicas, del Universidad, Madrid*. 1915, **13**, 1–168.

Coggeshall, J. C. The landing response and visual processing in the milkweed bug *Oncopeltus fasciatus*. *Journal of Experimental Biology*, 1972, **57**, 401–413.

Collett, T. S. Visual neurones in the anterior optic tract of the privet hawk moth. *Journal of Comparative Physiology*, 1972, **78**, 396–433.

Collett, T. S., & Land, M. F. Visual control of flight behaviour in the hoverfly *Syritta pipiens* L. *Journal of Comparative Physiology*, 1975, **99**, 1–66.

Cruse, H. Versuch einer quantitativen Beschriebung des Formensehens der Honigbiene. *Kybernetik*, 1972, **11**, 185–200.

Cruse, H. An application of the cross-correlation coefficient to pattern recognition of honey bees. *Kybernetik*, 1974, **15**, 73–84.

Davis, W. J. Functional significance of motoneuron size and soma position in swimmeret system of the lobster. *Journal of Neurophysiology*, 1971, **34**, 274–288.

Duelli, P. A fovea for e-vector orientation in the eye of *Cataglyphis bicolor* (Formicidae, Hymenoptera). *Journal of Comparative Physiology*, 1975, **102**, 43–56.

Eckert, H. Optomotorische Untersuchungen am visuellen System der Stubenfliege *Musca domestica* L. *Kybernetik*, 1973, **14**, 1–23.

Etienne, A. S. Analyse der Schlagauslösenden Bewegungsparameter einer punktförmigen Beuteattrappe bei der *Aeschna*-Larve. *Zeitschrift für vergleichende Physiologie*, 1969, **64**, 71–110.

Geiger, G. Optomotor responses of the fly *Musca domestica* to transient stimuli of edges and stripes. *Kybernetik*, 1974, **16**, 37–43.

Goldsmith, T. H., & Bernard, G. D. The visual system of insects. In M. Rockstein (Ed.), *The physiology of Insecta*. Vol. II. (2nd ed.) New York: Academic Press, 1974.

Goodman, L. J. The landing responses of insects I. The landing response of the fly *Lucilia sericata* and other Calliphorinae. *Journal of Experimental Biology*, 1960, **37**, 854–878.

Götz, K. G. Optomotorische Untersuchung des visuellen Systems einiger Augenmutanten der Fruchtfliege *Drosophila*. *Kybernetik*, 1964, **2**, 77–92.

Helversen, O. von. The relationship between difference in stimuli and choice frequency in training experiments with the honeybee. In R. Wehner (Ed.), *Information processing in the visual systems of arthropods*. Berlin: Springer, 1972.

Hertz, M. 1929–34. Die Organisation des optischen Feldes bei der Biene. I. *Zeitschrift für vergleichende Physiologie*, **8**, 693–748. II; ibid, **11**, 107–145. III ibid. **14**, 629–674.

Horridge, G. A. Optokinetic memory in the crab, *Carcinus*. *Journal of Experimental Biology*, 1966, **44**, 233–245. (a)

Horridge, G. A. Optokinetic responses of the crab *Carcinus* to a single moving light. *Journal of Experimental Biology*, 1966, **44**, 263–274. (b)

Horridge, G. A. (Ed.) *The compound eye and vision of insects*. New York: Oxford Univ. Press, 1975.

Horridge, G. A. Insects which turn and look. *Endeavour*, 1977, *1* (New Series), 1–10. (a)

Horridge, G. A. Looking at insect eyes. *Scientific American*, July 1977, 108–120. (b)

Horridge, G. A., & Burrows, M. Tonic and phasic systems in parallel in the eyecup responses of the crab *Carcinus*. *Journal of Experimental Biology*, 1968, **49**, 269–284.

Horridge, G. A., Mimura, K., & Hardie, R. Fly photoreceptors III. Angular sensitivity as a function of wavelength and the limits of resolution. *Proceedings of the Royal Society of London, Series B,* 1976, **194**, 151–177.

Horridge, G. A., Scholes, J. H., Shaw, S., & Tunstall, J. Extracellular recordings from single neurones in the optic lobe and brain of the locust. In J. E. Treherne (Ed.), *The physiology of the insect central nervous system*. New York: Academic Press, 1965. Pp. 165–202.

Jander, R. Die optische Richtungsorientierung der roten Waldameise (*Formica rufa* L.). *Z. vergl. Physiol.* 1957, **40**, 162–238.

Jander, R. Visual pattern recognition and directional orientation in insects. Annals of the N.Y. Academy of Sciences, 1971, **188**, 5–11.

Jander, R., & Volk-Heinrichs, I. Das strauschspezifische Visuelle Perceptorsystem der Stabheuschrecke (*Carausius morosus*). *Zeitschrift für vergleichende Physiologie*, 1970, **70**, 425–477.

Kien, J. Motion detection in locusts and grasshoppers. In G. A. Horridge (Ed.), *The compound eye and vision of insects*. New York: Oxford Univ. Press, 1975. Pp. 410–422.

Kirschfeld, K. The visual system of *Musca*: Studies on optics, structure and function. In R. Wehner (Ed.), *Information processing in the visual systems of arthropods*. Berlin: Springer, 1972. Pp. 61–74.

Labhart, T. Behavioral analysis of light intensity discrimination and spectral sensitivity in the honey bee, *Apis mellifera*. *Journal of Comparative Physiology*, 1974, **95**, 203–216.

Land, M. F. Head movements and fly vision. In G. A. Horridge (Ed.), *The compound eye and vision of insects*. New York: Oxford Univ. Press, 1975. Pp. 469–489.

Land, M. F., & Collett, T. S. Chasing behaviour of houseflies (*Fannia cannicularis*). A description and analysis. *Journal of Comparative Physiology*, 1974, **89**, 331–357.

Laughlin, S. B. The function of the lamina ganglionaris. In G. A. Horridge (Ed.), *The compound eye and vision of insects*. New York: Oxford Univ. Press, 1975. (a)

Laughlin, S. B. Receptor function in the apposition eye: An electrophysiological approach. In A. W. Snyder & R. Menzel (Eds.), *Photoreceptor optics*. Berlin: Springer, 1975. Pp. 479–498. (b)

Lindauer, M. Pattern recognition in the honey bee. In W. Reichardt (Ed.), *Processing of optical data by organisms and by machines*. New York: Academic Press, 1969. Pp. 510–543.

Lutz, F. E. Apparently non-selective characters and combinations of characters, including a study of ultraviolet in relation to the flower-visiting habits of insects. Annals of the N.Y. Academy of Sciences, 1924, **29**, 181–283.

Maffei, L., & Fiorentini, A. The visual cortex as a spatial frequency analyser. Vision Research, 1973, **13**, 1255–1267.

Maldonado, H. The diematic reaction in the praying mantis Stagmatoptera biocellata. Zeitschrift für vergleichende Physiologie, 1970, **68**, 60–75.

Maldonado, H., & Barros-Pita, J. C. A fovea in the praying mantis eye. I. Estimation of the catching distance. Zeitschrift für vergleichende Physiologie, 1970, **67**, 58–78.

Maldonado, H., Rodriguez, E., & Balderrama, N. How mantids gain insight into the new maximum catching distance after each ecdysis. Journal of Insect Physiology, 1974, **20**, 591–603.

Mast, S. O. Photic orientation in insects with special reference to the drone fly, Eristalis tenax and the robber fly Erax rufibarbis. Journal of Experimental Zoology, 1923, **38**, 109–205.

Mazochin-Porshnyakov, G. A. Die Fähigkeit der Bienen visuelle Reize zu generalisieren. Zeitschrift für vergleichende Physiologie, 1969, **65**, 15–28.

Meyer, H. W. Geometric und funktionelle Spezialisierung des optischen Abtastrasters beim Bachwasserläufer (Velia caprai). Journal of Comparative Physiology, 1974, **92**, 85–103.

Mimura, K. Units of the optic lobe, especially movement. In G. A. Horridge (Ed.), The compound eye and vision of insects. New York: Oxford Univ. Press, 1975. Pp. 423–436.

Mimura, K. Some spatial properties in the first optic ganglion of the fly. Journal of Comparative Physiology, 1976, **105**, 65–82.

Mittelstaedt, H. Control systems of orientation in insects. Annual Review of Entomology, 1962, **7**, 177–198.

Northrop, R. B. Information processing in the insect compound eye. In G. A. Horridge (Ed.), The compound eye and vision of insects. New York: Oxford Univ. Press, 1975. Pp. 378–409.

O'Shea, M., & Williams, J. L. D. The anatomy and output connection of a locust visual interneurone; the lobula giant movement detector (LGMD) neurone. Journal of Comparative Physiology, 1974, **91**, 257–266.

Perez de Talens, A. F., & Ferretti, C. T. Landing and optomotor responses of the fly. Musca. In G. A. Horridge (Ed.), The compound eye and vision of insects. New York: Oxford Univ. Press, 1975. Pp. 490–512.

Pinter, R. B. Frequency and time domain properties of retinular cells of the desert locust (Schistocerca gregaria) and the house cricket (Acheta domesticus). Journal of Comparative Physiology, 1972, **77**, 383–397.

Poggio, T., & Reichardt, W. A theory of pattern-induced flight orientation of the fly Musca domestica. Kybernetik, 1973, **12**, 185–203.

Reichardt, W. Autokorrelations Auswertung als Funktionsprinzip des Zentralnervensystems. Zeitschrift für Naturforschung, 1957, **126**, 448–457.

Rilling, S. Mittelstaedt, H., & Roeder, K. D. Prey recognition in the praying mantis. Behaviour, 1959, **14**, 164–172.

Schnetter, B. Visuelle Formunterscheidung der Honigbiene im Bereich von Vier- und Sechsstrahlsternen. Zeitschrift für vergleichende Physiologie, 1968, **59**, 90–109.

Schnetter, B. Experiments on pattern discrimination in honey bees. In R. Wehner (Ed.), Information processing in the visual system of arthropods. Berlin: Springer, 1972. Pp. 195–200.

Schwalb, H. H. Beitrage zur Biologie der einheimischen Lampyriden Lambyris noctiluca Geoffr. und Phausius splendidula Lee, und experimentelle analyse Ihres Beutegang—

und sexualverhaltens. *Zoologisches Jahrbucher, abteilung für Systematik*, 1960, **88**, 399–550.

Snyder, A. W. Acuity of compound eyes: Physical limitations and design. *Journal of Comparative Physiology*, 1977, **116**, 161–182.

Snyder, A. W., & Miller, W. H. Photoreceptor diameter and spacing for highest resolving power. *Journal of the Optical Society of America*, 1977, **67**, 696–698.

Snyder, A. W., Stavenga, D. C., & Laughlin, S. B. Spatial information capacity of compound eyes. *Journal of Comparative Physiology*, 1977, **116**, 183–207.

Strausfeld, N. J. *Atlas of an insect brain*. Berlin: Springer, 1976.

Thorson, J. 1966. Small signal analysis of a visual reflex in the locust. Part 1. Input parameters, *Kybernetik* **3**, 41–52. Part 2. Frequency dependence, ibid. 53–66.

Trujillo-Cenóz, O., & Melamed, J. Light and electron microscope study of one of the systems of centrifugal fibers found in the lamina of muscoid flies. *Zeit. Zellforsch. Mikros. Anat.*, 1970, **110**, 336–349.

Wallace, G. K. Visual scanning in the desert locust *Schistocerca gregaria*. Forskal. *Journal of Experimental Biology*, 1959, **36**, 512–525.

Wehner, R. Dorsoventral asymmetry in the visual field of the bee *Apis mellifera*. *Journal of Comparative Physiology*, 1972, **77**, 256–277. (a)

Wehner, R. Pattern modulation and pattern detection in the visual system of Hymenoptera. In R. Wehner (Ed.), *Information processing in the visual systems of arthropods*. Berlin: Springer, 1972. Pp. 183–194. (b)

Wehner, R. Pattern recognition. In G. A. Horridge (Ed.), *The compound eye and vision of insects*. New York: Oxford Univ. Press, 1975. Pp. 75–113.

Wehner, R., & Wehner von Segesser, S. Calculation of visual receptor spacing in *Drosophila melanogaster* by pattern recognition experiments. *Journal of Comparative Physiology*, 1973, **82**, 165–177.

Wiersma, C. A. G., & Hirsch, R. Contrast induced zones as the basis of optomotor memory in the crab *Pachygrapsus*. *Journal of Comparative Physiology*, 1975, **102**, 173–188.

Wilson, M. Angular sensitivity of light and dark adapted locust retinula cells. *Journal of Comparative Physiology*, 1975, **97**, 323–328.

Wolf, E. The visual intensity discrimination of the honey bee. *Journal of General Physiology*, 1933, **16**, 407–422.

Zettler, F. Die Abhängigkeit des Übertragungsverhaltens von Frequenz und Adaptationszustand: gemessen am einzelnen Lichtrezeptor von *Calliphora erythrocephala*. *Zeitschrift für vergleichende Physiologie*, 1969, **64**, 432–449.

Chapter 2

PERCEPTUAL DEVELOPMENT: OBJECT AND SPACE

T. G. R. BOWER

I. INTRODUCTION

The study of perceptual development has a long theoretical history but a relatively brief experimental one. As long ago as 1940 the theoretical controversies were dismissed as meaningless and sterile (Boring, 1950). Indeed they were doomed to remain so until experimental possibility caught up with theoretical sophistication. This has happened in the relatively recent past, bringing unforeseen changes in theoretical possibilities rather than support for either of the classical theories (Bower, 1974a; E. J. Gibson, 1969).

II. TWO CLASSIC THEORIES OF PERCEPTUAL DEVELOPMENT

The two original opponents are *nativism* and *empiricism*. In its extreme form, nativism would maintain that a perceptually naive organism would have all of the perceptual capacities of a mature, experienced organism. In this theory, experience and practice are irrelevant to the emergence of perceptual skill. The perceptually naive organism need not be newborn.

Lack of experience after birth is seen as irrelevant in this context. For example, sight restoration experiments should result in a normally functioning organism regardless of the age at which the operation is done.

Extreme empiricism would maintain a very different set of propositions about perceptual development. In this theoretical context the perceptually naive organism, does not have any of the capacities of the experienced organism. While the experienced organism can respond to distal variables (Brunswik, 1956), the naive organism is restricted to the proximal variables that specify distal variables; thus while we see objects arrayed in three dimensions around us, the visually naive organism sees nothing more than an evanescent flux of retinal images. In this theory the shift from proximal to distal responding depends on specific opportunities for specific kinds of practice, the details varying somewhat from one theory to another.

These then are the two classic opponents. They are still influential and indeed, despite their patent absurdity, have adherents even today. The two theories are clear enough that tests are not difficult, given the availability of the appropriate experimental technology. The relevant experiments should concentrate on neonate organisms, organisms of various ages, and organisms given special or limited experience. Within this framework, researchers have looked at a large variety of problems. In this chapter I shall look at two, the problem of the perceptual constancies and the problem of intersensory coordination. Both demonstrate the theoretical oppositions and the methodological issues that arise in the study of perceptual development.

A. Theoretical Issues

The theoretical issues in the study of the perceptual constancies are relatively clear. Adults are capable of a whole range of constancies, position, size, shape, etc., in all of which some aspect of the perceptual response remains invariant, faithful to some aspect of the distal stimulus, despite gross changes in the mediating proximal stimulus. Clearly, an empiricist theory must predict that early in development constancy will be absent, with the perceptual response determined by the proximal variations rather than by the distal invariants; with greater experience response will tend more and more to the distal and less and less to the proximal.

1. THE EMPIRICIST HYPOTHESIS

These predictions are relatively clear and well formed. To test the empiricist hypothesis two sets of age trend comparisons are required, one assessing the accuracy of distally oriented responses, the other assessing the accuracy of proximally oriented responses. If we take size constancy as an example, the age trend should show with increasing age an *increasing* ability to detect size invariance with change in distance and a *decreasing* ability to detect proximal–retinal size variation with change in distance. I cannot overemphasize the importance of the joint age trends. Neither alone provides a test of an empiricist or any other hypothesis. Misunderstanding of this point has led to a surplus of confused writing on the subject.

2. BRUNSWIK, CRUIKSHANK, AND OTHER INVESTIGATORS

There are a number of classic studies of this issue. Not one provides any comfort for an empiricist hypothesis. Brunswik (1956) reviews several of the classic studies. It is clear from the data that he reviews that "thing" constancy (accuracy of perception of distal variables) improves to a peak of perfection around 11 years of age and then declines. Perception of proximal variables, by contrast, improves steadily with age. While young children are clearly capable of distal detection, they seem totally incapable of perception of proximal variables, a pattern of results totally opposite to that predicted by an empiricist hypothesis.

The net result of these kinds of studies was a shift in the locus of the debate from the whole developmental sequence to its earliest stages. In part this represented a retreat to the armchair, for the earliest stages of development seemed comfortably beyond experimental attack. Not for long, however, for in 1941 Cruikshank, in a much misquoted study, dealt empiricism yet another body blow.

Cruikshank's basic observational procedure was to present either a 19-cm rattle to a baby at a distance of 25 cm or a 57-cm rattle at a distance of 75 cm. The two rattles were thus the same retinal size although at different distances. Her youngest subjects were 10 weeks old, the oldest were between 36 and 51 weeks of age with samples at every 2 weeks between these extremes. In her younger subjects, the large rattle elicited only 9% as many reaching attempts as the small, closer rattle. At 19 weeks, the large, far rattle elicited 46% as many reaching attempts as the small, closer rattle. By 35 weeks, the percentage had fallen to 6%, thereafter there were no reaching attempts at all for the far rattle. Thus at no age did these babies confuse the large, far rattle with the small, closer rattle. Their reaching was guided more by the distal difference than the proximal equivalence. It is possible that the relatively high percentage of reaches elicited at intermediate ages by the larger, further object was a function of communication attempts (see Bower, 1974a).

To those who took the trouble to read Cruikshank's study, it again served merely to shift the argument to a yet earlier phase of development. With the seeming absence of motor responses at this stage, research was forced to focus on discrimination paradigms, paradigms that have problems of interpretation built into them. Even given these problems, which I shall review subsequently, there is little comfort for an empiricist hypothesis in these studies.

Bower (1966) studied size and shape constancy within this framework, using the conditioning paradigm laid out in Table I. In generalization trials there was more generalization to the distally equivalent stimulus than to the proximally equivalent stimulus. Similar results were obtained for shape. Using an habituation method and a similar paradigm, Day and MacKenzie (1973) found results again indicating that the perceptual process in young infants is distally rather than proximally oriented (Fig. 1). Essentially identical results were obtained by Caron, Caron, and Carlson, (1977) although the authors do not seem to realize it (see the following discussion). However, as Bower, Broughton, and Moore (1970) pointed out the interpretation of such results depends on taking a rather old-fashioned view of proximal stimulation. Table I lists proximal equivalence only in terms of retinal size: Clearly that is not the only retinal variable that changes in this situation. Indeed if any distal difference is to be detected there must be some proximal difference to mediate it. Furthermore as J. J. Gibson (1950) has argued so persuasively, if there is a distal invariance it is highly likely that there is a proximal invariance to mediate it. This means, as Bower *et al.* (1970) pointed out, that there must be some ambiguity in the results of experiments using discrimination methods. Caron *et al.* (1977) have, nevertheless, gone further and have asserted that discrimination experiments can be used to demonstrate that perceptual response in early infancy is in fact proximal rather than distal, that young infants respond to retinal variables rather than the distal variables with which they are correlated. Their experiment used a complex habituation paradigm (Table II). The key variables of course are the differences

TABLE I
CONDITIONING PARADIGM USED BY BOWER (1966)[a]

	CS	GS1	GS2	GS3
Size	1	1	3	3
Distance	1	3	1	3
Distally equivalent to CS	Yes	Yes	No	No
Proximally equivalent to CS	Yes	No	No	Yes

[a] Size constancy was investigated with cubes of different distances from the infants. The Conditioned Stimulus (CS) was 30 cm × 30 cm × 30 cm and 1 m away. Generalization Stimuli (GS) were 30 cm × 30 cm × 30 cm or 90 cm × 90 cm × 90 cm and 1 or 3 m away.

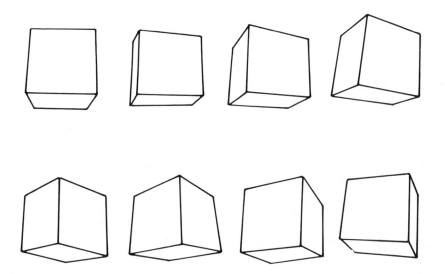

Fig. 1. This figure shows the same cube in eight different orientations. [After Day & MacKenzie (1973).]

TABLE II

HABITUATION PARADIGM USED BY CARON *ET AL.* (1977)[a]

	1	2	3	4	5	6
Distal Habituation Stimulus	□	□	□	⊻	⊽	□
Proximal Habituation Stimulus	□	⬭	⬭	□	⊽	□
Recovery Stimulus (distal = proximal in all cases)	□	□	□	□	□	□
Recovery of looking in secs.	.7	4.4	4.6	8.9	3.5	3.4

[a] After Caron, Caron, and Carlson (1977).

between the habituation stimuli and the recovery stimulus. In distal terms the stimuli, save the first and last, differed either in shape or slant or, as in habituation stimulus 4, in both. In proximal terms they differed in terms of the associated proximal stimuli. Comparing the proximal stimuli with the distal stimuli will give an indication of slant.

If we take a conventional view of proximal stimulation—in terms of retinal images and the variables that specify slant—we arrive at the interesting result that the recovery stimulus most different in distal terms, stimulus 4, is the least different in proximal terms. It would thus appear that a conventional empiricist theory would predict minimal recovery with stimulus 4: A conventional nativist theory would predict maximal recovery with stimulus 4. As the results show, recovery after stimulus 4 was nearly twice as great as recovery after any other stimulus, a result that would seem totally in line with a conventional nativist theory. However, this conclusion depends on acceptance of a conventional view of proximal stimulation, a view that the authors of the study explicitly reject. They argue, following Gibson, that the true proximal stimuli are the higher order variables that specify shape and slant; since these, as yet unspecified, variables in theory covary perfectly with distal variables, the results for Caron *et al.* support the view that the young child responds to proximal rather than distal variables. In fact, the experiments support no such thing; they are quite ambiguous on this point, as they must be, given a theory that argues for perfect covariation between distal and proximal. No simple discrimination experiment can ever separate response to proximal from response to distal within a Gibsonian theory of proximal stimulation. As I have pointed out elsewhere (1974a) a complex experiment would be required in which a distal object was specified in one time frame by one set of proximal variables, say the monocular parallax variables, and, in a second time frame, by a different set of proximal variables, say the binocular variables. One would thus have distal invariance over the two time frames with proximal change between the two time frames. If there was response invariance across the two episodes one would have clear evidence for distal perception. If not, one would have clear evidence for the opposite point of view. Unfortunately I have been unable to bring any such experiment to any decisive conclusion. In the absence of such a study, one is forced to rely on consensual data of a different sort, data from natural response experiments.

A natural response experiment, as the name implies, depends on responses from the organism's normal repertoire that have some "natural" distal appropriateness. In the context of space perception any behavior that must be spatially precise can be taken as an indicator response. Unfortunately there are few if any appropriate behaviors in the repertoire of young human infants. The establishment of a response as valid raises as many theoretical problems as it is intended to solve. Since the issue is of more relevance in the context of intersensory coordination, I shall postpone discussion of it until after I have reviewed that topic.

B. Intersensory Coordination

Historically speaking, intersensory coordination is the topic that separates nativism and empiricism most precisely. Beginning with Molyneux's proposed experiment, theorists of the latter persuasion have argued for the initial separation of the senses, with specific experience required for the stitching together of the senses. There is a whole history of research built around the testing of this assumption. However, as I have argued elsewhere (Bower, 1974a), the research is built on a myth, the myth of adult intersensory coordination. Intersensory coordinations can be described in various ways, for example, as a set of expectations, that sounds will have sources that can be seen or touched, that tangible events can be seen, and vice versa, and so on. These expectations can be couched in more or less precise terms; for example, the statement that the felt extent of an object should match its seen extent is a more precise statement than the second expectation listed previously. Common observation, and the little experimentation there has been, should make it obvious that adult intersensory coordination is not at all precise. As far as visual–tactual coordination is concerned, experiments from J. J. Gibson (1937) through Rock and Harris (1967) have shown that when vision and touch are put into conflict, vision dominates, and the tactual information is either lost or modified to conform with the visual input. This could not happen in a coordinated system; there would either be double awareness or a compromise percept (Bower, 1974b). Neither of these results happens in adult humans, whether the conflict involves size or shape.

Nor is there any evidence of coordination from studies in which vision and audition are put into conflict (Bertelson, 1978). The rule again seems to be that vision dominates, with no discrepancy perceived at any level, and no compromises either. Research by McGurk and Macdonald (1976) indicates the possibility of compromise when there is a contradiction in the visual and audible specification of speech content.

Another line of research indicates that there can be transfer of information from one modality to another, principally touch to vision, so that an object presented to one modality can be matched with one from an array presented to the other (e.g., Caviness, 1964). McGurk's research, alluded to in the preceding paragraph, could be interpreted as evidence of transfer as well, although available evidence does not make it clear whether the compromise percept was heard or registered in some amodal fashion.

All of these data together indicate that while there is intersensory coordination in adult humans it is not the tight, precise system that many theorists have assumed. The status of the adult system is important. Nativists and empiricists differ on the route to the adult status. Empiricism clearly should argue that the intersensory coordination observed in inexperienced organisms should be even less than that to be observed in mature adult humans: Nativists clearly must predict that the level attained by experienced adults should be equally well attained by inexperienced infants. I think it a hopeful sign that neither of these predictions has been validated by the available research.

C. Developmental Research

Developmental research falls into two classes, one comparing the efficiency of transfer of information from one modality to another, the other looking at the more basic intersensory expectations as just described. Some transfer has been demonstrated in infants of 8 months, a feat of marvelous technical skill (Bryant, Jones, Claxton, & Perkins, 1972). There is evidence that with increasing age, the transfer becomes more efficient, (E. J. Gibson, 1969). None of this is at all untoward and indeed fits with the generally confused picture we saw in the case study of the spatial constancies. However, when we look at intersensory coordination in much younger infants a more interesting picture emerges. The original and the best studies of intersensory expectancy and intersensory coordination have looked at auditory–visual coordination. Here the relevant expectancy is that a sound will have a source, which can be seen. The relevant experiment is simple: Does presentation of a sound elicit eye movements? Note that mere elicitation is all that is necessary to demonstrate expectancy. Accurately oriented eye movements demand transfer of information, a higher order requirement. It is clear that sounds do elicit eye movements in newborn babies (Pratt, Nelson, & Sun, 1930). Furthermore it is clear that there is transfer of information at least about direction and probably about extent as well. Eye movements tend to go in the direction of sound sources (Butterworth & Castillo, 1976; Turkewitz, Birch, Moreau, Levy, & Cornwall, 1966; Wertheimer, 1961). The further the sound source is off the midline, the larger the eye movements elicited, until a cut off is reached where the turn requires too much effort. (Alegria & Noirot, 1978; Macfarlane, 1977). These findings are so well established that I am amazed that anyone still wishes to challenge them. McGurk, Turnure, and Creighton (1977), however, claim that they could find no evidence of auditory–visual coordination in young infants. So far as I know the inability of McGurk *et al.* to obtain eye movements in response to auditory stimulation is unique. It is extremely easy to obtain "no response" from young infants. There are a range of perinatal conditions that predispose this result, as well as the more well-documented state variables.

The more interesting objection to the interpretations I have been offering is the argument that if it occurs at all it is "only" a reflex (e.g., McGurk *et al.*, 1977). At first glance the argument is mindless. A reflex demands structure, and the genesis of structure is what we are discussing in this chapter. In any event McGurk's experiment shows that the behavior is not a reflex in any classic sense of the word. What then is the word reflex supposed to imply? If it means anything it implies, I suppose, a lack of awareness; the babies' eyes turn to the source of a sound but there is no expectation that there will be anything there to see. There have been a few experiments designed to test this hypothesis. Before describing them I would like to look at the implications of the reflex hypothesis, for it neatly introduces the third classic theory of perceptual development, the *differentiation* theory.

III. THE DIFFERENTIATION THEORY OF PERCEPTUAL DEVELOPMENT

What does it mean if a baby's eyes turn toward the source of a sound, with no specific sensory expectations? If true, this hypothesis implies that the baby has a perceptual structure that registers events in some amodal space: The output of the structure could be described as "there is something happening $x°$ to my right (or left or whatever)." The corresponding structure in adults would have a rather different output: "I hear a sound coming from something $x°$ to my right." The adult output is clearly far more specific than the proposed infant output. In other words it is more specified or differentiated. There are psychologists who would argue over the precise meaning of words such as specified or differentiated. I am using them in the precise sense given them by Russell (1910) a sense introduced to psychologists by Bateson (1972). A statement, p, is more specific than another statement, q, if they have the relationship:

$$p \rightarrow q; q \rightarrow (p \vee \bar{p}); \bar{q} \rightarrow \bar{p}$$

where "$\rightarrow$", "v," and "$^{-}$" are respectively symbols for logical *implication, or,* and *negation*.
This is spelled out in more detail (see p. 93).

A differentiation theory of perceptual development thus proposes that in development the output of perceptual structures becomes more and more precise, more and more detailed, more and more specific. In this way the theory is totally opposed to classic nativism and classic empiricism, both of which emphasize the sensory specificity of early experience. For empiricism and nativism any evidence of nonsensory, or what one can call amodal, elicitation of response is a considerable embarrassment.

Previously I mentioned that there were some experiments that had tried to examine this issue either implicitly or explicitly. An explicit attempt was made by Aronson and Rosenbloom (1971) using a surprise paradigm.

A. Experiments Investigating Sensory Expectations

Many sounds come from a visually defined locus in space; the human voice normally proceeds from a human mouth. Aronson and Rosenbloom investigated the infant's response to a dissociation of these two variables. Infants sat facing their mothers who talked to them from behind a sound-proof screen. The mother's voice was relayed to the infant via a pair of balanced loudspeakers, one to either side of the infant. After some time, the mother's voice was displaced so that is appeared to come from a point 3 feet to the right or left of her mouth. Three-week-old infants were extremely disturbed by the dislocation, indicating that they expect voices, perceived as such, to come out of faces, perceived as such, a result contrary to the hypothesis I have been advancing here.

This result has been challenged by McGurk and Lewis (1974) who found no evidence of upset consequent upon dissociation. It could be argued that their presentation technique was never consonant in that the sound source was never in the same place in perceptual space as the perceived face. Results generally supporting Aronson and Rosenbloom have been obtained by Lyons-Ruth (1975) using a similar paradigm. Nonetheless the results are somewhat controversial.

That there is some intersensory specificity at early ages has been shown by Carpenter (1975). Her experiments also used face–voice dissociation, the mother's face, a stranger's face, the mother's voice and the stranger's voice being presented in consonant or dissonant combinations. The dissonant combinations clearly produced upset in 2-week-old subjects.

An experiment of this kind, however, can hardly be conclusive since it is clearly dealing with the outcome of a learning process. Surely no one would wish to assert that babies are born with any knowledge of the appearance of their mother's face or of the sound of her voice!

Testing the specificity of sensory expectations without relying on learned expectations is clearly not easy. The various studies of early imitation do provide challenging data on that point, implicitly at least, in one clear direction. It is quite clear that infants in the newborn phase can imitate a variety of gestures, including facial gestures (Dunkeld, 1977;

Maratos, 1973; Meltzoff & Moore, 1977). Since the youngest subject in such experiments was, I believe, 17 minutes old, learning is clearly irrelevant. The fascinating point here is that the imitation is quite specific; when the model's mouth opens, the baby's mouth opens; when the model's eyes widen, the baby's eyes widen, and so on. This would seem to indicate a highly specific mapping between vision and the proprioceptive senses. Interestingly, however, the authors of the best study of imitation, Meltzoff and Moore (1977) interpret this as evidence of amodal coordination that is not sensorily specific. Their reasons for this are complex; I confess I do not fully comprehend them. Nonetheless it would appear that some of the data on early imitation point away from early sensory specificity toward an amodal perception of the world.

B. Perceptual Descriptions and the Theory of Types

If there is at least a prima facie case for saying that the perceptual world of the newborn child is less differentiated than that of the adult, what precisely does this mean? Previously, differentiation or specificity was defined in terms of the theory of types. Compare the statements:

1. I hear a sound on my right.
2. Something happened on my right.
3. Something happened.

The relationship between them is

$$1 \rightarrow 2; 2 \rightarrow 3.$$

However, the direction of implication is not symmetric. In particular it is *not* the case that

$$3 \rightarrow 2; 2 \rightarrow 1.$$

The relationship between the sentences probably will raise no hackles. However, if that relationship is supposed to reflect the perceptual process, as I suppose it does, then one must anticipate some objections. Clearly if a sound is registered, it must be registered by the ears. However, while that is certainly true, registration does not imply awareness. Furthermore, neurophysiological research (Barlow, 1961; Hubel & Wiesel, 1962) should have familiarized us with the idea that information transfer within the nervous system is accomplished by massive loss of detail, with "higher" levels bearing the same relationship to "lower" levels that is embodied in the asymmetry laid out previously (Fig. 2). There would even appear to be units in the nervous system that respond to direction of stimulation irrespective of modality (Fishman & Michael, 1973; Murata, Cramer, & Bach-y-Rita, 1965).

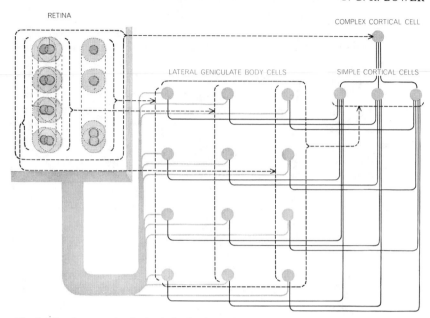

Fig. 2. Visual processing by brain begins in the lateral geniculate body that continues the analysis made by retinal cells. In the cortex, "simple" cells respond strongly to line stimuli, provided that the position and orientation of the line are suitable for a particular cell. "Complex" cells respond well to line stimuli but the position of the line is not critical and the cell continues to respond even if a properly oriented stimulus is moved, as long as it remains in the cell's receptive field. Broken lines indicate how receptive fields of all these cells overlap on the retina; solid lines, how several cells at one stage affect a single cell at the next stage. [From "The visual cortex of the brain," by D. H. Hubel. Copyright © 1963 by Scientific American, Inc. All rights reserved.]

What does this mean for theories of perceptual development? It involves mainly a radical change in our conception of what could be innate. The two classic theories argue for extreme sensory specificity at the beginning of development. The theory outlined in the preceding paragraphs argues for the opposite, *perceptual specificity*. The structures that are innate are those that register significant environmental events, such as occurrence, existence, location, change of location, relative size, hardness or softness perhaps; the system does *not* register lights or sounds or smells or touches, or any of the other specific energies of nerves.

In its extreme form the theory I am proposing here does not claim intersensory coordination in young infants; rather it claims perfect intersensory substitutability. This is an area of research that seems likely to burgeon in the near future. Unfortunately there are, as yet, few data on it. The hypothesis in question suggests that the perceptual system does not respond to inputs from specific senses as such; rather it responds to changes and patterns of change that can be presented through any modality. Consider an object approaching the observer. As it gets closer, its image on the observer's retina expands continually. But a process of this form can be abstracted without reference to the sensory channel through which it is perceived. That kind of change pattern could be presented through any sensory modality, given sufficient technical ingenuity.

It is at this point in the argument that the therapeutic application came to mind. For years there have been devices available for the blind that present information about the spatial position of objects as sound messages. These devices have not been popular with blind adults, and only about 5% of the blind population can use even the best of them. Teachers of the blind believe only the most intelligent blind children can learn to translate the sounds given by such machines into useful information about the world. If, however, the hypothesis about intersensory coordination advanced previously is correct, then, provided the information is given early enough in development, the baby should simply latch on to the information provided, with no special learning required at all.

The little that is known about the development of blind children suggests that they come into the world with the same high degree of intersensory coordination as the sighted child. They "look" toward sound sources, they "look" at their hands, they reach for noisemaking objects, just as sighted babies do. Unlike sighted babies, the blind child is given little or no information about the third dimension. He has no way of correcting growth-induced errors in his reaching. It is little wonder that the early coordinations die away, often forever. If the blind child is born with a perceptual system ready to seize on abstract information of a certain form, no matter what its method of presentation, the baby should be able to use a wholly artificial source of information, provided it had the same formal properties as natural information. It should be no more difficult for a blind child to use artificial auditory information than for a sighted child to use vision.

I reached this point in my research in 1972. The next 2 years were spent in abortive attempts to make a suitable machine and in having reservations about the whole enterprise. The reservations stemmed from the consideration that no really sensitive echolocation device could be made that presented stimuli that were at all "natural." Thus if evolution had acted to produce very specific sensory structures, the child would have no inbuilt, genetic headstart in learning to interpret the "unnatural" sounds from available echolocation devices. If that were the case, one would do more for the baby by giving him an echolocation device, which although less sensitive relied on natural sounds, such as human voices, finger snaps, and the like. The use of such sounds has been possible throughout evolution so there is a possibility that the child would have a start on making sense of them. On the other hand, I had become convinced by the internal logic of the opposite argument that evolution has functioned to produce perceptual structures that initially will respond to any modality of input, provided that it has the right formal characteristics.

In California, in 1974, I had the opportunity to test the hypothesis. It was explained to the parents of a 16-week-old blind baby, who were willing to take the risks involved. The New Zealand company, Wormald Vigilant, supplied an echolocation device free of charge. The device that provided the babies in these experiments with sound information about their environment is a modification of one invented by Professor Leslie Kay now at Canterbury University in New Zealand. Telesensory Systems of California agreed to modify it free of charge.

After extensive study of the bat's ultrasonic echolocation system Professor Kay devised a pair of spectacles for blind adults incorporating an ultrasonic aid. The aid continuously irradiates the environment with ultrasound and converts reflections from objects into audible sound. Ultrasound was chosen because the size of an object that will produce an echo is inversely proportional to the frequency of the sound source. Ultrasound will thus generate echoes from smaller objects than will audible sound. The conversion from ultrasound to audible sound codes the echo in three ways. The pitch of the audible signal is arranged to indicate the distance of the object from which the echo came—high pitch means distant objects, low pitch near ones. The amplitude of the signal codes for the size of the irradiated object (loud–large, soft–small), and texture of the object is represented by the clarity of the signal. In addition, the audible signal is "stereo" so direction to the object is perceived by the difference in time of arrival of a signal at the two ears.

In many ways the first session was the most exciting of all. An object was introduced and moved slowly to and from the baby's face, close enough to tap the baby on the nose. On the fourth presentation we noticed convergence movements of the eyes. These were not well controlled, but the baby was converging as the object approached and diverging as the object receded. On the seventh presentation the baby interposed his hands between face and object. This behavior was repeated several times. Then he was presented with objects moving to right and left; he tracked them with head and eyes and swiped at the objects. The smallest object presented was a 1-cm cube dangling on the end of a wire, which the baby succeeded in hitting four times.

The mother stood the baby on her knee at arms' length, chatted to him, telling him what a clever boy he was, and so on. The baby was facing her and wearing the device. He slowly turned his head to remove her from the sound field, then slowly turned back to bring her in again. This behavior was repeated several times to the accompaniment of immense smiles from the baby. All three observers had the impression that he was playing a kind of peek-a-boo with his mother, and deriving immense pleasure from it.

The baby's development after these initial adventures remained more or less on a par with that of a sighted baby. Using the sonic guide the baby seemed able to identify a favorite toy without touching it. He began two-handed reaches around 6 months of age. By 8 months the baby would search for an object that had been hidden behind another object. At 9 months he demonstrated "placing" on a table edge and a pair of batons. None of these behavior patterns normally is seen in congenitally blind babies. More important, so far as I know, no blind adult has been able to learn such skills with the guide.

IV. MECHANISMS OF DEVELOPMENT

This chapter thus far has been almost exclusively concerned with what is or could be innate. The issue of how the structures that are innate become the structures of the normal experienced adult has been left to one side. This seems necessary to me because there is no way one can describe transitions between states without some description of the initial and terminal states. Unfortunately the description of initial state is still controversial. However, associated with the theories of initial state that we have been describing are appropriate theories of transition. One of these, the maturation or growth theory of development, the logical associate of nativism, can be dismissed without much ado. It has been clear since von Senden (1932) compiled his reports that the perceptual system does not grow normally in the absence of normal input. Von Senden's data contradict an extreme empiricist position, too; the perceptual system does not remain static, ready to use input whenever it comes in. In the absence of normal input there is change that prevents utilization of input when it does come.

These data from humans set a frame within which we can consider the basic problems of neural growth that underlie perceptual development. Neural structures do change postpartum; the nature of the changes is a function of the inputs the structures are given.

These outline statements may seem heterodox to those psychologists familiar with no more recent neuroembryology than the brilliant, pioneering work of Sperry (1956). Sperry's work seems to show precisely that function had no rule in neural growth, the whole process being determined by chemical specificities of purely genetic origin. Some psychologists have argued that Sperry's work is of little relevance to human concerns since his experimental organisms, amphibians, are evolutionarily so far removed from man. This kind of critique or defense mechanism has little validity. The basic biological processes of growth seem to have remained invariant across the panoply of evolution. Nonetheless the theory derived from Sperry's work can be criticized on conceptual and empirical grounds. The conceptual critique stems from advances in molecular biology that have shown in some detail just how many of the connections in the nervous system could be coded in the genome. The DNA present in the nucleus of the fertilized egg may at most code a few million proteins. There is little variation between mouse, chimpanzee, and man. If we recall that the visual system of man has upwards of 9 million synaptic connections, we can see how unlikely it is that each of these connections is formed by a specific, individual protein match. The most important data on this point, for me anyway, are those reviewed by Changeux and Danchin, (1976); working with populations of genetically identical organisms, investigators have found marked differences in the neural organization of the sensory areas. Since these organisms were genetically identical, they offer a direct disproof of a chemospecificity theory; clearly environmental influences, as yet undescribed, are modulating the processes of gene expression. Gaze (1970) and his coworkers have elucidated some of these modulations in a brilliant series of experiments. One of the most interesting of these involves hemiretinal transplants (Fig. 3). In the frog the tectal projections from the hemiretinae are arranged in an extremely orderly fashion (Fig. 4). What happens when the input from an eye comes from two nasal hemiretinae? Do the inputs concentrate in the area normally reserved for nasal inputs, as the chemospecificity theory would predict, or do they occupy more than their normal share? The answer is quite clear; they spread out to occupy far more of the tectal area than they normally would (Gaze, 1970). Despite this the animal behaves as if no more than the normal tectal area had been covered. Specifically if

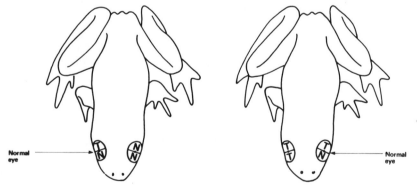

Fig. 3. Hemiretinal transplantation. To make a compound eye in the frog, eyes from different animals are cut in half and transposed as shown. N = nasal half; T = temporal half.

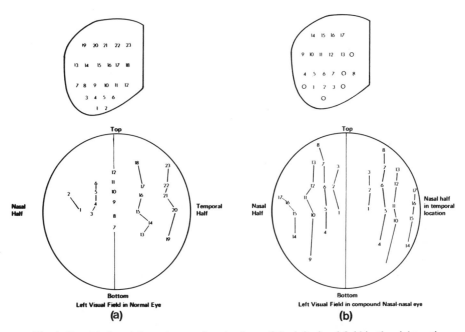

Fig. 4. Part (a) shows the retinotectal projections of the left visual field in the right optic tectum of a normal frog eye. These were determined by inserting electrodes into the right optic tectum, and then presenting stimuli at different positions in the visual field. Thus it can be shown that a stimulus at, for example, Position 6 in the visual field projects from the retina to Position 6 on the contralateral optic tectum. In the normal eye each half of the retina projects to half of the optic tectum. Part (b) shows the retinotectal projections from the right optic tectum of a compound nasal–nasal eye. Comparison with the normal situation shows that the projections have spread over the available tectum, so that each half effectively projects to the whole of the optic tectum. Small open circles show positions for which no responses could be obtained. [After Gaze (1970).]

shown an object on the right falling on the normal nasal area the animal snaps in the correct location: if shown an object on the left falling on the transplanted nasal area, the animal still snaps to the right, to the area that would have been appropriate had that transplanted piece of nasal retina still been nasal retina rather than temporal retina.

Effects such as this are not peculiar to these very abnormal experimental situations. They occur in the course of normal growth where retinotectal connections are continually remade, with the behavior controlled by them remaining invariant.

What are we to conclude from these studies? They do offer an explanation of why the effects of abnormal input early in development may be irreversible; the areas of the brain normally available for normal inputs may be taken over by abnormal inputs, and thence become unavailable for anything else. But more importantly, it would seem to me, these studies index a pattern of development from general to specific of the kind just outlined. It is clear that early in development the eye of the frog is specified to an extent that each hemiretina "knows" whether it is nasal or temporal, signifying an object on the right or an object on the left. The subsequent development, with increasing tectal representation, can only specify that initial decision into a more detailed decision, an object $x°$ to the right, an object with yellow stripes $x°$ to the right and so on. Laid out in type statements, as on page 93, the pattern of development is exactly that hypothesized by a differentiation theory.

Applied to the human case this kind of model implies innate specification of a few higher order perceptual variables; with development these become more detailed sensory–perceptual variables. The kinds of things that might be innate are those relating to information about spatial position and change in spatial position, particularly the kind of information that can be represented supramodally. For example, radial direction depends on a time–intensity code; this code can be transmitted through ears, nose or skin (Békésy, 1967) although only with difficulty can this variable be seen as relevant in vision (Dvorak, 1872; Lee, 1970; Mach, 1885). Change of position in the third dimension can be represented as a change in the rate of change of stimulation (Fig. 5); such changes can be presented through any modality: young infants can pick them up through ear or eye. With growth the kind of information preserved in its transfer through the nervous system will grow. The pattern of growth will depend on the inputs given. With much of the brain unspecified at birth, the specification that does occur will reflect the information content supplied to the developing brain. If some normal input is lacking, the brain areas normally reserved for it will be taken over by other functional systems, which should then become hyperfunctional. There does seem to be some evidence in favor of this proposition (Furth, 1964, 1971; Oleron, 1953; Oleron & Herren, 1961; von Senden, 1932; Supa, Cotzin, & Dallenbach, 1944; Worchell & Dallenbach, 1947). In case of restoration of function after a period of development the functions most likely to be preserved are precisely those higher perceptual functions that are posited to be specified at birth. Again there seems to be evidence in favor of this proposition (von Senden, 1932).

The neural bases of these functions are to me obscure although work with the war wounded may clarify the matter.

In any event there seems little reason to stick to a constructionist view of perceptual growth, far less a static nativist view. The guiding principle of development appears to be differentiation with increased specification. As

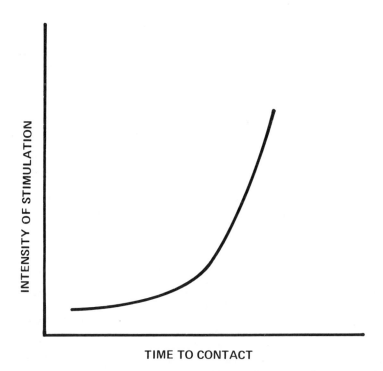

TIME TO CONTACT

Fig. 5. An approaching object represented without reference to the sensory channel through which it is perceived. Whether auditory, visual, or tactile input is used, intensity of stimulation increases as the time to contact decreases.

I have tried to indicate in this chapter, a differentiation theory offers more exciting practical experimental possibilities than either of the others. It is in accord with the flood of information coming from molecular biology (see, e.g., the review by Changeux and Danchin, 1976). Lastly, but unfortunately, it is a developmental theory whose basic parameters remain to be specified; we have only the vaguest clue about the psychological events that *cause* differentiation; we know more about the molecular events in differentiation than we do about their psychological causes. As rarely in the history of research on perception, theoretical and practical demands point in the same direction, offering a challenge I hope we can accept.

References

Alegria, J., & Noirot, E. Neonate orientation behaviour towards the human voice. *Early Human Development*, 1978.

Aronson, E., & Rosenbloom, S. Space perception in early infancy: Perception within a common auditory-visual space. *Science*, 1971, **172**, 1161–1163.

Barlow, H. B. The coding of sensory messages. In W. H. Thorpe & O. L. Zangwill (Eds.), *Current problems in animal behaviour*. Cambridge, England: Cambridge Univ. Press, 1961.

Bateson, G. *Steps towards an ecology of mind*. New York: Ballantine Books, 1972.

Békésy, G. von. *Sensory inhibition*. Princeton, New Jersey: Princeton Univ. Press, 1967.

Bertelson, P., 1977. Assimilation of auditory-spatial to visual-spatial information. Paper read at 21st International Congress of Psychology, Paris, July 1976. Presses Universitaires de France, 1978 (in press).

Boring, E. G. *A history of experimental psychology* (2nd ed.). New York: Appleton, 1950.

Bower, T. G. R. The visual world of infants. *Scientific American*, 1966, **215**, 80–92.

Bower, T. G. R. *Development in infancy*. San Francisco: Freeman, 1974. (a)

Bower, T. G. R. The evolution of sensory systems. In R. B. MacLeod and H. L. Pick (Eds.), *Perception: Essays in honor of J. J. Gibson*. Ithaca: Cornell Univ. Press, 1974. (b)

Bower, T. G. R., Broughton, J. M., & Moore, M. K. Infant responses to approaching objects: An indicator of response to distal variables. *Perception & Psychophysics*, 1970, **9**, 193–196.

Brunswik, E. *Perception and the representative design of psychological experiments*. Berkeley: Univ. of California Press, 1956.

Bryant, P. E., Jones, P., Claxton, V., & Perkins, G. M. Recognition of shapes across modalities by infants. *Nature*, 1972, **240**, 303–304.

Butterworth, G., & Castillo, M. Coordination of auditory and visual space in newborn infants. *Perception*, 1976, **5**, 155–161.

Caron, A. J., Caron, R. F., & Carlson, V. R. Do infants see objects or retinal images? Shape constancy revisited. Paper read at SRCD meeting, New Orleans, March 1977.

Carpenter, G. Mother's face and the newborn. In R. Lewin (Ed.), *Child Alive*. London: Temple Smith, 1975.

Caviness, J. A. Visual and tactual perception of solid shape. Unpublished doctoral dissertation, Cornell University, 1964.

Changeux, J-P., & Danchin, A. Selective stabilisation of developing synapses as a mechanism for the specification of neuronal networks. *Nature*, 1976, **264**, 705–712.

Cruikshank, R. M. The development of visual size constancy in early infancy. *Journal of Genetic Psychology*, 1941, **58**, 327–351.

Day, R. H., & MacKenzie, B. E. Perceptual shape constancy in early infancy. *Perception*, 1973, **2**, 315–321.

Dunkeld, J. The development of imitation in infancy. Unpublished doctoral dissertation. Univ. of Edinburgh, 1977.

Dvorak, V. Uber Analoga der personlichen differenz zwischen beiden Augen und den Netzhaufstellen desselben Auges. *Sitzb. Ges. Wiss.* 1872, 65–74.

Fishman, M. C., & Michael, C. R. Integration of auditory information in the cat's visual cortex. *Vision Research*, 1973, **13**, 1415–1419.

Furth, H. G. Conservation of weight in deaf and hearing children. *Child Development*. 1964, **34**, 143–150.

Furth, H. G. Linguistic deficiency and thinking: Research with deaf subjects 1964–69. *Psychological Bulletin*, 1971, **76**, 58–72.

Gaze, R. M. *The Formation of nerve connections*. London: Academic Press, 1970.

Gibson, E. J. *Principles of perceptual learning and development*. New York: Appleton, 1969.

Gibson, J. J. Adaptation with negative after-effect. *Psychological Review*, 1937, **44**, 222–244.

Gibson, J. J. *The perception of the visual world*. Boston: Houghton Mifflin, 1950.

Hubel, D. H. & Wiesel, T. N. Receptive fields, binocular interaction and functional architecture in the cat's visual cortex. *Journal of Physiology*, 1962, **160**, 106–154.

Lee, D. N. Spatio-temporal integration in binocular-kinetic space perception. *Vision Research*, 1970, **10**, 65–78.

Lyons-Ruth, K. Integration of auditory and visual space information during early infancy. Paper presented at SRCD meeting Denver, April 1975.

Macfarlane, A. *The psychology of childbirth*. London: Open Books; Cambridge, Massachusetts: Harvard Univ. Press, 1977.

Mach, E. *The analysis of sensations*. New York: Dover, 1959 (originally published 1885).

Maratos, O. The origin and development of imitation in the first six months of life. Unpublished doctoral dissertation, Univ. of Geneva, 1973.

McGurk, H., & Lewis, M. Space perception in early infancy: Perception within a common auditory-visual space? *Science*, 1974, **186**, 649–650.

McGurk, H., & Macdonald, J. Hearing lips and seeing voices. *Nature*, 1976, **264**, 746–748.

McGurk, H., Turnure, C., & Creighton, S. J. Auditory visual coordination in neonates. *Child Development*, 1977, **48**, 138–143.

Meltzoff, A. N., & Moore, M. K. Imitation of facial and manual gestures by human neonates. *Science*, 1977, **198**, 75–78.

Murata, K., Cramer, H., & Bacy-y-Rita, P. Neuronal convergence of noxious, acoustic and visual stimuli in the visual cortex of the cat. *Journal of Neurophysiology*, 1965, **28**, 1223–1240.

Oleron, P. Conceptual thinking of the deaf. *American Annals of the Deaf*, 1953, **98**, 304–310.

Oleron, P., & Herren, D. L'acquisition des conservations et le langage: Etude comparative sur des enfants sourds et entendants. *Enfance*, 1961, **14**, 203–19.

Pratt, K. C., Nelson, A. K., & Sun, K. H. *The behavior of the newborn infant*. Columbus, Ohio: Ohio State Univ. Press, 1930.

Rock, I., & Harris, C. S. Vision and touch. *Scientific American*, 1967, **216**, 96–104.

Russell, B. La théorie des types logiques. *Revue de Metaphysique et de Morale*, 1910, **18**, 263–301.

Senden, M. von. *Space and sight*. London: Methuen, 1960 (originally published 1932).

Sperry, R. W. The eye and the brain. *Scientific American*, 1956, **194**, 48–52.

Supa, M., Cotzin, M., & Dallenbach, K. M. Facial vision—perception of obstacles by the blind. *American Journal of Psychology*, 1944, **57**, 133–183.

Turkewitz, G., Birch, H. B., Moreau, T., Levy, L., & Cornwell, A. C. Effect of intensity of auditory stimulation on directional eye movements in the human neonate. *Animal Behavior*, 1966, **14**, 93–101.

Wertheimer, M. Psycho-motor coordination of auditory-visual space at birth. *Science*, 1961, **134**, 1692.

Worchell, P., & Dallenbach, K. M. Facial vision—perception of obstacles by the deaf-blind. *American Journal of Psychology*, 1947, **60**, 502–553.

Chapter 3

TRANSFORMATIONS ON REPRESENTATIONS OF OBJECTS IN SPACE*

LYNN A. COOPER AND ROGER N. SHEPARD

I. INTRODUCTION

Perception is not just a process of passive registration in which an external stimulus gives rise to a corresponding internal representation in an automatic and invariable way. What is perceived on a given occasion depends not only on the pattern of stimulation at the sensory receptors but also on the preceding context and on the expectancies and states of motivation and attention of the perceiver (Bruner, 1957; Neisser, 1967).

*Preparation of this chapter was supported by National Science Foundation Grants BMS75–15773 to Lynn A. Cooper and BMS75–02806 to Roger N. Shepard. We are indebted to a number of our colleagues and students—Joyce Farrell, Sherry Judd, Bob Glushko, Jim Levin, Steve Palmer, and Peter Podgorny—for permitting us to discuss their recent research in this chapter.

Indeed, the very same physical stimulus can give rise to two or more quite distinct perceptual interpretations, as is demonstrated most strikingly by the well-known reversible, or ambiguous, figures such as the duck–rabbit, rat–man, wife–mother-in-law, or Necker cube (Jastrow, 1900, p. 295; Neisser, 1967, pp. 61, 142, 144, respectively).

In fact, a significant perceptual interpretation of a stimulus sometimes emerges only after the active completion of additional, optional mental operations of transformation or comparison, or both. Thus, the ambiguous silhouette studied by Rock (1956) tends to be seen as a dog or as a head with a chef's hat depending upon whether the silhouette is imagined as being rotated 45° clockwise or counterclockwise, respectively. Likewise, a piece of a jigsaw puzzle may be perceived as capable of fitting into a certain hole only after imagining the piece appropriately rotated and translated across the puzzle.

In the case of the visual perception of objects in space, a particularly important class of mental operations comprises those corresponding to reversible spatial transformations. In addition to the uniform expansion or contraction most typically associated with the approach or recession of an object, these spatial transformations include translations, reflections, and rotations of an object as a rigid whole. They also include more complex structural manipulations, such as those of assembling or disassembling, or of folding or unfolding, in which parts of an object or system of objects are imagined to move in relation to other parts.

The study of such mental transformations is of interest from two complementary standpoints. First, it can lead to new information about a class of mental operations that appears to be quite different in character from the class of more discrete, symbolic, or linguistic operations that has, for some time, been the center of attention in the fields of cognitive psychology and artificial intelligence. Second, any new information about how internal representations of external objects behave under spatial transformations might clarify the nature of those internal representations themselves. In the case of visual perception, for example, such information can provide insights into the nature and degree of structural resemblance or isomorphism that an internal representation bears—either to the three-dimensional distal object that it represents, or to the very different two-dimensional proximal stimulus from which, necessarily, that representation must be constructed.

A. Some Historical Roots of Contemporary Research

The notion of mental transformations on internal representations of objects in space can be traced back at least to the British empiricists

Locke, Berkeley, Hume, and the two Mills. For according to these philosophers, internal representations (ideas) are of three types: (*a*) direct sensory impressions, as in perception; (*b*) faint, or less "vivacious," copies of previous sensory impressions, as in memory; and (*c*) transformations, decompositions, and recombinations of these faint copies, as in imagination and associative thought. To quote from Hume (1748), "To form monsters, and join incongruous shapes and appearances, costs the imagination no more trouble than to conceive the most natural and familiar objects." He further states that "all this creative power of the mind amounts to no more than the faculty of compounding, transposing, augmenting, or diminishing the material afforded us by the senses and experience [Section II of the *Enquiry concerning the human understanding*, pp. 15–16].

From our present perspective, the British empiricists fell short in failing to recognize that

1. Although "the material" of imagination may be afforded us by sensory experience, the "faculty" by which this material is transformed operates on the basis of some rather definite rules.
2. Such transformations do "cost the imagination" some effort and time.
3. This time, and hence these rules, can be experimentally investigated in the laboratory.

The specific case of imagined spatial transformations was later discussed more explicitly by the eminent physiological and physical scientists Helmholtz and Mach. As Hemholtz put it in 1844,

> Memory images of purely sensory impressions may . . . be used as elements of thought combinations without it being necessary, or even possible, to describe these in words. . . . Equipped with an awareness of the physical form of an object, we can clearly imagine all of the perspective images which we may expect upon viewing from this or that side, and we are immediately disturbed when such an image does not correspond to our expectations [see Warren & Warren, 1968, pp. 252–254].

In 1886, Mach presented irregular forms of geometrically identical shape to illustrate that, when two such forms are presented side by side in the same orientation, their identity of shape is immediately apparent but that, when one form is sufficiently rotated with respect to the other, their "identity of form is not recognizable" without additional "intellectual operations [Mach, 1959, pp. 106–109]."

Galton's (1883) *Inquiries into human faculty and its development* might be regarded as the beginnings of the empirical study of such intellectual operations. However, until quite recently, investigations of mental imagery and spatial manipulations, following Galton, have relied heavily on introspection or self-report as the method of data generation, and on intergroup correlation as the technique of data analysis. Thus Gordon's (1949) test of imagery control simply asked for *yes* or *no* answers to questions such as "Can you see a car standing in front of a garden gate?" "Can you now see the same car lying upside down?" and so on. Since neither the experimenter nor the subject has any objective criterion for assessing the results of the subject's mental operations, the *yes* or *no* responses are apt to be strongly influenced by such extraneous factors as set, interpretation of instructions, demand characteristics of the experiment, and response bias. And, although such self-report tests of imagery do correlate to some extent with some measures of personality, or spatial abilities, or both (Richardson, 1969, pp. 50–58), these correlations tell us little or nothing about the structural nature of the internal representations or of their transformations.

The rapid development of mental testing and the concomitant study of individual differences in cognitive functions, particularly by Thurstone and his followers, has from the 1930s onward provided us with a rich variety of much more objective tests of abilities to perform various sorts of spatial operations. Again, however, the analyses have been based exclusively upon correlations between overall performances of individuals or groups on entire subtests composed of many different items, and so have shed relatively little light on the *processes* underlying any one subject's performance on any one item. Nevertheless, many of the mental tasks of two- and three-dimensional rotation, surface development or paper folding, and hand identification that we shall be reviewing have been in part inspired by some of the earlier tests devised by Thurstone and others (see, e.g., Bennett, Seashore, & Wesman, 1959; Michael, Zimmerman, & Guilford, 1951; Smith, 1964; Thurstone, 1938).

Quite independently of this psychometric work, experimental psychologists pursued their own more behaviorally oriented investigations into the recognition of, generalization to, or discrimination between spatially transformed stimuli by human adults, children, and animals. For the most part, these behavioral studies have used measures, such as number of errors or number of trials to criterion, that again provide little information about the processes taking place on any one trial. Indeed, the subject's performance often was not even conceptualized in terms of a process of active internal transformation. More typically, it was regarded, instead, as a matter of passive or automatic stimulus generalization based, say, on the number and salience of the sensory elements shared between the stimuli. Most of the studies in this tradition do not provide very direct evidence concerning transformational processes as such and, for this reason, will not be further considered here. Descriptions of much of this work can be found in several available surveys (see, e.g., Corballis & Beale, 1970; Freedman, 1968; Howard & Templeton, 1966; Rock, 1973).

The most dramatic progress in the study of mental operations on spatial objects and, hence, the bulk of the work that we shall be reviewing here, has taken place relatively recently. This work has focused more directly on the internal cognitive processes that presumably underlie both the behaviors observed in laboratory experiments and the performances recorded on mental tests. Indeed, although the chronometric techniques that have proved to be such powerful tools in cognitive psychology generally (cf. Clark & Chase, 1972; Posner, Boies, Eichelman, & Taylor, 1969; Sternberg, 1966, 1969) had their early beginning in Donders' (1868) introduction of the subtraction method for analyzing reaction times, these techniques have been used to study spatial operations only during the 1970s. We turn now to a closer consideration of this development.

B. Current Experimental Paradigms and Measures

In most of the experimental paradigms that we shall be considering, time measurements have played the central role. Such measurements have been of two principal types. One measures the time required to respond to a spatially transformed object after it has been presented or, alternatively, to prepare for such a transformed object before it has been presented. The other measures the time to make a discriminative *same–different* response to a transformed test stimulus for which one has already prepared *when* that test stimulus is then presented. The time estimated by the first type of measurement is considered to include, as its principal component, the time to carry out the spatial transformation of interest. If the subject has successfully carried out this mental transformation, the time estimated by the second type of measurement should include only the comparison and response times.

In some paradigms, the transformation times are not measured directly. Instead, these times are estimated by experimentally varying the time available for carrying out a particular mental transformation. The point below which the subject's ability to complete that transformation breaks down then reveals itself in a marked increase in latency or errors of response, or both, to an ensuing test stimulus. Or, in a quite different paradigm based on the perceptual phenomenon of apparent movement, the breakdown takes the form of a disintegration of the illusion of coherent motion of the object as a rigid whole.

Data other than time estimates can also furnish useful information concerning mental transformations. Error rates must be monitored to ensure that the timed operations were in fact completed successfully (Sternberg, 1969). In addition, analysis of those errors that do occur, into their various types, can yield evidence concerning the structural form of an internal representation (Conrad, 1964; Shepard, Kilpatric, & Cunningham, 1975) or concerning what structural information is preserved in the internal representation (Mandler & Johnson, 1976; Mandler & Stein, 1974; Sachs, 1967). Still other types of data—including records of eye fixations (Just & Carpenter, 1976) and, possibly, evoked cortical potentials—show promise for investigating the representation of objects and their transformations in space.

Clearly, the paradigms for the study of mental transformations are potentially quite diverse. However, in most of the experiments that we shall review, the subject's basic task on each trial was to make one of two binary responses (e.g., to operate either a right- or a left-hand switch) as rapidly as possible following the presentation of a visual test object, depending upon whether or not that test object met some prespecified condition. Most commonly, the prespecified condition was that the test object be identical to a certain reference object with respect to its intrinsic structure, but without regard to possible extrinsic differences produced by a transformation chosen from a particular class of spatial operations.

C. Theoretical Issues

The most central issue raised by mental transformations on spatial objects concerns the nature of those transformations. Are they best described in terms of analytic processes of sequential search, recoding, and discrete manipulation of symbolic structures, which have been so vigorously applied in the study of verbal learning, semantic memory, and problem solving (see, e.g., Anderson & Bower, 1973; Kintsch, 1974; Minsky, 1975; Newell & Simon, 1971; Pylyshyn, 1973; Norman & Rumelhart, 1975), or do they require a fundamentally different kind of conceptualization based on holistic, analog modeling of continuous external processes (see, e.g., Attneave, 1972, 1974; Cooper, 1976; Kosslyn, 1975; Shepard & Metzler, 1971; Shepard, 1975; Sloman, 1971)? In order to address this issue in an incisive way, we need to draw the distinction more sharply without going to the implausible extremes of supposing either that the analytic processes should be strictly verbal or that the analog processes should be strictly continuous. The way of drawing the distinction that we have previously advocated hinges on whether or not the intermediate states of the internal transformational process have a demonstrable one-to-one correspondence to intermediate states through which the external object would pass in undergoing an appropriate physical transformation (Cooper & Shepard, 1973a; Shepard, 1975).

A second and closely related issue concerns the nature of the internal representations that are mentally transformed. Are these representations the result of an analysis and recoding of the visual stimuli into some discrete lists of features, verbal descriptions, or other propositional structures, or are they the result of the internal formation of some sort of more holistic, isomorphic models of the corresponding physical stimuli? This question of the nature of the representation is closely interwined with the question of the nature of the mental transformations performed on the representation. Certainly, the compatibility between the type of representation and the type of process that acts on that representation will be greatest if both are of an analytic, symbolic character or both are of a holistic, analog character. Evidence for the analog nature of imagined spatial transformations may therefore provide indirect evidence for the holistic nature of the representations transformed, and vice versa.

A possibly related issue concerns the degree to which the internal events or processes in question resemble those of perception, on the one hand, or those of linguistic (or at least symbolic) recoding, on the other. Relevant to the first alternative are any parallelisms between phenomena of merely imagined spatial transformations and phenomena of the actual perception of such transformations. We shall consider, in particular, some phenomena intermediate between those of purely internally controlled imagination and those of wholly externally driven perception; namely, certain illusions of apparent translational and rotational movement.

II. ROTATIONAL TRANSFORMATIONS

A. Basic Chronometric Paradigms and Principal Results

1. THE TIME TO COMPARE TWO OBJECTS DIFFERING IN ORIENTATION

Shepard and Metzler (1971) reported the first in a series of chronometric studies that have yielded remarkably orderly data concerning the internal representation of rotational transformations. On each trial, a pair of computer-generated perspective line drawings of three-dimensional objects was presented. Subjects were required to indicate as rapidly as possible whether or not the two objects had the same inherent three-dimensional shape, regardless of the orientations in which the two objects were portrayed. Each object was composed of 10 cubical blocks attached face to face to form one of 10 structurally distinct asymmetric armlike forms with three right-angled bends.

On a random half of the trials the two objects were of identical three-dimensional shapes. They then differed, if at all, by one of 10 angles of rigid rotation in 20° steps between 0 and 180° inclusively—either in the plane of the picture itself, or in depth. On the remaining random half of the trials the two objects were of inherently different shapes. In addition to a possible rotation, they always differed by a reflection in three-dimensional space.

The two principal results for the half of the trials on which the two objects were the same are evident in Fig. 1. First, the mean time required to determine that the two objects were of the same three-dimensional shape increased in a strikingly linear manner with the angular difference between the orientations of the two objects in the pair. Second, the slope and intercept of the best-fitting linear function was not greater for the pairs differing by a rotation in depth than for the pairs differing by a rotation in the picture plane.

Subsequent analyses and experiments reported by Metzler and Shepard (1974) led to the following additional findings:

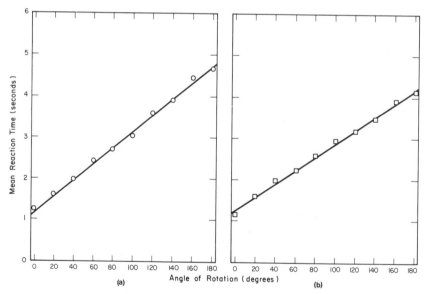

Fig. 1. Mean time to determine that two objects have the same three-dimensional shape as a function of the angular difference in their portrayed orientations, plotted separately for pairs differing by (a) rotation in the picture plane (circles) and (b) rotation in depth (squares). [From Metzler & Shepard (1974). Reprinted by permission.]

1. The linearity and approximate equivalence of slope so evident in the group data (Fig. 1) were consistently present in the data for the individual subjects and for each of the individual objects.
2. Results of the same linear form were also obtained whether or not the axis of rotation was known in advance of each trial, and whether or not corresponding ends of the two objects were color-coded to reduce the need for a preliminary search process.
3. Detailed analysis of pairs differing by depth rotations of the same angles (40° or 60°) revealed that mean reaction time was determined largely by the angle of rotation in three-dimensional space and relatively little, if at all, by the presence or absence of a topological equivalence between the two-dimensional perspective projections actually presented.

In a later experiment, using simplified objects with only seven cubes and only two right-angled bends, Metzler (1973; see Metzler & Shepard, 1974) established the following further results:

1. When the angular difference between objects of inherently *different* shape was defined as the minimum angle of rotation needed to bring just the (more salient) top parts of the two objects into congruence, then reaction time was again found to be a linearly increasing function of this angular difference—just as was earlier found for objects having the *same* three-dimensional shape.
2. When, toward the end of a block of trials, a few pairs were unexpectedly introduced in which the prevailing direction of the rotational difference was reversed, the reaction-time distribution became bimodal.

For these unexpectedly reversed pairs, which differed either by 225° if one rotated in the previously prevailing direction or by 135° if one rotated in the opposite but shorter direction, there were two distinct peaks—one aligned with the mode for the standard 135° pairs, and the other centered on a linear extrapolation of the reaction-time function past 180° out to 225°. (See Metzler & Shepard, 1974, p. 182, Fig. 16.)

The consistently linear increase in reaction time with angular difference, together with the bimodality beyond 180°, has been taken by Shepard and Metzler as support for their claim that a comparison is made by a transformational process that passes over a trajectory in which (*a*) the whole trajectory itself, and not just the static relation between its two end states, determines the reaction time; and (*b*) the times required to traverse successive portions of the trajectory are additive. The further facts that, for a given angular difference, the reaction times are not significantly increased either (*a*) when the rotations are in depth, rather than merely in the picture plane; or (*b*) when the two-dimensional projections are no longer topologically equivalent have been taken by them as evidence that the internal representation that is transformed along the trajectory preserves structural information pertaining more to the external three-dimensional object than to the two-dimensional retinal image (Metzler & Shepard, 1974; Shepard, 1975; Shepard & Metzler, 1971).

By monitoring eye fixations in the Shepard–Metzler task, Just and Carpenter (1976) obtained additional information concerning the internal processes preceding the subject's overt response on each trial. The sequence of fixations could often be divided into three distinct and successive patterns: a first, indicative of a search for corresponding ends of the two objects; a second, indicative of the rotational transformation itself; and a third, indicative of a process of decision as to sameness or difference. Although the times associated with the first and last phases (search and decision) both increased with the angular difference between the two objects, by far the greatest increase was attributable to the intervening transformational process.

In addition, these analyses provided insights into the internal processes that occurred when the two objects were different and, also, when the subjects responded incorrectly. Not unexpectedly, since a difference between the two objects would presumably be detected during the decision phase (Shepard & Metzler, 1971, p. 703), the major increase in reaction time for such different pairs was assignable to this phase. In addition, the eye-fixation records indicated that, when a match was not obtained during the decision phase, the subject sometimes repeated the entire three-phase process. Most interestingly, these records provided rather compelling evidence that incorrect responses frequently resulted from establishing an incorrect correspondence between the ends of the two objects during the initial search phase.

2. THE TIME TO RESPOND DISCRIMINATIVELY TO A ROTATED OBJECT

The increase in reaction time with angular difference in orientation is also found when subjects are required to respond discriminatively to a single rotated stimulus. Cooper (1975) trained subjects to discriminate standard from reflected versions of each of eight random polygons (similar to those studied by Attneave and Arnoult, 1956) when the two versions were always presented in the same arbitrarily chosen orientation. The shapes were then shown individually in any one of six orientations in the picture plane, and subjects were required to indicate as rapidly as possible whether each presented version was standard or reflected, regardless of its orientation. As in the experiments by Shepard and Metzler, reaction time increased linearly with angular departure—though in this experiment the departure was from a previously trained orientation rather than from the orientation of a second, simultaneously presented object. The highly reliable linear function for the group of eight subjects as a whole (shown by the open circles at the top of Fig. 2) was representative of the functions obtained for individual subjects as well as for individual polygons. Standard responses were a constant 60 msec faster than reflected responses, and error rates were generally 4% or less.

With stimuli that, in the uncontrolled preexperimental life of the subject, have been highly overlearned in a small range of similar canonical orientations, the reaction-time functions, though still monotonic, often depart from strict linearity. Thus, in experiments similar to that of Cooper

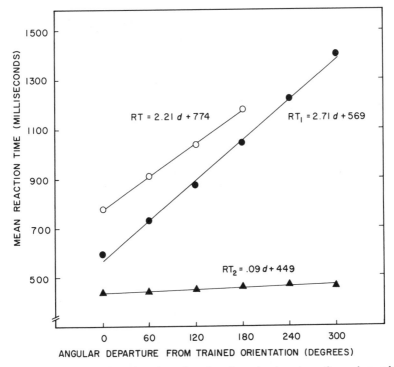

Fig. 2. Mean reaction time plotted as a function of angular departure of a random polygon from a previously learned orientation. (Group data: $N = 8$.) The uppermost function (open circles) shows the time to respond to a test form with no advance preparation. The middle function (solid circles) shows the time to prepare for an upcoming test form. The bottommost function (solid triangles) shows the time to respond to a test form following advance preparation. [From Cooper (1975).]

(1975), Cooper and Shepard (following some preliminary work by Shepard and Klun) found that reaction time for discriminating normal from backward versions of individually presented, rotated alphanumeric characters increased monotonically but nonlinearly with the angular departure of the character from its conventional upright position. The rate of increase was greatest as the position of complete 180° inversion was approached. (See Fig. 3 and Cooper & Shepard, 1973a, b).

Systematic dependence of reaction time on orientation has not been confined to tasks in which visual shapes must be discriminated from their mirror images. Corballis and Roldan (1975) have reported that the time needed to determine whether visual dot patterns are symmetrical about a line increases approximately linearly with the angular departure of this line of symmetry from the vertical orientation. This finding implicates a process of rotational transformation as one component of the symmetry judgment.

3. THE TIME TO PREPARE FOR AN OBJECT IN A SPECIFIED ORIENTATION

If a process of mental rotation is used in responding discriminatively to a previously presented rotated object, then a similar sort of rotational transformation may also be used in preparing for a to-be-presented rotated object. Cooper and Shepard (1973a, b) explored this possibility by providing subjects with advance information concerning the identity and the orientation of an upcoming rotated test character for varying amounts of time. Identity information, which consisted of an outline drawing of the upcoming alphanumeric character shown in the upright position, was presented for a fixed duration of 2 sec. Orientation information, which consisted of an arrow pointing to the position in which the top of the test character was to appear, was then presented for one of four durations ranging from 100 msec to 1 sec. Immediately upon the offset of the orientation cue, a rotated test character was presented in that orientation and subjects were required to determine as rapidly as possible whether it was normal or backward.

The results of this experiment, shown in Fig. 3, are consistent with the notion that subjects prepared for the presentation of the test stimulus by mentally rotating an internal representation of the designated character from the upright position into the designated orientation. When sufficient time was provided for completion of this preparatory rotational transformation, reaction time was rapid and constant for all test-character orientations. When the duration of the orientation cue was reduced, reaction time increased with departure of the test character from the upright

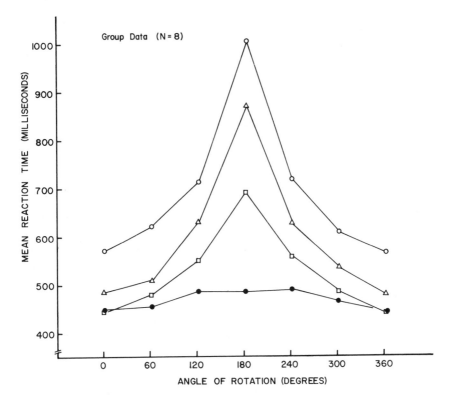

Fig. 3. Mean reaction time plotted as a function of clockwise angular departure of a test character from the upright position. (Group data: $N = 8$.) The four functions were obtained from conditions in which both identity information and orientation information were presented in advance. Duration of orientation information ranged from 100 msec to 1000 msec. [From Cooper & Shepard (1973a).] (○): 100 msec; (△): 400 msec; (□): 700 msec; (●): 1000 msec.

position, indicating that for larger departures subjects were not able to complete the preparatory rotation prior to the onset of the test stimulus.

Cooper (1975) modified this basic paradigm to investigate directly the time required to prepare for a rotated test form. As in the Cooper–Shepard experiment, advance information was provided; however, the duration of the orientation cue was controlled by the subject rather than by the experimenter. The subject was instructed to imagine a random polygon, indicated in outline by an identity cue, rotated into an orientation indicated by a tilted arrow. Rotations were to be imagined in a certain specified direction—clockwise or counterclockwise. When the subject had completed this process of preparation, he so indicated by pressing a button. The test form immediately appeared, and the subject was required to determine as rapidly as possible whether it was a standard or a reflected version of the previously learned shape. Thus, two reaction times—preparation time and discrimination time—were recorded on each trial.

The results of this experiment, shown as solid circles and triangles in the earlier Fig. 2, indicate that preparation time increases linearly with the angular departure of the test form from the learned orientation. Furthermore, discriminative reaction time was not affected by the orientation of the test form, indicating that subjects were indeed prepared for the presentation of the test form when they so indicated. The fact that, when direction was specified in advance, preparation time increased linearly all the way out to 300°, shows that subjects prepared for the upcoming test stimulus by carrying out a mental rotation in the specified direction. In addition, the slope of the linear preparation-time function (solid circles) was quite close to the slope of the previously obtained reaction-time function (open circles) for these same subjects and polygons. This similarity in slope suggests that similar processes of mental rotation underlie the *response* to a rotated object that is already presented and the *preparation* for a rotated object that is not yet presented.

4. THE TIME TO RESPOND TO AN OBJECT WHILE IMAGINING IT IN ROTATION

In a variation of the paradigm just described, the subject is instructed to imagine a specified object rotating in a specified direction. At a randomly selected time during this ongoing mental rotation, a test object is presented in some orientation and the subject is required to indicate whether it is standard or reflected as rapidly as possible. Cooper and Shepard (1973a) used this procedure by instructing subjects to imagine an alphanumeric character rotating in a blank circular field at a rate externally paced by means of auditory commands corresponding to six successive orientations about the circle. At an unpredictable point in the sequence, a visual test character appeared. The two principal results were as follows:

1. When the test character was presented in the expected orientation (i.e., the orientation corresponding to the current auditory command), discriminative reaction time was short and relatively independent of the (expected) angular departure of the tested orientation from upright.
2. When the test character was presented in an unexpected orientation, discriminative reaction time increased linearly with the angular difference between the tested orientation and the orientation corresponding to the current auditory command.

Hay (1975) performed an experiment resembling that of Cooper and Shepard, in that subjects were probed with a normal or backward alphanumeric character while imagining it in continuous rotation. However, the orientation expected from moment to moment, instead of being externally controlled by auditory commands, was controlled by the subject's own manual rotation of a disk (invisible in the dark) on which the luminous probe was to appear. As in Cooper and Shepard's experiment, reaction time was short and essentially independent of orientation when the probe appeared in the orientation expected at the moment of presentation, but increased markedly with departures from that orientation.

Metzler (1973; see Metzler & Shepard, 1974) instructed subjects to carry out, at a self-determined rate, a mental rotation of a three-dimensional object previously depicted by a perspective line drawing. Following some delay, a test picture was presented of an object in a rotated orientation, and the subject determined as quickly as possible whether the two successively depicted objects were the same or different in shape. The delay between the first and second pictures was selected to correspond to the mean rotation time estimated for that subject and that angular departure from a previous experiment. Thus, in Metzler's experiment all test objects were presented in expected orientations, and for the majority of the subjects reaction times were virtually constant, regardless of the angular difference between the orientations of the first and second stimuli.

Cooper (1976) performed a further experiment that combined the following features:

1. Subjects imagined a random two-dimensional polygon rotating in a circular field at a self-determined rate.
2. Test shapes were presented at both expected and unexpected orientations.
3. The points in time during the mental rotation at which test shapes were presented were selected on the basis of estimated rotation rates for these subjects and these shapes from a previous experiment (Cooper, 1975).
4. On a small proportion of the trials, test objects were presented in orientations, not previously presented to these subjects, that were halfway between the six familiar 60° orientations.

The results are displayed in Fig. 4. The right-hand panel shows that, when the test stimulus departed from the orientation that the subject was predicted to be imagining at the time of the test, reaction time increased linearly with the angular departure of the test stimulus from that expected orientation. The left-hand panel shows that the reaction times to

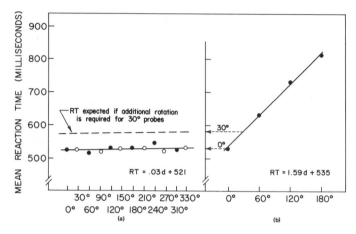

Fig. 4. (a) Mean reaction time as a function of angular departure of a test probe from a previously learned orientation for trials on which the probe was presented in an expected orientation. (Group data: $N = 6$.) Open circles (O) show 30° (unfamiliar) probes, and solid circles (●) show 60° (familiar) probes. (b) Mean reaction time as a function of angular departure of a test probe from the expected orientation. [From Cooper (1976). Reprinted by permission of the Psychonomic Society.]

those test stimuli that, according to the previously estimated rates of mental rotation, were presented at expected orientations were uniformly short and independent of departure from the trained orientation. Indeed, the reaction times to the new 30° probes were no longer than those to the familiar 60° probes. If the subjects had been preparing only for test stimuli at the familiar 60° orientations, reaction times to the intermediate 30° probes should have been elevated by the time corresponding to a 30° rotation; that is, to the broken horizontal line. Apparently, in preparing for objects in successive orientations rotated by 60°, subjects always passed through states of preparation for the intermediate 30° orientations.

5. THE TIME CONSTANTS FOR APPARENT ROTATIONAL MOVEMENT

At the outset we argued that perceptual interpretations sometimes depend upon the performance of mental transformations, including those corresponding to rotations. The extent to which the mental transformations themselves are perceptual in nature remains an open question. Of particular relevance to this question is some recent work on an illusion of *apparent* rotational movement. For, although the subjective experience of this illusion is unmistakably perceptual in character, the time constants estimated for this illusion exhibit a pattern that is similar to the pattern

that Shepard and Metzler (1971) first reported for the less directly perceptual task of mental rotation.

In order to induce an illusion of apparent rotation, on each trial Shepard
and Judd (1976) presented each of two perspective views of the same
three-dimensional objects in continuous alternation in the same spatial
location and without an interstimulus interval. The perspective views
were chosen from the set, portraying ten-cube objects, originally used by
Shepard and Metzler. The rate of alternation was varied from trial to trial
according to a random sequence. For each presented rate, the subject
gave a rating of the quality of the experienced movement on a numerical
scale of 1–3, defined by three anchor points: A rating of 1, for the
perception of a continuous rotation, back and forth, of the three-
dimensional object as a coherent, rigid whole; a rating of 2 for nonrigid or
noncoherent motion or vibration; and a rating of 3 for flickering superposition without spatial movement. Ratings by tenths were permitted between
these three integer values.

Despite the random order of presentation of rates, the ratings shifted
monotonically with rate, from 1 for slow rates to 3 for the highest rates
presented. The minimum duration of each field at which the monotone
rating profile intersected the rating level of 1.5 (halfway between rigid
and nonrigid rotation) was taken as an estimate of the time constant for
breakdown of the illusion of rigid apparent rotation. Figure 5 displays the
mean time constants estimated in this way for the group of ten subjects.
As can be seen, although in absolute level these times are much shorter
than those obtained by Shepard and Metzler (1971) in their less perceptual

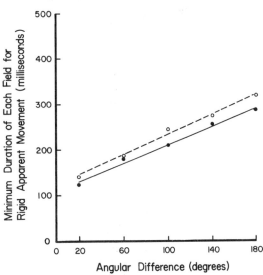

Fig. 5. Mean field duration at
which rigid apparent rotational motion breaks down plotted as a function
of angular difference. Solid points (●)
show durations for pairs of objects differing by a rotation in depth, open
points (○) show durations for pairs of
objects differing by a rotation in the
picture plane (– – –): $T_p = 1.10\phi +
121$; (—): $T_D = .97\phi + 112$. [From
Shepard & Judd (1976). Copyright ©
1976 by the American Association for
the Advancement of Science.]

task of mental rotation, the relative pattern is very much the same; time increases linearly with angular difference between the two orientations and with the same slope for rotations in depth and in the picture plane. Shepard and Judd conjectured that the same, basically perceptual mechanism may underlie both phenomena, but that the process proceeds much more rapidly when it is driven externally than when it is generated and controlled internally.

B. Theoretical Implications

1. IMPLICATIONS FOR THE NATURE OF THE PROCESS

We have been referring to the process of preparing for or responding to a rotated visual object as a *mental rotation*. Our usage is based on the notion that the process is in some specifiable sense an internal analog of an actual physical rotation of an external object. The specifiable sense intended is that the process passes through a trajectory of intermediate states, between the beginning and the end of the process, and that these intermediate states have a one-to-one correspondence to the intermediate stages in the external rotation of an object. The one-to-one correspondence need not be one of structural isomorphism between the internal representation undergoing the mental rotation and the external object undergoing the physical rotation. Rather, the correspondence entails only that, for each intermediate state, the subject is especially prepared for the presentation of the external object in a corresponding physical orientation. Precisely, what is rotating in a mental rotation is the unique external orientation in which the object must be presented in order for the subject to make the most rapid discriminative response (cf. Cooper & Shepard, 1973a; Metzler & Shepard, 1974; Shepard, 1975).

a. ADDITIVITY OF TIMES ALONG THE TRANSFORMATIONAL TRAJECTORY. The linear increase in reaction time and preparation time with angular difference, which is consistently found under specifiable conditions, provides one kind of evidence that mental rotation is an analog process in this sense. For this linearity implies that, for any three orientations A, B, C, with B between A and C, the time needed to compare visual objects in orientations A and C is an additive combination of the time needed to compare them in orientations A and B and the time needed to compare them in orientations B and C. This in turn provides indirect evidence that, in passing between orientations A and C, the process passes through an intermediate state corresponding to orientation B.

Important further evidence is provided by (*a*) the bimodality of the distribution of reaction times when the shortest direction of rotation to achieve congruence is unexpectedly reversed (Metzler, 1973; Metzler & Shepard, 1974); and, more conclusively, (b) the linear extrapolation of the reaction-time function beyond the maximum obtainable angular disparity of 180° (all the way out to 300°) when the direction of mental rotation is specified in advance (Cooper, 1975, and the present Fig. 2). These results establish that the process does indeed take place over a definite trajectory (corresponding to a particular direction of rotation). Moreover, they establish that the total time to complete the process depends upon the length of the particular trajectory taken and not merely on the static relation between its two end points.

b. RESPONSE TIMES TO TEMPORALLY UNPREDICTABLE PROBES. More direct evidence for the claim that mental rotation is an analog process comes from those experiments in which the correspondence between intermediate internal and external states was tested by presentation of external probes at experimentally determined times and orientations during the course of the process. If the internal process is specifically one of rotation, then reaction times should be shortest to test probes presented in orientations that change progressively with time.

In all experiments of this type, discriminative reaction time was short and constant when the test probe was presented in the changing orientation for which the subject was expected to be maximally prepared, regardless of its angular departure from a previously learned or canonical position. This was true when the rate of mental rotation was externally paced (Cooper & Shepard, 1973a) or manually controlled by the subject himself (Hay, 1975), and also when the subject was free to rotate at his own rate and test probes were presented in accordance with a previous estimate of that subject's rate (Cooper, 1976; Metzler, 1973; Metzler & Shepard, 1974).

One could argue that subjects were able to respond with uniform rapidity to probes presented in the expected orientation because they had learned to generate representations of test objects in familiar or frequently tested orientations. Alternatively, subjects could have achieved the required discrimination by extracting rotationally invariant features of the test objects, rather than by performing a mental rotation. Two aspects of the data discredit these possibilities:

1. Cooper (1976) demonstrated that responses to probes presented in expected orientations frequently seen before were no faster than responses to probes presented halfway between these familiar positions (see Fig. 4, left-hand panel). If subjects were generating internal representations of the test objects in only the previously experienced orientations, then reaction times to the unfamiliar probes should have been uniformly longer.

2. Cooper (1976) and Cooper and Shepard (1973a) showed that reaction time to test probes presented in an unexpected orientation increased linearly with the angular departure of the tested orientation from the expected orientation. The linearity of these reaction-time functions suggests that subjects performed an additional mental rotation after the presentation of the unexpected test probes.

In any case, if subjects were achieving the required discrimination by extracting rotationally invariant features of the test objects, then reaction times should have been equal to probes presented in expected and unexpected orientations.

In summary, the experiments discussed indicate quite directly that the internal process underlying the observed reaction-time data passes through an ordered series of states which have a one-to-one correspondence to the intermediate stages in the rotation of an external object. Thus, this internal process qualifies as a mental analog of an external rotation. At present, it is not possible to determine whether the process of mental rotation is strictly continuous or proceeds in a series of discrete steps. Cooper's (1976) finding of equivalently fast reaction times to unfamiliar test objects presented halfway between the familiar 60° orientations suggests that the size of any component steps must be at least as small as 30°.

2. IMPLICATIONS FOR THE NATURE OF THE REPRESENTATION

Whether the internal representation to which the process of mental rotation is applied is a structurally isomorphic *mental template,* a more abstract *structural description* (cf. Reed, 1973; Sutherland, 1973), or some intermediate kind of schematic structure is currently far from resolved. Nonetheless, some empirical results and theoretical considerations place significant constraints on the nature of possible models of the internal representation.

a. SPEED AND PRECISION OF DISCRIMINATION FOLLOWING PREPARATORY MENTAL ROTATION. Cooper (1975) and Cooper and Shepard (1973a, b) have shown that, following a preparatory mental rotation, discriminative reaction time to a test object is uniformly rapid (about 300–500 msec), regardless of the orientation of the test object. In addition, Cooper and Shepard (1973a, b) demonstrated that the time needed to compare a mentally rotated internal representation with a test object was only slightly longer than the time needed to compare two externally rotated objects presented successively and in the same orientation. These discriminative reaction times are much too rapid to allow for coding or decoding of verbal descriptions of the complex visual shapes. The same point is made by the phenomenon of apparent rotational movement, studied by Shepard and Judd (1976), which is not only very rapid but also subjectively perceptual in character.

The transformed internal representation also appears to preserve considerable spatial structure of the complex visual shapes. This is demonstrated most clearly in a study by Cooper and Podgorny (1976) in which there were test probes differing from the standard random polygons by various degrees of random perturbation, as well as test probes differing by an overall reflection. The entire stimulus set is illustrated in Fig. 6. For each of the five standard shapes, the perturbations varied in rated similarity to the standards, with *D1* perturbations being most similar to the standards and *D6* perturbations being least similar.

The relevant results of this experiment can be summarized as follows:

1. Discriminative reaction times and error rates were not systematically related to complexity of the test probe (cf. Fig. 7, upper two panels).
2. For the group data, *different* reaction times and error rates decreased monotonically with increasing dissimilarity between the

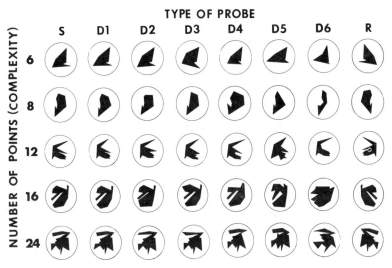

Fig. 6. The complete set of shapes used by Cooper and Podgorny. Standard shapes at five levels of complexity are shown in the leftmost column, reflected versions are shown in the rightmost column, and perturbations varying in rated similarity to the standards are shown in the middle six columns. [From Cooper & Podgorny (1976). Copyright 1976 by The American Psychological Association. Reprinted by permission.]

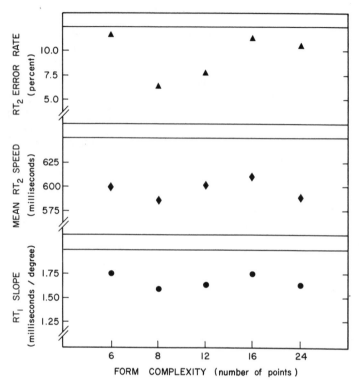

Fig. 7. Mean discriminative error rate (uppermost panel, triangles), mean discriminative reaction time (middle panel, diamonds), and mean slope of the preparation-time function (bottom panel, circles) plotted as a function of complexity of random polygons.

standard shape and the randomly perturbed test probes. Nonetheless, error rates were negligible and reaction times were quite rapid (about 500 msec) to D3 through D6 probes (cf. Fig. 6).

These findings indicate that the internal representation does preserve a significant degree of the spatial structure of its external counterpart. Certainly, the internal representation is not highly reduced or schematic, consisting of only a small set of visual features of its corresponding external object, for such a reduced representation would not permit such rapid and accurate discrimination of shapes differing in such subtle and unpredictable ways.

b. ABSENCE OF EFFECT OF COMPLEXITY ON RATE OF MENTAL ROTATION. Recently, several investigators have suggested that discrete, propositional data structures provide an appropriate format for the internal representation of visual objects (e.g., Palmer, 1975; Pylyshyn, 1973). In particular, network structures like those used in recent models of semantic memory (see Norman & Rumelhart, 1975) could be applied to the representation of visual information. Features and relations among features of a visual object could be represented by nodes and links between nodes in the network. Levin (1973) has described how a rotational transformation could be applied to a representation of this sort. In Levin's formulation, rotation is accomplished by successively changing orientation information at each node of the internal representation.

This model accomodates the finding that reaction time increases with the angular difference between two visual objects or the angular departure of a single visual object from a learned orientation. In addition, however, the model predicts that the time required for rotational transformation of a representation should increase with the complexity of the object represented. For, as the number of nodes in the internal representation increases, more time will be needed to update the orientation information at each node at each step of the rotation. Indeed, this dependence of rotation time on object complexity is predicted by all models which assume that the internal representation of a visual object is operated upon serially, piece-by-piece or feature-by-feature.

In contrast to this prediction, the results of the Cooper–Podgorny experiment described previously were that complexity had no effect on rate of preparatory rotation, on discriminative reaction time, or on error rate (Fig. 7). If the internal representations undergoing mental rotation were always reduced to the same level of internal complexity, then the failure to find an effect of external complexity on rotation rate could be explained. But, under this account, discriminative reaction time and error rate should have increased with complexity. This is because internal representations of more complex visual objects would then be less adequately represented by the uniformly schematic internal representations. Hence, the findings of Cooper and Podgorny suggest that the internal representations undergoing mental rotation are holistic in nature and are integrally transformed.

c. ABSENCE OF EFFECT OF SPECIFICALLY RETINAL FEATURES. The studies using perspective pictures of three-dimensional objects led to two findings with closely related implications for the nature of the internal representations of such objects. First, for pairs of objects differing by a given angle of rotation, comparison time was found to be no shorter for pairs of pictures related by a rigid rotation of the pictures themselves than for pairs of pictures related by the two-dimensionally nonrigid deformation corresponding to a rotation of the three-dimensional object in depth. Second, when the objects differed by a given angle in depth, comparison time was relatively independent of whether the two-dimensional pictures were at least equivalent to each other under a continuous deformation or whether they differed by a topological discontinuity as well (Metzler & Shepard, 1974). These results, together with the similar more recent results on apparent rotational movement obtained by Shepard and Judd (1976), indicate that the internal transformational process is relatively insensitive to the surface features of the two-dimensional retinal images. Shepard and Metzler have argued that the internal representations that are mentally transformed embody, principally, the structure of the three-dimensional object portrayed in the two-dimensional pictures.

C. Further Issues

1. CONDITIONS UNDER WHICH MENTAL ROTATION OCCURS

a. INABILITY TO PREPARE FOR THE ORIENTATION OF AN UNKNOWN OBJECT. As we have seen, when provided with advance information concerning both identity and orientation of an upcoming test object, subjects can prepare in such a way as to make responses to the ensuing object uniformly rapid. regardless of the extent of the object's rotation. Yet, earlier work of Rock and others (reviewed in Rock, 1973), in which recognition of rotated objects was tested with or without a rotation of the subject's head, has suggested that subjects might have difficulty preparing for a rotated orientation as such; that is, when the identity of the object is not known in advance.

Cooper and Shepard (1973a) addressed this question directly by providing subjects with advance information concerning only the orientation of an upcoming test character (see, also, Cooper & Shepard, 1975). Under these conditions, reaction time for determining the (normal-backward) version of the ensuing test character increased monotonically with the angular departure of the character from the conventional upright orientation. Moreover, the shape of the reaction-time function was essentially the same as that obtained in the absence of any advance information. Similar results have been obtained by Corballis and Roldan (1975), who reported that advance information concerning the orientation of a dot pattern has no effect on the shape of the function relating reaction time for detecting symmetry to orientation of the pattern. Apparently, subjects are able to prepare for the rotated presentation of a concrete object only by carrying out a mental transformation on the internal representation of that object, and not by mentally rotating an abstract frame of reference.

b. ROTATION OF OBJECTS VERSUS ROTATION OF THE OBSERVER. A further question concerns the ability of an observer to imagine the rotation of an object or array of objects versus the ability of an observer to imagine himself moved around the object or array. Piaget and Inhelder (1956, 1970) have called the second sort of problem the *perspective problem*, whereas the first sort of problem can be called the *rotation problem* (cf. Huttenlocher & Presson, 1973). Piaget and his colleagues have claimed that children are able to solve rotation problems at an earlier age than that required for the solution of perspective problems.

Huttenlocher and Presson (1973) systematically investigated the relative difficulty that children experience with these two types of rotational transformations. They reported that children of ages 8 and 10 are considerably more accurate in determining the outcome of rotating an array of objects with respect to an observer fixed in space than they are in determining the outcome of rotating an observer around an array of objects fixed in space. Furthermore, the difficulty of the perspective problem is reduced substantially if the child is permitted to physically move to the position of another observer, rather than having to anticipate the appearance of an array from the position of that other observer without actually moving.

The situation appears to be somewhat similar for adults. Hintzman (personal communication) presented subjects with a circular display consisting of an arrow and a dot at different locations around the perimeter. Subjects were instructed to indicate the direction from themselves that the target dot would be if they themselves were in the orientation indicated by the arrow. If subjects imagined themselves in the orientation of the arrow and preserved this imagined orientation from trial to trial, then reaction time for determining the direction of the target dot from the arrow should increase with the extent of rotation between the arrows from one trial to the next. No such evidence was found. Rather, reaction time increased with the angular difference between the orientation of the arrow and the upright position. Subjects seemed to determine the direction of the target dot by imagining the visual display rotated until the arrow reached the upright position and then indicating the transformed orientation of the target dot. Although this experiment does not show that subjects are unable to imagine themselves rotated with respect to a visual display, it does suggest that rotation of a display with respect to the fixed observer is the preferred mode of transformation.

Some possibly related observations have recently been made by Attneave and Farrar (1975). These investigators required subjects to answer questions about the locations and orientations of objects in a linear array. One group of subjects was allowed to inspect the array for a period of time and was then required to respond to the test questions in terms of the positions that the objects would have if the array were placed behind the subjects' heads. In this condition, several of the subjects reported that they answered the questions by "mentally translating" the array from behind to in front of them. Other subjects reported viewing the objects as if they had "eyes in the back of their heads." None of the subjects reported imagining themselves rotated to face the objects or moved behind the objects.

c. ROTATION RELATIVE TO RETINAL OR TO ENVIRONMENTAL UPRIGHT. A related question concerns whether rotational transformations are carried out to achieve congruence with the retinal or the gravitational upright orientation, when these two orientations differ. In their study of the detection of symmetry of dot patterns, Corballis and Roldan (1975) dissociated the retinal and environmental uprights by testing the subjects under three conditions of head tilt—45° to the left, 45° to the right, and upright. In the upright position, reaction time for detecting symmetry increased with the angular departure of the dot pattern from the gravitationally (and retinally) vertical orientation. Under conditions of head tilt, reaction time increased with the angular departure of the pattern from the retinally vertical orientation. These findings suggest that subjects mentally rotated the patterns into congruence with the retinally determined upright position in order to make the judgment of symmetry.

This conclusion contrasts with considerable evidence suggesting that a variety of perceptual judgments are made relative to gravitational (rather than to retinal) upright. For example, Rock and Leaman (1963) asked subjects which of two patterns—one symmetrical about the environmentally vertical axis and one symmetrical about the environmentally horizontal axis—was more similar to a pattern symmetrical about both axes. The pattern symmetrical about the vertical axis was nearly always selected, even when the head was tilted. And Attneave and Olson (1967) found that reaction time to environmentally horizontal and vertical lines was quicker than to oblique lines, even with the head tilted. In addition, transfer of responses associated with lines was excellent when subjects were required to give the same response to a line in the same environmental orientation, but much poorer when subjects were required to give the same response to a line in the same retinal orientation. In a subsequent study, however, Attneave and Reid (1968) found that when subjects were explicitly instructed to adopt a retinal frame of reference, transfer of responses based on retinally invariant orientation was facilitated.

Rock (1973) has argued that a disoriented pattern must be "corrected"—perhaps by some sort of mental rotation. However, whether the corrective rotation is to the upright orientation with respect to the environment, as Rock suggests, or with respect to the retinal framework, may depend upon a variety of factors, including the nature of the judgment, the instructions, and the stimuli. Corballis and his associates have recently obtained evidence concerning this last factor. Whereas they had found that reaction time depended primarily on retinal orientation for detection of symmetry of unfamiliar dot patterns (Corballis & Roldan, 1975), they have now established that reaction time depends primarily on environmental orientation for discrimination between standard and reversed versions of familiar alphanumeric characters, as in the Cooper–Shepard task (Corballis, Zbrodoff, & Roldan, 1976). Possibly, as they suggest, familiar objects with a standard orientation in the external world tend to be referred to the gravitational coordinate system, whereas unfamiliar patterns tend to be referred to the retinal coordinate system.

d. ROLE OF ROTATIONAL TRANSFORMATIONS IN OBJECT IDENTIFICATION. The results reviewed so far do not imply that the *identification* of a familiar object is achieved only after first mentally rotating it to match some canonical representation in long-term memory. Most familiar objects, such as plants and animals, tables and chairs, letters and numbers, may well be identifiable on the basis of redundant distinctive features of size, color, texture, presence or absence of straight or curved edges, etc., that are relatively invariant under rotation. Thus, the uppercase letter *R* may be identified quite immediately as an *R*, even when presented upside down, on the basis of its enclosed space, two free ends, and so on. It may be that a mental rotation is required only for more demanding discriminations—as when one object is the exact mirror image of the other (Cooper, 1975; Cooper & Shepard, 1973a; Shepard & Metzler, 1971) or is but a very slight distortion of the other (Cooper & Podgorny, 1976).

It is true that presentation in nonstandard orientations has been found to impair recognition or interpretation of letters of text (Kolers, 1968; Kolers & Perkins, 1969a, b) and, most strikingly, of human faces and of cursive writing (Bradshaw & Wallace, 1971; Hochberg & Galper, 1967; Rock, 1973, 1974; Yin, 1969). But this may be because the necessary feature analyses proceed more efficiently when the features are in their usual orientation, not because a mental rotation is carried out. Indeed, the maximum angular disorientation of 180° does not necessarily produce the most impaired recognition (e.g., Dearborn, 1899; Gibson & Robinson, 1935).

Cooper and Shepard (1973a) found that presentation of advance information concerning only the identity of a rotated alphanumeric character lowered the entire function relating reaction time to orientation by about 100 msec, without changing the shape of the function from that found with

no advance information. They concluded that, in the no-information condition, about 100 msec were required to identify the character, regardless
of its orientation. Cooper and Levin (unpublished data) have obtained
preliminary evidence lending more direct support to this claim. Subjects
were presented with a transformed letter or number whose identity remained unambiguous under rotation or reflection, and they were required
to identify vocally the visual pattern as rapidly as possible. Identification
was equally rapid and accurate at all picture-plane orientations.

Seemingly, then, mere identification of familiar but disoriented objects
does not usually require a corrective mental rotation of measurable duration. It is only when the identity of the object becomes ambiguous under
rotation (as in the study by Rock, 1956) or when a more difficult discrimination is required (as in the work, reviewed above, by Cooper, Shepard, and
others) that clear evidence for the occurrence of mental rotation emerges.

2. STIMULUS FACTORS AND RATE OF MENTAL ROTATION

a. ORIENTATION OF THE AXIS OF ROTATION. Any two different orientations of the same object in three-dimensional space define a unique axis of
rotation. Accordingly, the question arises as to whether the time to compare two identically shaped objects depends upon the orientation of this
uniquely defined axis. We have already commented on the theoretical
significance of Shepard and Metzler's (1971) finding that mental rotations
about the line-of-sight axis were no faster than those about a vertical axis.
Nevertheless, there may be some dependence of rate upon the orientation
of the axis with respect to the gravitational framework. In subsequent
work, Metzler (1973; see Metzler & Shepard, 1974) found that mental
rotation about an axis within the picture plane is slightly more rapid when
that axis is vertical than when it is horizontal or oblique. However, this
difference is small at best and has not always emerged (see the following
text).

More important than the absolute orientation of the axis in space is the
relative orientation of that axis with respect to the object rotated. In
particular, Metzler's (1973) results indicate that mental rotation is appreciably faster when the axis of rotation coincides with a natural axis of the
three-dimensional object itself, e.g., with the axis of the longest or central
row of cubical blocks forming that object (see Metzler & Shepard, 1974).

b. TWO- VERSUS THREE-DIMENSIONALITY OF THE OBJECTS. A remaining
puzzle concerns the vast difference in rates of mental rotation estimated by
Shepard and Metzler (1971) for their perspective drawings (about 60°/sec)

and by Cooper (1975) and Cooper and Podgorny (1976) for their random polygons (about 400–600° sec^{-1}). The most obvious difference between the two cases is that objects in the first case are perceived as three-dimensional, whereas those in the second are perceived as two-dimensional. Podgorny (1975) found that mental rotation was faster for the Cooper polygons than for the Shepard–Metzler objects, even when the procedures and modes of presentation were identical, and the same subjects served in both conditions. However, the ratio between the estimated rates for the two types of stimuli under these more comparable conditions was reduced from about 7 : 1 to about 2.5 : 1. Since it is not clear whether this remaining 2.5 : 1 ratio is attributable to the difference in dimensionality or to some other difference between the two kinds of stimuli, investigators have attempted to manipulate the perceived dimensionality of the objects while holding other stimulus factors constant.

In a second experiment, Podgorny (1975) compared the rate of rotation of three-dimensional objects like those used by Shepard and Metzler (1971) with the rate of rotation of two-dimensionalized versions of these same objects (i.e., outline polygons of the Shepard–Metzler objects). All rotations were in the picture plane, and the same subjects served in both the two-dimensional and the three-dimensional conditions. Estimated rate of mental rotation was no faster in the two-dimensional than in the three-dimensional condition. In both cases alike, the rates were between the slow rates reported by Shepard and Metzler (1971) and the fast rates reported by Cooper (1975) and Cooper and Podgorny (1976).

Cooper and Farrell (in preparation) attempted, in a somewhat different way, to manipulate perceived dimensionality while holding constant the number of line segments making up each picture. The two-dimensional objects were depicted by hexagonal shapes divided into six equal sections, with simple geometric symbols in three of the adjacent sections. The three-dimensional objects were depicted by perspective drawings of cubes, with geometric symbols on three faces of each cube. On each trial, two figures of either type were presented in different orientations in the picture plane. Subjects were instructed to determine whether the configuration of geometric symbols on the faces or sections of the two objects was the same or different. Once again, reaction time increased linearly with the angular difference between the two objects in each pair, but the slope of the reaction-time function was not different for two- and three-dimensional objects. Indeed, in a subsequent experiment by these same investigators no reliable differences were found among rates of rotation for two dimensional objects in the picture plane, three-dimensional objects in the picture plane, three-dimensional objects about a vertical axis in depth, and three-dimensional objects about a horizontal axis in depth. Thus, there is as yet no strong or systematic evidence supporting the conjecture that perceived dimensionality determines the rate of mental rotation.

c. Simultaneous versus successive presentation of rotated objects. A procedural difference may go further toward accounting for the dramatic difference in rotation rates reported by Shepard and Metzler (1971) and those reported by Cooper (1975) and Cooper and Podgorny (1976). In the case of the former experiment, the two visual objects to be compared were presented simultaneously, whereas in the latter experiments a single visual object was compared with a memory representation of a standard version of the object.

Podgorny (1975) evaluated this procedural difference by presenting two visual objects differing in orientation either simultaneously or successively. Reaction time for determining whether or not the two objects were the same in shape increased linearly with the angular difference in their orientations under both modes of presentation. However, for the same subjects and same objects, both the slope and the intercept of the reaction-time function obtained with simultaneous presentation were substantially greater than those obtained with successive presentation. The difference in intercept can be explained by the fact that, with simultaneous presentation, the subject must encode both objects in the pair. With successive presentation, only the time to encode the second or test object enters into the measured reaction time. The difference in slope indicates that mental rotation is also slower with simultaneous presentation. Analyses of eye fixation (cf. Just & Carpenter, 1976; Metzler & Shepard, 1974) suggest that a strategy of feature-by-feature rotation and comparison, induced by simultaneous presentation, may require more time than rotation of a well-learned, holistic internal representation followed by comparison with a standard representation in memory.

3. Individual Differences in Rate of Mental Rotation

a. Differences among normal adults. In the major studies of rotational transformation previously described, reaction time has been found to increase with angular difference for individual subjects, as well as for the group means. However, considerable differences have always been found in the rates of rotation estimated for individual subjects. For example, estimated rates for individual subjects ranged from about 30–70°/sec in the first and from about 20–60°/sec in the second of the two experiments reported by Metzler and Shepard (1974), using the same sort of three-dimensional objects, and from about 320–840°/sec in Cooper's (1975) experiment using random polygons. Within each of these three different sets of eight subjects there was thus a two-and-a-half to three-fold variation in rate of rotation. Moreover, such differences in rate for individual subjects (as well as for individual objects or types of objects) appear to be quite stable over time (Cooper, 1975, 1976; Cooper & Podgorny, 1976). So far, however, consistent evidence for any strong dependence of rate upon sex or handedness of the subjects in these studies has not been striking (see, in particular, Metzler & Shepard, 1974).

b. DIFFERENCES BETWEEN SPECIAL POPULATIONS. More compelling evidence for organismic factors affecting mental rotation has come from studies of groups specially selected on the basis of age, psychiatric classification, or brain damage. Using mental rotation tasks like those of Metzler and Shepard (1971), rates of rotation have been estimated to be lower and response times considerably more variable for young children (Marmor, 1975) and for the elderly (Gaylord & Marsh, 1975). Evidence of mental rotation in children less than about 7 years of age is of some interest in view of Piaget and Inhelder's (1970) contention that "kinetic imagery" does not emerge until 7 or 8. An extensive literature bearing on rotational transformations in various clinical populations has been reviewed by Royer and Holland (1975).

Of particular relevance to the question of the extent to which mental rotation is specifically visual or essentially amodal are studies investigating mental rotation in the blind (Carpenter & Eisenberg, 1978; Marmor & Zaback, 1976). Interestingly, for blind subjects, reaction time for determining whether or not two tactually presented objects are the same in shape also increases linearly with the angular difference between the orientations of the objects. Although Marmor and Zaback report that congenitally blind subjects are slower than subjects who are normally sighted or who became blind only later in life, evidence as to the degree of such slowness is as yet quite limited.

III. OTHER SPATIAL TRANSFORMATIONS

In this section, we consider the nature of mental operations that correspond to spatial transformations other than rotation. These transformations include size changes, translations, reflections, and structural transformations in which the form of an object is changed or parts of an object are synthesized into a whole. As in the case of rotational transformations, evidence concerning the time to carry out these other mental transformations has played a central role in assessing both the nature of the transformations themselves and the nature of the internal representations undergoing or resulting from such transformations.

A. Transformations of Size

1. SIZE SCALING IN THE COMPARISON OF PRESENTED OBJECTS

Bundesen and Larsen (1975) presented pairs of random, two-dimensional polygons differing in the ratio of their linear sizes. The time required to determine that the two polygons were the same in shape increased linearly with the ratio of the sizes. These results suggest that determination of identity of shape necessitated a mental expansion or contraction of the size of one object in the pair to correspond to the size of the other object.

Sekuler and Nash (1972) required subjects to determine as rapidly as possible whether two successively presented rectangles were the same or different in shape. The ratio of the linear sizes of the two rectangles could assume one of seven values; furthermore, when the two rectangles were the same in shape, they differed by a 90° picture-plane rotation on half of the trials. The time to determine that the two rectangles were the same in shape increased approximately linearly with the ratio of their sizes. When the two rectangles differed by a 90° rotation, average reaction time was a constant 70 msec longer than when the two rectangles were presented in the same orientation. These findings implicate the operation of a mental size-scaling process that is independent of a rotational transformation.

2. SIZE SCALING IN THE DETECTION OF PROPERTIES OF IMAGINED OBJECTS

Kosslyn (1975) has used a somewhat different paradigm to study mental size transformations. Subjects were asked to imagine a verbally designated animal (e.g., *cat*) and were then required to judge as rapidly as possible whether or not a particular property (e.g., *claws*) was appropriate for the imaged animal. Relative size of the imaged animal was manipulated both directly, by instructing subjects to imagine the animal as one of four designated sizes, and indirectly, by instructing subjects to imagine the animal standing next to a large or a small context animal. For both types of size manipulation, the time to determine whether or not the property was appropriate to the imaged animal decreased as the size of the imaged animal became larger, even when size and complexity were varied independently. These findings were interpreted as supporting the notion that detection of properties contained in relatively small images required a mental operation of size scaling (i.e., a mental expansion or "zooming in" on the critical portion of the imaged animal).

B. Translations

1. MOTION OVER A MENTAL IMAGE

One type of translational mental operation involves scanning, or mentally "moving across," an internal representation of an object or array. Kosslyn (1973) instructed subjects to generate mental images of line drawings of oblong objects that were horizontal or vertical in orientation (e.g., a car or a tower, respectively). Subjects were then asked to verify as rapidly as possible whether or not each imaged object contained a particular property (e.g., a headlight or a door). The group of subjects of interest was instructed to focus attention on a designated end of the image before attempting to verify the presence or absence of the test property. For these subjects, verification time increased linearly with the distance of the verified property from the point of initial focus. Thus, it appears that subjects can mentally fixate one part of an image and then scan over the internal representation to determine whether or not the image contains the test property. This mental scanning seems analogous to the physical process of scanning from one end to the other of an externally presented picture. However, under different conditions, Lea (1975) found that when physical distance and the number of features or spatial locations scanned were varied independently, reaction time was affected only by the latter of the two variables. (For somewhat conflicting results, see Kosslyn, Ball, & Reiser, 1978.)

2. TRANSLATIONAL APPARENT MOVEMENT

Since Korte (1915), it has been known that the temporal separation between two successive stimuli needed for an optimal appearance of translational movement increases as the spatial separation between the stimuli increases. This relationship between time and extent of spatial transformation is similar to that obtained both in studies of apparent rotational movement and in studies of mental rotation. In an important series of experiments based on a doctoral dissertation by Corbin (1942), Attneave and Block (1973) demonstrated that, with the retinal separation between two stimuli held constant, the time interval required for optimal apparent movement varies with the phenomenal separation between the stimuli. Phenomenal separation was manipulated by use of a perspective gradient that produced an illusion of slant of the stimulus plane and also by varying the physical deviation of the stimuli from the frontal plane. Results indicated that the internal representation of space in which the apparent translational movement was occurring was an analog of three-dimensional space. The correspondence of these results with those obtained in the studies of rotational transformations by Shepard and Judd (1976) lead us to suppose that mental operations of a similar nature underlie both cases.

C. Sequences of Rigid Motions

1. MULTIPLE TRANSFORMATIONS IN OBJECT IDENTIFICATION

Imagined spatial transformations are not necessarily restricted to single operations varying only in extent. Subjects may sometimes have to carry out sequences of different kinds of spatial operations. For example, Cooper and Shepard (1975) asked subjects to identify a line drawing as either that of a left or a right hand when the hand might appear in any of six orientations in the picture plane and, in each of these orientations, might display either the palm or the back. In some experimental conditions, subjects were instructed to prepare for the test hand by imagining a designated side (palm or back) of a designated hand (left or right) in a designated orientation. When the test hand and the imagined hand differed, subjects apparently performed one or more mental transformations in order to achieve a match between the internal representation of their own designated hand and the visually presented hand. The reaction times suggested that when a match was not achieved, an internal representation of the other, nondesignated hand was mentally rotated from a canonical "fingers-up" orientation into the orientation of the test hand. If this transformation failed to achieve a match with the visually presented hand, then a second mental transformation of flipping the internal representation was performed. The discrimination of left from right hands thus seems to afford a rather clear example in which the identification of an object may depend upon the mental completion of a combination of spatial transformations.

2. REFLECTIONS AND ROTATIONS

Shepard and Feng (see Shepard, 1975) instructed subjects to imagine, with eyes closed, specified spatial operations on specified letters, and to report the identity of the resulting character (so that, for a 90° rotation, they should report that N becomes Z). Picture-plane rotations of 180° took more time than those of 90°, and reflection about the horizontal axis took roughly the same time as reflection about the vertical. Interestingly, the combined operation of reflection about the vertical axis followed by reflection about the horizontal axis took the longest time of all, even though the result was always identical to that of one 180° rotation in the picture plane. This again illustrates the point that the time is determined by the trajectory of the transformational process, not by the relation between the end points.

Reflections of two-dimensional objects (like the flipping of a hand from palm to back) can be regarded as 180° rotations out of the picture plane. In further work following their initial study of apparent rotational movement (Shepard & Judd, 1976), Shepard and Judd have found that when two mirror images of the same random polygon are alternately presented at an appropriate rate, subjects report seeing the object flipping back and forth in depth. Moreover, the rate of alternation at which such rigid apparent movement breaks down evidently is about the same as the rate at which the breakdown occurs for alternation between two such shapes differing by a 180° rotation in the picture plane.

D. Structural Transformations

1. MENTAL MOVEMENT OF PARTS RELATIVE TO A WHOLE

Shepard and Feng (1972) measured the time that subjects took to carry out a sequence of mental folds in an initially flat pattern of squares. Two of the squares in each pattern were marked with arrows, and subjects were required to determine as rapidly as possible whether or not the arrows would meet if the pattern were folded up into a cube. In both of two experiments, reaction time increased linearly with the total number of folds (weighted by the number of squares moved in each fold) that would be necessary to bring the arrows into physical coincidence. Thus, it appears that mental operations on objects in space simulate the corresponding physical operations even when those operations change the structure of the object operated upon and must be carried out in a quite definite sequence.

3. MENTAL ASSEMBLY OF PARTS INTO A WHOLE

A potentially rich experimental paradigm is one in which subjects mentally synthesize a structural whole out of parts that are separately introduced, either visually or by verbal description. Following the mental synthesis, a test figure is presented, and the subject must determine as rapidly as possible whether or not the synthesized representation and the test figure match. Generally, the time needed to perform the mental synthesis and the time needed for comparison with the test figure are measured separately.

Evidence for some limitations on the abilities of subjects to synthesize wholes out of individually meaningful parts were initially obtained by Klatzky and Thompson (1975), using schematic facelike forms containing either two or three features. The features in the first stimulus were either presented within a single facial outline or distributed over two or three outlines. Subjects studied this initial display as long as they wished, and following a variable interstimulus interval a single test face was presented. *Same–different* reaction time increased with the number of facial outlines presented in the first display, indicating that subjects had not fully synthesized the individual components into a unified representation. However, in subsequent work by these same investigators, in which more abstract geometrical objects were to be mentally constructed out of inherently less meaningful components, subjects were apparently successful in synthesizing integrated internal representations (Thompson & Klatzky, 1978).

Palmer (1974) presented subjects with two spatially separated figures composed of three line segments that could be synthesized into a single figure composed of six segments. Examples of Palmer's displays are shown in Fig. 8. As can be seen, the three-segment components differed in their goodness as structural units of the synthesized six-segment figure. (See Palmer, 1974, for a complete discussion of the nature of goodness of

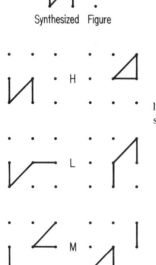

Synthesized Figure

Fig. 8. Three-segment components of high, medium, and low goodness which, when synthesized, form the six-segment figure shown at the top. [From Palmer (1974).]

subparts of visual figures and a general discussion of the role of structural organization in perception.) As soon as a subject had synthesized a pair of three-segment figures into a single six-segment figure, he so indicated by pressing a button. Immediately thereafter, a test figure was presented and the subject was required to determine as rapidly as possible whether the test figure was the same as or different from the mentally synthesized internal representation. The time required for mental synthesis was found to decrease with increasing goodness of the components to be synthesized. For at least some of the subjects, moreover, discriminative reaction time to a given whole figure was constant for all levels of goodness of the components from which it was synthesized, indicating that a complete mental synthesis had indeed been achieved.

Palmer (1974) has proposed the following analysis of the mental operations required for the synthesis. First, the three-segment components are mentally translated into the same spatial location. Second, these mentally translated components are linked together. Finally, the linked representation is restructured into figurally good subunits. Presumably, goodness of the original three-segment components facilitates all three of these mental operations. Thus, pairs of three-segment components with high goodness values are easy to move, require few linkages, and need little if any regrouping. According to this analysis, mental synthesis includes, in addition to analog operations of spatial movement, discrete modifications in the resulting internal structure.

In another type of mental assembly task, Glushko and Cooper (in press) required subjects to construct a mental image of a figure composed of squares and triangles, purely on the basis of a verbal description of the figure. The time required to carry out the mental construction increased with the number of component squares and triangles to be assembled. But discriminative reaction time to the ensuing visual test figure was rapid and independent of figural complexity. Moreover, the discriminative reaction times from this condition were highly similar to those obtained from a control condition in which two figures to be compared were both visually presented, one after the other. Evidently, rather than preserving the surface form of the descriptions from which they derived, representations constructed from verbal descriptions embodied the spatial organization of their component structural units.

IV. CONCLUDING REMARKS

Our understandings of mental transformations on internal representations on objects in space and of the role of such transformations in perception have advanced considerably since the early qualitative descriptions of such mental processes offered by the empiricist philosophers or by their scientifically oriented successors, Helmholtz and Mach. Particularly during the last decade, such spatial transformations as expansion or contraction, translation, reflection, rotation, folding, and joining of parts into wholes have been discovered to take times, when carried out purely mentally, that strongly suggest an internal simulation of the corresponding physical process in the external world. Such mental processes undoubtedly play a prominent role in creative thinking and problem solving, and in fields such as design, architecture, engineering, physics, and stereochemistry, in which spatial relations are central. They also appear to underlie our abilities, in everyday life to (a) make the subtle discriminations necessary to identify certain objects, such as left or right hands; and (b) prepare in advance for rapid and appropriate response to an object in an anticipated position or orientation. The introspective indication that these mental processes have an intimate connection with perception is supported by the finding that, at each stage of the mental process, one is perceptually most prepared for the corresponding external object in the corresponding state of spatial transformation.

References

Anderson, J. R., & Bower, G. H. *Human associative memory*. Washington, D.C.: Winston, 1973.

Attneave, F. The representation of physical space. In A. W. Melton & E. Martin (Eds.), *Coding processes in human memory*. Washington, D.C.: Winston, 1972.

Attneave, F. How do you know? *American Psychologist*, 1974, **29**, 493–511.

Attneave, F., & Arnoult, M. D. The quantitative study of shape and pattern perception. *Psychological Bulletin*, 1956, **53**, 452–471.

Attneave, F., & Block, G. Apparent movement in tridimensional space. *Perception and Psychophysics*, 1973, **13**, 301–307.

Attneave, F., & Farrrar, P. The visual world behind the head. Unpublished manuscript, Univ. of Oregon, 1975.

Attneave, F., & Olson, R. K. Discriminability of stimuli varying in physical and retinal orientation. *Journal of Experimental Psychology*, 1967, **74**, 149–157.

Attneave, F., & Reid, K. Voluntary control of frame of reference and shape equivalence under head rotation. *Journal of Experimental Psychology*, 1968, **78**, 153–159.

Bennett, G. K., Seashore, H. G., & Wesman, A. G. *Manual for the differential aptitude tests*. (3rd ed.) New York: Psychological Corporation, 1959.

Bradshaw, J. L., & Wallace, G. Models for the processing and identification of faces. *Perception and Psychophysics*, 1971, **9**, 443–448.

Bruner, J. On perceptual readiness. *Psychological Review*, 1957, **64**, 123–152.

Bundesen, C., & Larsen, A. Visual transformation of size. *Journal of Experimental Psychology: Human Perception and Performance*, 1975, **1**, 214–220.

Carpenter, P. A., & Eisenberg, P. Mental rotation and frame of reference in blind and sighted individuals, *Perception & Psychophysics*, 1978, **23**, 117–124.

Clark, H. H., & Chase, W. G. On the process of comparing sentences against pictures. *Cognitive Psychology*, 1972, **3**, 472–517.

Conrad, R. Acoustic confusions in immediate memory. *British Journal of Psychology,* 1964, **55,** 75–84.

Cooper, L. A. Mental transformation of random two-dimensional shapes. *Cognitive Psychology,* 1975, **7,** 20–43.

Cooper, L. A. Demonstration of a mental analog of an external rotation. *Perception & Psychophysics,* 1976, **19,** 296–302.

Cooper, L. A., & Farrell, J. E. Effects of stimulus structure on rate of mental rotation. Paper in preparation, 1978.

Cooper, L. A., & Podgorny, P. Mental transformations and visual comparison Processes: Effects of complexity and similarity. *Journal of Experimental Psychology: Human Perception and Performance,* 1976, **2,** 503–514.

Cooper, L. A., & Shepard, R. N. Chronometric studies of the rotation of mental images. In W. G. Chase (Ed.), *Visual information processing.* New York: Academic Press, 1973. Pp. 75–176. (a)

Cooper, L. A., & Shepard, R. N. The time to prepare for a rotated stimulus. *Memory & Cognition,* 1973, **1,** 246–250. (b)

Cooper, L. A., & Shepard, R. N. Mental transformations in the identification of left and right hands. *Journal of Experimental Psychology: Human Perception and Performance,* 1975, **104,** 48–56.

Corballis, M. C., & Beale, I. L. Bilateral symmetry and behavior. *Psychological Review,* 1970, **77,** 451–464.

Corballis, M. C., & Roldan, C. E. Detection of symmetry as a function of angular orientation. *Journal of Experimental Psychology: Human Perception and Performance,* 1975, **1,** 221–230.

Corballis, M. C., Zbrodoff, J., & Roldan, C. E. What's up in mental rotation? *Perception & Psychophysics,* 1976, **19,** 525–530.

Corbin, H. H. The perception of grouping and apparent movement in visual depth. *Archives of Psychology,* 1942, **273,** 1–50.

Dearborn, D. V. N. Recognition under subjective reversal. *Psychological Review,* 1889, **6,** 395–400.

Donders, F. C. On the speed of mental processes (W. G. Koster, trans.). *Acta Psychologica,* 1969, **30,** 412–431. (Original German publication, 1868).

Freedman, S. J. *The neuropsychology of spatially oriented behavior.* Homewood, Illinois: Dorsey Press, 1968.

Galton, F. *Inquires into human faculty and its development.* London: Dent, 1883.

Gaylord, S. A., & Marsh, G. R. Age differences in the speed of a spatial cognitive process. *Journal of Gerontology,* 1975, **30,** 674–678.

Gibson, J. J., & Robinson, D. Orientation in visual perception: The recognition of familiar plane forms in differing orientations. *Psychological Monographs,* 1935, **46,** No. 6; Whole no. 210.

Glushko, R. J., & Cooper, L. A. Spatial comprehension and comparison processes in verification tasks. *Cognitive Psychology,* in press.

Gordon, R. An investigation into some of the factors that favour the formation of stereotyped images. *British Journal of Psychology,* 1949, **39,** 156–167.

Hay, J. C. Mental rotation guided by manipulation. Paper presented at the 16th annual meeting of the Psychonomic Society, Denver, Colorado, November 6, 1975.

Hochberg, J., & Galper, R. E. Recognition of faces: I. An exploratory study. *Psychonomic Science,* 1967, **9,** 619–620.

Howard, I. P., & Templeton, W. B. *Human spatial orientation.* New York: Wiley, 1966.

Hume, D. *An enquiry concerning human understanding.* Chicago: Open Court, 1907. (Original publication, 1748).

Huttenlocher, J., & Presson, C. C. Mental rotation and the perspective problem. *Cognitive Psychology*, 1973, **4**, 277–299.

Jastrow, J. *Fact and fable in psychology*. Boston: Houghton Mifflin, 1900.

Just, M. A., & Carpenter, P. A. Eye fixations and cognitive processes. *Cognitive Psychology*, 1976, **8**, 441–480.

Kintsch, W. *The representation of meaning in memory*. Hillsdale, New Jersey: Lawrence Erlbaum, 1974.

Klatzky, R. L., & Thompson, A. L. Integration of features in comparing multi-feature stimuli. *Perception & Psychophysics*, 1975, **18**, 428–432.

Kolers, P. A. The recognition of geometrically transformed text. *Perception & Psychophysics*, 1968, **3**, 57–64.

Kolers, P. A., & Perkins, D. N. Orientation of letters and errors in their recognition. *Perception & Psychophysics*, 1969, **5**, 265–269. (a)

Kolers, P. A., & Perkins, D. N. Orientation of letters and their speed of recognition. *Perception & Psychophysics*, 1969, **5**, 275–280. (b)

Korte, A. Kinematoskopische Untersuchungen. *Zeitschrift für Psychologie*, 1915, **72**, 194–296.

Kosslyn, S. M. Scanning visual images: Some structural implications. *Perception & Psychophysics*, 1973, **14**, 90–94.

Kosslyn, S. M. Information representation in visual images. *Cognitive Psychology*, 1975, **7**, 341–370.

Kosslyn, S. M., Ball, T. M., & Reiser, B. J. Visual images preserve metric spatial information: Evidence from studies of image scanning. *Journal of Experimental Psychology: Human Perception and Performance*, 1978, **4**, 47–60.

Lea, G. Chronometric analysis of the method of loci. *Journal of Experimental Psychology: Human Perception and Performance*, 1975, **1**, 95–104.

Levin, J. Network representation and rotation of letters. Unpublished manuscript, Univ. of California, San Diego, 1973.

Mach, E. *The analysis of sensation* (C. M. Williams, trans.). New York: Dover, 1959. (Original publication, 1886).

Mandler, J. M., & Johnson, N. S. Some of the thousand words a picture is worth. *Journal of Experimental Psychology: Human Learning and Memory*, 1976, **2**, 529–540.

Mandler, J. M., & Stein, N. L. Children's recognition of reversals of geometric figures. *Child Development*, 1974, **45**, 604–615.

Marmor, G. S. Development of kinetic images: When does the child first represent movement in mental images? *Cognitive Psychology*, 1975, **7**, 548–559.

Marmor, G. S., & Zaback, L. A. Mental rotation by the blind: Does mental rotation depend on visual imagery? *Journal of Experimental Psychology: Human Perception and Performance*, 1976, **2**, 515–521.

Metzler, J. Cognitive analogues of the rotation of three-dimensional objects. Unpublished doctoral dissertation, Stanford Univ., 1973.

Metzler, J., & Shepard, R. N. Transformational studies of the internal representation of three-dimensional objects. In R. Solso (Ed.), *Theories in cognitive psychology: The Loyola Symposium*. Potomac, Maryland: Lawrence Erlbaum, 1974. Pp. 147–201.

Michael, W. B., Zimmerman, W. S., & Guilford, J. P. An investigation of the spatial relations and visualization factors in two high school samples. *Educational and Psychological Measurement*, 1951, **11**, 561–577.

Minsky, M. A framework for representing knowledge. In P. Winston (Ed.), *The psychology of computer vision*. New York: McGraw-Hill, 1975. Pp. 211–280.

Neisser, U. *Cognitive psychology,* New York: Appleton, 1967.

Newell, A., & Simon, H. A. *Human problem solving.* Englewood Cliffs, New Jersey: Prentice-Hall, 1971.

Norman, D. A., & Rumelhart, D. E. *Explorations in cognition.* San Francisco: Freeman, 1975.

Palmer, S. E. Structural aspects of perceptual organization. Unpublished doctoral dissertation, Univ. of California, San Diego, 1974.

Palmer, S. E. Visual perception and world knowledge: Notes on a model of sensory-cognitive interaction. In D. A. Norman & D. E. Rumelhart (Eds.), *Explorations in cognition.* San Francisco: Freeman, 1975. Pp. 279–307.

Piaget, J., & Inhelder, B. *The child's conception of space.* New York: Humanities Press, 1956.

Piaget, J., & Inhelder, B. *Mental imagery in the child.* New York: Basic Books, 1970.

Podgorny, P. Mental rotation and the third dimension. Unpublished senior honors thesis, Stanford Univ., 1975.

Posner, M. I., Bosies, S. J., Eichelman, W. H., & Taylor, R. L. Retention of visual and name codes of single letters. *Journal of Experimental Psychology Monograph,* 1969, **79,** (1), Part 2.

Pylyshyn, Z. What the mind's eye tells the mind's brain: A critique of mental imagery. *Psychological Bulletin,* 1973, **80,** 1–24.

Reed, S. K. *Psychological processes in pattern recognition.* New York: Academic Press, 1973.

Richardson, A. *Mental imagery.* New York: Springer, 1969.

Rock, I. The orientation of forms on the retina and in the environment. *American Journal of Psychology,* 1956, **69,** 513–528.

Rock, I. *Orientation and form.* New York: Academic Press, 1973.

Rock, I. The perception of disoriented figures. *Scientific American,* 1974, **230,** (1), 78–86.

Rock, I., & Leaman, R. An experimental analysis of visual symmetry. *Acta Psychologica,* 1963, **21,** 171–183.

Royer, F. L., & Holland, T. R. Rotational transformation of visual figures as a clinical phenomenon. *Psychological Bulletin,* 1975, **82,** 843–868.

Sachs, J. S. Recognition memory for syntactic and semantic aspects of connected discourse. *Perception & Psychophysics,* 1967, **2,** 437–442.

Sekuler, R., & Nash, D. Speed of size scaling in human vision. *Psychonomic Science,* 1972, **27,** 93–94.

Shepard, R. N. Form, formation, and transformation of internal representations. In R. Solso (Ed.), *Information processing and cognition: The Loyola Symposium.* Hillsdale, New Jersey: Lawrence Erlbaum, 1975. Pp. 87–122.

Shepard, R. N., & Feng, C. A chronometric study of mental paper folding. *Cognitive Psychology,* 1972, **3,** 228–243.

Shepard, R. N., & Judd, S. Perceptual illusion of rotation of three-dimensional objects. *Science,* 1976, **191,** 952–954.

Shepard, R. N., Kilpatric, D. W., & Cunningham, J. P. The internal representation of numbers. *Cognitive Psychology,* 1975, **7,** 82–138.

Shepard, R. N., & Metzler, J. Mental rotation of three-dimensional objects. *Science,* 1971, **171,** 701–703.

Sloman, A. Interactions between philosophy and artificial intelligence: The role of intuition and non-logical reasoning in intelligence. *Artificial Intelligence,* 1971, **2,** 209–225.

Smith, I. M. *Spatial ability.* London: Univ. of London Press, 1964.

Sternberg, S. High-speed scanning in human memory. *Science*, 1966, **153**, 652–654.

Sternberg, S. Memory-scanning: Mental processes revealed by reaction-time experiments. *American Scientist*, 1969, **57**, 421–457.

Sutherland, N. S. Object recognition. In E. C. Carterette & M. P. Friedman (Eds.), *Handbook of perception*. Vol. III. *Biology of perceptual systems*. New York: Academic Press, 1973.

Thompson, A. L., Klatzky, R. L. Studies of visual synthesis: Integration of fragments into forms. *Journal of Experimental Psychology: Human Perception and Performance*, 1978, **4**, 244–263.

Thurstone, L. L. Primary mental abilities (Psychometric Monograph, No. 1). Chicago: Univ. of Chicago Press, 1938.

Warren, R. M., & Warren, R. P. *Helmholtz on perception: Its physiology and development*. New York: Wiley, 1968.

Yin, R. K. Looking at upside-down faces. *Journal of Experimental Psychology*, 1969, **81**, 141–145.

Chapter 4

PERCEPTION OF MOTION*

MYRON L. BRAUNSTEIN

I. INTRODUCTION

Motion perception occurs in three-dimensional space. Rigid perspective transformations are almost always perceived as motions in depth, and depth is also perceived in many nonperspective and nonrigid transformations. Rigid motions may be grouped into four categories for convenience of discussion, though combinations of these motions are undoubtedly more common in everyday vision. First, there are the rotations about axes perpendicular to the line of sight. These are referred to as *rotations in depth*, as this transformation is characterized by continuous changes in the relative distances of parts of the rotating object from the observer. Second, there are the motions of objects towards or away from the observer, referred to as *translations in depth*. The third category, which is probably the least familiar, is that of rotations about the line of sight.

* This chapter is based, in part, on research supported by National Science Foundation Grant GB-40207.

HANDBOOK OF PERCEPTION, VOL. VIII

Although referred to as *rotations in the plane*, this transformation is not necessarily confined to a single frontal plane. The rotating object itself may be three dimensional. Every point on the object, however, moves in a plane perpendicular to the line of sight. Similarly in the fourth category, *translations in the plane*, either a two- or a three-dimensional object may be in motion, but each point on the object moves in a plane perpendicular to the line of sight. The next four sections will discuss the perception of these motions. A fifth section will deal with the relatively new research area of nonrigid motion.

II. ROTATIONS IN DEPTH

A. Minimal Conditions

Wallach and O'Connell (1953) posited that simultaneous changes in the length and direction of contours in the proximal stimulus are both necessary and sufficient for the perception of rotary motion in depth. This hypothesis was based on a series of experiments in which wire forms and solid objects were rotated about a vertical axis between a point light source and a translucent screen and observed from the opposite side of the screen. The perception of depth in these shadows, which appeared two-dimensional when the objects were stationary, was termed the *kinetic depth effect*. A rod that was fastened to a vertical shaft and was neither perpendicular nor parallel to the shaft—see Fig. 1(a)—is an example of an object which, when rotated about a vertical axis, cast a shadow that changed in length and direction. This display was judged to be rotating in depth by all subjects. A rod that was perpendicular to the shaft as in Fig. 1(b) and cast shadows that changed in length only, was judged to be rotating in depth by only 25% of the subjects. Displays of wire forms with concealed edges, which cast shadows that changed in direction only, as in Fig. 1(c), were not reported to be rotating in depth by any subjects.

The length and direction changes did not have to occur in visible

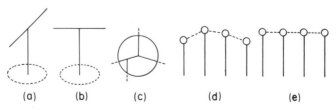

(a)   (b)   (c)   (d)   (e)

FIG. 1.   Examples of rotating objects studied by Wallach and O'Connell (1953).

contours, according to the Wallach–O'Connell hypothesis, but could occur in imaginary lines connecting parts of rotating configurations. Imaginary lines connecting shadows of spheres mounted on shafts differing in height—see Fig. 1(d)—simultaneously change in length and direction when the configuration is rotated about a vertical axis, but imaginary lines connecting shadows of spheres mounted at equal heights—Fig. 1(e)— change in length only. All subjects reported perceptions of motion in depth in the first case, but only 3 of 15 naive subjects did so in the second case.

Although the sufficiency of simultaneous length and direction changes for the perception of rotary motion in depth was clearly demonstrated by Wallach and O'Connell, the necessity of both changes for that perception has remained open to question. Even in Wallach and O'Connell's experiments there were some reports of rotary motion in depth for displays in which contours changed in length only. These were attributed to possible past experience with similar displays that included simultaneous length and direction changes. An alternative explanation is that the perception of rotary motion in depth is more likely with simultaneous length and direction changes, especially when conflicting information is present, but is not really a necessary condition for that perception. The small proportion of depth responses obtained by Wallach and O'Connell with separate length changes may have been due to the indications of flatness present in their display and viewing situation, such as the borders of the screen and the lack of binocular disparity and differential accommodation.

There is, in particular, an accumulation of evidence that length changes alone are sufficient to elicit reports of rotary motion in depth. White and Mueser (1960) rotated two identical pegs between a light source and a translucent screen, as illustrated in Fig. 2(a). With the tops and bottoms of the pegs concealed by the borders of the screen, the only proximal changes were in the distance between the pegs. Imaginary lines representing these distances would change in length only. The mean duration of

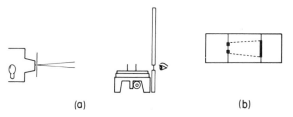

(a)   (b)

FIG. 2.   (a) Apparatus used to study the accuracy of kinetic depth perception; and (b) displays in which imaginary connecting lines would change in length and direction. [After White & Mueser (1960).]

three-dimensional reports for this display exceeded half of the observation period. This finding contradicts Wallach and O'Connell's hypothesis that simultaneous length and direction changes are necessary for the perception of rotary motion in depth. There are two likely reasons for White and Mueser's contradictory finding:

1. The subjects in White and Mueser's experiment viewed the displays monocularly through a prism, an arrangement that reduced some of the flatness indications present in Wallach and O'Connell's experiments.
2. White and Mueser's experiment included displays—see Fig. 2(b)—in which imaginary lines could be constructed that simultaneously changed in length and direction. These were combined with the stimuli displaying separate length changes in a random sequence, making it possible for previous experience with simultaneous changes to affect responses to the separate changes.

According to Wallach and O'Connell (1953), depth perception in displays having shadows that change in length only is enhanced by the memory of previously observed displays having shadows that simultaneously change in length and direction.

In a study by Johansson and Jansson (1968) two-thirds of the responses to a line changing in length only described perceptions of rotary motion in depth. The probable reasons for this proportion of depth responses being higher than that found by Wallach and O'Connell for length changes are similar to the reasons given above for White and Mueser's results:

1. The line in Johansson and Jansson's study was displayed in a dark room at a distance of 8 m. Although binocular viewing was used, the effects of lack of disparity and of differential convergence, as well as that of accommodation, were reduced by the viewing distance. The darkness of the room concealed the borders and texture of the screen.
2. The stimuli in Johansson and Jansson's experiment included lines simultaneously changing in length and direction. This could have allowed a memory effect to influence the responses to the separate length changes.

The sufficiency of length changes for the perception of rotary motion in depth was tested directly by Braunstein (1975). The possibility of a memory effect operating within the experimental situation was eliminated by presenting subjects with length changes only. The patterns consisted of one to four segments of a horizontal line. The segments, and the spaces between them, changed in length in accordance with one of three waveforms:

1. The lengths increased and decreased at a constant rate (as in Johansson and Jansson's study).
2. The lengths changed sinusoidally as in a parallel projection of rotary motion (approximating the waveform studied by Wallach and O'Connell and White and Mueser).
3. The lengths changed sinusoidally in accordance with a polar projection of rotary motion (as would occur in direct vision of a near object).

The three waveforms are shown in Fig. 3. The overall percentages of responses indicating perceived rotary motion in depth were 48%, 65%, and 84%, respectively, for the three waveforms. For four of the displays, showing three or four segments changing length sinusoidally, this proportion exceeded 90%. Clearly, length changes alone can elicit consistent reports of perceived rotary motion in depth, especially if the waveform of these changes realistically simulates the waveform projected by rotary motion in direct vision.

A sinusoidal waveform is not essential to the occurrence of nearly unanimous reports of rotary motion in depth when simultaneous length and direction changes are displayed. Johansson and Jansson (1968) obtained reports of rotary motion in depth on 99% of the trials for displays of lines simultaneously changing in length and angular orientation. Both changes occurred at a constant rate. Constant velocities were also used in a series of studies by Börjesson and von Hofsten (1972, 1973) of the perceptual effects of two- and three-dot motion patterns. The two-dot motion patterns were drawn from a factorial combination of three levels of common motion and three levels of relative motion. Common motion was defined as identical simultaneous translations of both dots in the frontal plane. The three levels of common motion were (a) no common

(a) LINEAR   (b) PARALLEL   (c) POLAR

FIG. 3. A segmented line (a) expanding and contracting linearly; (b) rotating and displayed with a parallel projection; and (c) rotating and displayed with a polar projection.

motion; (b) horizontal common motion; and (c) vertical common motion. The common motion vectors are illustrated in the column headings of Fig. 4. Relative motion was defined as horizontal translations of the two dots in the frontal plane that were equal in magnitude but opposite in direction. The three levels of relative motion were (a) no relative motion; (b) concurrent relative motion (dots moving toward and away from a common point); and (c) nonconcurrent relative motion (dots moving along parallel paths, toward and away from a common line). The relative motion vectors are illustrated in the row headings of Fig. 4. The motions displayed to the subjects were the vector sums of the relative and common motions. Subjects viewed the displays binocularly through an optical device that focused the image at infinity, minimizing flatness indications based on accommodation. Each dot moved back and forth at a constant velocity, disappearing from view briefly at each end of its motion path

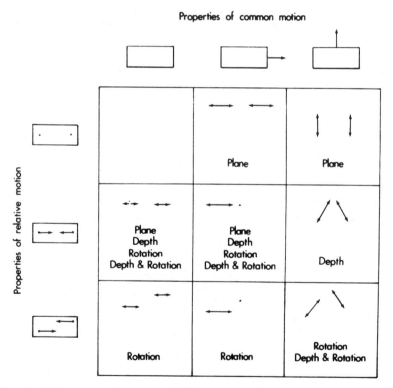

FIG. 4.   Main perceptual reports evoked by two-dot motion patterns. [After Börjesson & von Hofsten (1972).]

before changing direction. The results of the two-dot experiments are summarized in Fig. 4. Rotary motion in depth was the dominant perceptual report whenever there was nonconcurrent relative motion. Nonconcurrent relative motion would produce a simultaneous length and direction change for an imaginary line connecting the dots. Translatory motions in depth were the dominant report when a concurrent horizontal motion was combined with a common vertical motion. Reports of motion in depth occurred for other stimulus combinations, but were not dominant.

The results summarized in this section lead to the following conclusions about the minimal conditions required for the perception of rotation in depth:

1. Simultaneous length and direction changes in the proximal stimulus lead almost invariably to this perception, whether these changes occur in visible contours or in imaginary lines between pattern elements. Linear as well as sinusoidal rates of length change are effective. The pattern may be as simple as two dots in parallel relative motion.

2. Length changes alone are sufficient for eliciting reports of rotation in depth, but the proportion of such responses is noticeably reduced by indications of flatness in the viewing situation or in the display (such as a visible frame, effective binocular vision, a visible screen texture, or a linear rate of length change). A rate of length change that accurately simulates polar projections of rotating objects elicits consistent reports of rotation in depth, even in the absence of simultaneous direction changes.

B. Perceived Direction of Rotation

Some of the studies using shadow-projection techniques to examine the conditions under which rotary motion in depth is perceived found ambiguity in the perceived direction of rotation (Miles, 1931; Wallach & O'Connell, 1953). These studies used distant light sources that produced approximately parallel projections of the rotating objects. No such ambiguity of perceived direction of rotation was found when the light source was relatively close to the rotating object (Gibson & Gibson, 1957), producing a polar projection. Braunstein (1966) compared the accuracy of direction judgments with parallel and polar projections using computer-generated displays of random dot patterns rotating about a horizontal or vertical axis. Direction of rotation judgments for the parallel projections were at a chance level (51% correct), but for the polar projections averaged 90% correct. This confirmed the findings of separate studies that had used either polar or parallel projections: Accuracy of direction judgments was affected by the distance of the projection point in the display system, ranging from high accuracy with a polar projection point to chance performance with a parallel projection.

A somewhat separate line of research revealed another factor affecting the accuracy of judgments of direction of rotation: the shape of the rotating object. This line of research was based on Ames's (1951) finding that a rotating trapezoid appeared to oscillate under certain viewing conditions, although the motion of a rotating rectangle was correctly perceived under the same conditions. He considered the rotating trapezoid illusion to be a major demonstration of the validity of his transactional theory of perception. According to this theory, the observer, having had considerable experience requiring action to be taken with respect to doors and windows, has learned to interpret particular trapezoidal retinal projections as representing particular positions of these rectangular objects relative to his line of sight. Consequently, the observer unconsciously assumes the momentary retinal projections of the rotating trapezoid to be those of a rectangle at varying slants. The vertical side having the longer retinal projection is therefore judged to represent the closer side at all times, as would be the case for a rectangular object. But as the object is actually a trapezoid, the longer projection may represent the more distant side during the half of the rotation cycle when the larger side is more distant. This can result in a misperception of the relative distance of the two sides during half of the rotation cycle. Furthermore, according to the transactional explanation, rotation is perceived when the horizontal extent of the projection decreases. The direction of rotation is determined by which side appears further away during this decrease. If the left side appears farther away, for example, clockwise rotation (considered from above) would be perceived. This explanation, then, holds misperceived direction of rotation to be due to misperceived slant of the rotating object.

The transactional explanation of the rotating trapezoid illusion fails to account for the apparent changes in size and shape that occur during rotation of the trapezoid. Ames reported these observations and presented a reasonable explanation in terms of the projective geometry of the display. The projections of the longer side are larger when it is physically closer than when it is more distant (but appears closer), with the converse being true of the shorter side. The projections of the rotating trapezoid are therefore systematically different for the veridical and nonveridical portions of the rotation cycle. They could not represent the projection of an oscillating rectangle unless the rectangle changed size and shape while oscillating. As the transactional theory rests on past experience, its explanation of this aspect of the trapezoid illusion leads to the unreasonable implication that observers have more experience with doors and windows that change their physical size and shape as the observer moves around them than they have with trapezoidal doors and windows.

Most other explanations of the rotating trapezoid illusion have been similar to the Ames explanation in attributing misperceived direction of rotary motion to misperceived slant, differing only in their explanations of the misperceived slant (Pastore, 1952; Graham, 1963; Power & Day, 1973). Although judgments of static slant have been shown to be affected by the same stimulus variables that affect misperceived direction of rotary motion (Power & Day, 1973), this is not direct evidence that judgments of static slant determine the direction of rotation judgments. There is considerable evidence, on the other hand, that dynamic information dominates static information in slant judgments (Braunstein, 1976, Chap. 5). It seems unlikely that judgments of static slant would determine judgments of direction in a dynamic situation.

The two lines of research summarized above showed accurate judgment of direction to be affected by both the viewing distance and the shape of the rotating object. Braunstein and Payne (1968) studied the interaction of these two factors, using computer-generated motion-picture sequences of rectangles and trapezoids that were displayed either with a parallel projection or with polar projections simulating viewing distances from 1.5 to 4.5 times the width of the rotating form. Accuracy in judging direction did not exceed chance levels for the parallel projections, but the type of errors varied with the form. For each 360° rotation, the responses for the rectangle consisted of approximately 25% accurate judgments, 25% inaccurate judgments, and 50% judgments of oscillation. These are the percentages that would be expected if a direction were randomly assigned to the form for each 180° cycle. In contrast, the trapezoid was judged, in the parallel projection displays, to be oscillating during every 360° cycle. With polar projections, accuracy increased with decreasing projection-point distance for both forms, but increased more rapidly for the rectangle than for the trapezoid.

The rectangle and trapezoid sequences in Braunstein and Payne's experiment differed in at least three ways: (a) the angles between the horizontal and vertical contours; (b) the lengths of the vertical contours; and (c) the position of the axis of rotation relative to the vertical contours. As in the Ames demonstrations, the axis was centered between the vertical contours of the rectangle but was displaced towards the shorter end of the trapezoid. Braunstein (1971) used displays based on a factorial combination of these three variables (Fig. 5), each produced with projection point distances equal to 2.5, 5, 10, 20, or 40 times the width of the form. Accuracy of direction judgments increased with decreasing projec-

MYRON L. BRAUNSTEIN

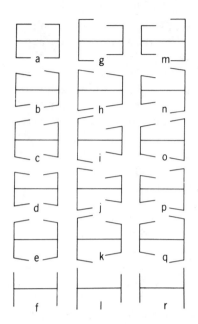

Fig. 5. Forms combining rectangular and trapezoidal features. [After Braunstein (1971).]

tion distance for each form. Accuracy was highest for the forms most like rectangles, such as form *a*, and lowest for those most like trapezoids, such as forms *h* and *o*. For other forms, accuracy was ordered primarily by angle relationships. Accuracy was higher, for example, for forms *g* and *m*, which have unequal vertical contours but have right angles than for forms *b* and *c*, which have equal vertical contours, but have acute angles enclosing one contour and obtuse angles enclosing the other. These results, combined with similar findings by Börjesson (1971), demonstrated that the differences in accuracy among judgments of rotary motion for rectangles and trapezoids was due primarily to the difference in the angles enclosing the vertical contours, rather than to the relative lengths of these contours. The displacement of the axis of rotation had a secondary effect on direction judgments.

The principal research findings regarding the perception of direction of rotary motion may be summarized as follows:

1. The accuracy with which the direction of rotation of any form is judged decreases with increasing projection-point distance, dropping to chance as this distance approaches infinity (a parallel projection).
2. The decrease in accuracy with increasing projection-point distance is most rapid for forms having one vertical contour enclosed by acute angles and the other enclosed by obtuse angles, and least rapid for forms having both vertical contours enclosed by right angles.

3. The decrease in accuracy with increasing projection-point distance is more rapid when the axis of rotation is off center than when it is at the horizontal center of the form (for rotation about a vertical axis).

These results can be explained in the following way: Whenever one side of a rectangle approaches the observer, the projections of the angles enclosing that side decrease, whereas the projections of the angles enclosing a receding side increase. The same is true of a trapezoid if it is within a certain distance of the observer—this distance depending on its width and the relative heights of its vertical sides. If a relatively distant trapezoid is observed, however, the projections of the acute angles always decrease as the overall projection contracts horizontally, regardless of whether the enclosed side is approaching or receding from the observer. This is true even in a parallel projection. Similarly, the projections of the obtuse angles always increase during overall horizontal contraction, regardless of whether the enclosed side is approaching or receding. If subjects used perceptual processes in which decreases in the projections of contour angles caused the enclosed side to appear to be approaching and increases in these projections caused this side to appear to be receding, they would judge direction of rotation correctly for rectangles as long as these angle changes were detectable. If increased viewing distance rendered these changes undetectable, or completely absent (as in a parallel projection), chance direction judgments would be expected. Accuracy would decrease more rapidly with viewing distance for a rotating trapezoid, but the errors would be predictable, even for a parallel projection. Judgments would be accurate when the side enclosed by acute angles was advancing during overall contraction of the form and inaccurate when that side was receding under that circumstance. This would lead to predictable judgments of oscillation. The hypothesis that direction of rotation is perceived on the basis of changes in the projected magnitudes of contour angles thus accounts for the second of the three findings listed, and could be the principal factor underlying the first finding.

When a rotating rectangle or trapezoid that is close to the observer leaves the frontal plane, the approaching side accelerates more rapidly than the receding side. If the two sides are not equidistant from the axis of rotation, the side farther from that axis will also tend to accelerate more rapidly than the opposite side. As the form increases in distance from the observer, the relative contribution of the advance or recession of a side in determining relative acceleration diminishes, until in a parallel projection, relative acceleration is determined entirely by the relative distance of the sides from the axis of rotation. If subjects perceive the more rapidly accelerating vertical side to be advancing, direction judgments would drop to chance levels with increasing viewing distance for forms having an axis of rotation at the horizontal center. If the axis of rotation were displaced toward one of the vertical sides, the errors in direction judgments with increased viewing distance would be predictable: The side more distant from the axis of rotation would always be perceived as advancing during overall horizontal contraction, giving rise to consistent judgments of oscillation. This would be true even for a parallel projection. Judgments based on the relative accelerations of the vertical sides would thus account for the third finding listed, and would contribute to the first finding. A model that postulates that subjects perceive direction of rotation on the basis of detectable changes in the projections of contour angles and otherwise perceive direction on the basis of the relative acceleration of the vertical sides has been shown to account for the quantitative results of Braunstein and Payne (1968) and Braunstein (1971) and the qualitative results of almost all other studies of rotating rectangles and trapezoids (Braunstein, 1972).

III. TRANSLATIONS IN DEPTH

Proximal size changes are almost invariably perceived as motions toward or away from the observer when other distance information is reduced. The Ames balloon demonstration provides a dramatic example of this. Balloons located at a constant distance from the observer appear to approach when inflated and to recede when deflated (Kilpatrick, 1952). Proximal size changes are equally effective in eliciting judgments of motion in depth, whether they result from distal size changes or from distance changes. Distal size changes can even prevent the perception of distance changes. An approaching diaphragm can be made to appear stationary, for example, by reducing its size at a rate which produces a constant proximal size (Kilpatrick & Ittelson, 1951).

Johansson (1964) found that equal increases or decreases in both the horizontal and vertical dimensions of a square resulted in reports of perceived translatory motion in depth for almost every subject (66 of 67). He explains his findings with a model based on reversed projections, in which proximal changes are assumed to be projected into the third dimension, with form changes perceived only when the proximal changes are not geometrically possible perspective transformations of a constant form. Some portion of the proximal change, however, may not be projected into the third dimension in the type of display studied by Johansson. Marmolin (1973a) found that a constant portion of the proximal size change was perceived as a distal size change, with the remaining proximal change perceived as a motion in depth. There were individual differences in the proportion of proximal size change that was attributed to distal size change, as evidenced by a negative correlation across subjects between measures of perceived size change and measures of perceived motion in depth.

Perceptions of translations in depth can also be elicited in the absence of visible contours by proximal expansions and contractions of random dot patterns. Braunstein (1966) displayed simulated translations in depth of two random dot patterns: dots confined to a circle perpendicular to the line of sight and dots confined to a sphere with the line of sight passing through its origin. The projected size and shape of each dot remained constant as the distances between the dots expanded or contracted. The pattern always filled the field of view. Both patterns were perceived as translating in depth by over 90% of the subjects when polar projections of the simulated translations were displayed.

In Börjesson and von Hofsten's (1972, 1973) studies of two- and three-dot motion patterns, reports of perceived translations in depth were dominant for patterns in which the dots moved alternately toward and away from a common point (see Fig. 4), as long as the paths of the dots were not confined to a common line. When the paths were confined to a common line, and the proximal changes were thus limited to one-dimension, the motion patterns were ambiguous. The dots in these patterns moved in their paths at constant velocities. Von Hofsten (1974) found that a single moving dot was perceived as translating in depth if the motion pattern displayed the rapid accelerations and decelerations that would occur in a polar projection of a dot alternately approaching and receding. As in the case of rotation in depth previously discussed, the ambiguity of a one-dimensional proximal change can be resolved by presenting a proximal velocity function that corresponds to a particular motion in depth. Also, as in the case of rotation in depth, the rate of change becomes unimportant when the changes occur in both dimensions of the proximal pattern (Marmolin, 1973b).

IV. ROTATIONS IN THE PLANE

There has been very little research specifically concerned with the perception of rotary motion in the frontal plane. The research that has so far been conducted has dealt with two problems: (a) the tendency of certain two-dimensional patterns undergoing rotary motion in the plane to take on the appearance of three-dimensional objects undergoing motion in depth; and (b) the perceptual extraction of rotary motion in the plane from complex proximal motions. These problems are related, but their relationship has not been examined.

The tendency of certain two-dimensional patterns to appear three-dimensional while rotating in the frontal plane has become known as the *stereokinetic effect* (Musatti, 1924). Examples of patterns that produce this effect are shown in Fig. 6. The basis of the effect is not well understood, but some tentative conclusions are possible. First, the process of rotation itself enhances perceived depth, regardless of the pattern, by decreasing indications of flatness. The surface texture, for example, becomes less perceptible during rotation. Second, certain patterns, especially those composed of circles and ellipses, assume a three-dimensional appearance in a two-stage process:

1. In the first stage, the pattern is not perceived as rotating with the turntable. Instead, some parts of the pattern may appear stationary while other parts may appear to change in orientation, rather than undergo complete rotation. Parts of the pattern may also appear to change their relative velocities. Figures that lack easily discriminable orientations, like circles, tend to retain their apparent shape, but other figures, like ellipses, may appear to change in shape during rotation.

2. In the second stage, a rigid or nonrigid object is perceived, usually rotating about an axis at some angle to the line of sight. The perceived axis itself may appear to be rotating about the line of sight. Exactly how the perception of motion in depth comes about in the second stage is uncertain, but it seems to be based on the nonveridical changes in the apparent relative positions and velocities of parts of the pattern that occur in the first stage.

Wallach, Weisz, and Adams (1956) offered an explanation of the stereokinetic effect that is consistent with the two-stage hypothesis. The stereokinetic effect was held to be an instance of the kinetic depth effect, and to thus require the presence of real or imaginary contours that simultaneously change in length and direction. Although there are no objective changes in the length and direction of contours or of imaginary lines connecting parts of the pattern during rotation, the nonveridical orientation changes that occur in the first stage may lead to *perceived* length and direction changes. Figure 7 shows two circles before and after a 90° rotation of the pattern. If the subject, in the first stage, perceives the inner circle as moving down and to the right and, at the same time,

FIG. 6.   Examples of stereokinetic displays. [Based on designs by Fred Duncan.]

FIG. 7. Length and direction changes for an imaginary line connecting perceived parts of a stereokinetic pattern. [After Wallach *et al.* (1956).]

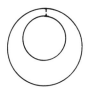

perceives the outer circle as remaining stationary, there is then an imaginary line connecting perceived parts of the pattern that would change in length and direction. A more precise analysis along these lines, applying Börjesson and von Hofsten's (1972, 1973) vector model to the output of the first stage rather than to the proximal motions, might be enlightening.

Rotary motion in the plane may be perceived as a component of a more complex motion. When a dot is rotated about a center that is itself translating horizontally—see Fig. 8(a)—subjects report perceiving the cycloidal path that the dot actually describes. When a second dot is added at the center of rotation, as in Fig. 8(b), the peripheral dot is reported to be rotating in the plane with the center of rotation translating horizontally (Johansson, 1974b). This is an important example of the perceptual separation of common and relative motions (Johansson, 1950, 1973; Börjesson & von Hofsten, 1975). Both dots in the two-dot case share a common translatory motion vector, but only the peripheral dot has a rotary motion vector. The relative motion of the two dots is therefore rotary, whereas the common motion is translatory. The analysis of complex motions into relative and common components by the visual system results in the perception of the peripheral dot as rotating and the center dot as translating when both dots are present. This perceptual separation of the rotary and translatory components does not occur when the peripheral dot alone is displayed, even though its objective motion is exactly the same.

Börjesson and von Hofsten (1975) studied combinations of rotary motion in the plane with parallel and concurrent relative motion (see Fig. 9). Their earlier results (1972, 1973) had shown that parallel relative motion generally lead to reports of rotary motion in depth, and concurrent relative motion to reports of translatory motion in depth. As predicted, combinations of rotary motion with parallel relative motion, concurrent relative motion, or both, generally led to reports of rotation in the plane,

FIG. 8. Typical perceptions of cycloidal motion (a) without a visible point at the center of rotation; and (b) with a visible point at the center.

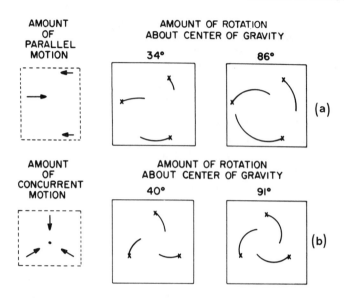

FIG. 9. Rotary motion in the plane combined with (a) parallel relative motion; and (b) concurrent relative motion. [After Börjesson & von Hofsten (1975).]

combined with either rotation in depth, translation in depth, or both rotation and translation in depth. When different magnitudes of rotary, parallel, and concurrent motion vectors were introduced, an unexpected interaction occurred. When the rotary motion vector was large, most responses described rotation about an oblique axis combined with translation in depth. A reduction in the magnitude of either the parallel vector or the rotary vector decreased the frequency of reports which included the corresponding perceptual component (rotation in depth or rotation in the plane, respectively), but this decrease was almost twice as great when the rotary vector was the one reduced. This may have occurred because some portion of the rotary motion component itself resulted in the perception of motion in depth, in accordance with the stereokinetic effect. Although the stereokinetic effect would not have been a factor in the initial patterns in the Börjesson and von Hofsten study, as the dots were equidistant from the center of rotation, the effect could have been introduced when this initial equidistance was altered by the parallel relative motions. The further exploration of these complex interactions may serve as a starting point for relating studies of stereokinetic depth to those studies concerned with the extraction of rotary motion from more complex proximal motions.

V. TRANSLATIONS IN THE PLANE

A. Stimulus Conditions

A single dot moving at a constant proximal velocity is consistently reported to be translating in the frontal plane (von Hofsten, 1974). Other velocity functions, as we have seen, may elicit reports of rotary or translatory motions in depth. Patterns of two or more dots moving at constant velocities are also reported to be translating in the frontal plane if all of the dots move at the same velocity (Börjesson & von Hofsten, 1972, 1973; Braunstein, 1966, 1968). The situation is more complex when the dots or other pattern elements move at different velocities. If the pattern consists of a small number of dots, such as two or three, the dots may be perceived either as moving independently or as moving relative to one another. Which perception occurs is probably determined by the proximity of the dots, in accordance with the adjacency principle (Gogel, 1974). If there are two dots moving at constant but different velocities, and these dots are perceived to be moving independently, the situation may be described as a case of motion parallax. Both dots appear to be moving in paths perpendicular to the line of sight, but the two paths appear to be at different distances from the observer. The dot with the greater proximal velocity is not always reported to be closer, and depth reversals occur during the observation of such two-dot patterns (Gibson, Gibson, Smith, & Flock, 1959). Patterns consisting of two or three dots that are sufficiently close may be perceived as a unit. The dots may appear to be the endpoints of a rod in the two-dot case, or the corners of a triangle in the three-dot case. When this occurs, relative proximal motions of the dots elicit reports of perceived motion in depth. Dots moving in parallel paths at different velocities (i.e., undergoing parallel relative motions), for example, may appear to be rotating in depth (Börjesson & von Hofsten, 1972, 1973).

When a pattern consists of a larger number of dots, each moving at a constant velocity but with the velocities varying among the dots, the dots are reported to be at varying distances, moving in paths perpendicular to the line of sight (Braunstein, 1968; Gibson et al., 1959). If each dot is moving at one of two velocities, the dots having the greater proximal velocity are not always reported to be closer (Gibson et al., 1959). Relative depth is unambiguous, however, when a gradient of velocities is presented. A gradient of decreasing velocity from the bottom to the top of a projected display, for example, consistently elicits reports of a textured surface that is slanted away from the observer at the top and is translating horizontally (Braunstein, 1968; Gibson et al., 1959).

B. Perception of Relative Velocity

Brown (1931) had subjects compare the velocities of forms moving in two illuminated fields observed monocularly in an otherwise dark room. All of the dimensions of field A were twice those of field B, but field A was twice as far from the subject. The proximal sizes of the fields were therefore equal. Velocity was judged equal in the two fields when the physical velocity in A was twice that in B, a condition that yields equal proximal velocities in the two fields. This result suggests that subjects equate perceived velocity on the basis of proximal velocity in the absence of distance information. There is, however, an alternative explanation (Gogel, 1973).* When there is no information about distance in the experimental situation, perceived distances are supplied by the observer in accordance with the specific distance tendency. As these subjectively supplied distances tend to be consistent within (and often among) subjects, velocity matches are produced as if the fields were at equal distances. Such matches would appear to be based on the equating of proximal velocities, as perceived velocities based on subjectively equal distances would be proportional to the proximal velocities.

A second finding by Brown appears inconsistent with the hypothesis that velocities are judged in accordance with the apparent distance of the moving objects. When fields A and B are displayed at the same distance, with field A again twice as large as B, field A must still display twice the physical velocity of B before the velocities in the two fields are judged equal. This result, which Brown called *velocity transposition*, was not considered to be based on differences in the apparent distances of the fields, as viewing was again monocular in a dark room. This conclusion, however, is not valid. Although there was no information available about the actual distances of the fields, there was information in the experimental arrangement that would cause the smaller field to have a greater *apparent* distance. The relative size of the fields would be expected to indicate relative distance, in the absence of more effective distance information (Gogel & Sturm, 1972). If field B appeared to be at twice the distance of field A, field A would have to be set at twice the velocity of field B in order for the apparent distal velocities to be equal. This was the obtained result. The transposition effect can thus be ac-

---

* Gogel's discussion is in the context of size perception. It can be applied to velocity perception under the assumption that perceived velocity is based on a combination of perceived space and perceived time, with size perception affecting the space component. Other evidence (Lappin, Bell, Harm, & Kottas, 1975; Rosenbaum, 1975) supports the alternative view that velocity is perceived directly. For this reason, the logic of Gogel's argument has been applied here to the direct perception of velocity.

counted for by the use of relative proximal size to locate the moving forms at different relative distances in three-dimensional space and the judgment of distal velocity on the basis of these apparent distances (Gogel, 1970). Support for the hypothesis that the transposition effect is based on apparent distance is found in another of Brown's findings: The transposition effect was reduced when the motion fields were viewed in daylight illumination, and the effect was reduced still further when binocular vision was allowed. These conditions provided information about the actual distances of the fields, contradicting the apparent distances suggested by their relative sizes. Binocular viewing in daylight, however, did not eliminate the transposition effect. Other variables, in addition to apparent distance, may contribute to the effect.

Smith and Sherlock (1957) suggested that Brown's subjects may not have been judging velocity at all, but may have been judging the frequency with which the moving objects disappeared from the field. In most of Brown's experiments, the spacing between the moving objects was proportional to the field and object size. If one field was twice as large as another, the objects would leave both fields at equal frequency only when the physical velocity of the objects in the larger field was twice that in the smaller field. Smith and Sherlock showed that subjects can judge frequency directly in moving fields, supporting their hypothesis that the transposition effect is due to the judgment of frequency, rather than velocity, in Brown's experimental arrangement. Brown presented two types of evidence against this possibility. First, conditions in which the spacing between elements was made irregular, and frequency judgments presumably made more difficult, did not show any reduction in the transposition effect. Second, there was some transposition effect present when both fields were made equal in the dimension in which the motion took place, but were made unequal in the perpendicular dimension. There would have been no transposition effect in that condition had it been based entirely on the frequency of disappearance of the objects.

Rock, Hill, and Fineman (1968) presented direct evidence that subjects judged distal velocity on the basis of the apparent distance of the moving objects. Two luminous circles, at different distances from the observer, were moved vertically. The distances were in a 4 : 1 ratio. No frame was displayed. Viewing was either binocular, or monocular with an artificial pupil. In the binocular condition, subjects set the physical speed of the more distant circle to 1.3 times that of the closer circle, compared to a predicted ratio of 1 : 1 if the distal velocities had been accurately matched. In the artificial pupil condition, the ratio obtained was 3.7 : 1, where 4 : 1 would have indicated a velocity match based on equal apparent distance (a proximal stimulus match). The method used in this study was criticized by Kaufman (1974, p. 390) on the grounds that the onset and offset positions of the circles provided an implicit frame for the motion field, which could have produced the transposition effect in the binocular condition. In the artificial pupil condition, the field of view was restricted and the implicit frame partially obscured. The possible presence of an implicit frame does not contradict the apparent-distance hypothesis presented here, however, as the implicit frame would have provided relative size information corresponding to the binocular information on distance. Obviously, further research is needed on the factors affecting relative velocity perception. Frame size, frequency of appearance and disappearance of the moving forms, and apparent distance need to be varied independently. Modern stimulus-control techniques, using artificially generated binocular motion displays, should make it possible to assess the separate and combined contributions of these factors to judgments of relative velocity.

C. Perception of Constant Velocity

In studies of velocity perception, the motion of a form at a constant physical velocity across some defined area has been typically regarded as an event that can be described by a single judgment of perceived velocity. This procedure implicitly assumes that a constant physical velocity results in a constant perceived velocity. Combining evidence from three different methods, Runeson (1974, 1975) has shown that this assumption may not be a valid one. In one method, paired comparison judgments were made as to which of two moving spots displayed the more constant velocity. The velocity functions included constant velocity, constant deceleration, and constant increasing and decreasing acceleration. The functions of decreasing acceleration were selected most often as the more constant in appearance. In a second method, subjects were trained to graph the apparent velocity of a moving spot as a function of time. Functions of constant velocity, constant deceleration, and constant and increasing acceleration were again presented, but natural-motion functions were substituted for the decreasing-acceleration functions studied with the first method. The natural-motion functions were decreasing-acceleration functions that leveled off asymptotically to constant velocities, as would motions produced by constant force in air or liquid. Of the graphs drawn by subjects indicating constant velocity, most were drawn in response to the natural-motion functions. The graphs drawn in response to the constant-velocity functions typically showed a stepwise deceleration from a higher initial velocity to a lower constant velocity (Runeson, 1974).

The third method was a prediction-of-collision task (Runeson, 1975). Two forms were presented, one moving in a horizontal path and the other moving in a vertical path. The horizontally moving form was occluded before it reached the intersection of the paths, and subjects were asked to judge whether it reached that point before or after the vertically moving form. Functions of constant velocity, acceleration, deceleration, and natural motion were displayed for the horizontally moving form. The form was occluded either one quarter of the way or halfway to the intersection point. With early occlusion and constant velocity, subjects judged the horizontally moving form to be arriving at the intersection point sooner than it actually was. This result would be expected if too high a velocity was perceived at the start of the motion, and that velocity was extrapolated. Judgments were more accurate with the constant-velocity function and late occlusion. There was no difference in accuracy for early versus late occlusion for the natural-motion functions. These results supported the conclusions reached with the graph method: Natural motion functions appeared to have constant velocities, but functions of physically constant velocity appeared to decelerate stepwise.

Runeson's results with the prediction-of-collision task appear to be in conflict with those of Rosenbaum (1975), who also used a prediction task. Rosenbaum obtained accurate predictions with constant-velocity functions, and found no effect of the time or distance for which the motion was visible prior to occlusion. His method, however, differed from Runeson's in several ways:

1. Subjects were asked to indicate when a horizontally moving object would pass behind a marker on the occluding screen, rather than to judge which of two moving forms first reached an intersection point.
2. A three-dimensional object (table-tennis ball) rather than a two-dimensional form was used.
3. Probably most important, the object appeared in motion from behind an edge of the screen, rather than starting at rest from a position visible to the subject.

Runeson (1974) found no difference between conditions in which a form was shown initially at rest and conditions in which a form appeared in motion within the area visible to the subject, but no comparison has yet been made between displays in which a form gradually emerges from behind an edge and displays in which a form appears in motion all at once within the field of view. This distinction may be important in determining whether physically constant velocity is perceived as constant or as undergoing stepwise deceleration. The entry of a form that is already in motion into the field of view may suggest that the start of the motion event has been occluded. If the motion event is perceived as a natural motion, the decreasing acceleration portion may be assumed occluded. The visible portion of the event may then be perceived as the constant-velocity portion of the natural-motion function. This would lead to accurate extrapolation of functions of constant velocity for forms which enter the field of view in motion from behind an edge.

The natural-motion stereotype, Runeson (1975) suggests, may be of ecological value in that allows the perceiver to extrapolate the velocity of forms undergoing natural starts even when the form is occluded after it begins to move. The use of this stereotype, then, may be an example of a heuristic perceptual process that has the advantage of allowing the observer to predict the future position of an object, even when the available visual information is degraded. (For discussion of the use of heuristic perceptual processes to overcome degraded information see Braunstein, 1976, Chap. 7).

VI. NONRIGID MOTIONS

Reports of nonrigid, or elastic, motions occurred in many of the studies of rigid motion discussed in the previous sections, but these were generally incidental to the main concerns of those studies. The perception of nonrigid motion was the subject of an investigation by Jansson and Johansson (1973). They were concerned in particular with bending, which they defined as a partially rigid motion. Their proximal stimuli were quadrilaterals that alternated between a square and one of six other shapes, as shown in Fig. 10. They explained their results (see Fig. 10) on the basis of a principle of minimum object change. According to this principle, a rigid distal motion is perceived whenever the proximal transformation is a geometrically possible projection of an object undergoing a rigid motion. When the proximal stimulus is not a possible projection of a fully rigid motion, but is a possible projection of a bending motion, bending is the dominant percept. This is because bending, as opposed to such alternatives as stretching, is the percept that involves the least amount of object change. There are several difficulties with this explanation. First, rigid motions are often perceived when these motions are not geometrically possible causes of the proximal stimulus. Neither of the stimuli in the Jansson and Johansson study for which rotation was the dominant percept could have been produced in direct vision as the projection of a rigid rotation. Second, rigid motions are not always perceived when geometrically possible. The proximal stimulus resulting from the rotation of a trapezoid is a geometrically possible projection of a rotating

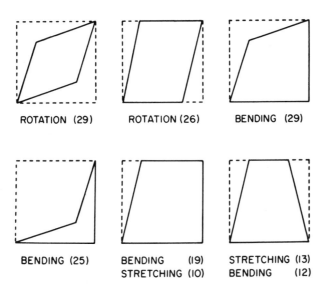

FIG. 10. Proximal stimuli that varied between outline squares (dashed lines) and other quadrilateral shapes (solid lines). The dominant perceptual reports are shown with their frequencies ($N = 30$). [After Jansson & Johansson (1973).]

trapezoid, but it is not a possible projection of the rigid oscillation of a rectangle. As we have seen, however, the dominant percept for a rotating trapezoid at a sufficient distance from the observer is that of an oscillating form, often of an oscillating rectangle that changes its apparent dimensions while oscillating. The perception of oscillation in the rotating trapezoid can be explained on the basis of perceptual processes that act directly on information in the proximal stimulus. Similar processes may account for the percepts resulting from the six proximal changes in Fig. 10. For example, a hypothesis that equal angular changes in diagonally opposite corners leads to the perception of rotation, whereas motion of a single corner leads to the perception of bending, can account for the results presented in that figure. These are not likely to be the actual processing rules. The discovery of those rules will have to await the accumulation of a great deal more data on the perception of nonrigid motions. The maintenance of minimal object change probably does play a role in perceptual processing, but it would seem to be a less direct role than that suggested by Jansson and Johansson. Perceptual processes have developed in an environment in which object change tends to be limited. Once developed, however, these processes are automatically applied to the proximal stimulus. A criterion of minimal object change does not enter into each perceptual judgment. The application of a perceptual process to an unusual stimulus situation, such as a rotating trapezoid, can thus result in perceived object change even when there is a rigid motion that is a geometrically possible interpretation of the proximal stimulus.

The overall motions of a living organism are nonrigid, but some of these motions may be represented by a hierarchy of rigid motions. Johansson (1973) has described such a hierarchy for a walking human form: The hips and shoulders move relative to the static background; the knees and elbows move relative to the hips and shoulders; the feet and hands move relative to knees and elbows. Johansson found that human locomotion can be identified from a display of from 10–12 spots describing the relative motions of the main joints. A walking form was correctly identified by all subjects, even when the overall common horizontal translatory motion was eliminated, giving the appearance of a person walking on a treadmill. Unfamiliar common motions, such as rotation of the overall image in the frontal plane, did not reduce the frequency of correct identifications. In a subsequent study (Johansson, 1974), an exposure time of .2 sec was found to be sufficient for 100% correct identification of a walking form. This persistence of 100% correct recognition with alterations in the overall common motion of the walking form and with brief exposures led Johansson (1973, 1974a) to conclude that this perception was based on a mechanical, automatic analysis of the proximal stimulus, applied at an early stage in perceptual processing. Previous learning was rejected as an explanation of the analysis of the motion pattern into a hierarchy of common and relative components, though learning may indeed be a factor in the recognition of the relative components following initial analysis.

References

Ames, A. Visual perception and the rotating trapezoidal window. *Psychological Monographs*, 1951, **67** (7, Whole No. 324).

Börjesson, E. Properties of changing patterns evoking visually perceived oscillation. *Perception & Psychophysics*, 1971, **9**, 303–308.

Börjesson, E., & von Hofsten, C. Spatial determinants of depth perception in two-dot motion patterns. *Perception & Psychophysics*, 1972, **11**, 263–268.

Börjesson, E., & von Hofsten, C. Visual perception of motion in depth: Application of a vector model to three-dot motion patterns. *Perception & Psychophysics*, 1973, **13**, 169–179.

Börjesson, E., & von Hofsten, C. A vector model for perceived object rotation and translated in space. *Psychological Research*, 1975, **38**, 209–230.

Braunstein, M. L. Sensitivity of the observer to transformations of the visual field. *Journal of Experimental Psychology*, 1966, **72**, 683–689.

Braunstein, M. L. Motion and texture as sources of slant information. *Journal of Experimental Psychology*, 1968, **78**, 247–253.

Braunstein, M. L. Perception of rotation in figures with rectangular and trapezoidal features. *Journal of Experimental Psychology*, 1971, **91**, 25–29.

Braunstein, M. L. Perception of rotation in depth: A process model. *Psychological Review*, 1972, **79**, 510–524.

Braunstein, M. L. *Minimal conditions for the perception of rotary motion*. (Report No. W80). Irvine, California: Univ. of California, School of Social Sciences, 1975.

Braunstein, M. L. *Depth perception through motion*. New York: Academic Press, 1976.

Braunstein, M. L., & Payne, J. W. Perspective and the rotating trapezoid. *Journal of the Optical Society of America*, 1968, **58**, 399–403.

Brown, J. F. The visual perception of velocity. *Psychologische Forschung*, 1931, **14**, 199–232.

Gibson, E. J., Gibson, J. J., Smith, O. W., & Flock, H. Motion parallax as a determinant of perceived depth. *Journal of Experimental Psychology*, 1959, **58**, 40–51.

Gibson, J. J., & Gibson, E. J. Continuous perspective transformations and the perception of rigid motion. *Journal of Experimental Psychology*, 1957, **54**, 129–138.

Gogel, W. C. The adjacency principle and three-dimensional visual illusions. In J. C. Baird (Ed.), *Human space perception: Proceedings of the Dartmouth conference*. *Psychonomic Monographs Supplement*, 1970, **3** (13, Whole No. 45), 153–169.

Gogel, W. C. The organization of perceived space: I. Perceptual interactions. *Psychologische Forschung*, 1973, **36**, 195–221.

Gogel, W. C. Relative motion and the adjacency principle. *Quarterly Journal of Experimental Psychology*, 1974, **26**, 425–437.

Gogel, W. C., & Sturm, R. D. A test of the relational hypothesis of perceived size. *American Journal of Psychology*, 1972, **85**, 201–216.

Graham, C. H. On some aspects of real and apparent visual movement. *Journal of the Optical Society of America*, 1963, **53**, 1019–1025.

von Hofsten, C. Proximal velocity change as a determinant of space perception. *Perception & Psychophysics*, 1974, **15**, 488–494.

Jansson, G., & Johansson, G. Visual perception of bending motion. *Perception*, 1973, **2**, 321–326.

Johansson, G. *Configurations in event perception*. Uppsala: Almqvist & Wiksell, 1950.

Johansson, G. Perception of motion and changing form. *Scandinavian Journal of Psychology*, 1964, **5**, 181–208.

Johansson, G. Visual perception of biological motion and a model for its analysis. *Perception & Psychophysics*, 1973, **14**, 201–211.

Johansson, G. *Spatio-temporal differentiation and integration in visual motion perception*. (Report No. 160). Uppsala, Sweden: Univ. Of Uppsala, Department of Psychology, 1974. (a)

Johansson, G. Vector analysis in visual perception of rolling motion. *Psychologische Forschung*, 1974, **36**, 311–319. (b)

Johansson, G., & Jansson, G. Perceived rotary motion from changes in a straight line. *Perception & Psychophysics*, 1968, **6**, 193–198.

Kaufman, L. *Sight and mind*. New York: Oxford Univ. Press, 1974.

Kilpatrick, F. P. (Ed.) *Human behavior from the transactional point of view*. Hanover, New Hampshire: Institute for Associated Research, 1952.

Kilpatrick, F. P., & Ittelson, W. H. Three demonstrations involving the perception of movement. *Journal of Experimental Psychology*, 1951, **42**, 394–402.

Lappin, J. S., Bell, H. H., Harm, J., & Kottas, B. On the relation between time and space in the visual discrimination of velocity. *Journal of Experimental Psychology: Human Perception and Performance*, 1975, **1**, 383–394.

Marmolin, H. Visually perceived motion in depth resulting from proximal changes. I. *Perception & Psychophysics*, 1973, **14**, 133–142. (a)

Marmolin, H. Visually perceived motion in depth resulting from proximal changes. II. *Perception & Psychophysics*, 1973, **14**, 143–148. (b)

Miles, W. R. Movement interpretations of the silhouette of a revolving fan. *American Journal of Psychology*, 1931, **43**, 392–405.

Musatti, C. L. Sui fenomeni stereocinetici. *Archivio Italiano di Psicologia*, 1924, **3**, 105–120.

Pastore, N. Some remarks on the Ames oscillatory effect. *Psychological Review*, 1952, **59**, 319–323.

Power, R. P., & Day, R. H. Constancy and illusion of apparent direction of rotary motion in depth: Tests of a theory. *Perception & Psychophysics*, 1973, **13**, 217–223.

Rock, I., Hill, A. L., & Fineman, M. Speed constancy as a function of size constancy. *Perception & Psychophysics*, 1968, **4**, 37–40.

Rosenbaum, D. A. Perception and extrapolation of velocity and acceleration. *Journal of Experimental Psychology: Human Perception and Performance*, 1975, **1**, 395–403.

Runeson, S. Constant velocity—not perceived as such. *Psychological Research*, 1974, **37**, 3–23.

Runeson, S. Visual prediction of collision with natural and non-natural motion functions. *Perception & Psychophysics*, 1975, **18**, 261–266.

Smith, O. W., & Sherlock, L. A new explanation of the velocity-transposition phenomenon. *American Journal of Psychology*, 1957, **70**, 102–105.

Wallach, H., & O'Connell, D. N. The kinetic depth effect. *Journal of Experimental Psychology*, 1953, **45**, 360–368.

Wallach, H., Weisz, A., & Adams, P. A. Circles and derived figures in rotation. *American Journal of Psychology*, 1956, **69**, 48–59.

White, B. J., & Mueser, G. E. Accuracy in reconstructing the arrangement of elements generating kinetic depth displays. *Journal of Experimental Psychology*, 1960, **60**, 1–11.

Chapter 5

COLOR IN CONTOUR AND OBJECT PERCEPTION*

ROBERT M. BOYNTON

I. PREFACE

The original topic of this chapter was color in *form* and object perception. But the perception of form, as related to color, has received scant attention. For example, despite thousands of references in his encyclopedic coverage of the visual perception of form, Zusne (1970) does not even list the word *color* in his index.

* The preparation of this chapter was supported, in part, by Grant EY 01541 from the National Eye Institute. I also wish to thank Dr. Philip Kaushall for his critical reading of an earlier version of the manuscript, which led to numerous improvements.

There are two further reasons for the change from *form* to *contour*. First, the perception of contour necessarily underlies that of form. Second, I have had a long-standing interest in contours that are formed by chromatic differences (Boynton, 1973).

Readers interested in a broader and more conventional coverage of surface color perception should consult Beck's (1972) excellent monograph on the subject. Also recommended is Evans's (1974) monograph on the perception of color.

As the *Handbook of Perception* moves closer to completion, it becomes progressively more likely that a topic considered in one of these later volumes will have already undergone considerable discussion in one or more of the earlier ones. Where the subject of this chapter is concerned, the following materials are particularly relevant:

Chapter	Volume	Author	Title
1	V	LeGrand (1975b)	History of Research on Seeing
2	V	LeGrand (1975a)	Measurement of the Visual Stimulus
5	V	DeValois & DeValois (1975)	Neural Coding of Color
8	V	Dodwell (1975)	Pattern and Object Perception
9	V	Boynton (1975)	Color, Hue, and Wavelength
14	I	Boynton (1974)	The Visual System: Environmental Information
16	III	Abramov & Gordon (1973a)	Vision
17	III	Abramov & Gordon (1973b)	Seeing

To avoid redundancy, as well as to keep this chapter within its assigned limits, I will refer frequently to most of these eight chapters, using a system where, for example, (16-365) would indicate that relevant information will be found starting on page 365 in Abramov & Gordon's (1973a) Chapter 16.

II. INTRODUCTION

A. The Problem of Defining Physical Surface Color

From early childhood, we are easily able to recognize a property of objects, usually associated with their surfaces, that we call *color*. No child, and relatively few adults, will doubt that the color is on (or sometimes, *in*) objects.* If asked to explain where the color goes if the lights are extinguished or his eyes are closed, a child will explain (using his own terms) that the color is still there but certain other conditions must be realized in order to discern it. The problem of where the color is—whether in the observer, the light, or the object—has been the subject of endless philosophical debate, and it is not my aim to enter this semantically booby-trapped territory here. Color perception must be explained in terms of relations among these three domains.

I will nevertheless begin by asserting that there is a sense in which color is a pure object property. *Physical surface color* depends upon the nature and configuration of those molecules of an object that are near enough to the surrounding medium, ordinarily air, to have a significant interaction with light. In describing the perceived color of a rose seen under artificial light, Wright (1968) puts it this way:

> The lamp is in fact ejecting millions of photons of light quanta per second and subjecting the rose to an intense random bombardment by these minute particles of energy. What happens when they batter themselves against the petals? Some bounce off, some penetrate a little way into the petal and are scattered back again, some penetrate so far that they escape on the other side. All this will depend on the molecular and atomic dimensions of the structures they encounter and on their own particular energies and frequencies [p. 109].

A more exact physical treatment of how light interacts with matter, with a special emphasis on the colors that we see, is given by Weisskopf (1968) as one of the articles in an excellent special issue of *Scientific American* devoted to light (see also 9-318). A full and detailed description of all properties of a surface that are related to its color is a practical impossibility. At best, we can hope merely to identify some measurable properties of the surface that correlate with our perception of its surface color. Because any practical set of measurements falls well short of a complete physical description, it would be misleading to denote physical surface color strictly in terms of such measurements.

An alternative that will be adopted here is to describe physical surface colors in terms of the color perceptions that they arouse in a human observer having normal color vision (1-17, 5-119, 16-328, 17-363). It is hazardous to do this, because there is an unfortunate tendency, to which we are all at least occasionally susceptible, to confuse description with explanation. If asked how we see an object as red, we might be tempted to

---

* The perception of color as seen in translucent objects and liquids will not be considered in this chapter.

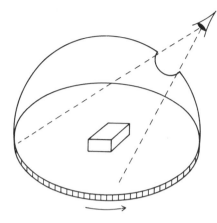

FIG. 1.   A standard condition for viewing an object and judging its *perceived* surface color. When *physical* surface colors are designated by color names in this chapter, it is their *perceived* color under these standard conditions of viewing that is indicated.

reply (as a child almost certainly will) that we see it as red because it *is* red. This, of course, is not very helpful. Another difficulty is that the object will not necessarily look red, even if there is a good source of illumination and an observer with normal color vision. For example, the object would look black if seen in the presence of a much brighter surround. One nevertheless can say that the object is "really" red in the sense that, *given the proper conditions*, it will so appear.

B. Standard Condition for Viewing Physical Surface Colors

The reader is therefore asked to imagine* the standard condition illustrated in Fig. 1. Illumination is provided by a hemisphere of uniform luminance. The object whose surface color is to be described is placed in the center of a horizontal circular plane lying below the luminous hemisphere as if lying on flat ground illuminated by cloudy sky. An observer peeks through a hole in the hemisphere, located at an angle of 45° with respect to the plane, and through this hole he sees most of the plane, but none of the "sky." The plane is free to rotate, doing so at a rate of 12 rpm. The plane is covered by a 40% neutral reflecting surface, one that diffusely reflects all wavelengths equally. The hemispherical source emits an

---

*   No such standard conditions for the purpose of specifying color seem previously to have been proposed. The *IES Lighting Handbook* (1972) comes close to suggesting that it might be a good idea. After discussing, on pages 5-1 and 5-2, the various usages of color terms, the *Handbook* states: "When assumed standard conditions are the same, then there is less need for distinguishing between the three meanings, the [film] *color*, [physical] *color of object*, and *perceived color of object*." But no standard condition is proposed.

equal-energy spectrum sufficient to cause a luminance of 100 cd/m² of the neutral reflecting surface.

In this chapter, when *physical* surface colors are described by the use of color names, consider the color term to apply strictly to what would be seen by an observer with normal color vision in this standard situation.

An alternative to the standard condition, it might be thought, would be to view the surface through a reduction screen in the manner first described by Katz (1911), and thereby render it into a "film" color. This is not satisfactory, because we are trying to define object or surface color, and not film color. A color seen through a reduction screen loses both its object and surface properties. Furthermore, an arbitrary decision would be needed regarding the luminance of the reduction screen, since this severely affects the appearance of a film color.

C. Perceived Surface Color

Perceived surface color (as opposed to physical surface color) is quite another matter. When this expression is used, the reference is to the color that the surface of an object seems to have under whatever particular set of circumstances actually prevail. Like physical surface colors, these cannot exist abstractly as the kind of detached color that one sees through a reduction screen or in Maxwellian view.

The distinction between physical and perceived surface color can perhaps be made clearer by considering the following question: Does the color of an object, such as a red book, disappear if the lights are turned off? From the standpoint of perceived object color, it surely has disappeared, because nothing at all is seen. If the lights are turned back on, and we redirect our gaze toward the object, it will then be seen as having the same color as before. But suppose that a green book had been surreptitiously substituted during the dark period. Now, when the lights are turned on, we immediately recognize the change. Therefore there must be something about the book, per se, that is related to its perceived color, and it is this property to which a name such as *green* may be given, strictly in the sense of physical surface color.

The foregoing illustrates that, even when physical surface color does not change, perceived surface color is nevertheless susceptible to substantial alteration. Turning the lights out is an extreme example.* More

---

* Turning the lights *down* to scotopic levels where only rods can function also eliminates the normally perceived color (17-359). However, in a long series of papers, of which that of Stabell and Stabell (1975) is an example, these authors have clearly shown that priming the scotopic visual system by prior exposure to bright colored lights permits the perception of

often than not, other more subtle changes occur, because perceived surface color turns out to depend upon the illuminant, surround conditions, vantage point of the observer, surface slant, and many other variables (Beck, 1972). Consequently, although perceived surface color seems solely to be a property of the object, this is not the case. Yet the correspondence between perceived surface color and physical surface color is sufficiently close under widely varying conditions that the impression of color as a fixed property of an object is usually maintained. Objects do not often seem to change their colors in wild and unpredictable ways, and if they do, we usually attribute the problem to the condition of viewing and not to the object itself.

III. SURFACE PROPERTIES

The interactions that take place between light and a surface are much more complex than suggested above. Current thinking holds that the photons of light that are reflected from a surface are not even the same ones that are incident upon it (Weisskopf, 1968). Light, composed of vibrating physical particles (photons), interacts with other physical particles that make up the surface. If a photon is absorbed, its energy may be converted into heat, and if so, that is the end of that quantum of light. The *reflectance* of a surface depends upon the percentage of incident photons that are reflected. What this really means is that only some of the incident photons resonate with physical particles in such a way as to produce absorption with reradiation at the same wavelength.† Diffuse reflectance

---

hue under conditions where the subsequent stimulation is scotopic, and therefore is effective only upon rods. This perhaps could be called "scotopic color vision." But it is deficient in the sense that any two stimuli that are equally effective upon rods, no matter how the visual system is primed (and therefore no matter how the stimuli appear), will presumably continue to match exactly. In other words, no *discriminations* are possible that are based strictly upon differences in the spectral distributions of the lights, and therefore there is no real chromatic vision. Another characteristic of object perception that makes scotopic color vision possible is called *memory color* (Bartleson, 1960). We continue under dim light to see the grass as green because we "know" it is green. But if someone painted the grass pink while keeping the same scotopic reflectance, it would continue to appear green.

† The very word *reflection* seems to imply a commonsense view that light coming back from a surface is part of the same light that was incident upon it. Usually it does not matter. After all, if the wavelength does not change, no eye or physical instrument could discriminate between this simpler situation and the actual one. Where the distinction does matter is in connection with the phenomenon of *fluorescence,* where the reradiated light is of a different (usually longer) wavelength than that which is incident. This gives rise to surface colors capable of "reflecting" more light than what is incident upon them! Although this

FIG. 2.   This diagram represents a layer of pigment containing reflecting particles of more or less random size and orientation. Some of the incident light is specularly reflected at the top surface; other rays enter the medium. Light is both transmitted through and reflected from the internal particles; multiple interactions are likely. This light, if it emerges from the medium, will do so at an unpredictable angle. [Adapted from Wright, 1958.]

occurs when a microsurface is rough (see Fig. 2); this introduces a random element that causes the angle of reflectance, considered at the single-photon level, to be unpredictable. With high intensities of illumination, these probabilities translate into definite distributions of relative reflectances as a function of angle, as shown in Fig. 3.

The physically measurable property of a surface that most closely correlates with the perception of its color is diffuse spectral reflectance (14-296).† Such reflectance is necessary in order for a surface to be perceived at all. For example, when the edges of a high-quality, dust-free plane mirror are suitably disguised, only *specular* reflection occurs. (This

sounds paradoxical, it occurs because spectral light is defined in terms of radiant energy weighted according to our visual response to it (2-41). When fluorescence occurs, some of the incident light is in the ultraviolet, where the sensitivity of the eye is zero, whereas the reemitted (reflected) light is converted to the longer wavelengths to which the eye is sensitive. Such surfaces, being brighter than is otherwise physically possible, often seem to glow, producing an appearance that Evans (1964, 1974) calls "fluorence" (see also 2-341).

† A good treatment of this subject will be found starting on page 175 of *The Science of Color*, written by the Committee on Colorimetry of the Optical Society of America and published by Thomas Y. Crowell Co., Inc. in 1953. Although the chapters on the anatomy and physiology of color vision, and also those on psychological concepts, are seriously out of date, most of the remainder of this book is still well worth reading.

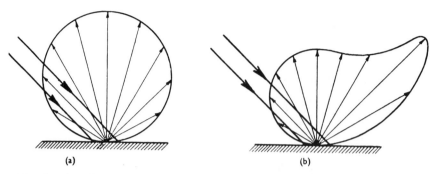

Fig. 3. A perfectly diffuse surface has the characteristics shown in (a). Many surfaces have characteristics like (b), which includes a prominent lobe of reflectance at the specular angle. [From W. D. Wright, *The measurement of color*. New York: Macmillan, 1958.]

means that the angle of reflection of each photon is equal to the angle of incidence.) The perceptual result, as we all know, is that instead of seeing the mirror as a surface, we perceive virtual images of objects, seen as if behind the mirror (14-299). A perfectly diffuse surface, on the other hand, appears exactly the same from all angles of view, no matter what the geometry of illumination. This gives the surface a constant property, one that is important not only for helping to demarcate it as a surface, but also for establishing its color.

Almost all surfaces have components of both specular and diffuse reflectance. For example, diffusely reflected light specifies the surface of a dusty mirror, and, except for some exotic materials seldom encountered outside of laboratories, most surfaces exhibit a lobe of reflectance that is centered upon, though not restricted to, the specular angle of reflection (see Fig. 3). Many surfaces simultaneously exhibit significant components of both types of reflectance. The shiny surface of a new automobile provides an excellent example.* If the car is red, this is because it has a component of diffuse reflectance that favors long wavelengths. If the car is also shiny, this is because of a strong specular component that is attributable to the very smooth, yet partially reflecting surface of the

---

* The practitioners who need most to understand the details of surface reflection are those in the graphic arts and photographic industries. The effort in color reproduction is to modify the reflectance of an initially white surface so that a variety of spectral distributions and luminances are produced in a highly controlled fashion across the surface of the color print. Despite the use of pigments by artists for thousands of years, the physical basis of so-called subtractive color mixture (where the incident white light is altered by its interaction with layers of pigments or dyes) has only recently become understood, and exact prediction is still difficult or impossible. See Yule (1967) for an excellent treatment of the principles of color reproduction.

paint. Light passing beneath this surface interacts with the more random pigment molecules below; if not absorbed, this component becomes diffusely reflected. Specular reflection is typically nonselective with wavelength.* Thus, a yellow light bulb on a used-car lot will look equally yellow whether imaged by specular reflection from the polished surface of a red, blue, or white car. In this way specular reflection provides critical information about the probable smoothness and hardness of a surface, and it also conveys information about the spectral nature of the light source that could be a valuable aid to gauging the quality of the illumination.

Although the directionality of reflected light is important, this forms a very complex subject and is not the most important characteristic of reflected light for the perception of color. What is important is the percentage of incident light that is diffusely reflected as a function of wavelength. At any particular wavelength, diffuse reflectance usually varies between about 5 and 90%. If the light source irradiating the surface is a mixture of all wavelengths and the surface is a nonselective reflector, the lightness of the surface will vary from black through gray to white as the percentage of reflectance increases. If the area is small relative to the surround, a reflectance less than about 10% will correlate with an appearance of black. A reflectance of 70% (or more) is perceived as white (LeGrand, 1968, p. 229). These perceived achromatic colors are remarkably independent, though not absolutely so, of the level of illumination. Thus, it is not the retinal illuminance produced by a patch of surface that primarily determines its lightness; rather, it is the relation between this retinal illuminance and that produced by other surfaces in the visual environment (5-161).

The perception of hue and saturation depends importantly upon the fact that many surfaces are selective reflectors, favoring the return of some wavelengths more than others. Some examples of spectral reflectances of typical printing inks are given in Fig. 4. Depending upon which parts of the spectrum are most strongly represented, the balance of activation of the three types of retinal cones is affected (9-337). The prediction of the appearance of the resulting color is fairly complicated and is best approached by first taking into account the relative amounts of light absorbed by these three types of cones. Given this information, chromaticity can be calculated (9-309), and this is somewhat predictive of what the

---

* There are important exceptions, especially the polished surfaces of certain metals. Polished gold, for example, reveals highlights that are the result of a specular reflection whose spectral characteristics modify the light from white toward yellow. See Weisskopf (1968) for an explanation of the physical basis for this.

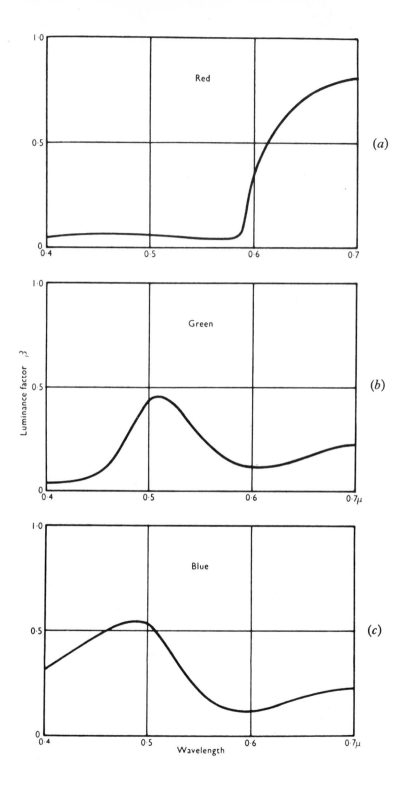

surface will look like. But chromaticity alone is not enough, as it does not specify the percentage of incident light reflected from the surface, which is correlated with lightness. For example, a bar of chocolate and an orange may have the same chromaticity, differing only in reflectance.

Chromaticity and percentage of reflectance, taken together, are sufficient to specify the properties of a diffuse surface that primarily determine its physical surface color. There are several systems of color samples, of which the Munsell is the most widely used in this country. Chips of color are arranged in an orderly way, with the chromaticity and reflectance of each chip also being specified (Wyszecki & Stiles, 1967, p. 478). Thus, it is possible to go from physical measurement to a palpable chip of color and to know the visual meaning of that measurement in terms of the perceived color of that chip. In the Munsell system, names and numbers are also assigned to each chip according to the scheme that is illustrated in Fig. 5.

The importance of reflectance for the perception of hue, even when the spectral distribution of the light (and therefore the chromaticity of the surface) is unchanged, is little short of astounding. Some colors, of which brown is a prime example, exist only for surfaces of low reflectance. If the bar of chocolate is brightly lit and viewed through a hole in a dark reduction screen, then its color will seem orange. This is an example of the fact that the perception of surface color depends, in part, upon the relations in the whole array, rather than merely upon the characteristic of the area being judged. If the illumination of the entire scene is changed, all parts of the scene are altered in the same proportion, so that relational aspects are unchanged. (A chocolate bar remains browner and darker than more neutrally colored objects.)

In order for the perceived surface color of an object to be a useful property, it must be able to transcend natural variations in illumination, which are huge. Thus, the adaptive significance of whatever mechanisms have evolved to allow such *color constancy* is surely clear, even though we shall see that the exact nature of these mechanisms remains elusive. The relative reflectances of the various objects in a scene are independent of illumination; so also is the relative spectral reflectance characteristic of any particular surface. We are easily able to judge—or perhaps directly to perceive—these relative properties and to discount, in some sense, the changing illumination. By contrast, we are ill-equipped to judge lighting, and most of us pay little attention to it.

FIG. 4.   Examples of spectral reflectance curves for red, green, and blue inks. [After Wright (1958).]

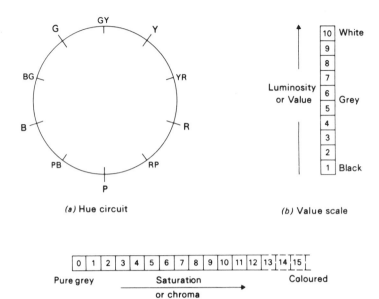

(a) Hue circuit

(b) Value scale

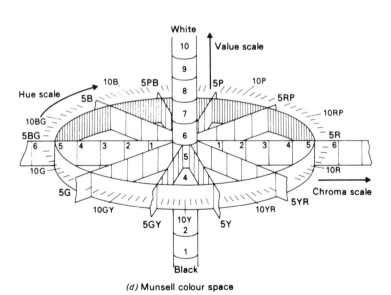

(c) Chroma scale

(d) Munsell colour space

FIG. 5. The Munsell color system. The value scale corresponds to the lightness of the sample which in turn is correlated with percent reflectance. Hue is represented around the rim, and chroma (saturation) by distance away from the center. [Reproduced from Padgham & Saunders (1975).]

IV. THE ILLUMINANT

A. We Do Not See Light

It is probably not generally appreciated that we usually do not, in fact, see light. If a person is standing in a scatter-free environment, light beams of enormous intensity can be projected laterally in front of his nose without anything being seen. Moreover, even a weakly illuminated scene across the room could still be appreciated, meaning that the light reflected from such a scene would be able to pass through the high-intensity lateral beam without being appreciably affected. When light enters the eye, it is almost always never perceived as such. Instead, what we see are the objects and surfaces that have been rendered visible by the presence of light. Light beams themselves can be observed by projecting them through a scattering medium, as happens, for example, when smoke is blown in front of a slide projector, or when atmospheric particles permit perception of solar rays against dark backgrounds. It is only the light scattered out of the beam that allows the beam to be seen, just as it is the light reflected from objects that allows them to be seen.

It is true that we perceive sources of lights, such as traffic signals, but such a percept is not as obvious as it may seem. A spot of light projected on a wall will be normally perceived as such, especially if the projector is visible and there is some scattering of light out of the beam. But if these cues are eliminated, and especially if a black ring is drawn around the edge of the projected spot (to eliminate any penumbra) the spot will be perceived as a source of light (if it is much brighter than the wall) or as a white piece of material (if its luminance could have been provided by a surface having a reflectance of at least 70%.

We may think that we perceive sunlight on a sunny day (and, in a sense, we do) but what we actually *see* is the presence of the sun, the bright blue sky, the high average brightness of things (to which we cannot entirely adapt), and the deep shadows. Add to this the warmth of the sun's radiant energy and we seemingly cannot help but perceive the world as if bathed in sunlight, even though we see none of the light that is doing the bathing.

B. Judging Illumination

Although we pay little attention to illumination, we evidently do successfully take account of the character of the illuminant. How do we do this? Sources are often in the field of view, and if so they may be directly viewed or seen in peripheral vision (specular reflection from objects provides a similar sort of information). But even in the absence of such information, the nature of illumination is usually discerned. Evans (1974, p. 194) discusses the matter as follows:

> Unless we see the actual light source itself . . . the only evidence of the nature of the illumination in a scene comes to us from its effects on the objects on which it falls. Yet these effects are usually sufficiently numerous . . . that we at once see the illumination directly. Perhaps the two major effects are the gradient of intensity (or lack of it) related to distance from the source and shape of objects and the nature and intensities of the shadows thrown by objects. Such effects are often called "clues" to illumination. While this is convenient terminology in explanations of how the perception can occur, it implies a detective-like attitude on the part of the observer that doesn't accord with the fact that he simply *sees* the illumination.

This situation surely is paradoxical: one "sees" something that certainly cannot, in any direct sense, be seen.

C. Color Rendering of Illuminants

Because physical surface color results from potentially reflecting light being removed, perception of surface color is not possible under monochromatic light, which can only be more or less removed, without change of character. Three monochromatic lights are the technical minimum required for reproducing almost any chromatic percept, but much of the information contained in the spectral reflection characteristic of a surface would be lost under such illumination, as explained in the legend of Fig. 6. The example given in Fig. 6 represents an extreme case, because surfaces do not physically exist having reflectance functions that change so rapidly with wavelength. Instead, it is in the physical nature of things that the spectral reflectance curves of natural surfaces are rather gently sloped and typically include substantial reflectance from all parts of the spectrum. Given that this is how things are, and that the natural illumination of the sun contains all visible wavelengths, it apparently has turned out to be evolutionarily possible to provide a wide gamut of color experience, and a high degree of discrimination of physical surface color, based initially on the absorption spectra of only three cone photopigments that broadly overlap. The ability to judge physical surface color (color constancy) tends to break down if the illuminant contains strong spectral lines or significant energy gaps in restricted spectral regions, or if the surface being irradiated has unusual reflectance characteristics. A system for predicting the color-rendering properties of illuminants has been proposed by Crawford (1959), who determined the amounts of various spectral

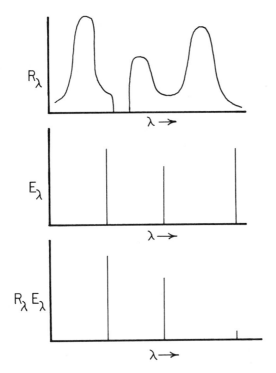

FIG. 6.   The curve at the top is intended to represent the relative spectral reflectance (R_λ) of a surface, as a function of the wavelength of light incident upon it. An illuminant having the unusual property shown by the middle panel would consist of three spectral lines having the relative energies (E_λ) that are shown. The light reflecting from the surface would be represented by the product ($R_\lambda E_\lambda$) as shown in the bottom panel. An essential characteristic of the surface, namely its high reflectance in three spectral regions, would in this case be totally lost. For good color rendering, a continuous and balanced spectrum is needed; if an equal-energy spectrum were substituted for that of the middle panel, the light returning from the object would have the same distribution with wavelength as that of the top panel.

bands that could be removed before observers noticed a difference in the scene that was being illuminated. For further treatments of this complex subject, see Wyszecki and Stiles (1967, p. 357) and also the IES Handbook (1972, pp. 5–18).

V. ADVANTAGES OF HAVING COLOR VISION

Why are so many people willing to pay four or five times as much to own a color television set as would be required to see the same scenes in black and white? An important reason, no doubt, is that color adds intrinsic beauty to what is seen. Because there is little firm scientific evidence related to this sort of thing, the affective and esthetic aspects of color will not be discussed further here. These are nevertheless fascinating subjects, and the forewarned reader may profit from the writing of Luckiesh (1938) and a profusely illustrated and very provocative volume by Birren (1963).

Above all, physical surface color is important because it provides information about an absolute property of a surface.* This information is limited, and cannot reveal everything that is measured in a spectral reflectance curve, because there are only three kinds of cones in the eye. For this reason, color is signaled at the first stage in reduced form, as three activity levels. One very important consequence of this fact is that *metameric* surface colors exist—these being colors that look alike to the eye, although physically they may be quite different (9–309). Two surfaces that look alike under one illuminant will not, in general, match under a different illuminant unless they are physically identical. Some physical surface colors are perceptually rather *stable;* that is, they do not seem to vary much with changes in illumination; others are notoriously *unstable* and change dramatically. There is no way to judge stability by viewing such pairs of surfaces under only one illuminant, for a stable and unstable color may happen to match exactly under that particular condition. Only by testing them under various lluminants, or by knowing their diffuse reflectances as a function of wavelength, can the stability of a physical surface color be judged.

VI. THE IMPORTANCE OF OBJECT COLOR

A. Identification

As a first example of a case where identification by color is important, consider watching a football game where both teams have light jerseys and dark pants that appear very similar on a black-and-white television screen. In such a case, following the action of the game proves very difficult. The problem is not one of discriminating that there are football players; it is rather one of classification. With color television and normal

---

* As Linksz (1964) remarks on page 163 of his provocative "An Essay on Color Vision," in quoting a remark of a friend of his: "I might call the black-and-white photograph of a friend a 'speaking' likeness, but I would hate to find him the photograph's color when I answer the doorbell."

color vision, one sees immediately that the jerseys of one team are, say, gray, and the others, pink; the dark pants in one case are blue, and in the other, maroon. Veridical surface color perception is however not necessary, so long as the perceived colors are discriminably different.

As another example, consider the following demonstration. I enter the office of a colleague and, with his permission, select at random a couple of dozen books from his shelf. I lay these out on a table in a disordered, partially overlapping fashion and ask him to retrieve the appropriate book as soon as possible after I state the name of the author and the title of the book. In one part of the experiment I allow him to see the books through goggles containing neutral filters that do not alter chromaticity. The rest of the time, I require him to wear red goggles of the same photopic density as the neutral ones. (By filtering out all but very long wavelengths, these reduce him to a state of virtual monochromatism). The result would probably be an increased response time with the red goggles. This example introduces the idea that the use of color cues in tasks involving search and recognition can be important (see Green & Anderson, 1956; Smith, 1962; Williams, 1966; Christ, 1975).

Judging the ripeness of a banana provides a third example of yet a different kind. Here the problem is not perceiving a banana, or (usually) being able to find one. The problem is instead to decide, by vision alone, whether it is edible. Here the importance of color vision is that it allows a valid prediction, obtainable without the need to touch or ingest the fruit, concerning one of its important properties—ripeness. And whereas one can, without color vision, surely find a book amongst a pile of books (though it takes longer), the color-blind individual would be helpless to judge the ripeness of a remote banana. Similarly, the physician could not judge the health of a patient by noting the color of his skin, gray skies would become confusable with blue ones, and so on.

The controlled use of physical surface color has been exploited artificially in a wide variety of contexts, for example, to identify wires and pipes. Such color coding virtually always proves helpful for those having normal color vision.

B. Discrimination

One time I happened to remark to a colleague how profuse the blossoms were on a magnificent tulip tree that grew next to Morey Hall at the University of Rochester. As soon as he told me that he could not see any blossoms, I knew that he was a red–green dichromat, probably a deuteranope (5-123, 17-366). From where we stood, the details of the leaves and blossoms were not readily discernible, and what I actually saw were small spots of orange scattered amongst many other spots of equally light and darker green. The most famous of screening devices for revealing red–green color blindness is a formalization of the tulip-tree test: In the Ishihara plates, the deviant dots that form a pattern for a normal observer do not do so for the dichromat, because they are not sufficiently different from one another for him to perceive the pattern.

A trick used to great advantage in the Ishihara plates and others like them is that of providing many microcontours in the form of the outlines of clearly separated colored dots that anyone can see. The "contour" that must be seen in order to pass the test is instead a superordinate Gestalt type of percept, which requires that one must disregard the physical contours of the pattern and utilize instead an ability to perceive a larger figure that depends upon the apprehension of similarly colored elements. It is highly probable that if the test figure were of uniform color, seen without any dividing line against a background of a different color, at least some red–green dichromats would see it. (This could result from individual differences or from difficulty in controlling printing inks.). In particular, any brightness difference (even a very small one) between figure and ground would form a contour. To avoid the possibility of discrimination based on lightness, Ishihara also cleverly varied the lightnesses as well as the chromaticities of his spots.

VII. COLOR AND CONTOUR

The perception of contour underlies the perception of form and is of critical importance for object perception (8-273, 14-293, 16-352, 17-383). Chromatic vision is usually not necessary for contour perception; this can easily be demonstrated by turning down the color control on a television display. Nevertheless, spectral differences sometimes carry contour information that would otherwise be lost at equal luminance.

Contours are sometimes seen as a result of a narrow band of reduced retinal contrast, which would be produced for example by viewing a utility wire or the strokes of a cartoonist. More often they result from differences in juxtaposed areas of retinal stimulation, as in the usual case of perceiving almost any kind of figure against a background. One way to examine this kind of contour in the laboratory is to juxtapose two fields and then manipulate their relative luminances. A fraction of a 1% difference, for large and carefully juxtaposed fields, is sufficient to perceive a perceptible contour (LeGrand, 1968, p. 276). The contour will grow in distinctness as the relative luminance difference is further increased.

One way to examine how purely chromatic differences affect contour is to juxtapose two fields that differ in chromaticity and then manipulate their relative luminances. Typically, although there is no luminance ratio at which the apparent contour separating the fields will disappear, the border is minimally distinct at equal luminance. Research on such minimally distinct borders has revealed that they depend almost exclusively upon the ratio of activation of "red" (R-) and "green" (G-)cones:* the more this ratio deviates from unity, the more distinct is the border (Tansley & Boynton, 1976). For small fields of low luminance, used in our work, the "blue" (B-)cones appear to make little or no contribution to contour and the two parts of the field seem to melt into one another. This result is consistent with spatial-modulation–transfer measurements made by Green (1968) and Kelly (1974) using psychophysical methods involving selective chromatic adaptation to isolate color mechanisms. They agree that the R- and G-mechanisms have spatial contrast transfer functions of about the same shape, and that the B-mechanism differs by having a much lower cutoff frequency. This in turn is consistent with the following findings:

1. Visual acuity in an observer having only B-cones is much less than for the normal observer (Green, 1972).
2. Normal observers, if tested with shortwave gratings on a bright yellow background (which isolates the B-mechanism) show a similarly reduced acuity (Brindley, 1970, p. 241; Green, 1968).

It would appear then that the R- and G-cones, in addition to making their contributions to color vision, are importantly involved in the detection of contour, and that the B-cones are not. Van der Horst, De Weert, and Bouman (1967) were the first to show that spatial chromaticity modulation from red to green produces a very different low-frequency behavior than does luminance modulation (see 17-381 for discussion of spatial modulation transfer functions, as obtained psychophysically). Luminance modulation exhibits low-frequency attenuation, which is believed to be caused by lateral inhibition in the retina (see Ratliff, 1974).

---

* Or L- and M-cones, to use the DeValois's designation. DeValois and DeValois (5-139) express extreme displeasure at the use of color names to designate the three cone types. For the photopigments that cones contain, there are at present even more equivalent names than there are for the cones themselves (see 9-336 for some of these). Personally, I prefer the names B- , G- , and R-cones. It seems highly probable that each of these types of cones, if stimulated uniquely, would unequivocally give rise to sensations of blue, green, and red. Therefore, I find these labels mnemonically convenient and not any more objectionable than the use of chromatic labels for activity in the opponent-color cells of the lateral geniculate nucleus, where DeValois and DeValois seem somehow to feel quite comfortable about using them.

Therefore, it is hard to see gradual transitions in brightness. This is not the case for modulation of chromaticity, which produces a flat curve at low frequencies, meaning that gradual transitions in chromaticity are relatively easy to see.

From the standpoint of perception, these results are consistent with the need to discount gradual liminance variations of the sort that are all around us. These occur because the inverse-square law, among other things, makes it almost impossible to illuminate a surface uniformly, even with great effort. In real life it virtually never happens (most illumination is at a slant), yet we are able to discern that a surface has uniform reflectance characteristics. Similar gradients in chromaticity are rare; when they do occur it is much more likely that the spectral reflectance of the surface is what is actually varying, so it becomes productive to be able to see the change in that way.

An explanation of these effects is possible, based on the idea that most of the lateral inhibition is between, rather than within, the R- and G-cone systems. In a recent experiment utilizing low-frequency sinusoidal flicker, Kelly (1975) investigated modulation sensitivity to *temporal* variations in luminance and chromaticity, using fields that were either uniform, as shown in Fig. 7(b) and 7(c), or vertically divided and modulated in counterphase, as shown in Fig. 7(a) and 7(d). For slow flicker (1 Hz), he found that splitting the field greatly enhanced sensitivity for luminance modulation—illustration in Fig. 7(a)—but reduced it considerably for chromaticity modulation—see Fig. 7(d). This result can be interpreted on the hypothesis that sensitivity to low-frequency luminance flicker is reduced by an inhibitory process that operates strongly between R- and G-mechanisms. The inhibitory messages themselves are assumed to follow low temporal frequencies well, and are in phase with the excitatory

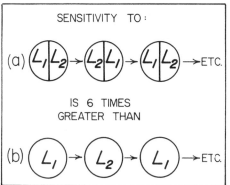
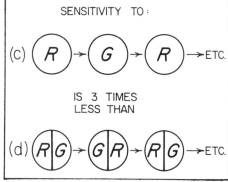

FIG. 7. Summary of experimental conditions and the results of Kelly (1975) on chromaticity and luminance flicker.

signal. Thus, they normally serve to limit the perception of low-frequency luminance flicker—Fig. 7(b). But when the two parts of the field are flickered out of phase—Fig. 7(a)—the inhibitory mechanisms cannot operate in their normal way along the border, and sensitivity to flicker is relatively enhanced by the absence of the inhibition that occurs throughout a uniform field.

In chromatic flicker with uniform fields, on the other hand, the repeated exchange of chromaticity does not permit the inhibition between R- and G-mechanisms to operate optimally, presumably because the inhibitory signals are out of phase with respect to the mechanisms that they would otherwise inhibit, as illustrated by Fig. 7(c). In this case, splitting the field—see Fig. 7(d)—restores the appropriate phase relationships for inhibition along the border and thereby reduces the sensitivity to chromaticity flicker. These effects are very large: In Kelly's experiment, the introduction of the split-field and counterphase flicker improved luminance discrimination by a factor of about 6, and reduced chromaticity discrimination by a factor of 3.

From the standpoint of physiology, it is reasonable to suppose that sharp contours are signaled by a differential activation of nearby R- and G-cones that lie on opposite sides of the image of the border. In the macaque monkey, DeValois found that almost all of the spectrally opponent cells (whose role in color vision has long been recognized) were also spatially opponent in a way that allowed them to signal color for large uniform fields, as well as contour, when contour is present (5-133). This seems to agree with the idea that R- and G-cones are mutually inhibitory, and that the purpose of such inhibition is to aid contour discrimination as well as chromatic perception. Consistent with this view, DeValois has also found cells that can discriminate color change, but not the direction of the change. He further suggests that color information goes two ways in the cortex—to color-specific paths and to so-called multiple-color cells that "use color (and luminance) information to detect form, but do not care what colors are involved (DeValois & DeValois, 1975, p. 139).

VIII. LIGHTNESS OF COLORS

Because surface colors necessarily depend upon removing some of the light that is initially available, one might suppose that colored objects would always look dark. Some of them of course do—those that reflect very little light. But others, such as the red surface represented by the spectral reflectance curve of Fig. 3(a) actually look quite light.

Underlying this phenomenon is the nonadditivity of brightnesses, sometimes called a failure of Abney's "law" (Guth, Donley, & Marroco, 1969). Consider a red field next to a yellow one and adjust its radiance until it appears equally as bright as the yellow. Now remove the red and use a green field instead to make the same kind of adjustment. Finally, reduce the intensity of the red and green fields, each by half, and optically superimpose them. The surprising result is that the mixture field looks much less bright than the yellow field. It also looks much less red or green than its components, the mixture field, in fact, looks yellow and resembles neither of them. The explanation, in theoretical terms, is that there is a subtractive signal obtained from the outputs of red and green cones that adds to brightness. Whenever the two types of cones are equally activated, this component of brightness is eliminated. If the balance swings greatly in one direction, as will be the case if the shortwave end of the spectrum is removed, as shown in Fig. 3(a), an extra brightness contribution initiated by the R-cones is released. Probably for this reason, the lightness of color prints and lithographs does not usually seem less than for black-and-white reproductions that physically reflect a higher percentage of the incident light.

IX. COLOR CONSTANCY

Using the language introduced earlier in this chapter, it could be said that we enjoy color constancy whenever physical surface color is correctly judged. Or, to put the matter a bit differently, perceived surface color continues to correlate well with physical surface color, despite changes in the illumination or other variables that may greatly alter the spectral distribution of light reaching the eye relative to what it would be under the standard condition by which we initially defined the idea of physical surface color. I have left this important topic for last, knowing that there would be little space left in which to discuss it.

It seems logically necessary to suppose that the visual field is tied together laterally, to form the basis of an intricate neural network that permits the rendition of the color of one patch of the visual scene in a context provided by all the rest. (Land has reminded us of this in his famous demonstrations.*) The neural machinery needed for doing such

* I strongly recommend Dean Judd's "Appraisal of Land's Work on Two-Primary Color Projections" which appeared a year or so after Land startled the uninitiated (1960). This scholarly paper puts Land's work in a proper perspective, by showing that (a) some of Land's claims were exaggerated; (b) relatively little of what he did was new; and (c) existing predictive systems could account for his results, as well as Land's own model. In addition, Judd's paper contains a brilliant discussion of many aspects of object–color perception that are treated in this chapter.

computations is under active investigation and probably exists both in the retina and the brain. Most of the retinal evidence, so far as physiology is concerned, comes from nonprimates, but it is at least anatomically established in man and monkey that horizontal and amacrine cells exist in the retina, and that they have the structure and connections to do the job (16-333). At the ganglion cell stage and beyond, the organization of the visual system in terms of receptive fields requires the mapping of many retinal locations onto single cells and also requires that each retinal location must influence the activity of many high-order cells. As already mentioned, many such cells have been investigated in the monkey that appear to encode both chromatic as well as spatial information. But it is not yet possible, at least for me, to understand the meaning of these data for the complex phenomena of color constancy. The discussion of these matters by DeValois and DeValois (5-151) is commendable and perhaps takes us as far as we can go with our present knowledge.

Color constancy, like all complex perceptual phenomena, appears to depend upon very many physiological mechanisms and psychological cues. But it is certain, from the most elementary demonstrations of *color contrast* (Evans, 1964) and *assimilation* (Helson, 1963) that there are strange lateral effects in color perception that have nothing directly to do with the nature of any illuminant (see also Pearson, Rubinstein, & Spivack, 1969).

Color constancy is by no means perfect; definite shifts in color perception occur for example in taking an object from sunlight into tungsten— incandescent illumination. The best equations that have been worked out predict the effects of illumination, and to account for the influence of surround colors are the empirical formulas of Judd (1940, 1960), which are based on the ideas that (*a*) illumination is taken into account; and (*b*) surfaces whose reflectances are above the overall adaptation level take on the hue of the illuminant, whereas those below have a complementary hue (a principle elucidated by Helson, 1938).

Among the possible physiological mechanisms, those concerned with selective chromatic adaptation are surely important for color constancy. The three types of cones or the mechanisms for which they constitute the input, or both, adapt nonlinearly. As a consequence, a light that is predominantly red adapts the R-cones more than the others, causing them to become less sensitive than before, so that the reddish cast that otherwise would be provided by the illuminant becomes less noticeable.

In summary, color constancy must depend upon many factors, including the indirect perception of the illuminant, local color-contrast effects, global determinations of adaptation level, selective chromatic adaptation, and probably other variables of a sensory nature. In addition, it has been shown that much more complex perceptual variables are also important.

Beck (1972) has proposed that "the perception of a surface color involves two separable components: the signals resulting from the operation of the sensory processes, and the integrative schemata for the perception of visual surfaces into which the signals are assimilated [p. 7]." In other words, the perception of the meaningful presence of real objects does not arise out of whole cloth but depends in the first instance upon basic sensory processing. Yet, once this perceptual structure is formed, it has the power to change perceived colors significantly in ways that cannot be directly accounted for in basic sensory terms.

X. EPILOG

The essential ideas brought forth in this chapter may be summarized as follows:

1. Doubtless, the reactions of our senses to natural objects are those that are most frequently and most generally perceived. For both our welfare and convenience they are of the most powerful importance.
2. What the eye sees is the mind's best guess as to what is out front.
3. The notion that the way we see objects is sometimes strongly influenced by our experience is, of course, correct; but *one must not represent as products of experience the primary innate functions of the visual system, which in fact constitute the very basis by which these experiences were originally acquired.*
4. When we open our eyes in an illuminated room, we see a manifold of spatially extended forms that are differentiated or separated from one another through differences in their colors. Colors are what fill in the outlines of these forms; they are the stuff out of which visual phenomena are built up.
5. In vision, we are not concerned with perceiving light rays as such, but with perceiving the external objects mediated by these radiations; the eye must inform us, not about the momentary intensity or quality of the light reflected from external objects, but about these objects themselves.
6. The colors of all natural bodies have no other origin than this: that they are variously constituted so as to reflect one kind of light in greater plenty than others.
7. The characteristic *properties* of natural objects, in spite of this name, do not denote something that is peculiar to the individual object by itself, but invariably imply some relation to a second object (including our organs of sense).

8. Self-regulation of light sensitivity is mediated by two different mechanisms: on the one hand by reciprocal interactions among areas of the somatic visual field, and on the other hand by the fact that with every persisting total illumination, the eye can be brought by a gradual change in state to a sort of equilibrium by virtue of which the average brightness of the visual field always remains about the same.

9. Reciprocal interaction consists in the fact that the momentary excitation of every single somatic element of the visual field partly determines the light sensitivity of the rest, and that, in turn, its own light sensitivity also depends in part upon the simultaneous excitation of the remaining elements.*

References

Abramov, I., & Gordon, J. Vision. In E. C. Carterette & M. P. Friedman (Eds.), *Handbook of perception*. Vol. III. New York: Academic Press, 1973. Pp. 327–357. (a)

Abramov, I., & Gordon, J. Seeing. In E. C. Carterette & M. P. Friedman (Eds.), *Handbook of perception*. Vol. III. New York: Academic Press, 1973. Pp. 359–406. (b)

Bartleson, C. J. Memory colors of familiar objects. *Journal of the Optical Society of America,* 1960 **50,** 73–77.

Beck, J. *Surface Color Perception.* Ithaca, New York: Cornell University Press, 1972.

Birren, F. *Color: A survey in words and pictures.* New York: University Books, 1963.

Boynton, R. M. Implications of the minimally-distinct border. *Journal of the Optical Society of America,* 1973, **63,** 1037–1043.

Boynton, R. M. The visual system: Environmental information. In E. C. Carterette & M. P. Friedman (Eds.), *Handbook of perception.* Vol. I. New York: Academic Press, 1974. Pp. 285–307.

Boynton, R. M. Color, hue, and wavelength. In E. C. Carterette & M. P. Friedman (Eds.), *Handbook of perception.* Vol. V. New York: Academic Press, 1975. Pp. 301–347.

Brindley, G. *Physiology of the retina and the visual pathway.* Batlimore: Williams & Wilkins, 1970.

Christ, R. E. Review and analysis of color coding research for visual displays. *Human Factors,* 1975, **17,** 542–570.

Crawford, B. H. Measurement of color rendering tolerance. *Journal of the Optical Society of America,* 1959, **49,** 1147–1156.

DeValois, R. L., & DeValois, K. K. Neural coding of color. In E. C. Carterette & M. P. Friedman (Eds.), *Handbook of perception.* Vol. V. New York: Academic Press, 1975. Pp. 117–166.

Dodwell, P. C. Pattern and object perception. In E. C. Carterette & M. P. Friedman (Eds.), *Handbook of perception.* Vol. V. New York: Academic Press, 1975. Pp. 267–299.

Evans, R. M. Variables of perceived color. *Journal of the Optical Society of America,* 1964, **54,** 1467–1474.

* All of the statements of this concluding section are essentially direct quotes. Numbers 3, 4, 5, 8 and 9 are statements of Ewald Hering, taken from the Hurvich and Jameson (1964) translation. They are found on pages 21, 1, 13, 18, and 18, in that order. Numbers 1 and 7 are from the Optical Society translation of Helmholtz's *Physiological Optics,* volume 3, page 21. Number 2 is from Judd (1960, p. 265), who attributes it, without further reference, to Adelbert Ames. Finally, No. 6 is from MacAdam's (1970) *Sources of Colour Science,* p. 15, as stated originally by Sir Isaac Newton.

Evans, R. M. *The perception of color.* New York: Wiley, 1974.

Green, B. F., & Anderson, L. K. Color coding in a visual search task. *Journal of Experimental Psychology,* 1956, **51,** 19–24.

Green, D. G. The contrast sensitivity of the colour mechanisms of the human eye. *Journal of Psychiatry,* 1968, **196,** 415–429.

Green, D. G. Visual acuity in the blue cone monochromat. *Journal of Psychiatry,* 1972, **222,** 419–426.

Guth, S. L., Donley, N. J., & Marrocco, R. T. On luminance additivity and related topics. *Vision Research,* 1969, **9,** 537–575.

Helmholtz, H. *Physiological optics* (edited by J. P. C. Southall). Rochester, New York: Optical Society of America, 1924.

Helson, H. Fundamental problems in color vision I. The principle governing changes in hue, saturation, and lightness of non-selective samples in chromatic illumination. *Journal of Experimental Psychology,* 1938, **23,** 439–476.

Helson, H. Studies of anomalous contrast and assimilation. *Journal of the Optical Society of America,* 1963, **53,** 179–184.

Hering, E. *Outlines of a theory of the light sense.* Translated by L. M. Hurvich & D. Jameson. Cambridge, Massachusetts: Harvard Univ. Press, 1964.

IES Lighting Handbook (5th ed.) New York: Illuminating Engineering Society, 1972.

Judd, D. B. Hue, saturation, and lightness of surface colors with chromatic illumination. *Journal of the Optical Society of America,* 1940, **30,** 2–32.

Judd, D. B. Appraisal of Land's work on two-primary color projections. *Journal of the Optical Society of America,* 1960, **50,** 254–268.

Katz, D. *The world of color.* Translated from the second German edition (1911) by R. B. MacLeod & C. W. Fox. London: Kegan, Paul, 1935.

Kelly, D. H. Spatio-temporal frequency characteristics of color-vision mechanisms. *Journal of the Optical Society of America,* 1974, **64,** 983–990.

Kelly, D. H. Luminous and chromatic flickering patterns have opposite effects. *Science,* 1975, **188,** 371–372.

LeGrand, Y. *Light, colour, and vision.* London: Chapman & Hall, 1968.

LeGrand, Y. Measurement of the visual stimulus. In E. C. Carterette & M. P. Friedman (Eds.), *Handbook of perception.* Vol. V. New York: Academic Press, 1975. Pp. 25–55. (a)

LeGrand, Y. History of research on seeing. In E. C. Carterette & M. P. Friedman (Eds.), *Handbook of perception.* Vol. V. New York: Academic Press, 1975. Pp. 3–23. (b)

Linksz, A. *An essay on color vision.* New York: Grune & Stratton, 1964.

Luckiesh, M. *Color and colors.* New York: Van Nostrand, 1938.

MacAdam, D. L. *Sources of color science.* New York: Wiley, 1970.

Optical Society of America, Committee on Colorimetry. *The science of color.* New York: Crowell, 1953.

Padgham, C. A., & Saunders, J. E. *The perception of light and colour.* New York: Academic Press, 1975.

Pearson, D. E., Rubinstein, C. B., & Spivack, G. J. Comparison of perceived color in two-primary computer-generated artificial images with predictions based on the Helson-Judd formulation. *Journal of the Optical Society of America,* 1969, **59,** 644–658.

Ratliff, F. (Ed.). *Studies on excitation and inhibition in the retina.* New York: Rockefeller Univ. Press, 1974.

Smith, S. L. Color coding and visual search. *Journal of Experimental Psychology,* 1962, **64,** 434–440.

Stabell, U., & Stabell, B. Scotopic contrast hues triggered by rod activity. *Vision Research,* 1975, **15,** 1115–1118.

Tansley, B. W., & Boynton, R. M. A line, not a space, represents the visual distinctness of borders formed by different colors. *Science,* 1976, **191,** 954–957.

Van Der Horst, G. J. C., De Weert, C. M. M., & Bouman, M. A. Transfer of spatial chromaticity-contrast at threshold in the human eye. *Journal of the Optical Society of America,* 1967, **57,** 1260–1266.

Weisskopf, V. F. How light interacts with matter. *Scientific America,* 1968, **219,** 60–71.

Williams, L. G. The effect of target specification on objects fixated during visual search. *Perception & Psychophysics,* 1966, **1,** 315–318.

Wright, W. D. *The measurement of colour.* New York: Macmillan, 1958.

Wright, W. D. *The rays are not coloured.* New York: Elsevier, 1968.

Wyszecki, G., & Stiles, W. S. *Color science.* New York: Wiley, 1967.

Yule, J. A. C. *Principles of color reproduction.* New York: Wiley, 1967.

Zusne, L. *Visual perception of form.* New York: Academic Press, 1970.

Part II

Representation of Temporal, Auditory, and Haptic Spaces

Chapter 6

TIME AND RHYTHM PERCEPTION

PAUL FRAISSE

I. INTRODUCTION: THE FIELD OF TEMPORAL PERCEPTION

Perception is information extracted from a stimulus that is present. Is it possible to speak of the perception of time? Time is only a concept that subsumes all the aspects of change in our environment as well as in our life. Changes are incessant. If one wants to analyze them, one has to admit that in change there are events that are like noticeable moments, or to say it differently, that are like figures on a ground.

Changes may be characterized by the following two aspects: (*a*) the succession and order of events; (*b*) the duration of the event, or the interval between two successive events.

HANDBOOK OF PERCEPTION, VOL. VIII

Physicists, for example, need to have these two types of data when they describe the changes in nature. To perceive time is in fact a general expression that means that succession and duration are both perceived.

But does the evolutive character of every change enable us to say (strictly speaking) that we perceive time? As a matter of fact, to ask this question in such terms is to have a wrong conception of perception. As Gibson (1966) notes: "Perception is an activity, not an instantaneous event [p. 143]." To make an analogy, if we consider change as a film, perception does not correspond to a freezing of the image. Perception always consists of perceiving an event of variable duration, and what we generally regard as perception corresponds to the recognition of some invariants (a color, a form, a phoneme, a taste, a smell, etc.). Every perception is the *perception of a changing world* from which we extract information because, to some extent, we are capable of integrating successive data. Kant had seen the originality of time and space (*a priori* forms of sensitivity, as he claimed) as the general modalities of all our perceptions.

In the nineteenth century, German philosophers thought it possible to speak specifically of a sense of time, and they even speculated about specific receptors. Some authors attributed space to vision, and time to audition, even though each of these perceptions has to some extent a space and a duration. Some psychologists, including Wundt and James, spoke of a *psychological present*, in the sense of a merely apparent, subjective, or phenomenal temporality. The psychological present, however, is nothing more than the temporal field in which a series of events is rendered present and integrated into a unique perception; evidence of the latter is given by perceptual responses (identification or discrimination).

Behaviorists abandoned the notion of the psychological present, probably because it had been analyzed in an introspective way. They ignored the possibility of studying it in an objective way, as with the spatial field. The temporal field, like the spatial field, is a set of stimulations; we do not perceive duration or space as such, but only the duration or the space of perceptual data, which thus enables us to define the extent of these fields. The phenomenal character of these perceptions should not prevent even a strict behaviorist from studying them, since every perception has a phenomenal character, be it a color, a timbre, a flavor, etc. The important point is to establish a correspondence between phenomenal and physical data and not to restrict the study to the gathering of introspective analyses. If every perception has a duration, the temporal field may be put in evidence every time the perceptual act is oriented towards the apprehension of successive events into a unit, such as an uninterrupted series of letters or digits, a rhythm, a melody, or a sentence.* It has been shown that this field is limited by the number of perceptible elements: 7 ± 2. G. Miller (1956) has shown that this number may correspond to isolated elements as well as to groups of elements (chunks). With adults, the temporal field is 7 letters (random presentation), but it becomes 25 syllables when letters form words and words form the semantic unit of a sentence (standard of Binet–Simon Scale).

The arrangement into chunks may be done on the basis of temporal proximity (groups of sounds or of letters) but cognitive factors also play an important role. For instance, the temporal field of the child, which does not differ very much from the adult's when rhythmical structures are considered, increases with age when cognitive processes intervene in the formation of chunks (Fraisse & Fraisse, 1937).

There remains one difficulty: how to differentiate the temporal field perceived at a given moment from the temporal perspectives that are constructed through our memory. Speaking metaphorically, I can glance at the past week or the last year, but these perspectives should not be confused with the temporal field that enables me to perceive the rhythm of a waltz or the words of a sentence. Evidently, memory intervenes in the coding of every perception, but perception differs from memory, in that it depends directly upon sensory data.

The perceived present, or psychological present, may be defined as the temporal extent of stimulations that can be perceived at a given time, without the intervention of rehearsal during or after the stimulation. The capacity of apprehension of successive stimulations is to be distinguished from long-term and short-term memory. The concept of short-term memory refers to the possibility of keeping in memory a series of bits of information for a duration that does not exceed several tenths of seconds. For instance, a phone number that is apprehended globally when heard for the first time is remembered through rehearsal. It could be argued that perception of a succession of events implies the storing in memory of former data so that they can be integrated with the most recent ones. Such an argument brings us back to an "instantaneist" conception of perception and does not permit distinguishing the storing of information from its apprehension.

If one admits a sensory register, one also has to admit that a perceptual activity has a duration such that data may be integrated, within a temporal

---

* This span, which corresponds to a perfectly correct perception, has to be distinguished from the memory span, which corresponds to what a subject is capable of reproducing after a single presentation of a series of events in which primacy and recency effects are observed.

limit. This limit can be measured by the temporal extent that corresponds to the capacity of apprehension. The capacity of apprehension in terms of elements varies with the possibility of their organization; such organization is only possible when the temporal proximity of the elements is increased, which explains the relative constancy of the higher limit of the psychological present.

On the basis of the number of perceptible elements (or chunks) and the maximum interval between each of them, the maximal duration of the perceived present is about 5 sec. This duration also corresponds to the duration of the enunciation of a sentence of 25 syllables, to the duration of the measure of the slowest adagio or, in poetry, to the duration of the longest verse.

What is this limit when only two stimulations are perceived? It is defined by the duration that prevents the integration of two stimulations into a perceptual unit. Think of the unity of a rhythm, for instance, the *tick–tock* of a clock. The sounds follow each other at the cadence of one per second and are grouped into a pattern of two sounds. If the cadence is slowed down, the grouping of two as one vanishes and only isolated sounds are perceived: *tick* then *tock*, then *tick*, then *tock*. Two close sounds belong to a same perceived present when the interval is approximately 1.8–2 sec.

The same observation applies to the notes of a short melody. When intervals are increased from 1.5 to 2 sec, there is no longer a melody but only isolated notes. Another example can be given, using a two-syllable word. Take the semantic unit *bitter*. If there is a small interval between *bit* and *ter*, the two syllables are still identified as one word, until the interval reaches 1.5–2 sec; at that moment, the two syllables are perceived independently and they can only be linked together by rehearsal of the first syllable. This 2-sec duration corresponds to the maximum temporal field, or to the perceptible duration, when there are only two stimulations. The same limit between the onset and the offset of the stimulation applies to continuous stimulations. Perception of time is thus restricted to 2 sec when there are only one or two events. This chapter will deal with facts that range within that duration, as most of the work on succession and duration use only one or two stimulations.

To limit the study to this duration prevents us from confusing two different modes of apprehension: direct estimation (when perception is involved) and estimation based on events stored in memory (when longer durations intervene). If the results obtained by different authors are often at variance, it is probably due to the fact that, in the same research, durations of less than a second and durations of several seconds were used.

Having said this, it has to be noted that there is no functional hiatus between perception of time and estimations based on memory in our life.

Information processing and, consequently, temporal information processing is a continuous process beginning with the recording of information and ending with this information being stored in long-term memory, but at the different levels of processing there are specific questions that arise and specific processes that play a role.

The distinction between a duration perceived on the basis of immediate data and a duration estimated on the basis of data stored in memory is found in contemporary work. Michon (1967b), for instance, spoke of time perception for short durations ranging approximately from 50 msec to a few seconds: "As long as it is not possible to specify the process involved in the estimation of short intervals, we may define time perception operationally as the ability of a subject to behave differentially in response to intervals of various durations, while experimentally noticeable use of cognitive, physiological or motor cues is absent [p. 3]." Ornstein (1969) distinguished four modes of time experience: (a) the present, short-term time, with the perception of short intervals and rhythm or timing; (b) duration, the past, long-term memory; (c) temporal perspective; (d) simultaneity and succession. He was personally interested in duration, for which he proposed the "storage-size" hypothesis. The same distinction was made by Miller and Johnson-Laird (1976) who proposed to speak of "now" to characterize the experience of short intervals of time such as the phenomenal present or the detection of rhythm.

Toda (1975) also distinguished two subsystems in the cognition of time. The primary system is always active, like respiration. It corresponds to the succession of our perceptions and acts and regulates our continuous adaptations, which very often have a temporal dimension. Temporal information is not stored in memory when it corresponds to expectations. "Only at occasional expectation as well as no expectation, the primary system transfers the task up to a higher cognitive subsystem for a real processing [Toda, 1975, p. 317]." The second system, which deals with stored information, has to solve temporal problems (embeddings of succession and durations, for instance) that the primary system cannot solve.

II. THE PERCEPTION OF SUCCESSION

Psychologists try to elucidate under what conditions succession becomes a perceptual datum. Succession that is reconstructed on the basis of mnemonic data (succession of the days of the week, seasons, personal or social events) has to be distinguished from succession that is perceived (i.e. when two or more stimulations are perceived as successive while still belonging to the same psychological present).

A. Unimodal Stimulations Located in the Same Place: The Critical Threshold of Fusion

Two successive stimulations of the same nature, be they visual, auditory, or tactile, that excite the same sensory receptors are perceived as combined into a unique stimulus below a threshold, which is called the critical threshold of fusion. Between succession and fusion, a continuous stimulation is perceived: flicker for vision, flutter for audition, vibration for touch. The critical frequency of fusion depends upon the intensity and duration of the stimulation. It is about 10 msec for audition and touch and 80–100 msec for vision (Piéron, 1952).

B. Unimodal Stimulations Spatially Adjacent

1. APPARENT MOVEMENT

When two successive stimulations (visual or tactile) occur in spatially close places, there is an interval where succession is no longer perceived, but where simultaneity is not yet perceived. The two stimulations become a continuous movement, called *apparent movement*, that goes from the place of the first temporal stimulation to the place of the second. This movement is not a laboratory phenomenon, it is the basis of perception of movement in films, in which movement is due to the projection of successive still views at the rate of 18 or 24 frames per second (stroboscopic movement).

Temporal limits of apparent movement are defined by Korte's law (1915) and depend upon the intensity and distance of the stimulations. Wertheimer (1912) considered that an interval of 60 msec between stimulations yielded optimal movement, a 200-msec interval giving rise to the perception of a clear succession. Perception of apparent movement is facilitated when two successive stimulations have a good continuity. It is also facilitated by a good figure–ground contrast (Pollack, 1966). It is improved with brief stimuli (shorter than 100 msec) and when the stimulus onset asynchrony is from 80 to 140 msec. When stimuli are presented for longer durations, the perception of apparent movement is better with an interstimulus interval (ISI) of 0 msec (Kahneman & Wolman, 1970).

The Gestalt school, which based its theory on the study of apparent movement, considered that this phenomenon revealed the existence of cortical short circuits. This hypothesis was rejected when the proof was given that apparent movement could occur in dichoptic vision with a stimulation of the right field of the right eye and the left field of the left eye (Piéron, 1933).

2. THRESHOLD FOR SIMULTANEITY

When successive stimulations become temporally closer (30 msec), they are perceived as simultaneous. Perceptual simultaneity has to be distinguished from objective, or physical, simultaneity.

Determining a threshold for simultaneity poses interesting problems when stimulations are integrated into a perceptual unit.

a. PERCEPTION OF SHAPE. If four dots corresponding to the apexes of a diamond are lighted successively, they are perceived as being simultaneous and delineating a shape for a maximum duration of 125 msec. Below this value, the relative duration of flashes and intervals is of no importance (Lichenstein, 1961). Within the range of 100–150 msec, if two identical superimposed and inversed triangles are projected, they are perceived as a hexagon, even though the stimuli have not been repeatedly presented, contrary to Lichenstein's conditions (Fraisse, 1966).

McFarland (1965a) found that integration of a form's line and angle parts requires different amounts of time in the same range. When the outline of a triangle is presented with line parts in sequence and interline intervals are varied, the threshold for succession in 84 msec. When the same form is presented with angle parts in sequence, the limiting interval for simultaneity is 71 msec.

D.A. Allport (1970) studied the paradoxical case of a white radius on a black disk that moves continuously and uniformly. If this area is lighted stroboscopically at a rate of more than 10 flashes per second, a set of light radii turning together as a group delineating a sector is perceived. Consequently, radii are perceived as simultaneous. It is possible to measure the duration for which this phenomenon occurs. Allport has shown that this duration depends upon the frequency and intensity of the stroboscopic lighting. It varies from 50 to 100 msec and the lower the intensity, the longer the duration seems.

b. PERCEPTION OF LETTERS. If six letters forming a word are successively presented, provided the total duration of presentation does not exceed 86 msec (Hylan, 1903), succession cannot be discerned. The same observation is true when the letters are presented normally, from left to right, or in the reverse order, from right to left. However, with more refined methods, McFarland (1965b) found that the threshold for succession was 57 msec with the normal order of presentation of three letter words and 64 msec with other orders of presentation.

Fraisse (1966, 1968) found that two groups of three letters presented in succession were perceived as being simultaneous when the total duration (from the onset of the first group to the outset of the second one) does not exceed 100 msec. With an interstimulus interval (ISI), the threshold is a bit lower. Eriksen and Collins (1967) superimposed two boards by means of a two-field tachistoscope. Each board had a random set of dots that when grouped together formed a meaningless syllable. The integration into one syllable was possible with a duration of 75–100 msec.

C. Heteromodal Stimulations

When two different stimulations (for example, sound and light) excite the senses, it becomes difficult to speak of perceived simultaneity. There is a zone of temporal indistinctness in which the subject is incapable of deciding whether stimuli are simultaneous or successive.

The old question of personal equation falls within this perspective. In his complication experiment, Wundt (1874) found that the error in localizing the position of a hand on a clock when a sound occurs could reach 100 msec by over- or underestimation. Hirsh and Fraisse (1964) found that the threshold for succession (and order as well) was about 60 msec with naive subjects. However, subjects trained for several weeks can lower their threshold to 20 msec, as Hirsh and Sherrick (1961) have shown. Trying to elucidate the reasons for this difference, Gengel and Hirsh (1970) suggested that Hirsh and Sherrick's results were due first to the repeated presentation of the same pair of stimuli before each response, and second to the fact that during training the progress of the subjects was especially important during the first few days. With trained subjects and with presentation of only one pair of stimuli before each response, the threshold was 30 msec.

From the results presented in Section II,A,B, and C, it is clear that the threshold for succession varies from 20 to 100 msec. It is all the higher when stimuli form a perceptual unit (e.g., a continuous sound, a geometric form, a word).

D. Temporal Order

Hirsh (1959) and Hirsh and Sherrick (1961) admitted that the threshold for succession may vary with the sensory modalities of stimulations, but found that the threshold for detecting the order of two stimulations is always 20 msec with trained subjects, for unimodal as well as for heteromodal stimuli (two sounds differing in pitch, two lights or two tactile stimulations spatially close, or a sound and a light). This threshold can be even lower when stimuli are sufficiently similar. Liberman, Harris, Kinney, and Lane (1961) found a threshold of 12 msec for the beginning of two formants in language.

E. Explanatory Systems

Two main hypotheses attempt to explain the results mentioned above. The first one is called the *psychological-moment hypothesis*, according to which data would be organized by a scanning process, and stimulations perceived in a short duration would not be differentiated. The second hypothesis is based on perception latencies.

1. THE PSYCHOLOGICAL-MOMENT HYPOTHESIS

W. James referred to this in his *Principles of Psychology* (1890). According to this hypothesis, which was taken up later by Wiener (1949) and developed by Stroud (1956), a scanning apparatus with a specific frequency would be set in the brain. This hypothesis assumes that all events perceived within a same psychological moment—the duration of which varies between 50 and 200 msec—are not temporally differentiated. Succession would be perceived only when two stimulations occurred at different moments. The results we have presented can be interpreted in these terms, and the following result supports this hypothesis particularly well: If the frequency of a visual, or auditory, or tactile stimulation exceeds a certain limit and does not yet reach the critical threshold of fusion, the apparent frequency does not increase beyond 8–12 stimulations per second. According to this hypothesis, several stimulations are integrated into a unit of which the period would be 80 msec (Bartley, Nelson, & Ranney, 1961; White, 1963). Some authors attempted to find a neurological support to this hypothesis, and considered to have found it in the following phenomena: The variability of cortical stimulations, the cerebral rhythms, and the mechanisms of synchronization, more particularly the α rhythm to which many studies have been devoted. The duration period of the α rhythm is about the same as that of the psychological moment. Some studies have indeed found a correlation between performance in tasks of discrimination of succession and frequency of α rhythms (Kristofferson, 1967; Murphee, 1954). Kristofferson (1967) and Kristofferson and Allan (1973) related the periodic process that determined the quantum of the psychological moment to an attention-switching theory. According to this theory, the discrimination of the successiveness of two events that are in separate channels is limited by the time required to switch attention from one channel to the other. The probability of this switching would be 1 when duration is equal to a quantum of time. Kristofferson and Allan claim that the same predictions could be made on the basis of their recent quantal onset–offset theory (see Section III,C,3) that refers to psychophysical time.

The hypothesis of the psychological moment is very appealing. It has also been proposed in order to explain the perception of duration (see Section III,C,4). Unfortunately, no physiological process has been identified. Depending upon authors and conditions, it would vary between 50 and 100 msec.* This hypothesis leads to predictions that do not differ radically from those derived from the analysis of stimulations latencies.

2. THE PERCEPTION-LATENCY HYPOTHESIS

This hypothesis takes into account the fact we have just evoked. If it is useful to relate the perception of succession and the duration of the physical interval between two stimulations, we have good reasons to think that the basis of perceptual judgment is the order of the stimulations and the interval between their arrival in the cortex. In other words, the latency of sensory processes has to be taken into account. For instance, a tactile stimulation of the thigh has to come 20–35 msec before the stimulation of the forehead in order to be judged as simultaneous (Klemm, 1925). This value is about the same as the difference in the duration of transmission of two influxes. The same problem arises every time a judgment on the succession of two sensations having a different latency has to be given; for example, when one has to make a judgment about the succession of a sound and a light. If simple reaction time is considered as an index of latencies, auditory reaction time is 40 msec shorter than visual reaction time. If then a sound and a light are simultaneously presented, the visual sensation will be posterior to the auditory sensation. It has been shown that when a sound is followed by a light, the threshold for succession and order is 60 msec and when a light is followed by a sound it varies from 90 to 120 msec (Hirsh & Fraisse, 1964). However, precise values of the threshold for order cannot be deduced from the differences in duration of reaction times (Gibbon & Rutschmann, 1969; Rutschmann & Link, 1964). This is not surprising, since the processes involved in judgments of succession and reaction times are different. However Rutschmann (1966) has explained the order of succession between two visual stimulations (one of them being central, the other peripheral) by the difference in latency between these two stimulations. The fact that perception of order depends on sensory latencies does not explain the irreducible limit of 20 msec that Hirsh and Sherrick (1961) found with unimodal stimulations for which latencies have no influence.

Consequently, Sternberg and Knoll (1973) hypothesized a decision

---

* The fact that the threshold for temporal acuity is sometimes lower is not a counterargument. After intensive practice, the subjects may find indices that are independent of the threshold for succession as such.

mechanism that would make a judgment on the basis of the order of arrival of stimuli, following decision rules that would have their own variability. If $\Delta(x, y)$ is the variability of two stimuli, x and y, and if $R_x(y)$ and $R_y(x)$ are the latencies (difference between the time of the stimulation and the time of the arrival in the brain) of each stimulus, the psychometric function of the order of succession $D(x, y) = R_x(y) - R_y(x) + \Delta(x, y)$ gives the probability of perceiving the order of two stimulations as a function of their physical gap. This function is expressed "as the convolution of the decision function with the distribution of arrival latencies differences between channels" [Sternberg & Knoll, 1973 p. 641]. The 20-msec threshold would correspond both to the latencies variability (when they have about the same value) and to the variability in the use of the decision criteria.

This model based on latencies permits us to take into account a variable that we have not yet mentioned, although it had an important role in the development of this question. What we have in mind is the law of prior entry thoroughly investigated by Wundt and Titchener and taken up later by Piaget in the law of centration. All conditions being otherwise equal, if two stimuli are presented, the stimulus to which attention is given seems to precede the other. It is a well-known phenomenon that has also been established in the auditory–tactile complication experiment (Stone, 1926) and in experiments with auditory stimuli (Ladefoged & Broadbent, 1960). According to Stone, this attentional bias can reach 46 msec. It is legitimate to think that the attention given to a stimulus reduces the latency, which then does not have to be considered as an invariable physiological datum.*

This hypothesis, together with other similar lines of reasoning, led some authors to claim the existence of a decision center. Efron (1963a,b), Corwin and Boynton (1968), Umilta, Stadler, and Trombini (1973), by measuring thresholds for succession of two visual stimuli presented dichoptically, have concluded that this center should be located in the dominant hemisphere.

Swisher and Hirsh (1972) threw a new light on this issue by comparing normal subjects with left-brain-damaged (aphasics) and right-brain-damaged patients. They measured the threshold for judgments of order of visual and auditory stimulations after repeated presentations of a same pair. Within a pair, stimuli were presented either in the same place or in a different one (to both ears with auditory stimulations).

Results varied with the sense modality, the location of stimuli, the

---

* Attention is either spontaneous (one stimulus is more attractive than the other), or voluntary. In most work on the threshold for succession, the effect of attention was not controlled. It is probably for this reason that similar experiments produced different results.

stimuli features, and the location of the lesion. Swisher and Hirsh have admitted that these results do not support the conclusion of Hirsh and Sherrick (1961), who suggested "some kind of time-organizing system that is both independent of and central to the sensory mechanisms [p. 431]." They found that deficits were more important in fluent aphasics with pairs of auditory stimuli, especially when given to the same ear. These subjects also had deficits with visual stimuli having the same location. Nonfluent aphasics present the same kind of deficit, but to a less important degree. Dextrally brain-damaged patients had slight deficits, but it was particularly difficult for them to order two sounds (one sound to each ear) differing in pitch. Swisher and Hirsh agree with Efron (1963a, b) that the left hemisphere is particularly concerned with stimuli that occur in the same place. Lesions of the temporal lobe—named appropriately—are probably responsible for the deficits of fluent aphasics. Several studies have also shown that the more posterior the lesion, the more important are the deficits in the ordering of visual stimulations.

Fraisse (unpublished) analyzed the variations of the threshold for order of a sound and a light in brain-damaged patients of various types. For some patients, the threshold was very high (from 200 to 800 msec), and there was no relationship between this deficit and the localization of the lesion. The only correlation found was between the extent of the lesion and the threshold value. Evidently, the larger the lesion, the more likely the possibility of damage in a precise center. But it is also reasonable to think that the larger the lesion, the more difficult it becomes to establish a temporal relationship between two sensations that correspond to distant zones of reception.

F. Conclusion

We have reviewed the different cases in which one passes from simultaneity (or continuity) to succession. Each case involves differing processes (inertia effect in the critical visual threshold of fusion; pregnance of cognitive type that increases the threshold for succession, etc.). But the threshold for succession is always at least 50 msec.

The present state or research in the field does not permit us to decide whether this threshold depends on a psychological moment or on the variability of latencies and the establishment of relationships between sensory information. The second hypothesis has the advantage of explaining various situations, but it does not account for the cases in which several successive stimulations are perceived as simultaneous (as in the experiments by Lichenstein, Fraisse, Allport, etc.).

III. THE PERCEPTION OF DURATION

Perhaps because time is a faint stimulus, as Pavlov liked to say, or because in the field of successiveness we cannot go backwards to check an estimation or a comparison (contrary to what is possible in the spatial field), the studies dealing with duration give results that depend very much on the method of investigation.

A. Methods

Four main methods are used in the study of the perception of duration: verbal estimation, production, reproduction, and comparison. These methods may be used for the study of both brief and long durations.

1. ESTIMATION AND PRODUCTION

Both methods use conventional time units. The estimation method requires that the subject, after being presented a stimulus having a certain duration, states its length in terms of time units (hours, minutes, seconds, or tenths of a second, depending on the range of durations that are used). Goldstone and his collaborators, since 1957, have used a variant of this method: they ask subjects to state whether a duration is longer or shorter than one second.

The production method requires that the subject produce a duration equal to a standard stimulation expressed in time units. Generally, correlations between production and estimation performances are negative, which is easy to understand. If a duration is overestimated, for instance, if a 5-sec duration is estimated as having a duration of 4 sec, it may be predicted that the production of 4 sec will result in a duration of 5 sec. This is particularly evident when the same subjects are asked to use both methods in the course of the same session, as in Carlson and Feinberg's study (1970).

2. REPRODUCTION AND COMPARISON

The two methods require that subjects compare two successive durations. With the method of reproduction, the subject reproduces a duration equal to a standard stimulation given previously. With the method of comparison, the subject has to say if the second duration is shorter or longer than the first.

For the past 10 years, the method of comparison has been increasingly used with an experimental paradigm that makes the task very similar to a signal-detection task. The subject has to compare several times two different durations that are hardly discriminable. It is then possible to compute the probability of correct responses. These comparisons may be done in two different conditions: the forced-choice (FC) condition, in which two stimuli are presented, and the single-stimulus (SS) condition, in which, after a phase of presentation, only one stimulus is presented. The former type of training may lead to systematic errors that are named time errors.

3. COMPARATIVE STUDY OF THE METHODS

a. ESTIMATION, PRODUCTION, AND REPRODUCTION METHODS. Estimation, production, and reproduction methods have been used by many authors. Hawkes, Bailey, and Warm (1961) compared the three methods, using durations varying from .5 to 4 sec for three sense modalities: touch, audition, and vision. Within a session, a subject used one method for one sense modality. The analysis of variance yielded a slightly significant difference between modalities, but no differences between methods. The correlation (Spearman's ρ) between production and estimation is $-.78$. Treisman (1963) compared methods of production and reproduction, using durations from .25 to 3 sec. He found a constant positive error with both methods: 10.8% with the reproduction method, 21.4% with the production method. The higher percentage of errors was observed observed with durations of .25 sec; errors decreased slowly with higher durations. Relative variability decreased when passing from short to long durations and was higher with the production method than with the reproduction one.

McConchie and Rutschmann (1971), with durations from .3 to 1 sec, compared the three methods. At the end of a session, the constant error was -5% with the reproduction method, -12.8% with the estimation method, and $+35.3\%$ with the production method. The differences among methods were thus quite significant, even though the experimenter introduced anchors (i.e., models—durations of 250 and 1200 msec were presented and explicitly labeled at various times throughout the experiment). Intrasubject variability was about 13% for reproduction, 20% for estimation, and 21% for production. Intersubject variability had approximately the same value. The reliability of measures was about the same for the three methods (.60 to .70). The correlation between reproduction and estimation was $+.03$, between reproduction and production $+.15$. There was a slight negative correlation between estimation and production $(-.31)$.

Some authors were interested in the variations of judgments in the course of trials. McConchie and Rutschmann (1971) found that estimations became shorter, productions became longer, and reproductions remained the same in the course of repetitions. Carlson and Feinberg (1970) compared the three methods by studying the variations of judgments throughout 10 successive sessions. They found that the results were very different when the same subjects used different methods and when the subjects differed. When the same subjects used the three methods, estimations decreased at the beginning and then increased up to an asymptote. The evolution of productions was very symmetrical (the correlation between estimation and production was −.86). If one considers that the task of reproduction corresponds to the estimation of a first duration followed by the production of a second duration, one may predict the evolution of reproductions as a function of estimations and productions. The results supported this hypothesis: Reproductions were rather stable throughout the sessions. The results were quite different when different groups of subjects were submitted to the three methods. With three independent groups of subjects, there was a clear increase in productions and a low decrease in estimations, whereas reproductions were stable and could not be predicted from estimations and productions. It must be noted that this study used durations varying from 1 to 10 sec, but that, unfortunately, the influence of durations was not analyzed. Warm, Foulke, and Loeb (1966) have studied the influence of successive productions using durations of .5, 3, 7, and 15 sec. They found a significant effect with 7 and 15 sec. but no significant effect with .5 and 3 sec. The method of reproduction gives the most stable results, provided that the standard duration is given before each response. If such a precaution is not taken, reproduction responses lengthen, as Falk and Bindra (1954), Brown and Hitchock (1965), and Von Sturmer (1966) have shown. It is generally admitted that when the standard duration is not given between judgments, the situation becomes monotonous and the subject has fewer and fewer time-relevant cues. Consequently, as the experiment progresses, the subject gives longer durations. Using a 5-sec duration, Von Sturmer (1966) found a significant tendency for the responses of reproduction to become longer throughout the sessions, and confirmed the role of monotony. When using an alerting stimulus (sound or light) in the course of trials, thus increasing the subject's vigilance, he observed that reproductions on alerted trials were significantly shorter than those on nonalerted trials.

b. TIME-ORDER ERROR. Reproduction and comparison imply that the stimulus to be reproduced or compared follows another one. As early as 1860, Fechner mentioned the influence of a time-order error related to the order in which two stimuli to be compared are presented. The influence of time-order errors has been shown to appear with different sense modal-ities, as Woodworth (1938) noticed. In most cases, time-order errors are negative (i.e., the second stimulus is overestimated). With the method of reproduction, the second stimulus is shorter than the first; with the com-parison method, the point of subjective equality is reached when the second stimulus is shorter than the first.

Time-order errors also intervene in the perception of durations, but the influence of this variable is not well established, since two effects have frequently been confused: the effect of the interval between stimulations (ISI) and the effect of the range of durations employed in one experiment. The range of stimulations has an influence on several sense modalities, and this effect results in the overestimation of smaller stimuli and the underestimation of larger stimuli. This effect, which also plays a role in the estimation of duration, as many studies have shown, may be explained by Helson's theory (1964) of adaptation level. The second stimulus is compared not with the first stimulus, but with a weighed mean of the stimuli employed. Thus, if the first stimulus is higher than the mean, the error is negative, and if it is smaller, the error is positive. This effect is most certainly related to the succession of stimuli, and it has to be distinguished from the time-order effect, which can be studied as such only in experiments where only one standard stimulus is presented to the same subject. Very few authors have taken this factor into ac-count.

The range of the ISI used in the same experiment may also play a role, especially with a rather long ISI. With brief durations (less than 500 msec) and a short ISI (up to 2–3 sec), Small and Campbell (1962), Carbotte (1973), Allan, Kristofferson, and Rice (1974) did not find any effect of the ISI. Allan et al. (1974) used two methods of comparison: the forced-choice (FC) and the single-stimulus (SS) conditions (Section, III,A,1). Both methods yielded the same results and the authors have suggested that in the FC condition the subjects have the same behavior as in the SS condition—they judge each stimulus separately as long or short. Con-sequently, the ISI would not play a role. But perhaps this explanation only applies to repeated comparisons of two identical durations.

The hypothesis most frequently admitted for explaining this error, Fechner's *fading image hypothesis* [which Köhler (1923) called the *fading trace hypothesis*], does not apply to rather long intervals (Ornstein, 1969). This hypothesis is very controversial because it does not explain the positive or null time errors that are sometimes observed. Some authors have tried to explain time errors by referring to after effects (Peak, 1940; Huppert & Singer, 1967) but they still give description instead of an explanation.

B. Perception of Duration and Content of Stimulations

Since duration is always a duration of a stimulus, it must be asked whether or not the nature of stimuli has an influence on perceived duration.

The variety of possible stimuli, of experiments performed, and of criteria used only allows us to present a provisional evaluation of the results obtained in this field.

1. INFLUENCE OF SENSE MODALITIES

Duration is a perceptual dimension of all our sensations. It is a well-established fact that this dimension is very imprecise in gustatory and olfactory sensations, whereas precise perceptions are possible with auditory, visual, and tactile sensations.

a. THE SENSITIVITY OF DISCRIMINATION. Goodfellow (1934) computed the variance of the differential fraction for auditory, visual, and tactile stimulations, using durations of about 1 sec, and obtained the following results:

Audition	6%
Touch	8%
Vision	10%

Most authors agree that auditory and tactile perceptions are more precise than visual ones.

b. APPARENT DURATION. All conditions being otherwise equal, an auditory stimulation seems longer than a visual one. Many studies (Behar & Bevan, 1961; Goldstone & Lhamon, 1974) have confirmed this result for a 1-sec duration. However, Loeb, Behar, and Warm (1966) found that correlations between median judgments of durations in the visual and auditory modalities were .70 (the subjects rated the duration of each stimulus on an 11-category verbal scale), and correlations between judgments of adjacent durations within each sense modality were .79. Inter- and intramodality correlations were very significant and of about the same value. These results support the hypothesis that perceptual judgments depend on a central process and that the conditions in which the input is delivered introduce only a systematic difference. On the other hand, the apparent duration of tactile and auditory stimuli do not differ (Ehrensing & Lhamon, 1966).

c. INFORMATION TRANSMITTED. Lhamon and Goldstone (1974) have found that auditory stimulations transmit more information (1.6 bit) than visual stimulations (1.20 bit), with durations varying from 150 to 1950 msec. However, this difference is observed with filled durations only (see Section III,C,2). This result reflects the sensitivity of discrimination— filled auditory signals are better discriminated than filled visual ones.

2. INFLUENCE OF THE CONTENT OF STIMULATIONS

a. FILLED AND EMPTY INTERVALS. Specialists of time have always been interested in this opposition. A filled interval is defined as the duration of a homogeneous stimulus (e.g., sound or light) as opposed to a duration defined by two boundaries (e.g., two clicks or two flashes). The boundaries do not introduce any systematic effect when they are brief, but when this is not the case, the effect of the duration of boundaries is added to the effect of the interval.

It should be noted that there are systematic interindividual differences. Some subjects overestimate filled durations, whereas others overestimate empty durations (Triplett, 1931; Gavini, 1959). Using an original method, Craig (1973) found some unexpected results. He presented subjects with pairs of filled stimuli of equal duration. The pairs of stimuli were vibrotactile, auditory, or visual. The subjects were required to adjust the interval between two stimuli until it appeared equal in duration to the duration of the first stimulus. With durations varying from 100 to 1200 msec. the subjects set an "unfilled interval too long by a constant amount [p. 101]" This constant was 596 msec for vibrotactile stimuli, 657 msec for auditory stimuli, and 436 msec for visual stimuli. This overestimation of empty time as compared to filled time does not seem to be due to the method, since this error is not observed when the subjects compare a pair of sounds to an interval filled with a white noise of the same apparent intensity.

Craig wondered whether this constant error of 500–600 msec would not correspond to the perceptual constant (Fraisse, 1963), which represents the time necessary to pass from one perception to another. Our interpretation is rather that the empty interval plays the role of the ground relative to the form constituted by the pair of stimuli. As Schultze (1908) has shown, a duration of at least 600 msec is necessary to perceive the time between two stimuli as an interval (see also Michon, 1967a, b). This ground effect would disappear when three filled intervals are presented.

b. STIMULATION INTENSITY. The more intense a stimulation, the longer the duration perceived. This is a trivial observation in the case of very brief stimulations, since there is integration of duration and intensity. However, G. Oléron (1952) observed the same phenomenon with durations of 350–1400 msec. Studies from the Stockholm laboratory have shown that the apparent duration increased as the logarithm of intensity for electrical (Ekman, Frankenhaeuser, Levander, & Mellis, 1966), vibro-

tactile (Ekman, Frankenhaeuser, Berglund, & Waszak, 1969), and auditory (Berglund, Berglund, Ekman, & Frankenhaeuser, 1969) stimulations. This latter work revealed that, with intensities varying from 57 to
104 dB, the slope of apparent duration noticeably increased when the
duration varied from 50 msec to 500 msec. Zelkind (1973), using durations
of 500–8000 msec, found comparable results with four different methods
(estimation, comparison, production, and reproduction).

c. FREQUENCY OF STIMULATIONS. Since the work of Hall and Jastrow
(1886), it has been admitted that a duration divided by multiple stimulations is estimated as being longer than a duration that is not divided. Most
studies observed this result with durations varying from 4 to 10 sec.
Fraisse (1965), who compared this phenomenon to the Oppel–Kundt
visual illusion, has established that the maximum effect of frequency
appears with a 2 Hz cadence for a 4-sec duration. The work of Matsuda
and Matsuda (1974, 1976) has not confirmed this result. They found that
the higher the frequency, the longer the duration perceived. The authors
admit, however, that with children, systematic effects are scarce, and
with adults the effects are irregular.

  With shorter durations, Buffardi (1971) and Thomas and Brown (1974)
have shown that divided durations are perceived as longer than empty
durations, and this effect increases with the number of divisions (i.e., with
their frequency). Buffardi used a method of comparison with auditory,
visual, and tactile modalities. The duration of about 1 sec was divided by
zero to five stimuli (i.e., there were from two to seven stimulations,
including the boundary stimulations). Thomas and Brown used durations
varying from 800 to 1600 msec, with three intercalated stimuli. Similar
results were found in the two experiments, whether the intervals were
regular or not. Buffardi, referring to Ornstein's (1969) model, suggested
that this result was due to the increase in the quantity of information, or in
the mental input. In Thomas and Brown's model, each subinterval is
separately encoded and the reproduced interval is the addition of subin-
tervals. This effect of temporal division should be compared to the effect
found by Mo (1971, 1974, 1975). When two stimuli are presented through a
tachistoscope during .5 sec, the stimulus that has more dots (five dots, as
opposed to three dots or one dot) seems to be longer. With the method of
comparison (Mo, 1974) the effect is very clear; it is not as strong with the
method of reproduction (Mo, 1975). Mo also refers to Ornstein's (1969)
model and to the content of memory stage.

  The explanation of these results in terms of interaction between the
perceived duration and the time necessary for processing information is
discussed further in Section III,C,4.

d. SPACE AND VELOCITY. The physical duration of a movement is proportional to the covered distance and inversely proportional to the velocity. Does this fundamental relationship hold for duration, space, and perceived velocity? This difficult problem has given rise to many studies. In considering these, it is important that static effects be distinguished from dynamic effects.

If empty durations are defined by light dots separated by a certain distance, the apparent duration is longer when the distance between stimuli is larger. This effect is not very important: If the covered distance is multiplied by 10, the increase in apparent duration is about 12%. Abbe (1936) named this effect the S effect and Cohen, Hansel, and Sylvester (1955) called it the Kappa effect. It also appears with tactile stimuli (Suto, 1952). It is symmetrical with the tau effect, lengthening the interval between two stimuli increases their apparent distance.

The Kappa effect is all the stronger as durations are briefer. It seems to decrease with the size of the visual angle corresponding to the distance. Sudo (1941) and Abbe (1971), using intervals bounded by the three apexes of the angles of the Müller–Lyer figure (Brentano's version) have shown that this effect was related to the perceived distance and not to the physical distance.

The experiments just mentioned prevented the production of an apparent movement by using long enough durations. In dynamic conditions, the space is delimited by the displacement of a moving stimulus. In this case, the duration is filled, and it is difficult to dissociate the space covered effect from the velocity factor.

Many studies have found that the perception of the duration of a movement is independent of space and velocity when s/v is constant. Several studies, however (Fraisse, 1962; Bonnet, 1968) have shown that the same duration was perceived as a little longer if space and velocity were increased two or three times. In other studies, (Matsuda, 1974) opposite results have been obtained: "The longer the physical path and velocity of a moving stimulus of constant duration, the lesser the duration of a comparison stimulus interval of constant spatial characteristics required to match the physical duration of the moving standard [p. 108]." A duration of 1500 msec is perceived as 20% shorter when space and velocity are multiplied by 3.

Matsuda studied this problem from a developmental point of view, working with groups of 6–7-year-olds and with 10-year-olds. The opposite effect was observed in the group of 6–7-year-olds: When space and velocity were multiplied by 3, there was about an 8% increase in apparent duration. Making the assumption that this procedure would create a cue-selection set, Matsuda used a 1500-msec duration in series where velocity was varied and distance kept constant and series where distance was varied and velocity kept constant. He observed that the velocity factor predominates in adults (faster velocity yielded a perception of less duration time), whereas in children the predominant factor is space (more space yielded a perception of more duration time), and velocity does not play an important role.

These studies explicitly refer to Piaget's (1970) and Fraisse's (1963) work on the comparison of the criteria used in the estimation and perception of time by children and adults. Piaget and Fraisse agree that in the perception of the duration of a movement very young children (under 6 years) are more sensitive to space than to velocity, but Piaget claims that for children, greater velocity led to long-duration perceptions, and that the reversal of this estimation would be characteristic of operational reasoning. Fraisse claims that in certain cases for younger children, greater velocities gave the impression of less time, but the main characteristic of children of that age is their inability to take into account the two cues of duration, especially when the information given by these cues is in contradiction (Fraisse & Vautrey, 1952). Children base their judgment on the most salient cues, and distance covered is one of them. In adults, the direct influence of space on the perception of duration would be predominant in static conditions in which time and space are the only perceptual data. When there is perception of velocity in addition, the influence of distance covered is less important than the effect of velocity (Newman & Lee, 1972).*

Psychophysicists of the Stockholm school have studied the interrelationships among scales of duration, space, and velocity. Svenson (1971) has verified that the equation $t = s/v$ is still valid when t, s, and v are estimated. In his experiment, the subjects were asked to estimate the duration, distance, and velocity of a moving object relative to a standard moving object that traveled 9 cm in 3 sec. For the three scales, the exponent had about the same value (.8), and there were very high correlations (.97) between the values of each parameter computed on the basis of the two other parameters and the direct empirical values. Results were obtained with durations varying from .5 to 8 secs., displacement of .8–9° angle, and velocity of 1.1–7.6°/sec.

---

* It should be noted that Cohen and Cooper (1962) have shown that if two parts of a long distance take the same physical time to be covered, the one which is longer and covered with the faster velocity seems to be the one that takes more time. In this case, more space ⇒ more time (and not, faster ⇒ less time). In this condition, it no longer concerns perception, and cognitive processes then become predominant. Could it be possible that cues of distance are more salient than cues of velocity?

C. Psychophysics of Perceived Durations

Psychophysical studies of time date back to the beginning of experimental psychology. However, very few unquestionable results were obtained, and this for several reasons. The early experiments were done with rather imprecise tools, their methodology was not very strict. In addition, the heterogeneity of durations was ignored. In other words, perceived durations were not differentiated from durations estimated by memory factors.

For these reasons, only the recent literature will be reviewed; in most cases, these studies deal with very short durations. Studies using durations of less than 100 msec (that is, durations below the critical duration) should be analyzed separately, since for such durations there is a reciprocal relationship between stimulus intensity and duration (Bloch's law). With these durations, it is very difficult to know whether duration is judged directly or indirectly (on the basis of the intensity of the perceived stimulus). However, it seems (cf. Allan & Kristofferson, 1974b) that confusion between duration and intensity only occurs with stimuli that are difficult to detect. Below the critical duration, differences in duration are perceptible, even when the intensity of the stimulus (visual or auditory, filled or empty) varies.

Taking into account the relationships between physical and perceived durations within the range of 100 msec–2 sec, three types of problems shall be distinguished.

1. SYSTEMATIC ERRORS AND THE INTERVAL OF INDIFFERENCE

As early as 1864, Höring found that short intervals were overestimated and long intervals underestimated. The notion of shortness or the length of intervals was based on introspective analyses. According to the studies by Vierordt (1868), Katz (1906), and Schultze (1908), three types of intervals can be distinguished from a phenomenal point of view: (a) Short intervals (less than 500 msec). Within that range, the succession of the two limits is perceived more easily than the duration of the interval; (b) Indifferent intervals (between 500 and 1000 msec), in which the limits and the interval form a unit; (c) Long intervals (from 1000 to 2000 msec), in which the perception of an interval predominates and it is difficult to bring the two limits within the same present.

Several studies have confirmed Höring's results concerning the overestimation of short intervals and the undersestimation of long ones, which implies the existence of an interval of indifference. But authors disagree about the duration of long and short intervals, and Bolton was right when he noted with surprise, as early as 1894, that, depending on the authors, the interval of indifference varied from .36 to 5 sec. Hollingworth (1909) and Helson's (1964) studies have provided good explanations for these fluctuations. In most psychophysical experiments there is an anchoring of estimates based on the central value of the stimuli employed. For example, Fraisse (1948a) found a point of indifference for 1.15 sec when he used durations varying from .2 to 1.5 sec, whereas it was 3.65 sec with durations varying from .3 to 12 sec. This anchoring effect can be eliminated if each subject estimates only one duration, as in Woodrow's (1934) experiment. He found a 6.2% overestimation of a 300-msec duration and a 2.1% underestimation of a 1200-msec duration with a 600-msec interval of indifference. With the same method, Stott (1935) found a 900-msec interval of indifference for filled durations.

We claim (Fraisse, 1963) that this interval of indifference has a direct relationship with the duration of the whole perceptual process. It would correspond to the continuation of two percepts with no overlapping and no interval.

2. DISCRIMINATION OF DURATIONS

How precise is the discrimination of duration? How does it change with the variations of durations? Is Weber's law—a classical reference—valid for durations? The results obtained in this domain have to be analyzed according to the methods employed.

a. METHOD OF REPRODUCTION. It is generally admitted that the measure of the discriminability of a stimulus is given by the variance of a series of reproductions. In the experiments previously mentioned, Woodrow (1934) obtained reliable results by asking different groups of subjects to reproduce different durations. He found the following values (ratio of the standard error to the mean):

Duration	Percentage
200 msec	10.3
600 msec	7.8
1000 msec	8.6
2000 msec	10.1
beyond 2000 msec–30 sec	16–17

From these values, it can be deduced that there is an optimum of discrimination for a 600-msec duration and that it decreases below and beyond this value. It could be argued that in this situation the motor factor has an influence. As we know, the natural tempo is about 600 msec. But it is difficult to know whether there is an interaction, and if this is the case, what is the cause and what is the effect?

b. COMPARISON OF TWO DURATIONS. The differential threshold is determined by presenting before or after a standard stimulus a series of smaller or larger stimuli. This threshold may be expressed in quartile deviation or in standard deviation.

Within the range of perceived durations, the results are homogeneous, as it may be seen in Fig. 1 that plots the results of the following authors:

Source	Year	Condition
Woodrow	1930	sounds, empty intervals
Stott	1933	sounds, filled intervals
Hawkes & Warm	1961	electric stimulations filled intervals
Small & Campbell	1962	sounds, filled intervals
Getty	1975	sounds, empty intervals

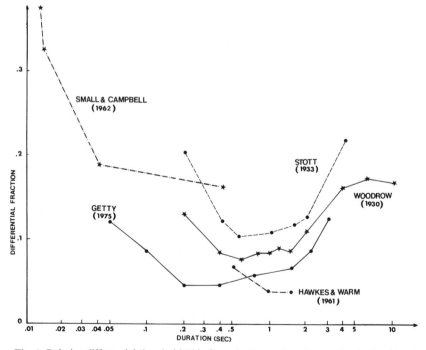

Fig. 1. Relative differential threshold (this figure is drawn after the results obtained by the authors quoted in the text).

Before comparing these results, it should be noted that these authors did not use the same algorithm in computing the differential fraction. In addition, the subjects did not receive the same amount of training. The striking point is that in all these studies, the differential fraction stayed nearly constant between 400 and 2000 msec. Getty (1975) found a constant differential fraction between 200 and 400 msec. All the authors mentioned above found a clear increase of this fraction with brief durations—less than 200 msec (see Small & Campbell, 1962). Studies that used durations longer than 2 sec (Woodrow, Stott, Getty) found an increase of the differential fraction. These results led some authors to claim that Weber's law was not valid for durations, except for those that fell within a narrow range. This range corresponds to the duration of perceived durations. If one considers the differential fraction without discarding very brief durations and durations longer than 2 sec, a U-shape distribution is found that corresponds to the curve obtained by applying Weber's law to various sensory dimensions.

Allan and Kristofferson (1974a) have contested these results in a series of publications. To understand the scope of their criticisms, it is necessary to recall that the signal-detection theory led to a new formulation of the problem of sensory discrimination. Creelman (1962), under the supervision of Tanner, was the first to apply the signal-detection theory to the study of duration. Instead of computing a discrimination threshold by varying ΔT, T being the standard, the probability of discriminating two durations T and $T + \Delta T$ for one or several values of ΔT is computed, with the forced-choice method or the single-stimulus method (Allan, Kristofferson, & Wiens, 1971; Kinchla, 1972). Generally, results are better with the forced-choice method than with the single-stimulus method, but Carbotte (1973) found identical results with both methods when using durations varying from 150 to 250 msec. These types of experiments require many sessions. Throughout each session, the subject compares two stimuli a hundred, if not a thousand, times, and he is informed about the correctness of each response.

With this method, Allan and Kristofferson (1974b) found that d' has a constant value for light flashes having durations of 70–1020 msec and for empty auditory intervals varying between 100 and 1600 msec. To interpret their data, they suggest a model of the discriminability of durations that does not depend on the duration itself, but rather on the variability of the latencies of the beginning and the end of the duration. It can be understood that these variabilities may indeed be independent of durations, but thousands of trials are necessary to obtain these results, and there is no real transfer from one duration to another—a surprising phenomenon according to the proposed model. Our personal feeling is that for each duration the subject succeeds in finding criteria for discriminating durations T and $t + \Delta T$ that are independent of the durations but specific of each time.

Very few authors have suggested quantitative models that explain the monotonic increase of discriminability with the increase of duration. Creelman (1962) hypothesizes that the subject makes his decision on the basis of an accumulation of pulses. The pulse source is a random emitter, "each with a fixed probability of firing at any time". The distribution of pulses for a given duration T would correspond to a normal distribution with mean and variance both equal to λT, where λ corresponds to the rate of pulse emission. Creelman suggests that when comparing two durations, T and $T + \lambda T$, the subject compares the number of pulses for each one. The basic formula for the detectability of a difference in duration is

$$d'_{1,2} = (2\lambda)^{1/2} \times \frac{\Delta T}{(2T + \Delta T)^{1/2}}.$$

This model has a purely hypothetical basis. Getty (1975) has compared predictions derived from this model to predictions derived from Weber's law. An adaptation of Creelman's model leads to the prediction of a constant decrease of the differential fraction with the increase of T, while Weber's law predicts, within a certain range, its constancy. Getty's conclusion is that Weber's law leads to better predictions than Creelman's model.

c. THE CHANNEL CAPACITY. The sensitivity of discrimination may be evaluated by the number of stimuli correctly identified in a set, using the method of absolute judgments. For instance, it is possible to ask the subject to identify a set of stimuli that were coded in a preliminary experiment and to measure the number of correct identifications. Is it then possible to estimate the quantity of information transmitted and the limit of the subject's capacity (considered as a channel of transmission)? This channel capacity is defined by the maximum number of stimuli that the subject identifies without error in a given set. The results obtained by Hawkes (1961a,b) with cutaneous electric stimulations, by Murphy (1966) and Bovet (1969) with filled auditory stimulations of 1000 Hz, and by Lhamon and Goldstone (1974) with empty and filled durations (with auditory and visual stimulations of approximately one second) are very concordant and enable us to claim that:

1. The channel capacity is about 1.5 bits for perceived durations (that is to say, a value equivalent to the information transmitted by three stimuli).
2. This capacity increases very slightly with the number of stimuli (i.e., with the entropy), but reaches a maximum when $N = 5$ or 6.

3. This capacity increases slightly with the range of stimuli. In Bovet's experiment (1974), with five stimuli, when the range of stimuli varies from 300 to 1650 msec, the number of bits of transmitted information is 2.63; with a range of 300–970 msec it is 1.74; and with a range of 970–1650 msec it is 1.64.
4. The channel capacity increases slightly with the amount of training (Hawkes, 1961a,b) and with the correction of the response after each trial (Murphy, 1966; Bovet, 1969).

However, it should be noted that even with all these possible increases, the channel capacity reaches two bits (that is to say, a transmitted information equivalent to four stimuli).* The only alphabet formed with durations, the Morse code, uses combinations of two durations: dot and line. Musical melodies are also based essentially on the interplay of two durations (Fraisse, 1974; see also Section IV,B,3).

3. THE PSYCHOPHYSICAL LAW

Since Fechner's work, there have been several attempts to establish the relationship between physical stimuli and their perceptual evaluation. This problem differs from the problem of discrimination in its principle. The discriminability of a 2-sec duration may be twice the discriminability of a 1-sec duration, but this does not imply that a 1-sec duration is perceived as exactly half of a 2-sec duration.

However, Fechner attempted to make one single problem of these two issues by postulating that the evaluation of stimulus intensity was based on the number of just noticeable differences (JND) that could be distinguished. If Weber's law is admitted (i.e., if one admits that the JND are doubled when the physical value is doubled), one admits a logarithmic relationship between physical and perceived data. This relationship relies on a postulate that could be verified only if a direct measurement of the intensity of sensations were possible. Since such a thing is not possible, subjective scales were constructed. These were of two types: interval scales and ratio scales.

Plateau (1872) invented the principle of interval scales; he proposed the method of bissection (which he called the *mean graduations*) that consisted of determining a sensation that was exactly equidistant from two other sensations. Edgell (1903) was the first to apply this method to the study of duration. He found that the value of the bissection was about the

---

* It is interesting to note that this limit disappears with a larger range of stimuli. With nine stimuli ranging from 500 to 5000 msec, subjects were able to identify 7.9 stimuli (Murphy, 1966). As Murphy remarked, subjects use counting and different cues of a cognitive type. This phenomenon underlines once more the difference between the range of perceived durations and longer durations.

value of the arithmetic mean of the two basic values, and not the geometric mean, as was predicted from Fechner's law.

Bovet (1968) has systematically applied this method, using durations varying from 300 to 1650 msec with auditory filled intervals of 1000 Hz; the results obtained from three subjects with a method of production through successive bissections are presented together with predictions based on a linear relationship:

Bissections	300	490	640	770	960	1110	1260	1420	1650
Predictions		470	640	810	980	1140	1310	1480	

It is clear that the results correspond to the predictions.

Ratio scales were devised by Stevens and applied to the study of duration. Within the range of perceived durations, two experiments using the method of fractionation judgments (determination of a stimulus that is half the standard stimulus) have led to the same results. In the expression $\psi = a\Phi^n$ the value of the exponent is 1.1 (Björkman & Holmkvist, 1960; Gregg, 1951). This value is probably a bit high because the upper limits of the standards were 4.8 and 7 sec. Gregg has shown that the overestimation of the values produced was especially clear with higher values. Michon (1967) has established that the exponent was .6 between 100 and 500 msec, and 1.1 between 500 and 2000 msec. Given the variability in the subjective measures, it is difficult to decide whether or not the exponent 1.1 differs significantly from 1; furthermore, Stevens (1967) gives this same value.

4. EXPLANATORY PROCESSES

How is duration evaluated? Duration is spontaneously taken into account in our behavior whenever it is relevant information: the duration of a signal, the time available to cross a street, the duration of phonemes on which meaning depends, the duration of notes in music that is the basis of rhythm and melody, etc.

Taking into account this cue implies that there exists a process capable of evaluating it. Spontaneous evaluation, the guide for our action, has to be distinguished from voluntary evaluation (judgment by methods of estimation, comparison, production, and reproduction). In a judgment task, the subject may use all possible cues provided by the situation. The problem is different when the durations to be judged encompass the perceptual range, and consequently require the intervention of memory processes.

The difference between judgment of perceived durations and longer durations is illustrated in a series of experiments based on the reproduction of approximately 1-sec durations. Children (Fraisse, 1948b) like the aged

(Lhamon, Goldstone, & Goldfarb, 1965) and mental patients (Dobson, 1954; Fraisse, 1952; Lhamon *et al.*, 1965) are capable of performing this task with success.* This perceptual capacity takes its full meaning when it is opposed to the difficulties, if not the incapacity, of the same subjects to evaluate longer durations. Five-year-olds have great difficulty in reproducing 20-sec durations: Either they do not understand the task, or they give very brief durations (they tap two times only) or even give random responses. Old-aged people keep the knowledge of durations, but differ very much from adults in their judgments of recent durations and in their temporal perspectives. Mental patients who are capable of perceiving 1 sec may suffer from temporal disorientations. The specific mechanisms of perceived durations differ from the mechanisms of longer durations.

a. THE BIOLOGICAL CLOCK. The most often proposed hypothesis to account for the perception of duration is the *biological-clock hypothesis*. A clock has two functions: On the one hand, it is the source of isochronous impulses that are counted in seconds, minutes, and hours by a mechanism; on the other hand, it is the apparatus that gives the time (i.e., that locates the present time in the nycthemeral rhythm).

When one speaks of a biological clock, one has in mind these two functions. Insofar as durations are concerned, the emphasis is put on the first function—that of a timer; when the nycthemeral cycle is referred to, the second function is emphasized. Many studies have put in evidence circadian cycles of our organism that provide conscious or unconscious cues about the time of the day. The most interesting studies were done in free-running conditions, on men totally isolated from the natural and social environment. They have shown the persistence of circadian rhythms, particularly the persistence of the rhythm of body temperature. To be more exact, the duration of the circadian rhythm becomes a little longer (about 25 hr). In most cases, behavior keeps its circadian structure (Colquhoun, 1971). Biological rhythms, or behavioral rhythms, provide us with cues for our temporal orientation in the course of the day (nutrition, sleep).

When perception of duration is concerned, the timer function of a clock is evoked. The first approach to this question consisted in trying to find its basis in biological systems having a brief period, such as heartbeats, respiration, and α rhythms. But no study succeeded in establishing a solid relationship between the frequency of these rhythms and the perception of duration [no more than with estimations of longer durations (see

---

* Here it is not a question of using the methods of estimation or production that require a reference to time units; such methods are based on a concept that children have not yet acquired.

Michon, 1967,b). Of course, the subject may explicitly count the number of respirations, or pulses, or even count at the cadence of one number per second to give himself a timer, but when one speaks of time perception, one refers to an unconscious mechanism of which the impulses would be counted by another unconscious mechanism. The mechanism would be the basis of our spontaneous behavior and of our judgments of duration.

What could be the time basis (i.e., the periodicity) of this clock? One could think of a very brief time basis, for instance, the msec. But no data support this hypothesis. A period of 100 msec, which corresponds to the perceptual moment, was put forward. The perceptual moment is meaningful for deciding phenomena of simultaneity (see Section II,E,1) but it has no physiological basis, and such a period seems to be too long to explain the perceptual discrimination of durations shorter than 100 msec. A fortiori, the 600-msec duration cannot be the time basis, since it is considered as the interval of indifference. Furthermore, we do not know anything about the possible mechanisms of this clock. Is there a neural formation that plays the role of a timer in a computer? Is it a specific property of neural tissues? Are they specific assemblings? Are they the fruit of heredity, or of experience?

The present knowledge in this field only allows us to make inferences based on the modifications of perception of time produced by biological modifications. François (1927) and Hoagland (1933) have shown that artificial or natural increases in body temperature increase the frequency of tapping in subjects asked to tap at the cadence of one tap per second. Temperature, then, could accelerate the speed of the clock.*

The effects of drugs confirm the effect of temperature; it has to be noted, however, that they were most often studied with longer durations than perceived durations (Goldstone, Boardman, & Lhamon, 1958). Barbituates produce overestimations and amphetamines underestimations, which may correspond to decelerations and accelerations of an internal clock.

b. MODELS. If several facts permit us to speak of a biological clock when long durations, such as a day, are concerned, nothing permits us to speak of a biological clock for the perception of brief durations. One may, however, hypothesize such a mechanism as a purely hypothetical process. On this basis it is possible to propose models and compare their predictions to observed behavior.

Creelman (1962) has proposed a theoretical decision model that ac-

* Pfaff (1968) found comparable effects with methods of production and estimation of 10–30-sec durations. Contradictory results obtained by modifying the external temperature are not relevant, since in such experiments the main factor is the discomfort of the situation (Lockhart, 1967).

counts for the discrimination of durations. We have already mentioned this concerning the psychophysical approach (see Section III,C,2). It is based on a "counting mechanism which operates on impulses generated over the relevant durations. The source of these impulses is assumed to be random. Limitations on performance come from uncertainty regarding the end points of the time interval and from limited memory [p. 582]."

Treisman's (1963) model hypothesizes regular impulses produced by a pacemaker, but the rate of the pulses depends on a specific arousal center. "A counter records the number of pulses arriving at a given point and transfers this measure to the store. Measures in the store can be retrieved by the comparator (decision mechanism) which compares retrieved measures with current counts made by the counter and selects responses for the response mechanisms to make [p. 19]."

It is also possible to postulate that the perceptual input is segmented into moments, each one corresponding to a mean number of pulses.

These models do not reveal anything about the counting mechanism itself. Counting is evidently a metaphor. What is the summation or integration process that forms the cues for judgments of duration?

c. DURATION OF INFORMATION PROCESSING. All the results mentioned in Section III,B,2 show that judgments of durations take into account not only specific cues, but also the content of durations. Roughly speaking, we could summarize the results concerning the content of duration as follows: From two stimuli, the one with the higher intensity, or the more divided (or the more extended), is perceived as longer than the one that has the same characteristics to a lesser degree. These effects are never proportional to the content of duration. A duration twice as intense is not perceived as twice as long. Duration is a basic stimulus modulated by its content. How could this be?

Modern psychologists attempt to explain the interaction of these two types of indices by information processing, which permits an analysis of the temporal stages of the perceptual act. Currently, the most elaborate theory is that of Thomas and Weaver (1975). It consists of relating processing time and perceived duration. "The key assumptions of this theory are that (1) in general temporal information is obtained from a timer (f processor) and a visual information (g processor). (2) Attention is shared between the f and g processors such as the output of the f processor becomes less reliable as the g processor captures more attention [p. 366]." In this case, the authors assume that the ratios between the processors are dependent on the range of durations.

It is true that the different stages of information processing consume a nonneglectible time. The sensory register can keep information during 200–300 msec. It has been established that the bigger the information load, the longer the processing of information necessary for recognition. But the difficult point is to define the quantity of information to be processed. Criteria of difficulty, complexity, familiarity and uncertainty do not necessarily lead to the same results.

Within durations shorter than 100 msec, the apparent duration depends upon several secondary factors (e.g., brightness of the stimulus, difficulty of identification). Thomas and Weaver (1975) used 40 and 80-msec durations and found that the duration of presentation of a three-letter word or of a meaningless syllable formed with the same letters is judged longer than an empty interval. If one considers that the perception of empty intervals depends only on a timer, then it should be admitted that the time spent in processing the letters is longer than the duration and independent of it. With the method of comparison, Avant, Lyman, and Antes (1975) found that a 30-msec stimulus seems all the briefer as it is more familiar. Familiarity would shorten the coding duration by a faster mobilization of the representation stored in memory. When there is a coding process, the duration of the visual information process would combine with the duration of the timing process and it can be admitted, following the proposal of Avant *et al.* (1975) that it is more difficult (and consequently takes longer) to recognize a meaningless syllable than a word.

Beyond 100 msec, within the limits of perception, the results mentioned above have shown that apparent duration increases with more stimulations. But, at least in the case of the number of elements (dots or letters), it has been verified that the duration of coding measured by the response latency (Fraisse et Smirnov, 1976) increased with the number of stimuli. In other cases, it is possible to think that there is an assimilation effect and, for instance, that a higher intensity causes the duration to be judged longer.

One result does not fit into this framework. Warm and McGray (1969), using the method of estimation, have shown that the presentation duration (1 sec) of short and frequent words was judged longer than that of long and infrequent words, the two variables adding their effect. They suggest that since the recognition threshold of short and frequent words is lower than the threshold of long and infrequent words, the quickest recognition of short and frequent words enables the subjects to be more attentive to the duration of presentation itself. They evoke the well-known fact that with long intervals a duration seems longer when attention is given to the duration itself, rather than to its content (Fraisse, 1963).

Referring again to Thomas and Weaver, it could be said that with such durations, timing (f) and visual information (g) processes are not combined. Furthermore, Thomas and Weaver explicitly postulate that the duration of visual information increases the duration of timing only when the first (f) is longer than the latter (g). The results obtained by Michon (1965) may be explained in the same way. He found that the timing of a series of responses at intervals of 2 sec did not depend on the uncertainty of stimuli (from one to six in number). On the other hand, he found the produced interval was all the shorter (i.e., overestimated) as the uncertainty of response was higher (from one to six). New experiments are necessary to relate in a more precise manner perception of duration and perception of the information processing. It is certain that when Ornstein uses the concept of cognitive storage size in order to explain the evaluation of durations longer than 3–4 sec, he is still in the perspective of information processing, but at a different quantitative and qualitative scale.

IV. THE PERCEPTION OF RHYTHM

To speak of rhythm is to speak of an ordering in temporal succession. Perceived rhythm (e.g., rhythm of the heart or of a waltz) in which ordering is given in a perceptual gestalt is contrasted to induced rhythm (e.g., the rhythm of tides, of days and nights, of seasons) in which ordering is reconstructed on the basis of experiences stored in memory.

To study rhythm is to investigate the relationship between objective conditions and the content of perceptions in which there is a temporal order.

A. Rhythmical Grouping

1. SUBJECTIVE GROUPING

A series of identical sounds (separated by equal intervals) heard for a certain time is spontaneously perceived as groupings of two, three, or four elements (Bolton, 1894). This phenomenon is also observed with light stimuli (Koffka, 1909). Wundt called it the *subjective rhythmization*. This phenomenon reveals that perception, and more particularly, the creation of an order within the succession, is an activity of the subject. It will be shown that this activity may be partly determined by objective orderings, but that the perception of a rhythm depends on the subject's activity.

It should be noted that subjective rhythm is created by the repetition of stimulations and gives rise to the repetition of a pattern in the course of time. This aspect will be specifically dealt with in Section IV,C.

a. CONDITIONS OF OCCURRENCE OF A SUBJECTIVE RHYTHM. Subjective rhythm occurs only when stimulations follow each other at a cadence such that they are distinct [115 msec, according to Bolton (1894)], but not so far apart that they are perceived as independent (1.58 sec, according to Bolton; from 1.5 to 2 sec, according to McDougall (1903) and Fraisse (1956) (see Section IV,B,1).

Within these limits, the most favorable interval seems to be about 400 msec, according to Meumann (1894). Fraisse (1956) found the same value when subjects were asked to produce spontaneous groupings of three or four tappings. This duration, however, depends on the extent of the grouping. Bolton (1894) has shown that the rate of stimuli preferred by the subjects when they make subjective groupings by two, three, or four is such that groupings have a duration of 1.59 sec for two sounds, 1.38 sec for three sounds, and 1.24 sec for four sounds. With a method of production of groupings, McDougall (1903) found that groupings by four and six were respectively 1.8 times and 2.2 times longer than groupings by two. Grouping is easier when the proximity of stimuli is greater.

b. Consequences of subjective grouping. Phenomenal changes in perception are associated with subjective grouping. The intervals between two successive groups seem to be longer than the intervals between elements. Gradually, the first element of each grouping seems to be accentuated (Bolton, 1894; Koffka, 1909), as can be seen when the subject is asked to produce taps while hearing stimuli, or to produce a subjective rhythm (Miyake, 1902; Stetson, 1905; Wirth, 1937).

2. The Perception of Groupings

a. Simple structures. A single periodical differentiation, be it qualitative or quantitative, introduced in a sequence of stimuli determines the nature of the groupings. A grouping ends with a longer stimulus or a longer interval. In most cases, a more intense stimulus or a stimulus differing in pitch begins the group, but sometimes terminates it (Bolton, 1894; McDougall, 1903; Meumann, 1894). Lengthening a sound does not have the same effect when the sound is small and when it is large. If it is small, the longer sound plays the role of an accentuated element and determines the beginning of the grouping; if it is large, the longer sound plays the role of an interval between two patterns and terminates the grouping (Woodrow, 1909).

It should be noted that this element, which may be stronger (S) or weaker (W), higher (H) or lower (L) plays the role of figure relative to other elements which play the role of ground. A sequence $SSSWSSSW$, etc. may be perceived as $WSSS$ or, less often, $SSSW$, but a reversal can also appear, as with spatially reversible figures, and it can become $SWWW$ or $WWWS$ (Fraisse, 1953).

The early studies on rhythm established the fact that the accent, whether subjective or objective, has an influence on the apparent duration of the interval that follows it. Since the accent sometimes ends the grouping, some authors, Woodrow (1909) among others, have considered the accent effect to be equivalent to the pause effect that it determined. But this interpretation does not explain why the accent is more often at the beginning of the group than at the end. As a matter of fact, Miyake (1902) and, later on, Schmidt (1939), have shown that two factors are responsible for the lengthening of certain intervals: (a) the pause at the end of a group; (b) the lengthening of the interval after the accented element. Accent and pause effects seem to result in an increase of 8–10% (Fraisse, 1956; Miyake, 1902). When the accent is at the end of the group, these two effects are cumulative.

A simple example will illustrate this point (Fraisse, 1956, p. 96). The subjects listened to a regular succession of a strong sound (100 dB) and a weak sound (75 dB) separated by 475-msec intervals. They were asked to produce tappings when hearing the sounds. 60% of the time, subjects perceived trochees (strong–weak) and 40% of the time, they perceived iambs (weak–strong). The intervals produced were as follows—Trochee: 484–452 msec.; iamb: 432–520 msec. With the trochaic structure, the pause and accent effects compensated each other, even though the accent effect was more important than the pause effect. With the iambic structure, the two effects were cumulative.

b. COMPLEX STRUCTURES. A complex structure is a temporal succession in which more than one element differs from the others. How is the perception of succession organized?

First of all, an effect found in all studies should be discarded: the effect of the initial elements on pattern organization, or the starting point effect. The first pattern presented has a tendency to impose itself (Handel & Yoder, 1975; Royer & Garner, 1966; Garner & Gottwald, 1968). This effect may be avoided either by gradually increasing the sound or by beginning the sequence at a high rate and gradually decreasing it (Royer & Garner, 1970).

Once this effect has been eliminated, it is observed that in a set composed of two types of elements, similar ones are grouped together. For instance, in the example given above, the sequence WWSS or SSWW may be perceived, while WSSW is more unlikely. When the structure is complex and longer (eight or nine elements), as in the experiments of Garner (1974) and his co-workers, all the identical elements, if they are perceived as contiguous, are grouped in a run that begins or ends the pattern. Preusser, Garner, and Gottwald (1970a,b) have distinguished two types of runs. They consider that in patterns composed of two elements, some are perceived as playing the role of a figure, others as the ground. The scope of the runs may be twofold, depending on their location. The authors speak of *run principle* if the longest run of identical elements is composed of figure elements, and of *gap principle* if the longest run is composed of ground elements. The run effect may be investigated by varying the nature of the distinction between two elements (Handel, 1974). With two sounds differing in frequency, it is observed that the lowest sound in 69% of the responses plays the role of a figure and begins the pattern. For instance, the perceived structure is *LLLLHHHH* 70% of the time and *HHHHLLLL* 26% of the time. With more complex patterns, if the longest run corresponds to low sounds, these sounds often become the ground, and then the run ends the pattern, *HLHLHLLL* is perceived 68% of the time and *LLLHLHLH* 20% of the time. There are, however, cases in which the run accent overcomes the run gap.

With two sounds differing in intensity, the strongest elements begin the pattern 71% of the time. The best possible organization is the one in which the pattern begins with one or several intense sounds and ends with a run of weak sounds. Patterns of *SWWSWWWW* or *SWSWSWWW* are observed in 92 and 93% of the responses, respectively, whereas there are eight possible different types of responses. With elements differing in duration, the figure element is the short one; 88% of the responses begin with a short element or with a series of brief elements. If different intervals are introduced in a series of identical elements, it is observed that the longest run without an interval begins the pattern.

In spite of the differences, the relative difficulty of the various patterns to be identified (measured by the number of responses that correspond to each pattern) is very similar, whether or not elements differ in intensity, frequency of interval (mean $\rho = .82$). The only exception concerns the difference in duration ($\rho = .48$). These patterns are always very difficult, but the 1:5 ratio between durations chosen in this experiment may be considered too high.

In these studies, the rate of the stimuli was about two or three per second and the total duration of a pattern was about 2 sec. It was perceived as a unified whole. If the rate is increased or decreased it is more difficult to identify as a whole, as Garner and Gottwald (1968) have shown for auditory and visual sequences.

It should be added that if, in a series of eight elements differing in pitch that follow at constant intervals, an element is accentuated or an interval lengthened, the pause permits the identification of the pattern twice as fast as the identification of the accent (Handel & Yoder, 1975).

Complex measures are much more difficult to perceive than simple measures. More precisely, the difficulty in perceiving the pattern increases with the number of perceived alternatives (Garner, 1974). Vos (1973) has established an index of complexity that is a product of the number of different elements, of the length of the pattern, and of the ratio between the shortest and the longest substructure. This index has the advantage of pointing out the main factors of complexity.

c. AUDITORY AND VISUAL STRUCTURES. Koffka (1909) has shown that there are subjective visual rhythms; but the rhythmization appears more slowly and the identification of patterns is more difficult with visual structures than with auditory ones (Garner, 1974; Handel & Yoder, 1975; Nazzaro & Nazzaro, 1970). The difficulty of the visual structuration may be due to the fact that the temporal character of visual stimulations is less defined or the immediate memory of forms is based on auditory coding, or both, even when the stimuli are presented visually (Atkinson & Shiffrin, 1968). It has been observed (Fraisse, 1948) that when subjects are asked to synchronize tappings with visual structures, their performance is better than when they verbalize each visual stimulus by a subvocal aid.

B. Structuration of Rhythmical Patterns

Pause, accent, and run are responsible for the organization of a series of regular or periodical stimuli into rhythmical groups. These factors are always related to temporal structures which shall now be mentioned.

1. SPONTANEOUS STRUCTURES

Subjects were asked to produce rhythmical patterns of five or six tappings and to organize them as they choose in order to avoid known rhythms; the following durations of intervals in the patterns were observed on 735 subjects:

Duration of interval (msec)	Percentage
Less than 200	15.5%
Less than 400	56.2%
Less than 600	77.2%
Less than 1000	92%
Less than 1800	98%

Two facts emerge from the tabular material. Short times of less than 400 msec, which correspond to the perception of a collection (see Section III, C,1), represent more than 50% of the durations, 92% of the durations are shorter than 1 sec, and only 2% are longer than 1.8 sec. This latter value seems to be the limit duration above which there is no longer a holistic perception of two elements.

b. RATIOS OF DURATIONS. At first glance, it seems that spontaneous structures are made of the succession of two types of duration: intervals that may be regarded as short durations (shorter than 400 msec), and long durations (longer than 400 msec).

If the ratio between two successive durations is computed by always selecting the ratio between the shortest and longest durations, a bimodal distribution is observed. There is a high percentage of absolute or relative equality with a ratio inferior or equal to 1.25 (see Fig. 2) and a second mode when the ratio is about 2. But these ratios are mostly observed with short–long or long–short sequences and very seldom with long–long sequences of two durations. Consequently, subjects produce simple structures with two types of temporal intervals. Within each type, a tendency to equalize the durations predominates assimilation. Between these two types, there is a clear *distinction* with a ratio of about 2:1.*

c. PATTERN DURATION AND ORGANIZATION. The production of spontaneous patterns shows that the relative mean duration increases with the length and complexity of the pattern: .67 for two tappings, 1.06 for three tappings, 1.84 for four and 2.68 for five. The opposite effect is seen with groups of isochronous sounds or tappings. If, after having answered at his spontaneous tempo, the subject is asked to change his tempo while keeping the same pattern, it is seen that when he accelerates, the long duration becomes shorter; the ratio long duration to short duration decreases to 1.8:1. When the subject slows down, short and long durations become longer, but as long as the subject says that he perceives the pattern, the ratio is about 1.55:1. The perceptual limit is observed with a pattern of four beats or three intervals for a 4.8 sec total duration (Fraisse, 1956).

2. DYNAMIC CHARACTER OF THE ORGANIZATION

Spontaneous structures that are dominated by the laws of assimilation and distinction of durations are not just a form of production more frequent than another. They are imposed by perceptual laws, as can be shown by asking the subject to reproduce other types of structures; the structures are produced with constant errors, as predicted by these laws. There is a real dynamic organization of patterns and the relative duration of one of the intervals is modified by the duration of the others. Consider-

---

* If the same subjects are asked to produce long sequences as arhythmic as possible, the duration of the longest intervals is about 1.8 sec, and the percentage of short durations is lower (35%). On the other hand, the distribution of ratios is unimodal, with a strong predominance of equal ratios between two successive durations. It is as though rhythmical patterns and arhythmic sequences were constituted by breaking a natural tendency to make successive intervals equal (law of economy).

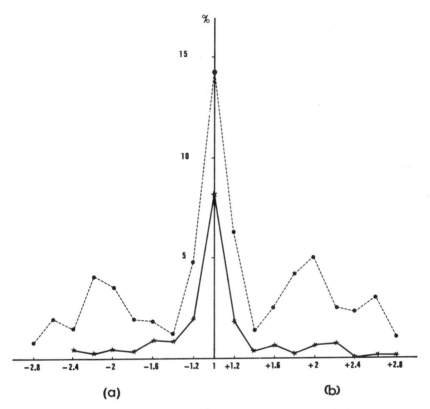

Fig. 2. The distribution of frequencies of ratios between two successive intervals: (a) between a short and a long interval (●----●); (b) between two long intervals (★—★).

ing the example of three intervals spontaneously produced and having durations of 180, 450, and 450 msec, we constructed series of models by varying either the duration of the first interval or the duration of the second interval. The subject listened to this pattern several times before producing it. The results, shown in Table I, show that the high ratios are overestimated, while those less than 1.5:1 are underestimated. These constant errors conform to the laws of assimilation and distinction and maintain the predominance of the structure of the two durations.

These laws do not characterize auditory patterns only. They are found in the silent reproduction of temporal visual forms (Fraisse, 1947). They are not related to motor laws either: they were found in graphic reproductions of spatial patterns presented during 300 msec. Systematic errors have about the same value. Thus these laws characterize all the perceptions of a pattern.

TABLE I

Evolution of Ratios between Intervals Reproduced
as a Function of the Model (csec)

Model duration	Reproductions	Ratio of first duration to second duration in model	Ratio of first duration to second duration in reproduction
18–45–45	17–50–49	2.50	3.00
24–45–45	20–52–54	1.90	2.50
30–45–45	27–56–53	1.50	2.10
36–45–45	39–45–46	1.25	1.16
42–45–45	44–44–46	1.10	1.00

Model duration	Reproductions	Ratio of second duration to third duration in model	Ratio of second duration to third duration in reproduction
18–21–45	19–21–54	2.13	2.57
18–27–45	19–28–58	1.67	2.03
18–33–45	17–42–53	1.36	1.26
18–39–45	17–46–48	1.15	1.04
18–51–45	17–52–51	1.13	1.02
18–57–45	18–59–52	1.27	1.14
18–63–45	18–63–52	1.40	1.21
18–69–45	17–67–55	1.53	1.22

3. Structures in Art

All the observations recorded in laboratory research are confirmed by the practice of the rhythmical arts, such as poetry, dance, and music.

In most cases, the structuration of patterns is realized by the use of pauses (especially in poetry and plainsong) and accents that mark the beginning or end of a pattern (the role of the rhyme in poetry, and of the accentuation of the first beat in music).

The duration of rhythms is very similar to the durations observed in experimental studies. According to Wallin (1901), the mean duration of English verses is 2.69 sec (ranging from .89–5 sec). The mean of measures in music is 3.43 sec (Sears, 1902). The structures used by poets in languages in which temporal structures predominate (e.g., Greek, Latin, Arabic, Persian) are created by contrasting brief and long durations, the long being the double of the brief, as Aristoxene of Tarentum (fourth century B.C.) noticed.* In modern music, the variety of notes extends

* In other languages (English, German, Italian, Spanish) rhythms are based on patterns of accents. In French, the number of syllables and the location of pauses and breaks dominate. But these are only the main tendencies. In all poetry, in fact, there are distinctions in duration, accent, and pause (see Fraisse, 1974).

from the sixty-fourth note to the whole note. If a page of music that has a unit of movement and of measure is considered, it is seen that the musician uses essentially two notes, the ratio of which is 2:1—most often the eighth note and the quarter note or the sixteenth note and the eighth note. These two notes represent 80–90% of all notes.* The shortest note is the most frequent (45–75%), and the longest one is the least frequent (12–44%). If one considers the duration of the notes for which the tempo is indicated, it is observed that the shortest note has durations that vary, according to the author and the tempo, from 150 to 410 msec, and the longest one from 300 to 860 msec. The correspondence with spontaneous patterns is very striking. We do not pretend to reduce art to psychology, but we do claim that the artist spontaneously takes into account perceptual laws, in the same way as architects take gravity into account when they build a bridge or an arch. But the essence of the artist is to use these laws in new creations that, to some extent, try to escape determinism.

If the performance of musicians trying to follow a sheet of music is analyzed (Gabrielsson, 1974), the performance of, for instance, a pianist or a drummer will be seen to be relatively stable, but the phenomenon of the accentuation of the first note (2–4 dB on the piano, 2–24 dB on the drum) will slightly modify the temporal values of the notes. An interesting point to be remembered is that "Punctuations were as a rule sharpened in the performances, that is, the punctuated eighth-note was made relatively longer, the sixteenth-note relatively shorter than according to the 3:1 ratio implied by the notation [p. 72]." It should be added that in this case, the 4 : 3 ratio between the quarter note and the punctuated eighth note is flattened. All musicians know how difficult it is to respect the durations of sharpened notes that introduce an intermediary duration.

This privileged use of two durations in music and poetry has to be compared to the fact, already mentioned, that we cannot easily identify more than two or three different durations.

C. Strings of Rhythmical Patterns

Rhythmical grouping, whether it derives from subjective rhythmization or from the production of patterns, seems to be a gestalt closed on itself (Fraisse, 1975). One group succeeds to another with an interval or pause that separates the Gestalt but that also relates them to form what Werner (1919) calls *Gestalt Verkettung* and Sander (1928) *Fugen Gestalt*.

1. PAUSES BETWEEN PATTERNS

Pauses are not random. In most cases, their duration is equal to or longer than the longest interval in the group (in 90% of the cases). This is

* The present computations were done on 14 randomly chosen samples of classical music.

an essential condition for an unambiguous perception of the pattern. However, it has no precise ratio with any interval. Its duration increases with the complexity of the pattern but never exceeds 2 sec. A higher duration would produce a segregation of patterns and interrupt the rhythmical string.

Pauses depend on the complexity of rhythmical patterns. On the other hand, it can be verified, in spontaneous productions or in reproductions with variable pause duration, that the pattern is independent of the pause, except when the pause is so brief that it leads to a restructuration of the string of elements; a long beat may then play the role of a pause. In reproduction tasks, it is noteworthy that it is necessary to direct the subject's attention to the pause duration that he would otherwise neglect because of his attention being oriented towards the pattern.

Pause, then, has not the same function as the durations that constitute rhythmical patterns. It is an interval that reinforces the salience of each pattern according to the laws of proximity, but it is also a link between patterns. The perception of rhythm is always the perception of successive forms that are often isochronous in art, but are always differentiated by the melodic, intensive, or temporal structuration.

2. PERCEPTUAL AND MOTOR RHYTHMS: SYNCHRONIZATIONS

Everybody has accompanied musical rhythms with tappings of the foot or the hand. One-year-olds rock, and 3–4-year-olds are capable of following a rhythm without error. These movements are synchronized (simultaneous) with the accentuated element of rhythmical patterns. When the adult is asked to tap as if it were a form or reaction to this element or to syncopate (i.e., to intercalate the series of tappings in the series of sounds), he can succeed, but he needs training. This example contrasts with the easiness of synchronization (Fraisse & Ehrlich, 1955).

a. SYNCHRONIZING WITH UNIFORM SERIES. In order to give a better analysis of this phenomenon, the simplest synchronization should be considered. If a subject is asked to produce tappings when hearing a series of isochronous sounds, as those of a metronome, synchronization is easy when sounds are separated by an interval of from 200 to 1000 msec. The time lag between sound and tapping never exceeds 4–6% of the interval, with a minimum around 600–800 msec* (Woodrow, 1932), which is less

---

* This minimum should probably be compared to the spontaneous tempo of repetitive movements (Fraisse, 1974). A spontaneous tempo depends on the movement which is done and particularly on the muscles involved. The spontaneous motor tempo has been studied

than the value of the threshold for succession. With a higher rate of sounds, the synchronization is altered because the control of tappings is no longer precise enough. The limit rate is 8.5 sounds per second (Seashore, 1938). If the rate is slower, when the interval is more than 2 sec, there is no longer synchronization. The subject oscillates between responses of anticipation and delayed responses, the interval between the stimulus and the response having about the same value as a reaction time.

Synchronization implies that the command of the movement is anticipated relative to the perception of the sound. In most cases, the tapping occurs about 30 msec before the sound. This phenomenon of anticipation has been observed by many authors (King, 1962; Fraisse & Voillaume, 1971).

b. SYNCHRONIZATION WITH RHYTHMICAL PATTERNS. In some cases, the subject tries to synchronize each tapping with each element of the stimulus while respecting durations and intervals (McDorman, 1962). The simpler the pattern, the better the kind of synchronization. The duration of the pattern must not be too short nor too long. Seventy percent of the responses are anticipatory responses.

Synchronization is rapidly established. If the subject has to produce tappings from the beginning of a series of rhythmical patterns as simple as iambs, synchronization is achieved by the third pattern. Three patterns are also necessary when the subject has to change his synchronization from one pattern to another (Fraisse, 1966). In other cases the subject tries only to tap synchronously with the first stimulus of the pattern (the accented one).

D. Experience of Rhythm

The conditions of the perception of rhythm are then the holistic grasping of a pattern and its linking with what follows. But the continuous audition of rhythms is not solely a perceptual activity; it gives rise to an experience of rhythm where a motor induction dominates, the characteristics of which we have just analyzed.

---

with a task consisting of tapping with a hand on a table or on a key. The spontaneous tempo varies from 350 to 880 msec, the most frequent value being 600 msec. Interindividual variance is higher than intraindividual variance, a fact that supports the idea that there is a personal tempo (Stern, 1900). Many spontaneous human activities fall within the same range of frequency, but they do not have noticeable correlations. The duration of a step is about 500 msec, of a heartbeat 750–800 msec; the interval between two movements of sucking, eight days after birth, varies from 600 to 1200 msec. Movements of chewing have about the same frequency; periodical contractions of orgasm in males and females occur every 800 msec (Masters & Johnson, 1966).

The experience of rhythm is an amalgam of perceptions of uniform or varied structures and movements, an amalgam that gives rise to emotional reactions. These three aspects were already noticed by Wundt, and Gabrielsson (1973a, b) investigated them thoroughly.

Gabrielsson selected three types of musical samples: (a) monophonic structures played on a piano or on a drum; (b) polyphonic structures, typical of dance. Rhythm was produced by percussion instruments, without melody; (c) complete musical patterns. The structures were repeated four or five times. Subjects were asked to give judgments of similarity of the patterns, and estimations using 92 adjectives selected for describing rhythms. Factor analysis and multidimensional analysis yielded three main aspects of rhythmical experience:

1. The cognitive perceptual aspects, or structural properties, were those of meter, accentuation, and basic pattern. Three dimensions predominated: accentuation–clearness, uniformity–variation, and simplicity–complexity.
2. Movement properties were those of rapidity and tempo, and forward movement (distinction between rhythms that were perceived to continue or even accelerate in their movement up to the first beat in the following measure and rhythms that were perceived to stop, decelerate, or be cut off somewhere in the measure). Movement characters were described by scales of the following types: dancing–walking, floating–stuttering, solemn–swinging, etc. In the same way, Gatewood (1927) found that musical works that gave an impression of movement were those in which the rhythmical character predominated, as opposed to those in which melody or harmony or timbre predominated.
3. Emotional aspects were described by the following pairs of adjectives: vital–dull, excited–calm, rigid–flexible.

A very similar method was applied to the study of rhythms in Swedish poetry (Linde, 1975). The correlation matrix between adjective ratings was subjected to principal component analysis. The first two components interpreted as dimensions of rhythms in a strict sense were labeled (a) regularity versus variation; and (b) melody versus lack of melody. Two other components were named: emphasis versus lack of emphasis and calmness versus agility. These dimensions may be compared to the ones found in music, but the importance of semantic aspects of poetry slightly masks structural aspects, and the importance of motor inductions in such cases is not observed.

References

Abbe, M. The spatial effect on time perception. *Japanese Journal of Experimental Psychology*, 1936, **3**, 1–52.

Abbe, M. Relation between time and space as field forces. *Psychologia*, 1971, **14**, 208–212.

Allan, L. G., & Kristofferson, A. B. Judgments about the duration of brief stimuli. *Perception & Psychophysics*, 1974, **15**, 434–440. (a)

Allan, L. G., & Kristofferson, A. B. Psychophysical theories of duration discrimination. *Perception & Psychophysics*, 1974, **16**, 26–34. (b)

Allan, L. G., Kristofferson, A. B., & Rise, M. E. Some aspects of perceptual coding of duration in visual duration discrimination. *Perception & Psychophysics*, 1974, **15**, 83–88.

Allan, L. G., Kristofferson, A. B., & Wiens, E. W. Duration discrimination of brief light flashes. *Perception & Psychophysics*, 1971, **9**, 327–334.

Allport, D. A. Temporal summation and phenomenal simultaneity: Experiments with the radius display. *Quarterly Journal of Experimental Psychology*, 1970, **22**, 686–701.

Atkinson, R. C., & Shiffrin, R. M. Human memory: A proposed system and its control processes. In K. W. Spence & J. T. Spence (Eds), *The psychology of learning and motivation*. Vol. 2. *Advances in research and theory*. New York: Academic Press, 1968.

Avant, L. L., Lyman, P. J., & Antes, J. R. Effects of stimulus familiarity upon judged visual duration. *Perception & Psychophysics*, 1975, **17**, 253–262.

Bartley, S. H., Nelson, T. M., & Ranney, J. E. The sensory parallel of the reorganization period in the cortical response in intermittent retinal stimulation. *The Journal of Psychology*, 1961, **52**, 137–147.

Behar, I., & Bevan, W. The perceived duration of auditory and visual intervals: Cross-modal comparison and interaction. *American Journal of Psychology*, 1961, **74**, 17–26.

Berglund, B., Berglund, U., Ekman, G., & Frankenhaeuser, M. The influence of auditory stimulus intensity on apparent duration. *Scandinavian Journal of Psychology*, 1969, **10**, 21–26.

Björkman, M., & Holmkvist, O. The time-order error in the construction of a subjective time scale. *Scandinavian Journal of Psychology*, 1960, **1**, 7–13.

Bolton, T. L. Rhythm. *American Journal of Psychology*, 1894, **6**, 145–238.

Bonnet, C. Le rôle des changements continus et discontinus dans l'estimation de la durée. *Année Psychologique*, 1968, **68**, 348–356.

Bovet, P. Echelles subjectives de durées obtenues par une méthode de bissection. *Année Psychologique*, 1968, **68**, 23–36.

Bovet, P. La méthode des jugements absolus en psychophysique. *Bulletin de Psychologie*, 1969, **XXII**, 631–639.

Bovet, P. Quantité d'information transmise dans la perception des durées brèves. Thèse de 3e cycle, Université René Descartes, Paris, 1974 (unpublished).

Brown, D. R., & Hitchcock, L., Jr. Time estimation: dependence and independence of modality-specific effects. *Perceptual and Motor Skills*, 1965, **21**, 727–734.

Buffardi, L. Factors affecting the filled, duration illusion in the auditory, tactual, and visual modalities. *Perception & Psychophysics*, 1971, **10**, 292–294.

Carbotte, R. M. Retention of time information in forced-choice duration discrimination. *Perception & Psychophysics*, 1973, **14**, 440–444.

Carlson, V. R., & Feinberg, I. Time judgment as a function of method, practice, and sex. *Journal of Experimental Psychology*, 1970, **85**, 171–180.

Cohen, J., & Cooper, P. New phenomena in apparent duration, distance and speech. *Nature*, 1962, **196**, 1233–1234.

Cohen, J., Hansel, C. E. M., & Sylvester, J. D. Interdependence in judgments of space, time, and movement. *Acta Psychologica*, 1955, **11**, 360–372.

Colquhoun, W. P. (Ed.) *Biological rhythms and human performance*. London, New York: Academic Press, 1971.

Corwin, T. R., & Boynton, R. M. Transitivity of visual judgments of simultaneity. *Journal of Experimental Psychology*, 1968, **78**, 560–568.

Craig, J. C. A constant error in the perception of brief temporal intervals. *Perception & Psychophysics*, 1973, **13**, 99–104.

Creelman, C. D. Human discrimination of auditory duration. *Journal of the Acoustical Society of America*, 1962, **34**, 582–593.

Dobson, W. R. An investigation of various factors involved in time perception as manifested by different nosological groups, *Journal of General Psychology*, 1954, **50**, 277–298.

Edgell, B. On time judgments. *American Journal of Psychology*, 1903, **14**, 418–438.

Efron, R. The effect of handedness on the perception of simultaneity and temporal order. *Brain*, 1963, **86**, 261–284. (a)

Efron, R. The effect of stimulus intensity on the perception of simultaneity in right and left handed subjects. *Brain*, 1963, **86**, 285–294. (b)

Efron, R. An invariant characteristic of perceptual systems in the time domain. In S. Kornblum (Ed.), *Attention and performance* (Vol. IV). New York: Academic Press, 1973. Pp. 713–737.

Ehrensing, R. H., & Lhamon, W. T. Comparison of tactile and auditory time judgments. *Perceptual and Motor Skills*, 1966, **23**, 929–930.

Ekman, G., Frankenhaeuser, M., Berglund, B., & Waszak, M. Apparent duration as a function of intensity of vibrotactile stimulation. *Perceptual and Motor Skills*, 1969, **28**, 151–156.

Ekman, G., Frankenhaeuser, M., Levander, S. & Mellis, I. The influence of intensity and duration of electrical stimulation on subjective variables. *Scandinavian Journal of Psychology*, 1966, **7**, 58–64.

Eriksen, C. W., & Collins, J. F. Some temporal characteristics of visual pattern perception. *Journal of Experimental Psychology*, 1967, **74**, 476–484.

Falk, J. L., & Bindra, D. Judgment of time as a function of serial position and stress. *Journal of Experimental Psychology*, 1954, **47**, 279–282.

Fraisse, P. De l'assimilation et de la distinction comme processus fondamentaux de la connaissance. In *Miscellanea Psychologica* A. Michotte. Louvain, Paris, Institut Supérieur de Philosophie: J. Vrin, 1947. Pp. 181–195.

Fraisse, P. Les erreurs constantes dans la reproduction de courts intervalles temporels. *Archives de Psychologie*, 1948, **32**, 161–176. (a)

Fraisse, P. Etude comparée de la perception et de l'estimation de la durée chez les enfants et chez les adultes. *Enfance*, 1948, *1*, 199–211. (b)

Fraisse, P. Les conduites temporelles et leurs dissociations pathologiques. *Encéphale*, 1952, **41**, 122–142.

Fraisse, P. La perception comme processus d'adaptation. L'évolution des recherches récentes. *Année Psychologique*, 1953, **53**, 443–461.

Fraisse, P. *Les structures rythmiques*, Louvain, Paris: Publications Universitaires de Louvain, Ed. Erasme, 1956.

Fraisse, P. Influence de la vitesse des mouvements sur l'estimation de leur durée. *Année Psychologique*, 1962, **62**, 391–399.

Fraisse, P. *The psychology of time*. New York: Harper, 1963.

Fraisse, P. L'Oppel-Kundt temporel ou l'influence de la fréquence des stimulations sur la perception du temps. *Psychologie Française*, 1965, **10**, 352–358.

Fraisse, P. Visual perceptive simultaneity and masking of letters successively presented. *Perception & Psychophysics*, 1966, **1**, 285–287.

Fraisse, P. L'intégration et le masquage de lettres présentées en succession rapide. *Année Psychologique*, 1968, **68**, 321–345.

Fraisse, P. *Psychologie du rythme*. Paris: Presses Universitaires de France, 1974.244p.

Fraisse, P. Is rhythm a gestalt? In S. Ertel, L. Kemmler & M. Stadler (Eds.), *Gestalttheorie in der modernen Psychologie*. Darmstadt: D. Steinkopff, 1975, Pp. 227–232.

Fraisse, P., & Ehrlich, S. Note sur la possibilité de syncoper en fonction du tempo d'une cadence. *Année Psychologique*, 1955, **55**, 61–65.

Fraisse, P., & Fraisse, R. Etudes sur la mémoire immédiate. I. L'appréhension des sons. *Année Psychologique*, 1937, **38**, 48–85.

Fraisse, P., & Smirnov, S. Response latency and the content of immediate memory. *Bulletin of the Psychonomic Society*, 1976, **8**, 345–348.

Fraisse, P., & Vautrey, P. La perception de l'espace, de la vitesse et du temps chez l'enfant de cinq ans. *Enfance*, 1952, **5**, 1–20, 102–119.

Fraisse, P., & Voillaume, C. Les repères du sujet dans la synchronisation et la pseudo-synchronisation. *Année Psychologique*, 1971, **71**, 359–369.

Francois, M. Contribution à l'étude du sens du temps. *Année Psychologique*, 1927, **28**, 186–204.

Gabrielsson, A. Adjective ratings and dimension analyses of auditory rhythm patterns. *Scandinavian Journal of Psychology*, 1973, **14**, 244–260. (a)

Gabrielsson, A. Studies in rhythm. *Acta Universalis Upsaliensis:* Abstracts of Uppsala Dissertations in Social Sciences, 1973. (b)

Gabrielsson, A. Performance of rhythm patterns. *Scandinavian Journal of Psychology*, 1974, **15**, 63–72.

Garner, W. R. *The processing of information and structure*. New York: Wiley, 1974.

Garner, W. R., & Gottwald, R. L. The perception and learning of temporal patterns. *Quarterly Journal of Experimental Psychology*, 1968, **20**, 97–109.

Gatewood, E. L. An experimental study of the nature of musical enjoyment. In M. Shoen (Ed.), *The effects of music*. London: Kagan, 1927.

Gavini, H. Contribution à l'étude de la perception des durées brèves: Comparaison des temps vides et des temps pleins. *Journal de Psychologie Normale et Pathologique*, 1959, **56**, 455–468.

Gengel, R. W., & Hirsh, I. J. Temporal order: the effect of single versus repeated presentations, practice, and verbal feedback. *Perception & Psychophysics*, 1970, **7**, 209–211.

Getty, D. J. Discrimination of short temporal intervals. A comparison of two models. *Perception & Psychophysics*, 1975, **18**, 1–8.

Gibbon, J., & Rutschmann, R. Temporal order judgment and reaction time. *Science*, 1969, **165**, 413–415.

Gibson, J. J. The problem of temporal order in stimulation and perception. *Journal of Psychology*, 1966, **62**, 141–149.

Goldstone, S., Boardman, W. K., & Lhamon, W. T. Effect of quinal barbitone, dextroamphetamine and placebo on apparent time. *British Journal of Psychology*, 1958, **49**, 324–328.

Goldstone, S., & Lhamon, W. T. Studies of auditory-visual differences in human time judgment. I. Sounds are judged longer than lights. *Perceptual and Motor Skills*, 1974, **39**, 63–82.

Goldstone, S., Lhamon, W. T., & Boardman, W. K. The time sense: Anchor effects and apparent duration. *The Journal of Psychology*, 1957, **44**, 145–153.

Goodfellow, L. D. An empirical comparison of audition, vision, and touch in the discrimination of short intervals of time. *American Journal of Psychology*, 1934, **46**, 243–258.

Gregg, L. W. Fractionation of temporal intervals. *Journal of Experimental Psychology*, 1951, **42**, 307–312.

Hall, G. S., & Jastrow, J. Studies of rhythm. *Mind*, 1886, **11**, 55–62.

Handel, S., & Yoder, D. The effects of intensity and interval rhythms on the perception of auditory and visual temporal patterns. *Quarterly Journal of Experimental Psychology*, 1975, **27**, 111–122.

Hawkes, G. R. Information transmitted via electrical cutaneous stimulus duration. *Journal of Psychology*, 1961, **51**, 293–298. (a)

Hawkes, G. R. Absolute identification of duration. *Perceptual and Motor Skills*, 1961, **13**, 203–209. (b)

Hawkes, G. R., Bailey, R. W., & Warm, J. S. Method and modality in judgments of brief stimulus duration, *Journal of Auditory Research*, 1961, **1**, 133–144.

Hawkes, G. R., & Warm, J. S. ΔT for electrical cutaneous stimulation. *Journal of Psychology*, 1961, **51**, 263–271.

Helson, H. *Adaptation-level theory: An experimental and systematic approach to behavior*. New York: Harper, 1964.

Hirsh, I. J. Auditory perception of temporal order. *Journal of the Acoustical Society of America*, 1959, **31**, 759–767.

Hirsh, I. J., & Fraisse, P. Simultaneité et succession de stimuli hétérogènes. *Année Psychologique*, 1964, **64**, 1–19.

Hirsh, I. J., & Sherrick, C. E., Jr. Perceived order in different sense modalities. *Journal of Experimental Psychology*, 1961, **62**, 423–432.

Hoagland, H. The physiological control of judgments of duration: Evidence for a chemical clock. *Journal of General Psychology*, 1933, **9**, 267–287.

Hollingworth, H. L. The inaccuracy of movement. *Archives of Psychology*, 1909, **13**, 1–87.

Höring, A. *Versuche über das Unterscheidungsvermögen des Hörsinnes für Zeitsgrössen*, Tubingue: 1864.

Huppert, F., & Singer, G. An after-effect in judgment of auditory duration. *Perception & Psychophysics*, 1967, **2**, 544–546.

Hylan, J. P. The distribution of attention. *Psychological Review*, 1903, **10**, 373–403.

James, W. *The principles of psychology*. New York: Holt, 1890.

Kahneman, D., & Wolman, R. E. Stroboscopic motion: Effects of duration and interval. *Perception and Psychophysics*, 1970, **8**, 161–164.

Katz, D. Experimentelle Beiträge zur Psychologie des Vergleichs im Gebiete des Zeitsinns. *Zeitschrift für Psychologie und Physiologie der Sinnersorgane*, 1906, **42**, 302–340, 414–450.

Kinchla, J. Duration discrimination of acoustically defined intervals in the 1- to 8-sec range. *Perception & Psychophysics*, 1972, **12**, 318–320.

King, H. E. Anticipatory behavior: Temporal matching by normal and psychotic subjects. *The Journal of Psychology*, 1962, **53**, 425–440.

Klemm, O. Über die Wirksamkeit kleinster Zeitunterschiede im Gebiete des Tastsinns. *Archive für Gesamte Psychologie*, 1925, **50**, 205–220.

Koffka, K. Experimental-Untersuchungen zur Lehre vom Rhythmus. *Zeitschrift für Psychologie*, 1909, **52**, 1–109.

Köhler, W. Zur Theorie de Sukzessivvergleichs und der Zeitfehler. *Psychologische Forschung*, 1923, **4**, 115–175.

Korte, A. Kinematoskopische Untersuchungen. *Zeitschrift für Psychologie*, 1915, **72**, 193–296.

Kristofferson, A. B. Successiveness discrimination as a two-state, quantal process. *Science*, 1967, **158**, 1337–1339.

Kristofferson, A. B., & Allan, L. G. Successiveness and duration discrimination. In S. Kornblum (Ed.), *Attention and Performance*. Vol. IV. New York: Academic Press, 1973.

Ladefoged, P., & Broadbent, D. E. Perception of sequence in auditory events. *Quarterly Journal of Experimental Psychology*, 1960, **12**, 162–170.

Lhamon, W. T., & Goldstone, S. Studies of auditory-visual differences in human time judgment. II. More transmitted information with sounds than lights. *Perceptual and Motor Skills*, 1974, **39**, 295–307.

Lhamon, W. T., Goldstone, S., & Goldfarb, J. L. The psychopathology of time judgment. In P. H. Hoch & J. Zubin (Eds.), *Psychopathology of perception*. New York: Grune & Stratton, 1965. Pp. 164–188.

Liberman, A. M., Harris, K. S., Kinney, J., & Lane, H. A. The discrimination of relative onset-time of the components of certain speech and non-speech patterns. *Journal of Experimental Psychology*, 1961, **61**, 379–388.

Lichenstein, M. Phenomenal simultaneity with irregular timing of components of the visual stimulus. *Perceptual and Motor Skills*, 1961, **12**, 47–60.

Linde, L. Perception of poetic rhythm. A dimension analysis. *Scandinavian Journal of Psychology*, 1975, **16**, 167–176.

Lockhart, J. M. Ambient temperature and time estimation. *Journal of Experimental Psychology*, 1967, **73**, 286–291.

Loeb, M., Behar, I., & Warm, J. S. Cross-modal correlations of the perceived durations of auditory and visual stimuli. *Psychonomic Science*, 1966, **6**, 87.

Mac Dorman, C. F. Synchronization with auditory models of varying complexity. *Perceptual and Motor Skills*, 1962, **15**, 595–602.

Masters, W. H., & Johnson, V. E. *Human sexual response*. Boston: Little, Brown, 1966.

Matsuda, F. Effects of space and velocity on time estimation in children and adults. *Psychological Research*, 1974, **37**, 107–123.

Matsuda, F., & Matsuda, M. Effects of frequency of intermittent stimuli on time estimation in children and adults. I. Sounds and lights. *Psychologia*, 1974, **17**, 206–212.

Matsuda, F., & Matsuda, M. Effects of frequency of intermittent stimuli on time estimation in children and adults. II. *Psychologia*, 1976, **19**, 11–22.

McConchie, R. D., & Rutschmann, J. Human time estimation: On differences between methods. *Perceptual and Motor Skills*, 1971, **32**, 319–336.

McDougall, R. The structure of simple rhythm forms. *Psychological Review, Monograph supplements*, 1903, **4**, 309–411.

McFarland, J. H. Sequential part presentation: A method of studying visual form perception. *British Journal of Psychology*, 1965, **56**, 439–446. (a)

McFarland, J. H. The effect of different sequences of part presentation on perception of a form's parts as simultaneous. *Proceedings of the 73th Annual Convention of the American Psychological Association*, 1965, 43–44. (b)

Meumann, E. Untersuchungen zur Psychologie und Aesthetik des Rhythmus. *Philosophische Studien*, 1894, **10**, 249–322, 393–430.

Miyake, I. Researches on rhythmic action. *Studies from the Yale Psychological Laboratory*, 1902, **10**, 1–48.

Michon, J. A. Studies on subjective duration. II. Subjective time measurement during tasks with different information content. *Acta Psychologica*, 1965, **24**, 205–212.

Michon, J. A. Magnitude scaling of short durations with closely spaced stimuli. *Psychonomic Science*, 1967, **9**, 359–360. (a)

Michon, J. A. *Timing in temporal tracking.* Soesterberg: Institute for Perception RVO-TNO, 1967. (b)

Miller, G. A. The magical number seven, plus or minus two: Some limits of our capacity for processing information. *Psychological Review,* 1956, **63,** 81–97.

Miller, G. A., & Johnson-Laird, P. N. *Language and perception.* Cambridge, Massachusetts: Harvard Univ. Press, 1976.

Mo, S. S. Judgment of temporal duration as a function of numerosity. *Psychonomic Science,* 1971, **24,** 71–72.

Mo, S. S. Comparative judgment of temporal duration as a function of numerosity. *Bulletin of the Psychonomic Society,* 1974, **3,** 377–379.

Mo, S. S. Temporal reproduction of duration as a function of numerosity. *Bulletin of the Psychonomic Society,* 1975, **5,** 165–167.

Murphee, O. D. Maximum rates of form perception and the alpha rhythm. *Journal of Experimental Psychology,* 1954, **48,** 57–61.

Murphy, L. E. Absolute judgments of duration. *Journal of Experimental Psychology,* 1966, **71,** 260–263.

Nazzaro, J. R., & Nazzaro, J. N. Auditory versus visual learning of temporal patterns. *Journal of Experimental Psychology,* 1970, **84,** 477–478.

Newman, C. V., & Lee, S. G. The effect of real and imputed distance on judgments of time: Some experiments on the Kappa phenomenon. *Psychonomic Science,* 1972, **29,** 207–211.

Oléron, G. Influence de l'intensité d'un son sur l'estimation de la durée apparante. *Année Psychologique,* 1952, **52,** 383–392.

Ornstein, R. E. *On the experience of time.* Harmondsworth: Penguin Books, 1969.

Peak, H. The time order error in successive judgments and in reflexes: II. As a function of the first stimulus of a pair. *Journal of Experimental Psychology,* 1940, **26,** 103–115.

Pfaff, D. Effects of temperature and time of day on time judgments. *Journal of Experimental Psychology,* 1968, **76,** 419–422.

Piaget, J. *The child's conception of time.* New York: Basic Books, 1970.

Piéron, H. Remarques sur la perception du mouvement apparent. *Année Psychologique,* 1933, **34,** 245–248.

Piéron, H. *The sensations.* New Haven, Connecticut: Yale Univ. Press, 1952.

Plateau, J. Sur la mesure des sensations physiques et sur la loi qui relie l'intensité de ces sensations à l'intensité de la cause existante. *Bulletin de l'Academie Royale de Belgique,* 1872, **33,** 376–388.

Pollack, R. H. Effect of figure–ground contrast and contour orientation on the temporal range of apparent movement. *Psychonomic Science,* 1966, **4,** 401–402.

Preusser, D., Garner, W. R., & Gottwald, R. L. Perceptual organization of two-element temporal patterns as a function of their component one-element patterns. *American Journal of Psychology,* 1970, **83,** 151–170. (a)

Preusser, D., Garner, W. R., & Gottwald, R. L. The effect of starting pattern on descriptions of perceived temporal patterns. *Psychonomic Science,* 1970, **21,** 219–220. (b)

Royer, F. L., & Garner, W. R. Response uncertainty and perceptual difficulty of auditory temporal patterns. *Perception & Psychophysics,* 1966, **1,** 41–47.

Royer, F. L., & Garner, W. R. Perceptual organization of nine-element auditory temporal patterns. *Perception & Psychophysics,* 1970, **7,** 115–120.

Rutschmann, R. Perception of temporal order and relative visual latency. *Science,* 1966, **152,** 1099–1101.

Rutschmann, R., & Link, R. Perception of temporal order of stimuli differing in sense mode and simple reaction time. *Perceptual and Motor Skills,* 1964, **18,** 345–352.

Sander, F. Experimentelle Ergebnisse der Gestaltpsychologie. *Bericht über den X-Kongress für experimentalle Psychologie in Bonn*. Iena: Verlag von gustav Fischer, 1928, Pp. 23–88.

Schmidt, E. M. Uber den Aufbau rhythmischer Gestalten. *Neue Psychologische Studien*, 1939, **14**, 6–98.

Schultze, F. E. O. Beitrag zur Psychologie de Zeitbewusstseins. *Archiv für die Gesamte Psychologie*, 1908, **13**, 275–351.

Sears, C. H. A contribution to the psychology of rhythm. *American Journal of Psychology*, 1902, **13**, 28–61.

Seashore, C. E. *Psychology of music*. New York: McGraw-Hill, 1938.

Small, A. M., & Campbell, R. A. Temporal differential sensitivity for auditory stimuli. *American Journal of Psychology*, 1962, **75**, 401–410.

Sternberg, S., & Knoll, R. L. The perception of temporal order: Fundamental issues and a general model. In S. Kornblum (Ed.), *Attention and performance*. Vol. IV. New York: Academic Press, 1973. Pp. 629–685.

Stetson, R. H. A motor theory of rhythm and discrete succession. *Psychological Review*, 1905, **12**, 250–270, 292–350.

Stevens, S. S. Intensity functions in sensory systems. *International Journal of Neurology*, 1967, **6**, 202–209.

Stone, S. A. Prior entry in the auditory-tactual complication. *American Journal of Psychology*, 1926, **37**, 284–287.

Stott, L. H. The discrimination of short tonal durations. Unpublished doctoral dissertation. Univ. of Illinois, 1933.

Stott, L. H. Time-order errors in the discrimination of short tonal durations. *Journal of Experimental Psychology*, 1935, **18**, 741–766.

Stroud, J. M. The fine structure of psychological time. In H. Quastler (Ed.), *Information theory in psychology*. Glencoe, Illinois: Free Press, 1956. Pp. 174–205.

Sudo, Y. On the effect of the phenomenal distance upon time perception. *Japanese Journal of Psychology*, 1941, **16**, 95–115.

Suto, Y. The effect of space on time estimation (S-effect) in tactual space. I. *Japanese Journal of Psychology*, 1952, **22**, 189–201.

Svenson, O. Interrelations and structure of judgments of velocity, time, and displacement in relative movement. *Reports from the Psychological Laboratories*. Univ. of Stockholm, no. **325**, June 1971.

Swisher, L., & Hirsh, I. J. Brain damage and the ordering of two temporally successive stimuli. *Neuropsychologia*, 1972, **10**, 137–152.

Thomas, E. A.C., Brown, I., Jr. Time perception and the filled-duration illusion. *Perception and Psychophysics*, 1974, **16**, 449–458.

Thomas, E. A. C., & Weaver, W. B. Cognitive processing and time perception. *Perception & Psychophysics*, 1975, **17**, 363–367.

Toda, M. Time and the structure of human cognition. In J. T. Fraser & N. Lawrence (Eds), *The study of time*. New York: Springer-Verlag, 1975. Pp. 314–324.

Treisman, M. Temporal discrimination and the indifference interval: Implications for a model of the "internal clock." *Psychological Monographs*, 1963. 77(13), (Whole no. 576).

Triplett, D. The relation between the physical pattern and the reproduction of short temporal intervals: A study in the perception of filled and unfilled time. *Psychological Monographs*, 1931, **42**(4, Whole No. 187), 201–265.

Umilta, C., Stadler, M., & Trombini, G. The perception of temporal order and the degree of excentricity of the stimuli in the visual field. *Studia Psychologica*, 1973, **15**, 130–139.

Vierordt, K. *Der Zeitsinn nach Versuchen*. Tubingue: Laupp, 1868.

Von Sturmer, G. Stimulus variation and sequential judgments of duration. *Quarterly Journal of Experimental Psychology*, 1966, **18**, 354–357.

Vos, P. G. Pattern perception in metrical tone sequences. Unpublished thesis, Univ. of Nijmegen, 1973.

Wallin, J. E. W. Researches on the rhythm of speech. *Studies from the Yale Psychological laboratory*, 1901, **9**, 1–142.

Warm, J. S., Foulke, E., & Loeb, M. The influence of stimulus-modality and duration on changes in temporal judgments over trials. *American Journal of Psychology*, 1966, **79**, 628–631.

Warm, J. S., & McCray, R. E. Influence of word frequency and length on the apparent duration of tachistoscopic presentations. *Journal of Experimental Psychology*, 1969, **79**, 56–58.

Werner, H. Rhythmik, eine mehrwertige Gestaltenverkettung. *Zeitschrift für Psychologie*, 1919, **82**, 198–218.

Wertheimer, M. Experimentelle Studien über das Sehen von Bewegung. *Zeitschrift für Psychologie*, 1912, **61**, 161–265.

White, C. T. Temporal numerosity and the psychological unit of duration. *Psychological Monographs*, 1963, **77**(12, Whole No. 575),p. 37.

Wiener, N. *Cybernetics or control and communication in the animal and the machine*. New York: Wiley, 1949.

Wirth, W. Die unmittelbare Teilung einer gegebenen Zeitstrecke. *American Journal of Psychology*, 1937, **50**, 79–96.

Woodrow, H. A quantitative study of rhythm. *Archives of Psychology*, 1909, **14**, 1–66.

Woodrow, H. The reproduction of temporal intervals. *Journal of Experimental Psychology*, 1930, **13**, 473–499.

Woodrow, H. The effect of rate of sequence upon the accuracy of synchronization. *Journal of Experimental Psychology*, 1932, **15**, 357–379.

Woodrow, H. The temporal indifference interval determined by the method of mean error. *Journal of Experimental Psychology*, 1934, **17**, 167–188.

Woodworth, R. S. *Experimental Psychology*. New York: Holt, 1938.

Wundt, W. *Grundzüge der physiologischen Psychologie*. Leipzig: Engelmann, 1874.

Zelkind, I. Factors in time estimation and a case for the internal clock. *Journal of General Psychology*, 1973, **88**, 295–301.

Chapter 7

AUDITORY PATTERNS: STUDIES IN THE PERCEPTION OF STRUCTURE*

MARI RIESS JONES

I. INTRODUCTION

A. Background

The sense of expectancy and of motion that so often accompanies hearing certain musical passages is phenomenologically interesting. In fact, it is remarkable how often the word *motion* crops up in writings about the human response to abstract auditory patterns. From such unlikely bedfellows as Helmholtz (1954, p. 370), Mach (1914, p. 284), and Koffka (1935, p. 433), as well as from Lashley in his grand exposition of serial order (1951), there has been recurrent interest in the idea of motion-related responding. However, rarely has this interest led to lasting conceptions about perceptions of auditory patterns. Indeed, as the basis

* The author is indebted to Anthony Greenwald, Neal Johnson, Lester Krueger, and Dean Owen whose comments on an earlier version of this chapter assisted in its revision. Research involved in preparing this chapter was supported, in part, by Grant BMS-74-21492 from the National Science Foundation.

for a general theory the idea of psychological motion, or activity, has fared little better. Directed activity in perception and thought formed the core of the Wurzburg school's reaction to Wundt's passive associationism. But formalizations of such activity in this century have been slow to develop, in part because successive waves of behaviorism and "pure" memory models have not encouraged development of activity-oriented approaches and, in part, because Gestalt theoriests have been reluctant to quantify responding in ways that threaten the treatment of stimuli as wholistic patterns. As a result, whenever the study of auditory patterns has emerged into the mainstream, it has been admired for its portrayal of powerful phenomena, but finally ignored as too complex. The history of studies in rhythm presents a clear example of this. From Wundt's time until Koffka's writings in the 1930s, rhythmic perceptions recurrently captivated the attention of psychology's best minds (see, for example, Boring, 1942, p. 583–586; Gabrielsson, 1973a). But in spite of splendid illustrations of rhythmic organization, their implications were subsequently eclipsed by the general tenor of behaviorism and, more recently, by the mechanistic orientation of information-processing research. Nevertheless, there are signs of renewed interest not only in rhythmic phenomena, but also in the general problem of structure in temporal sequences. As a result, there has been progress in attacking one major cause of the sporadic neglect of this area, namely the problem of defining "patternness" itself.

Properly, a pattern is a nonrandom sequence of events, in this case, sounds, that can be meaningfully extended. The rub comes in defining *meaningful*. Historically, lack of criteria for identifying a pattern has given a crazy-quilt appearance to the field, which is dotted with whimsical studies based on abstract sound patterns varying from strings of pronounceable nonsense syllables to 12-tone music. Fortunately, recent advances in nomenclature and specification of structure promise coherence in this area. Curiously, these same advances are also suggesting new ways of formalizing psychological activity. For these reasons, the introductory sections of this chapter dwell on nomenclature and definitions. These sections are important not only because they lay a foundation for understanding basic structural properties of patterns, but also because they allow an evaluation of theories subsequently described in which psychological activity becomes tied to pattern structure.

B. Serial Structure in Time: Presentation Rate and Relative Timing

Auditory patterns are sequences of sounds in real time. Because of this we often have less control over the onrush of auditory events than upon visual–spatial arrays that can be visually retraced. Auditory patterns may unfold as slowly as .10 of an event per second or as quickly as 10 or 20 events per second. Presentation rate is a function of event duration and of interevent intervals (IEI); it refers to the unit time taken by n events. Presentation rate is different from relative timing. It refers to whether a sequence is presented rapidly or slowly, on the average. Relative timing refers to the distribution of different durations. Within some unit time, successive sounds may all be of equivalent duration and equally spaced in time, or their durations may differ. If durations of events and the intervals between them stay constant, then there is no objective basis for variation in relative time. But if, for example, one sound is always twice as long as another, then the relative time of the two sounds differs, and if changes in durations are regular a rhythmic grouping of sounds becomes apparent. Take a pattern of two sounds: A and B. If every third sound is twice as long as the others, regardless of the pattern's presentation rate, the resulting sequence has a temporal structure: B—A—B————B—A—B———— and so on.

Rhythm can be specified apart from presentation rate because the former refers to relative event times within a given unit, while the latter refers to the total time taken by n events. In part, this distinction corresponds to the musical distinction of tempo and meter.* What complicates the understanding of rhythm is that an accent structure almost always goes hand-in-hand with specifications of relative timing. An accented sound, denoted a, is one that a listener singles out from other (unaccented) sounds. Rhythmic form occurs when time between successive accents does not change as a sequence unfolds. The problem of what creates an accent for the listener is a difficult one, because a variety of circumstances, including event durations themselves, create subjective accents (Cooper & Meyer, 1960; Fraisse, 1956; Handel & Yoder, 1975). Thus, in the foregoing pattern, the lengthened sound itself may be perceived as an accent leading to an accent structure of *uua uua,* etc. That is, in this rhythmic form the sounds B—A—B———— are grouped together subjectively and listeners report the first two sounds as unaccented and the lengthened B———— sound as accented. This is called an *end-accented* rhythmic form and is denoted (*uua*). Other ways of creating accents involve changes in a certain sound's pitch or intensity and often these changes will cause listeners to hear accents that begin a group (Woodrow, 1909). A *beginning-accented* rhythm is denoted by *au* or *auu.* As it turns

---

* The treatment of rhythmic form in terms of relative timing and accent does not preclude the possibility that people perceive meter and durational aspects of auditory patterns as separate dimensions, but it does suggest that accent structure may not be perceived independently of durational patterns. Some recent work suggests that these distinctions hold for some auditory sequences (Gabrielsson, 1973b).

out, rhythmic grouping helps listeners cope with the onrush of sounds in auditory patterns. As such, rhythmic structures reflect a fundamental and pervasive organizing process that is largely temporal in nature.

C. Serial Structure in Terms of Relations: Advances in Pattern Specification

In addition to rhythmic grouping, listeners detect other structure in temporal patterns. Consider a sequence of spoken digits: 1,3,5,3,5,7 etc. At some level relations between successive events (e.g., between 1 and 3) somehow "capture" the attention and lead into the next events. These relations are nonsemantic constraints, and the entire pattern can be conceived as a series of such relations. Clearly a definition of *relation* is necessary before the structure of an entire pattern can be specified. The purpose of this section is to define relation and to describe some kinds of serial relations that exist. To do this it is necessary to distinguish between a serial pattern and the set (s) of sounds that make up a pattern or group of patterns. The set s may consist of 2, 3 $\cdots$ S events (i.e., digits, tones, etc.). Thus if nine digits are used to construct a pattern, then $s = \{1, 2, \cdots 9\}$ and $S = 9$. Next, it is necessary to define a relation:

1. NOMENCLATURE: RELATIONS AS ORDERED SETS

A useful framework within which to cast event–event relations has been elaborated by Simon (1972). It involves the Cartesian set product of s, namely the $s \times s$ set of all ordered pairs of members of s. Examples of two product sets are shown in Figure 1. In Figure 1(a) a set of consonants $s = \{N, P, \cdots G\}$ is used, and in Fig. 1(b) a digit set $s = \{1, 2, \cdots, 5\}$ is crossed with itself. In both cases the resulting matrix contains ordered pairs. A relation is a subset of ordered pairs in the product set. If the

	N	P	X	L	G
N	(N,N)	(N,P)	(N,X)	(N,L)	(N,G)
P	(P,N)	(P,P)	(P,X)	(P,L)	(P,G)
X	(X,N)	(X,P)	(X,X)	(X,L)	(X,G)
L	(L,N)	(L,P)	(L,X)	(L,L)	(L,G)
G	(G,N)	(G,P)	(G,X)	(G,L)	(G,G)

(a)

	1	2	3	4	5
1	(1,1)	(1,2)	(1,3)	(1,4)	(1,5)
2	(2,1)	(2,2)	(2,3)	(2,4)	(2,5)
3	(3,1)	(3,2)	(3,3)	(3,4)	(3,5)
4	(4,1)	(4,2)	(4,3)	(4,4)	(4,5)
5	(5,1)	(5,2)	(5,3)	(5,4)	(5,5)

(b)

Fig. 1. Examples of two set products obtained by taking all ordered pairs of events that result from crossing s with itself (i.e., $s \times s$). Part (a) gives the set product for $s = N, P, X, L, G$ and (b) gives the set product for a digit alphabet where $s = 1, 2, 3, 4, 5$.

members of a subset share a common property and if that property comes to represent the entire subset, then a rule defines the relation set. Thus, a rule is an abstraction with respect to all instances (i.e., ordered pairs) in a subset. Depending upon the nature of s, different kinds of relations and rules can emerge to define a pattern's structure. A means of classifying pattern relations is given next:

a. Nominal relations. If members of s lack order, then only nominal relations are found in resulting patterns. Consider the set of consonants given as s in Fig. 1(a). In the $s \times s$ set, two major subsets are *identical*, given by all ordered pairs with identical members: $\{(N, N), (P, P) \cdot \cdot \cdot \}$; and *different* given by the subset of ordered pairs whose members differ: $\{(N, P), (N, L) \cdot \cdot \cdot \}$. This means that structure in a whole pattern built from these five consonants, such as *GNPPXLPX*, may be described by different rules (e.g., G, N) or identical rules (e.g., P, P) as applied to successive letter pairs. The identity rule is a powerful rule, for it relates events at the level of physical equivalence. Listeners respond not only to successive identities as in (P, P), but also regular recurrences of the same sound, as in $X \cdot \cdot \cdot X$. In fact, periodic recurrence of certain events within a sequence such as louder sounds forms the basis of simple rhythmic structure.

b. Ordinal relations and interval relations. If members of s form at least an ordinal scale then this set is called an *alphabet*. The alphabet of letters, for example, forms an ordinal scale, so that instead of different relations, there are now relation sets that give greater $(+)$ and less $(-)$ rules in addition to identical rules. Thus, descriptions of letter patterns such as *ABMCDM* can be cast in terms of ordinal relations, as Simon (1972) has shown. But with interval scales, numbers can be assigned to differences between the ordered members of s, and more relations exist. With the set product of the digit alphabets ($s = \{1, 2, \cdot \cdot \cdot 5\}$) in Fig. 1(b), for example, the greater relation can be broken down into subsets such as $\{(1, 2), (2, 3) \cdot \cdot \cdot \}$ where all pairs represent instances of a $+ 1$ rule, or $\{(1, 3), (2, 4) \cdot \cdot \cdot \}$ for a $+2$ rule, and the less relation is replaced with subtracting relations such as $\{(2, 1), (3, 1) \cdot \cdot \cdot \}$ for a -1 rule. A complement, C, is also possible where for one member i, $C(i) = S + 1 - i$. Here C describes the relation set $\{(1, 5), (2, 4) \cdot \cdot \cdot \}$. The greater array of relations possible with an interval scale allows the specification of successive relations in the sequence 1,3,1,5, for example, as $+2$ (i.e., (1, 3)), -2 for (3, 1), and C for (1, 5).

The set-product nomenclature is important, for it lays a foundation for the specification of the *entire* structure of a pattern in terms of potentially meaningful relations. A preview of such an application may convince readers of its worthiness. Consider again the pattern 1,3,1,5. Because the digit alphabet possesses nominal and ordinal, as well as interval, properties, Jones (1974) has suggested that such a pattern may be meaningfully represented in terms of levels of structure that include all three types of relations. Not only can exact differences between successive digits be specified by the interval rules: $+2$, -2, and C, but so also may ordinal (greater, less) and nominal (identical, different) relations. Ordinal structure comes from treating adjacent differences merely in terms of greater $(+)$ and less $(-)$; this results in an intermediate structural level called pattern *contour* $(+ - +)$. Nominal relations form the simplest structural level. Often these relations involve strings of physically identical events (runs), or periodic identities, as with the recurrence of 1 in 1,3,1,5.

2. Unidimensional and Multidimensional Alphabets

For simplicity an alphabet, s, is taken as a collection of discrete and discriminable sounds that can be ordered along one psychological dimension as a unidimensional alphabet or along several as a multidimensional alphabet. Common unidimensional alphabets with sound patterns are often tied to physical features such as frequency or intensity, but usually alphabetic members must differ by more than is required by differential thresholds (e.g., Pinheiro & Ptacek, 1971). With patterns that involve several physical dimensions (e.g., frequency and intensity), the possibility of representing structure in terms of weighted combinations of unidimensional alphabets has received little attention (e.g., Handel, 1974), perhaps because it is more likely that structure arises from order abstracted from the total multidimensional set of sounds. This is clearly what happens with the abstract alphabets of conventional letter- and integer-symbol systems where recent advances in scaling (e.g., Shepard, Kilpatric, & Cunningham, 1975) suggest that alphabetic order is given by one or more subjective dimensions. Because we detect patternness in many types of auditory sequences it is apparent that a basis of structure must be flexible enough to encompass alphabets that are largely physical, as well as those that are derived and symbolic. Distinctions between symbolic and physical alphabets are important for several reasons:

1. Strategies may be a function of the nature of a pattern's alphabet. That is, the verbal labeling and rehearsal proposed by some (e. g., Estes, 1972) may occur only with symbolic alphabets such as letters, while perceptual learning of pattern structure presumed by others (e.g., Gibson, 1969; Restle, 1973) may be specific to sequences built from physical alphabets such as tones.

2. The speed with which people detect structure in auditory sequences will inevitably depend upon whether the events are distinguished along a physical dimension as they are with patterns of tones, or along some derived or conceptual dimension, as with spoken patterns of digits.

3. Because symbolic auditory sequences are spoken (e.g., letters, digits), they involve both an auditory speech pattern and conceptual symbolic structure. To the extent a speech code is involved, pattern structure at the auditory level of analysis may involve complex prelinguistic auditory relations. The possibility of greater involvement of the speech code with symbolic sequences has suggested to some that verbal symbolic patterns (e.g., spoken digits) and nonverbal physical patterns (e.g., music) may be processed in different hemispheres (Kimura, 1967). However, recent work with nonspeech patterns (e.g., Halperin, Nachson, & Carmon, 1973) indicates that a strict equivalence of the verbal–nonverbal distinction with left and right hemispheres, respectively, is misleading.

a. MUSICAL PATTERNS. Musical patterns are the best examples of orderly auditory patterns that we encounter regularly. Unfortunately, musical jargon often baffles the average psychologist. An attempt is made in this section to illustrate the relevance of certain musical phenomena and terminology to the study of auditory pattern perception.

Musical scales of pitch are, in fact, auditory alphabets that relate to logarithmetic differences in sound frequency. Three common pitch scales are shown in Table I, where the leftmost column lists frequencies of 13 musical notes that form a basic musical scale, the chromatic scale, listed in the third column of the table. In contrast to pure tones, which are rarely encountered outside the laboratory, musical tones are complex sounds composed of both a fundamental frequency, shown in Table I as F_0, and many harmonic frequencies F_j ($j = 1, 2, \cdots n$). A harmonic frequency is always an integer multiple of F_0. Thus, the first harmonic, F_1 of F_0, is always twice the frequency of F_0, and in general, $F_j = (j + 1) F_0$. It is the fundamental frequency, F_0, that determines the pitch of a harmonic tone. Notes whose fundamental frequencies correspond to harmonic ratios of 2 : 1 are separated in pitch by an interval called an *octave*. Thus, in the first column of Table I, the tone with an F_0 of 523.25 Hz, namely C′, is twice the fundamental frequency of C, which is 261.63 Hz, and is an octave higher in pitch. Within this octave interval several ordinal and interval alphabets of pitch exist. The chromatic scale is one that is interval scaled with respect to pitch because ratios of successive tone-frequency increments, ΔF, to the prior frequency are virtually constant at .0595.* Thus,

---

* Although the establishment of interval differences is important to the elaboration of scales and to an objective description of musical and pattern structure, in practice, listeners' representation of intervals may be imperfect.

TABLE I

THREE COMMON MUSICAL ALPHABETS

Frequency (F_0) in hertz	$\Delta F/F$ Semitones	Chromatic scale	C-major scale	Whole-tone scale	
				Note	Digit code
261.63		C	C	C	1
	.0594				
277.18		C#			
	.0595				
293.66		D	D	D	2
	.0595				
311.13		D#			
	.0595				
329.63		E	E	E	3
	.0595				
349.23		F	F		
	.0594				
369.99		F#		F#	4
	.0595				
391.99		G	G		
	.0595				
415.31		G#		G#	5
	.0594				
440.00		A	A		
	.0595				
466.16		A#		A#	6
	.0595				
493.88		B	B		
	.0595				
523.25		C'	C'	C'	1'

the chromatic scale divides an octave interval into 12 equal pitch intervals called semitones. From this scale, other scales are formed by skipping notes. Two of these, the familiar C-major scale and the whole-tone scale are also listed in Table I. The C-major alphabet is ordinal with respect to pitch because notes are separated by either one or two semitones.* An interval of two semitones is called a whole tone. The whole-tone scale can be treated as an interval alphabet with respect to pitch, because successive notes are separated throughout by whole-tone intervals.

* This presentation of musical scales is oversimplified because listeners finally may treat the C-major scale subjectively as if it were an interval scale. Moreover, in terms of frequency differences (in Hz) members of the chromatic and whole-tone scale are logarithmically related. For simplicity, the transformation of these scales to the interval digit code of Table I is not elaborated upon here.

It is apparent that musical scales give special status to octaves, each of which represents only a slice of the overall audible frequency range (20–20,000 Hz). Yet traditionally psychophysicists have assumed that pitch is uniformly determined by frequency, so that the higher a tone's frequency the higher its pitch, regardless of its location within an octave (Stevens & Volkman, 1940). How is this resolved? There is accumulating evidence that pitch of tones below 5000 Hz can be represented by two subjective dimensions, *tone height* and *tone chroma* (Attneave & Olson, 1971; Deutsch, 1975; Shepard, 1964). Tone height reflects the sense of high and low pitch that varies with overall frequency, wheras tone chroma reflects the relative position of a tone within some octave. Shepard (1964) suggests that the two dimensions jointly form a helix, with tone height given in a vertical scale and chroma in a surrounding circular alphabet. One implication of the circular chromatic alphabet is that diametrically opposed tones within it (e.g., notes C and F# in Table I) bear special relationships to each other that do not necessarily exist in a linear representation of the same array.

Tones within a given octave, therefore, differ in fundamental frequencies and harmonic structure, whereas tones in corresponding positions in different octaves have different fundamental frequencies but similar harmonic structures (Winckel, 1967). Special aspects of the harmonic structure of (complex) tones that last longer than 50 msec determine the uniqueness of tone chroma. That is, the relative intensities of harmonic frequencies vary with different sound-producing instruments. A frequency spectrum of a single, steady state, sound can show this graphically by portraying intensities of harmonics with varying line lengths. Take, for example, an idealized spectrum for a natural horn sounding a note with F_0 of 80 Hz, shown in Fig. 2(a). The third harmonic is relatively more intense than the fundamental, as indicated by a longer vertical line at 320 Hz. A higher note with F_0 of 240 Hz of different chromatic quality is shown in Fig. 2(b). Here, successively less intense harmonics at 480, 720, and 960 Hz are given by progressively shorter lines at these points. In fact, relative intensity is more realistically represented in terms of spectral regions, not discrete lines; the dotted *envelope* connecting the vertical lines in the spectra of Fig. 2(a) and 2(b) is probably a truer representation of their tonal structure. A majority of musical sounds have spectral envelopes with two or three major peaks that correspond closely to harmonic frequencies. Nonmusical sounds, including speech sounds, are also characterized by several major spectral peaks, but these are not directly related to harmonic frequencies.

These illustrations show us properties of isolated musical sounds. In music, many different sounds follow each other at rates of approximately

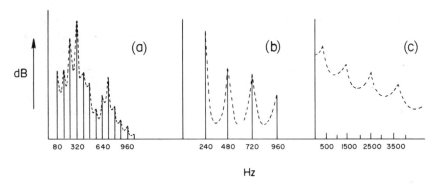

Fig. 2. Idealized frequency spectra of two sound producing sources. Parts (a) and (b) indicate regions of relatively more intense frequencies in the spectra of a natural horn sound notes with fundamental frequencies of 80 Hz and 240 Hz. [Adapted from Winckel (1967).] Part (c) shows the spectrum of the neutral vowel sound | ə | . [Adapted from Richardson & Meyer (1962).]

10 sounds per second in patterns that are much more complex than those currently studied in controlled situations by psychologists. But, despite their complexity, musical patterns combine rhythmic structure with relations built on tone height and tone chroma. Therefore, to the extent that the auditory patterns we do study capture these relations, we shall achieve a greater understanding of music perception. In fact, examples of auditory patterns presented in the remainder of this chapter will often, for simplicity, be treated in terms of musical alphabets, especially the whole-tone scale. For this reason, the last column of Table I references notes of this scale as a digit code. The reader is urged to become familiar with this code.

b. SPEECH. Like music, speech presents a rapid and continuously changing pattern of sounds occurring at rates of approximately 20 sounds sec^{-1} (Winckel, 1967) that is rhythmically organized (Martin, 1972). Unlike music, a meaningful alphabet for the auditory level of speech analysis has not been identified. Some (e.g., Jakobson, Fant, & Halle, 1969) have suggested that the smallest speech sounds identifiable in isolation (phonemes) are the basic units of acoustic speech patterns. In part, this is because, as steady-state sounds, phonemes can be categorized into a nominal scale based upon groups of distinctive features that arise from a multidimensional acoustic representation of speech sounds. Indeed, in terms of spectral structure, a comparison of phonemes with harmonic structure of steady-state musical sounds testifies to similar multidimensional representations of both types of sounds: A phoneme possesses a fundamental frequency and regions of relatively intense higher-order frequencies, just as a musical note possesses an F_0 and various intensities of harmonics. The spectral peaks in envelopes of phonemic sounds are called *formants*. Formants of consonants bear little resemblance to the harmonic structure of musical notes, but those of vowels are often strikingly similar. Take the vowel sound of *a* in *sofa*, for example,* which is /ə/. An idealized spectral envelope of /ə/, shown in Fig. 2(c), illustrates a first formant frequency at 500 Hz, and successively less intense peaks at 1500, 2500 Hz, and so forth. Often it is the formant properties of vowels and consonants, such as rapid changes in formant frequency (i.e., formant transitions), that offer the basis for phonemic categorization.

But real speech, like music, combines these sounds into rapidly changing patterns. And in the speech pattern, steady state acoustic properties of many phonemes are often modulated (Liberman, Delattre, & Cooper, 1952) leading some to abandon the search for an auditory alphabet of speech (e.g., Liberman, Cooper, Shankweiler, & Studdert-Kennedy, 1967). Others have sought to make sense of the speech pattern by exploring invariant auditory features within a spoken syllable (Cole & Scott, 1974). The rising or falling contours formed from successive formants over the syllable appear to provide information about the temporal order of phonemes within. It is possible that a complex of auditory scales along several dimensions may eventually contribute to an understanding of speech patterns at auditory or phonetic levels of structure, or both, but clear parallels to musical dimensions and alphabets are not apparent at this time. Nevertheless, it is inappropriate to rule out the possibility of some auditory alphabet before there exists a clearer understanding of the distinction between *alphabets,* on the one hand, and the use of alphabetic *rules* on the other. Because this understanding may come with the study of alphabetic structures in simpler, abstract, auditory patterns, the research covered in this chapter has relevance for theories of music and speech.

D. Theories

A simple auditory pattern built from the whole-tone scale (Table I in digit code) can be grouped in time as 1,2,3—2,3,4—6,5,4—5,4,3. If a listener hums a reproduction of this, his responses will typically be quick but grouped in time, and even if erroneous his sounds will correspond to certain relationships between the presented ones (e.g., 1,2,3—3,4,5). This sensitivity to relations in time and content documents the implausibility of psychological explanations that incorporate neither temporal organization nor context effects. Historically, the approaches most neglectful of these

---

* The phoneme sound denoted /ə/ represents the vowel sound of *a* in *sofa* or *u* in *putt*.

considerations have been behavioristic theories, wherein successive events are viewed as chained by S–R bonds, and models based on pure memory, where memory is primarily a function of the number of events admitted to some chamber of limited capacity. The traditional reluctance of psychologists to posit relations, however, is currently giving way to a recognition of the real challenges involved in representing meaningful psychological relations. As articulated much earlier by Lashley (1951), this challenge demands not only that we discover cognitive representations of relations that define patterns in time, but that we understand how these relations are detected and how they come to guide pattern reproduction. It was the speed and organization of pattern reproduction, like those of the hummed protocol above, that caught Lashley's fancy. They suggested to him the existence of an active central mechanism flexibly moving amidst preplanned schemes. What else could explain the rhythmic bursts, the nonrandom nature of errors, and the facility of remembering so many otherwise discrete sounds?

In response to this challenge, modern theorists have sought to characterize these preplanned schemes. In so doing, some have focused only upon rhythmic schemes and others only upon relations between events; all have been forced to assume the existence of elusive central mechanisms working amidst these schemes. Most are theories of temporal pattern perception and cognition, and not specifically theories of auditory pattern perception. All assume that abstraction of rules is finally a central, modality-independent process that is not tied to specifics of individual events. Finally, none have completely met the challenge of how patterns in time are centrally abstracted and cognitively transformed to finally guide response groupings that follow real-time properties of the original sequence. Theories are sketched in three categories: (a) the associative listener; (b) the structuring listener; (c) the structure-detecting listener, with emphasis upon the ways each links activity with pattern relations.

1. THE ASSOCIATIVE LISTENER

For associationism to cope with rapid serial responding there must be provision for the activation and direction of response groups. Estes (1972) has accomplished this with a hierarchically organized scheme. The hierarchy is an associative network that maintains, in immediate memory, representations of serial groups of sounds to which sets of responses may be attached. To represent the structure in 1,2,6,5, for example, events are associated (e.g., 1 with 2 and 6 with 5), then these groups are labeled (e.g., *up, down*), and the labels are rehearsed if time between events and/or event groups is sufficient. Activity, in the form of verbal rehearsal, then cements the serial order of labeled events (*up–down*). Rehearsal achieves this by contributing to the growth of an inhibitory network, which in turn directs serial reproduction by preventing intrusions of inappropriate responses during recall.

This theory arises from work with temporal letter patterns. As such, its emphasis on rehearsal as a source for inhibition of order errors seems misplaced with sequences of nonverbal events such as tones. Furthermore, because activity is confined to verbal rehearsal, pattern relations can only guide responding via labels such as *up* or *down*. This means that rules are abstracted primarily in the form of verbal mnemonics.

2. THE STRUCTURING LISTENER

Modern heirs to the Wurzburg tradition find directed activity in their listeners either as Gestalt restructuring or as imageless thinking given in programmed moves upon a memory alphabet.

For both Fraisse (1956) and Garner (1974), Gestalt principles describe the central preplanned scheme guiding responses. Fraisse has sought temporal parallels to spatial contour in an analysis of rhythmic structure. As a result of studies on the reproduction of tapping rhythms, Fraisse proposed two organizing principles: *assimilation,* which reflects the tendency of listeners to equalize similar durations in a series; and *differentiation,* which reflects the tendency to exaggerate other time differences. Together, these distorting principles lead people to produce taps in time that are grouped with equivalent short durations, in contrast to long temporal pauses.

Garner (1974) has placed less emphasis on temporal structures and more upon organization of sounds themselves in binary sequences. A listener is assumed to hear one of the two sounds as the figure, and the other as the ground. Two central organizing principles govern the way a listener then structures figure and ground categories: the run principle and the gap principle. The run principle has a listener reorganize incoming events so that the longest string of identical events (i.e., a run) of the *figure* element begins the pattern, whereas in a gap organization the longest run of the *ground* event is last. Thus, if *B* becomes the figure in the repeating pattern *ABBBAAB,* the run principle yields the representation *BBBAABA,* while the gap principle gives *BABBBAA.* Activity, in this view, comes in pattern reorganization. However, listeners actively reorganize pattern wholes in a conceptual fashion primarily at slow presentation rates. At rapid rates, reorganization occurs according to similar Gestalt principles, but somehow it becomes a passive perceptual process. Reorganization, whether conceptual or perceptual, is more difficult if run and gap rules conflict, resulting in many alternative organizations, than if they are compatible.

Directed activity is formalized in Simon's computer model (Simon & Kotovsky, 1963), which posits three psychological stages: rule discovery, rule representation, and interpretation. In the first stage, periodicities in a presented sequence (e.g., the period of M in $ABMCDM$) incite the listener to search his memory for a rule that relates events within the period (e.g., A, B). Listeners are assumed to have in memory not only the appropriate alphabet (s is the Roman alphabet in this case), but also a repertoire of rules about elements from this $s \times s$ set product. In the second stage, a located rule is represented in a cognitive program as an instruction to move from one alphabetic event to another (e.g., "next" of A is B). For Simon, this means the pattern is stored as a concept. In the third stage, the program is interpreted to produce the event series in real time. Because some complex pattern representations can be interpreted in one of several ways to reproduce the same sequence in real time, Greeno and Simon (1974) have maintained that this approach meets Lashley's ideal of a mechanism that moves flexibly amidst preplanned schemes. But an implication of this flexibility is that the three stages are not strictly dependent, so that the order in which a listener discovers the rules need not determine how he reproduces the pattern itself. In contrast to Garner's use of alternative organizations, this aspect of Simon's approach implies that different interpretations, or restructuring, of the same pattern whole contribute to a more adaptable listener.

3. THE STRUCTURE-DETECTING LISTENER

The role of background activity both from the listener and the environment suggest a third approach wherein a listener actively seeks invariant relations against a flux of constant change. Some impetus for this view comes from the theories of the Gibsons (E. J. Gibson, 1969; J. J. Gibson, 1966) who argue that object perception arises from the organism's detection of invariant higher-order physical relationships given by the object, such as its contour and texture. In visual object perception, such properties do not change, even as an object is transformed along physical dimensions (e.g., size or illumination) as a result of environmental change (e.g., object movement) or as a result of the organism's own activity (e.g., motion toward or from the object). In audition, some (e.g., Kubovy, Cutting, & McGuire, 1974; Mach, 1914) maintain that auditory patterns and melodies, by virtue of their various dimensions (e.g., frequency, intensity, time) and higher-order structural properties, are the objects of auditory perception.

Recently, Restle (1973; Restle & Brown, 1970) proposed that higher-order invariants that people detect in temporal patterns have to do with interval relations that exist between successive serial events. These rela-

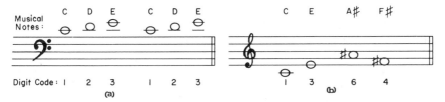

Fig. 3. Musical representation of the structure of two tone patterns. Panel a shows the pattern, 1,2,3,1,2,3, as notes from the whole tone scale; panel (b) similarly shows the pattern, 1,3,6,4. Both patterns have formulas given by combinations of rules presented in Fig. 5.

tions are best illustrated in certain types of serial patterns. The pattern 1,2,3—2,3,4—6,5,4—5,4,3 is one of these. A shift of one unit in the whole tone alphabet using a next (i.e., N^1) rule applied to 1,2,3 generates 2,3,4, but exact interval distances (i.e., +1) between component events within the subsets are unchanged. A complement rule, C, relates 1,2,3—2,3,4 to 6,5,4—5,4,3 on this alphabet where $S = 6$. The final pattern has a hierarchical formula $C[N^1(x)]$, where $x = 1,2,3$, that reflects the invariance of certain interval relations amidst transformations by N^1 and C of the events themselves. Such hierarchical schemes provide the basis for Restle's concept of psychological activity, which involves the detection and transformation of interval relations.

Jones (1974) has called attention to the role of invariant relations other than interval relations in an approach that conceives of levels of different relations, rather than hierarchical stratification of interval relations. A listener is assumed to progress from detection of nominal, or rhythmic, invariants to detection of ordinal, or contour, relations, and finally to abstraction of certain invariant interval rules. This progression is best understood by considering a pattern that has easily identifiable relations at each of these levels, namely 1,2,3,—1,2,3 (from the whole-tone scale, Table I); musically, it appears in Fig. 3(a). Because an initial sound is often perceived as an accent, the regular recurrence of 1 in 1,2,3—1,2,3 leads to the rhythmic form, *auu–auu*. Within and between rhythmic groups, higher-order structural invariants are detected if time permits. Thus a listener next detects contour in terms of ordinal rules of greater (+) and less (−): ++−++− that remain invariant within (i.e., +) and between (i.e., ++−) rhythmic groups. Finally, with time and/or practice, invariant interval differences emerge for the listener* and these are captured in the formula, $I\{N^1[N^1(1)]\}$ where I reflects the identity rule operating on 1,2,3

* Locking of a biological rhythm into environmental sequences has been technically termed *entrainment*.

to give 1,2,3. Other, more complex patterns such as that of Fig. 3(b) can be similarly represented in terms of rules that differ from Restle's. These rules, shown in Fig. 5, permit descriptions of organizational schemes that will describe pattern invariances based on nominal, ordinal, and/or interval relations primarily because they form mathematical groups. Combinations of these rules form the central schemes that permit Jones to describe a listener's activity as one of detecting certain kinds of predetermined invariances.

4. THEORETICAL SUMMARY

Each theory has sought to represent a listener's activity along different preplanned lines. In some cases, activity is circumspect, limited to rehearsal of hierarchically clustered symbols (Estes, 1972). In others, it is spelled out with rules as programmed instructions (Simon, 1972). For a few, activity is given in detecting invariants in one level of pattern structure against changes in others (Jones, 1974; Restle, 1973). Some similarities and differences among these approaches transcend theoretical categories:

1. In different ways, Jones, Restle, and Simon are more explicit in linking levels of pattern structure to proposed activities than are Estes and Garner.
2. Estes, Garner, and Jones have indicated circumstances in which activity takes time to be effective, and so make predictions about the role of pattern presentation rate, whereas others do not.
3. Fraisse, Garner, and Restle have concentrated upon structure in patterns built from physical dimensions such as tones, lights, or durations, whereas the theories of Estes, Jones, and Simon relate more to patterns of symbols such as letters or digits.
4. Fraisse, Jones, and Simon attempt to incorporate effects of pattern periodicities and/or rhythm into pattern perception, whereas others do not.

These comparisons suggest some issues that develop in the next section where research on pattern structure, presentation rate, and relative timing is considered.

II. CURRENT RESEARCH

Beneath the theoretical differences already outlined are classic problems that relate to perception of holistic patterns, expectancy, and the role of attention in rhythm. With the recent emergence of auditory pattern perception as an area of theoretical concern in its own right, the scattered research on sometimes unrelated topics has been replaced with more focused attention on (*a*) evaluation of pattern structure; (*b*) presentation rate; and (*c*) relative timing.

A. Pattern Structure

When single events form a sequence, effects of the collective context on the perception of individual members are so overwhelming (Deutsch & Roll, 1974; Guilford & Nelson, 1937; Fraisse, 1956) that Gestalt psychologists argue that patternness can only be understood in terms of the total pattern, and not isolated members. To show this, consider the sequence of whole tones, 2,3,2—3,4,2. Here the last sound is likely to be mistaken for a 3, because the prior context (2,3,2) encourages a listener to expect 3,4,3. Gestalt critics are surely correct in their claim that a pattern is not a simple sum of individual parts. Nevertheless, it may be possible to explore the structure of whole patterns in terms of special combinations of individual parts, if the parts themselves are conceived of as relations. That is, it is the consistency of $+1$ then -1 from 2,3,2 in 2,3,2—3,4,3 that makes this a good, or easy, pattern. In this manner, expectancy about forthcoming events is given by extrapolation of relations between encountered events. If this is so, then as the theories discussed in the previous section indicate, two important questions are what relations are most compelling and what schemas determine their extrapolations?

Methodologically, there are two approaches to answering these questions: (*a*) listeners revealing organizing principles in their *subjective* descriptions; and (*b*) listeners confronting *objectively* selected easy and hard pattern structures. Both have advantages and disadvantages. The former discourages formulation of interesting testable hypotheses, while the latter can be unduly restrictive. Both have been used successfully with binary patterns (0, 1), where the majority of research has been centered. With more complex patterns ($S > 2$), to which attention will be directed in the future, the subjective method may prove more unwieldy than the a priori manipulation of pattern structure.

1. PATTERNS THAT COMBINE NOMINAL RELATION: TWO APPROACHES TO PATTERN STRUCTURE

Binary or trinary patterns are usually formed by arrangements of respectively two or three arbitrarily selected sounds that usually vary on several acoustic dimensions. In these cases, pattern structure is given by combinations of nominal relations. With binary patterns, for example, some suggest that Gestalt principles govern overall arrangements of strings of identical events, while others contend that accent structure generates temporal expectancies about pattern length. Gestalt theorists have typically relied upon the subjective method, whereas proponents of the latter view objectively manipulate accent structure.

Royer and Garner (1966) sought to reveal the operation of run and gap principles on listeners' reorganization of repeating binary sound patterns using the subjective method. The patterns (shown in Table II) were begun at each of a pattern's eight serial positions. People listened until they could tap two keys in synchrony with the pattern sounds. Because sequences varied in structure, the authors predicted that those with conflicting run and gap principles (e.g., 11011010 of Table II) would be difficult for a listener to organize. If a listener revealed a run organization of one of these patterns by beginning to tap at the onset of the longest run of the figure element, the longest run of the ground element would not end the pattern, thus violating the gap principle. However, patterns with compatible run and gap principles (e.g., 11111110 of Table II) offer few alternative organizations and so should be easy. The number of alternative ways to organize each pattern given by compatibility of run–gap principles is shown in the fourth column of Table II. However, as a result of listeners' demonstrated variability in initiating key tapping at each of a pattern's serial locations, a subjectively weighted measure of alternative organizations called *response-point uncertainty* (RPU) was also determined. This is given in the fifth column. The impact of run–gap compatibility upon subjective organizations was supported by the finding that RPU correlated highly with performance difficulty as measured by the median delay in responding averaged over serial start locations (sixth column of Table II). This, and related work (e.g., Preusser, 1972), have supported Garner's interpretation that pattern structure is guided by human predisposition about the relative placements of strings of identical events.

A different interpretation of pattern structure comes from Martin (1972), according to whom good, or easy, patterns are those with equally spaced accents. If accent is taken as the *onset* of one of the two pattern events, then the accent structure (a, u) for Royer and Garner's patterns is given above each in Table II. The accent-structure hypothesis predicts that patterns (i.e., patterns 1 through 8 of Table II) with accents occurring at serial locations 1, or 1 and 3 and/or 5 should be easy because these are equidistant in time. A reconsideration of the data in Table II indicates that:

1. Most listeners began to respond at a pattern's accent point, as indicated by the modal response location for each pattern (underlined in the first column).
2. Listeners were quick to respond at the pattern's accent point for patterns 1 through 8.

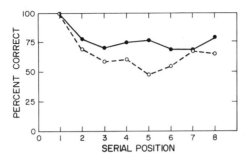

Fig. 4. Percent recall of events at each of eight serial positions for "good" (8G,●) and "poor" (8P,○) accent structures in a 4 sec delayed recall task. Each curve is averaged over four patterns. [Reproduced from Sturges & Martin (1974). Copyright 1974 by the American Psychological Association. Reprinted by permission.]

3. Other patterns were not quickly responded to, as the delays shown in the third column of Table II indicate.

The run–gap hypothesis and the accent-structure hypothesis often agree on which patterns are easy and which are difficult; they disagree on why. Martin's hypothesis parsimoniously predicts an interaction of accent structure with pattern length, whereas Garner's hypothesis does not. That is, accents must equally divide a whole sequence, and such a division is unlikely with patterns that are eight events long, but not with pattern composed of seven events. Sturges and Martin (1974) tested this prediction and found that rhythmic patterns of length 8 were more readily recognized than patterns of length 7 that were not uniformly divided in time by the same accent structure. Furthermore, listeners tended to forget poor accent patterns over a 4-sec delay, especially in central serial positions, but not good ones. Figure 4 presents delayed recall accuracy averaged over several good and poor patterns of length 8.

In summary, some evidence indicates that temporal regularity of certain events is important in the structure of binary sound patterns. One way of understanding accent structure of good patterns is in terms of recurrent nominal relations of fixed periods. The periodic recurrence of accented sounds defines an invariant property, or rule, that relates to the time dimension. This rule, when used, generates an expectancy about when a rhythmic pattern should end.

2. PATTERNS THAT COMBINE ORDINAL AND INTERVAL RELATIONS

Patterns that combine more than two sounds are potentially complex. We must consider not only how the events relate to the time dimension in

TABLE II

Two Hypotheses about Binary Pattern Structure[a]

Accent structure/ patterns	Accent–structure hypothesis		Run–Gap uncertainty hypothesis		
	Predictions	Observations	Predictions		Observations
	Serial location of accents[a]	Median delay of modal start response (sec)	Run–Gap alternatives	RPU	Mean of median delay over all starting locations
a u u u u u u u 1. 1̲ 1 1 1 1 1 1 0	1	16	2	1.32	21.9
a u u u u u u u 2. 1̲ 1 1 1 0 0 0 0	1	12	2	1.42	18.0
a u u u u u u u 3. 1̲ 1 1 1 1 0 0 0	1	16	2	1.45	20.5
a u u u u u u u 4. 1̲ 1 1 1 1 1 0 0	1	16	2	1.68	20.9
a u u u u a u u u 5. 1̲ 1 0 0 1 1 0 0	1, 5	11	2	1.27	13.0
a u u u u a u u u 6. 1̲ 1 1 0 1 1 1 0	1, 5	12	2	1.32	14.5
a u u u u a u u u 7. 1̲ 1 1 0 1 0 0 0	1, 5	26	2	1.89	34.9
a u a u a u a u 8. 1 0̲ 1 0 1 0 1 0	1, 3, 5, 7	12	2	.99	11.5
a u u u u a u a u 9. 1̲ 0 0 0 1 0 1 0	1, 5, 7	16	2	1.88	21.4
a u u u u u u a u 10. 1 1 1 0̲ 0 0 1 0	1, 7	24	3	2.02	33.4
a u u u u u u a u 11. 1 1 1 1 1 0̲ 1 0	1, 7	30	2	2.05	24.5

Pattern					
a u u u u a u u 12. 1̲1110100	1, 6	16	2	2.07	26.9
a u u u u a u u 13. 11110̲110	1, 6	16	3	2.11	24.1
a u u u u a u u 14. 110̲00100	1, 6	26	3	2.12	37.5
a u u u a u u u 15. 1110̲0110	1, 6	41	3	2.12	44.5
a u u u a u u u 16. 1110̲0100	1, 6	28	3	2.15	33.0
a u u a u u a u 17. 110̲10100	1, 4, 6	24	3	2.19	30.5
a u u a u u u a u 18. 1101001̲0	1, 4, 7	112	6	2.43	103.9
a u u a u u u a u 19. 1̲1011̲010	1, 4, 7	33; 49	6	2.73	48.8

[a] Comparison of an accent structure hypothesis (Martin) with the Run–Gap hypothesis (Garner). Patterns, taken from Royer and Garner (1966) are listed in the left-most column with accent structure (a, u) above each, and with the modal start location underlined. Columns 2 and 3 present, respectively, accent–structure predictions, in terms of serial locations of accents (a), and observations based on delay in responding of the modal start response for each pattern. Columns 4, 5, and 6 list, respectively, the objective number of different organizations possible from Run–Gap analysis, subjective uncertainty in pattern start points is RPU, and the median of the mean of response delays at all pattern start points. [Data are taken from Royer & Garner, 1966; reproduced with permission of the author and the Psychonomic Society, Inc.]

275

rhythm, but also how (if at all) they relate to each other along one or more alphabetic dimensions. Lack of criteria for pattern specification has drastically hampered the study of these patterns. What structural descriptions exist stem from work with visual–temporal patterns (e.g., Jones, 1974; Restle & Brown, 1970), although some come from analysis of music (e.g., Deutsch, 1969; Simon & Sumner, 1968). None, however, have generated a corpus of knowledge about the perception of complex auditory patterns. All agree that listeners readily detect certain abstract pitch relations that tend to involve the circular tone-chroma alphabet and, furthermore, that these relations can be generalized, as relations, to other octaves along the tone-height dimension (Deutsch, 1969, 1975). In fact, it is with respect to transposed melody that the issue of abstracting holistic pattern relations has been classically posed (e.g., Koffka, 1935). In shifting a whole-tone pattern such as 2,3—6,5—3,4—5,4 up an octave to 2′,3′,—6′,5′—3′,4′—5′, 4′, it is readily apparent even to the untrained listener that the auditory object, or melody, is preserved, although the individual parts (i.e., the tones) change.

What is preserved with pattern transposition? It appears that both the sequence of ordinal relations $(+ + - - + + -)$ and that of interval differences $(+1, +3, -1, -2, +1, +1, -1)$ between successive whole tones are unchanged with transposition, and listeners are able to use both to identify complex patterns. Pattern contour was found to determine short-term recognition of transposed five-tone auditory patterns, while exact interval differences determined listeners' identification of distorted versions of familiar folk tunes (Dowling & Fujitani, 1971). That is, depending upon the task, different invariant properties are abstracted from a given sequence as contour and interval rules.

It is for the future to discover how people use these structural levels: the nominal level in accent structure, the ordinal level in contour, and the interval level in melody. One system (Jones, 1974) that permits a priori manipulations of structural levels involves the mathematical groups of rules given in Fig. 5 for the whole-tone-pitch alphabet (chroma) of $S = 6$ where $s = \{1, 2, 3, 4, 5, 6\}$. Each rule is illustrated by its transformation of 1,2,3. Thus, $T(1,2,3)$ transposes 1,2,3 to 4,5,6 by $S/2$. Reflection, $R\ell$, of 1,2,3 gives 3,2,1, and $C(1,2,3)$ is 6,5,4. The Next, or N^J rules, are adding or subtracting rules, so N^1 (123) is 234 within s as defined, but $N^S(1,2,3)$ can shift the entire pattern up an octave (i.e., to s' on the tone height dimension) to 1′2′3′. When used in different combinations, these rules have the power to describe invariant pattern features at each level of structure. Some patterns will possess alternations, others symmetries, and still others interval invariances. Table III presents illustrative patterns for each of three cases of structural invariance: Case 1, or repeating

Formal Rule Definitions in terms of a given symbol, i			Rule Applications
Rule	Notation	Definition	Examples apply to unit, i, from alphabet : 123456
Identity	I	$I(i) = i$	$I(i) = 123$
Next	N	$N^j(i) = i + j$	$N^1(i) = 234 ; N^2(i) = 345$
Transpose	T	$T(i) = i + \Delta$	$T(i) = 456$
Complement	C	$C(i) = 2\Delta + 1 - i$	$C(i) = 654$
Reflection	RL	$RL(i) = \Delta + 1 - i \ (if\ i \leq \Delta)$ $RL(i) = 3\Delta + 1 - i \ (if\ i > \Delta)$	$RL(i) = 321$
Where $\Delta = S/2$ and S is alphabet size			Where $i = 123$ and $S = 6$

Fig. 5. Notation and definition of rules that describe relations within complex patterns are given in the three left columns. Examples of rule usage are given in the right panel. Note that rules are defined with respect to some alphabet of size S, but they may apply either to a single event, $i = 1, 2, 3, 4, 5,$ or 6, or to several events as when $i = 1,2,3$.

patterns, involves alternations of some unit (x) with another (not x). These patterns result from successive transforms of x by either T, $R\ell$, or C. Thus, repeatedly transposing 2,4 gives 2,4–5, 1–2, 4–5,1 as shown in Table III; Case 2 involves pattern arrangements of consistent contours, or symmetries, or both. These result from schemas that combine I, T, $R\ell$, and C. For example, 1,6—6,1—3,4—4,3, comes from successive application of C, then T, and C again to 1,6. A property of symmetrical patterns is invariant contour under a mirror-image transformation (See Table III, Case 2). Case 3 patterns use N^J to add or subtract either within the original set, s, or to transpose to other sets (s'). With repeated application of N^1 to 2,5, for example, interval differences between adjacent events in transformed pairs of the sequence, 2,5—3,6—4,1—5,2, remain $|3|$.

Little is known of the ability of any rule system to handle phenomena in auditory pattern perception, but there is evidence that each of the rules in Fig. 5 is detectable even in short-term auditory pattern recognition (Dowling, 1972). Nevertheless, it is the rules in combination that reveal special mathematical properties of the rule group pertaining to pattern invariances. Perhaps eventually expectancy can be cast in terms of such rule combinations so that a listener's anticipations are actually those extrapolations of ongoing pattern relations that retain rhythmic, contour, and/or interval invariances. In this sense, this system has greater breadth than

TABLE III

THREE CASES OF PATTERN STRUCTURE[a]

Start units X	Example patterns of successive rules applied to X	Predominant pattern features	Representation of pattern structure	
			Level of formal structure	invariant property formal description
Case 1:	Repeating patterns			
2,4	2,4 5,1 2,4 5,1 $\underline{T}\uparrow$ $\underline{T}\uparrow$ $\underline{T}\uparrow$	Alternations of X	Nominal:	period of nominal relation = 3 intervening events
1,2,3	1,2,3 6,5,4 1,2,3 6,5,4 $\underline{C}\uparrow$ $\underline{C}\uparrow$ $\underline{C}\uparrow$	Alternations of X	Nominal:	period of nominal relation = 5 intervening events
Case 2:	Pattern symmetries			
1,6	1,6 6,1 3,4 4,3 $\underline{C}\uparrow$ $\underline{T}\uparrow$ $\underline{C}\uparrow$	Invariant contour	Ordinal:	$(+)I(-)+(+)I(-)$
1,2,3	1,2,3 6,5,4 4,5,6 3,2,1 $\underline{C}\uparrow$ $\underline{R\ell}\uparrow$ $\underline{C}\uparrow$	Mirror contour	Ordinal:	$(+\,+)+(-\,-)I(+\,+)-(-\,-)$
Case 3:	Adding, subtracting patterns			
2,5	2,5 3,6 4,1 5,2 $\underline{N}^1\uparrow$ $\underline{N}^1\uparrow$ $\underline{N}^1\uparrow$	Invariant event distances	Interval:	$(|3|)^{+1}(|3|)^{+1}(|3|)^{+1}(|3|)$
1,2,3	1,2,3 3,4,5 1',2',3' 3',4',5' $\underline{N}^2\uparrow$ $\underline{N}^{s-2}\uparrow$ $\underline{N}^2\uparrow$	Invariant event distances	Interval:	$(|1|\,|1|)^{+2}(|1|\,|1|)^{+4}$ $(|1|\,|1|)^{+2}(|1|\,|1|)$

[a] Three pattern types (Cases 1, 2, 3) with generative rules in left columns have respectively different invariant features that relate to structural levels: nominal, ordinal, and interval.

others that have focussed either upon nominal structure, as with Garner's run–gap principles, or upon interval invariances, as in the case of Restle's theory.

While this section focuses upon pitch patterns, similar distinctions are possible with intensity differences. Rhythmic contour, for example, consists of special arrangements of intensity differences that can be viewed as Case-2 (or hierarchical) accent patterns (Martin, 1972). Patterns based not upon physical alphabets, but upon learned, symbolic ones (e.g., digits, letters) are also amenable to interpretations involving expectancies based upon physical features (e.g., Case 1, 2) or upon inferred rules (Case 2, 3). Unfortunately, research that relates in one way or another to these ideas is sparse.

B. Presentation Rate

One remarkable aspect of auditory patterns is their transposability along the time dimension: We readily recognize the same melody or spoken phrase at speeds both faster and slower than normal. Just as the pattern of pitches preserves its integrity when melody shifts an octave on the tone-height dimension, so also rhythmic character remains unchanged if temporal structure is shifted up or down on the time dimension within limits. It is important to stress that temporal transposition has its limits, for at very rapid rates listeners do fail to accurately integrate serial pattern structure (Peters, 1975). And at very slow rates, performance is also modified. Two theorists who have studied the effects of presentation rate most carefully suggest that two psychological processes underlie this performance. Both Estes (1972) and Garner (1974) distinguish a process of immediate perceptual representation of serial order operating at fast rates from a process involving relating successive events that occurs memorially at slower rates.

For Estes, immediate perception is hierarchically organized and veridical, with confusions of temporal order developing rapidly and overcome only by time-consuming rehearsal. On the other hand, Garner assumes that an immediate perceptual restructuring occurs at rapid rates, but that as time separates successive events, listeners must actively engage Gestalt principles to restructure the pattern. A primary difference between the two theories rests with Garner's commitment to interpreting pattern structure in terms of run–gap principles and Estes' lack of such a commitment. This difference results in Garner's prediction of an interaction of structure with presentation rate, whereas Estes' has no basis for such a prediction.

An important study by Garner and Gottwald (1968) permits evaluation of Garner's prediction by varying both presentation rate (from .8 events sec^{-1} to 8 events sec^{-1}) and structure in repeating binary patterns (145 Hz, 195 Hz). Structure was varied in 10 patterns, selected from Table II, by starting each either at a preferred start point (PSP), namely the modal start point underlined in Table II, or at a nonpreferred location (NPSP). Run–gap principles were consistent with PSP patterns, but not with NPSP patterns. The authors anticipated that at slower rates expectancies based on initial events would facilitate PSP pattern identification, but interfere with NPSP patterns. Because expectancy could not operate at rapid rates, fast patterns should be automatically integrated according to run–gap principles, but via a perceptual, rather than a conceptual, process.

Listeners heard a sequence until they could correctly identify it. Figure 6 shows mean time to identification as a function of rate and structure. Consistent with Garner's prediction, accurate identification of NPSP patterns took longer than PSP patterns at slow rates. And although the number of pattern repetitions required for identification increased steadily with rate, total observation time actually decreased to an optimum around 2.67 events per second and then increased with rate, as Fig. 6 shows. Such a pattern of results is difficult for Estes' theory because it (a) suggests the need for clearer specification of structure; and (b) indicates that as time for rehearsal decreases, overall performance is not proportionately degraded.

What is more surprising is that closer scrutiny of these data suggest that Garner's run–gap principles do not entirely capture the nature of the psychological processes that operate with changes in pattern presentation rate.

1. Presentation Rates between Two and Eight Events per Second

With regard to performance at 2.67 events per second, Garner and Gottwald remarked that listeners perceived events in definite groups

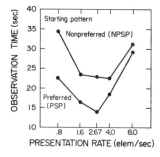

Fig. 6. Time taken (observation time) prior to listeners' correct identification of 10 repeating binary sound patterns presented at different rates as a function of pattern structure (PSP, NPSP). Patterns were started either at a preferred (i.e., modal) serial location (PSP), or at a difficult, previously determined, serial location (NPSP). [Reproduced from Garner & Gottwald (1968) by permission.]

(1968, p. 103). Subsequently, Preusser (1971) found that groups were formed according to the gap principle at rates between 2 and 4 events sec^{-1}, but at slower rates the run principle maintained. He suggested that this organizational shift was related to some timing mechanism that operated above 2 events sec^{-1}. Fraisse (1956) has been more explicit about the nature of such a timing mechanism. He maintains that between rates of 2 and 8 events sec^{-1}, the mechanism responsible for grouping serial events involves rhythmic organization.

Rhythmic organization means that the listener is responding primarily to structure in time, such as relative tone durations and time intervals between outstanding (i.e., accented) sounds. But if relative time is an important part of pattern structure, then the two-process distinctions given by Estes and by Garner are both incomplete. Neither mention relative timing.

The study of rhythm has a long history in psychology (cf., Boring, 1942; Fraisse, 1956; Gabrielsson, 1973a). Let us briefly consider the implications of a relative-timing hypothesis in the present context. One important aspect of our response to rhythmic structure is what it reveals about our ability to separate perceptions of time from perceptions of pitch or intensity. We simply cannot treat these dimensions independently (Fraisse, 1956; Martin, 1972; Woodrow, 1909). For example, if every third sound in a binary sequence of two pitches is intensified so that the accent structure is *auuauu* for the pattern presented at a constant rate with no pauses, listeners will nevertheless report hearing pauses before each accented sound: *auu* (pause) *auu* (pause), and so forth (Handel, 1974; Woodrow, 1909, 1951).

The dependency of accent structure and time structure was well illustrated in a study by Handel (1973). He inserted pauses irregularly into repeating binary patterns and found that listeners had difficulty identifying the sequences correctly, largely because they shifted the accent structure and misjudged pattern length relative to control conditions with regular or no pauses. Effects of purely temporal variations are difficult to explain for theories that neglect relative timing because they suggest that listeners' expectancies about pattern structure are at least partly temporal, having to do with forthcoming accents.

But temporal expectancy does play a role in Martin's accent-structure hypothesis. Listeners are assumed to extrapolate along the time dimension to sense when the next accent will occur. Accents vary in level, so that dependencies between relative time and accent level are hierarchically formalized. Within any good rhythmic pattern, the stronger accents must be separated from each other by correspondingly longer times, whereas weaker accents may fall close together in time. Therefore, regular pauses should not change this correlation of relative time and relative accent level, but irregularly placed pauses will disrupt it.

Martin has posed a sort of objective specification of rhythmic structure that others (e.g., Fraisse, 1956; Handel, 1974) have resisted, maintaining instead that rhythmic organization arises from a subjective synthesis of pattern dimensions to create simple gestalts. Both views treat patterns as wholes, but they disagree on the determinants of pattern organization. Nevertheless, all agree that sound patterns are quickly cast into a temporal framework, and in this respect, they represent departures from approaches that do not consider structure along the time dimension (e.g., Crowder, 1972; Garner, 1974).

In sum, just as there is evidence for a concept of relative pitch in melody, there is need for a concept of relative time to describe the rhythmic aspect of auditory structure. Furthermore, it is likely that these two concepts are not independent. Martin has formalized a dependency between the two in his accent-structure hypothesis. Martin's theory is based upon relationships between relative accent level and relative time, and so it implies that speeding up or slowing down the rate of an auditory pattern should have little effect on the ability to detect its structure. Within limits, this transposability is true, but as the next section illustrates, if a pattern is presented too rapidly, it is no longer perceived as a single rhythmic whole. This phenomenon reveals that Martin's hypothesis is incomplete.

2. PRESENTATION RATES GREATER THAN EIGHT
   EVENTS PER SECOND

Music and speech are fast-paced auditory patterns that occur at rates above eight events per second, so it is clear that somehow people preserve order amongst successive sounds with durations in the neighborhood of 100 msec. But it is important to try to understand what occurs at these rates in order to understand how and when serial order of rapid-fire sequences is preserved. At exceedingly rapid rates, for example, above 20 events $\sec^{-1}$, it appears from work with interrupted sounds that a listener's resolution of temporal order may come from pitchlike perceptions of fused sounds (Green, 1971; Miller & Taylor, 1948). But short of these rates, listeners' performance with fast auditory patterns depends upon (a) the physical nature of the events themselves; and (b) the presence and duration of IEI.

Certain tone patterns seem to retain their serial integrity as rate increases far better than sequences of unrelated environmental sounds where listeners are more apt to confuse event order (Bregman & Campbell, 1971; Broadbent & Ladefoged, 1959; Warren, Obusek,

Farmer, & Warren, 1969). Furthermore, when the loss of serial order does occur with tone patterns, errors are usually not random, whereas with noise sequences they are. In the latter case, only extended training and/or lengthened IEI reduce serial confusions (Divenyi & Hirsh, 1975; Warren, 1974).

Although tone patterns are more durable at fast rates than noise sequences, even tone patterns with good rhythmic structure are eventually confused by listeners if tones are contiguous and their durations fall much below 200 msec. That is, sequences with stronger accents, or pitch changes, correlated with longer time intervals are subject to what is known as *auditory streaming.* * This is the phenomenal breakup of a series into two or more co-occurring subpatterns or auditory streams. The phenomenon, first demonstrated by Miller and Heise (1950), has been nicely illustrated by Bregman and Campbell (1971) with patterns of three high tones ($H_1 = 2,500$ Hz; $H_2 = 2,000$ Hz; $H_3 = 1,600$ Hz) and three low tones ($L_1 = 550$ Hz; $L_2 = 430$ Hz; $L_3 = 350$ Hz). Each tone was presented once for 100 msec in two 600 msec repeating patterns: $H_1L_1H_2L_2H_3L_3$ and $H_1H_2L_1L_2H_3L_3$. Listeners reproducing a six-tone pattern could determine order either among the high tone set, or among low tones, but they could not interleave the sets to reconstruct the sequence as it was presented: They reported that high and low-tone groups occurred simultaneously! Cleavage occurred with the greatest physical difference, but serial order was preserved in subpattern contours (e.g., $H_1H_2H_2H_3$ and $L_1L_2L_3$) based on smaller physical differences.

Streaming is affected by the structure of a sequence, with certain contours (e.g., ascending pitches) being more resistant to cleavage than others (Divenyi & Hirsh, 1975; Heise & Miller, 1951). Furthermore, once a sequence is broken, listeners cannot attend to both subpatterns simultaneously, but identification of one or another improves as a function of the difference between pitch ranges of the two (Dowling, 1973). These facts about the effects of relational context upon streaming have implications for speech perception, in which the phenomenon is also reported to occur whenever large frequency changes between adjacent formants occur very rapidly (Cole & Scott, 1974). Dorman, Cutting, and Raphael (1975), for example, found that providing a connecting frequency contour between first formant frequencies of adjacent phonemes in synthetic speech prevented streaming and increased serial-order report accuracy. These frequency contours parallel *frequency glides* that connect different

---

* The phenomenon actually has been variously labeled as *trill threshold, primary auditory stream segregation,* and *rhythmic fission*, depending upon details of the circumstances under which it has been observed. *Pattern fission* seems to be a broader generic term that ties in with this chapter.

tones by gradually changing pitch levels. Bregman and Dannenbring (1973) demonstrated that frequency glides prevent streaming in abstract tone patterns.

Clearly, streaming represents an interesting phenomenon that deserves more theoretical attention. It is not a mysterious happening, but one we cope with daily as we hear several interleaved sound sequences and devote our attention to one, but are somehow aware of the background noise supplied by others. The parameters that determine streaming are not fully understood. But, from what is known, the phenomenon appears to depend upon both the presentation rate and the magnitude of pitch (or loudness) differences between events occurring at that rate. The greater the pitch differences, the more likely will a pattern stream at slower rates. Thus, good rhythmic patterns should be more resistant to streaming. This is because they correlate relatively small differences in pitch with relatively small changes in time, so that large pitch changes would rarely occur too quickly. Nevertheless, Martin's ideas on relative timing offer no criteria for the relationship between accent change and time in absolute terms, and so do not anticipate streaming. The phenomenon itself suggests that there is more to serial integrality than merely the correlation of relative time with relative accent level within the pattern context. Rather, for any time difference, there must exist a limited range of differences in pitch that can be serially integrated by listeners, and if a change of pitch is too great for that time interval, some lawful proportionality between pitch change and time change is destroyed and streaming occurs. Thus, streaming suggests a very simple, but novel, way of looking at serial-pattern structure: For a sequence to retain serial integrity over changes in rate, differences in pitch must shrink proportionately to correspond with changes in time as rate speeds up. This not only enlarges upon Martin's ideas of relative timing, but it formalizes the notion that the structure of an auditory sequence is carved from several related dimensions, including the time dimension. Jones (1976) has developed these ideas further.

III. CONCLUSION

The heavy concentration upon pattern definition found in this chapter reflects the author's bias that experimental progress in understanding perception of auditory patterns is only interpretable if some framework exists for understanding and manipulating what a pattern is. Because a useful framework is finally emerging, there is a promise of exciting strides in future research. One area that especially calls for attention is that involving listeners' detection of rules within complex auditory patterns. The developing interest in auditory streaming suggests that a complete definition of pattern structure must ultimately include time as one of several related dimensions along which relations are described.

It is apparent that a final evaluation of emerging theories in this young field is premature. The weight of current evidence favors theories that incorporate temporal expectancies and permit some representation of expectations about changes in pitch or intensity, or both, at nominal, ordinal, and interval levels of pattern structure. But it is equally apparent that there is not a surplus knowledge about exactly how such expectancies operate in retaining serial order. There are still far more questions than there are answers, and some of the questions are fundamental ones of general importance to psychologists that may, in fact, only be answerable within the context of research on structured auditory patterns. One of these has to do with the way people perceive structure in time, that is, rhythm. To date, we have no satisfactory answer to this question, which is at the heart of both speech and music perception. Another question has to do with how people can attend to two or more interleaved auditory patterns. Most of our daily auditory environment is composed of interleaved sound sequences, yet we manage to separate out different auditory streams and focus our attention. How is this achieved? At present, we can only pose such questions. Nevertheless, with some ideas about the appropriate dimensions of pattern structure and the manner in which relations can be manipulated, we can say that we are ready to begin the search for concrete answers.

References

Attneave, F., & Olson, R. K. Pitch as a medium: A new approach to psychophysical scaling. *American Journal of Psychology*, 1971, **84**, 147–165.

Boring, E. G. *Sensation and perception in the history of experimental psychology*. New York: Appleton, 1942.

Bregman, A. S., & Campbell, J. Primary auditory stream segregation and perception of order in rapid sequence of tones. *Journal of Experimental Psychology*, 1971, **89**, 244–249.

Bregman, A. S., & Dannenbring, G. L. The effect of continuity on auditory stream segregation. *Perception & Psychophysics*, 1973, **13**, 308–312.

Broadbent, D. E., & Ladefoged, P. Auditory perception of temporal order. *The Journal of the Acoustical Society of America*, 1959, **31**, 1539.

Cole, R. A., & Scott, B. Toward a theory of speech perception. *Psychological Review*, 1974, **81**, 348–374.

Cooper, G. W., & Meyer, L. B. *The rhythmic structure of music*. Chicago: Univ. of Chicago Press, 1960.

Crowder, R. Visual and auditory memory in language by ear and eye. In J. F. Kavanagh &

I. G. Mattingly (Eds.), *The relationships between speech and reading*. Cambridge, Massachusetts: MIT Press, 1972.

Deutsch, D. Music recognition. *Psychological Review*, 1969, **76**, 300–307.

Deutsch, D. The organization of short-term memory for a single acoustic attribute. In D. Deutsch (Ed.) *Short-term memory*. New York: Academic Press, 1975.

Deutsch, D., & Roll, P. L. Error patterns in delayed pitch comparison as a function of relational context. *Journal of Experimental Psychology*, 1974, **103**, 1027–1034.

Divenyi, P. L., & Hirsh, I. J. The effect of blanking on the identification of temporal order in three-tone sequence. *Perception & Psychophysics*, 1975, **17**, 246–252.

Dorman, M. F., Cutting, J. E., & Raphael, L. J. Perception of temporal order in vowel sequences with and without formant transitions. *Journal of Experimental Psychology: Human Perception and Performance*, 1975, **104**, 121–129.

Dowling, D. J. Recognition of melodic transformations: Inversion, retrograde, and retrograde inversion. *Perception & Psychophysics*, 1972, **12**, 417–421.

Dowling, D. J. The perception of interleaved melodies. *Cognitive Psychology*, 1973, **5**, 322–337.

Dowling, W. J., & Fujitani, D. S. Contour, interval, and pitch recognition in memory for melodies. *The Journal of the Acoustical Society of America*, 1971, **49**, 524–531.

Estes, W. K. An associative basis for coding and organization in memory. In A. W. Melton & E. Martin (Eds.), *Coding processes in human memory*. New York: Wiley, 1972.

Fraisse, P. *Structures rhythmiques*. Louvain: Univ. of Louvain, 1956.

Gabrielsson, A. Studies in rhythm. *Acta Universitatis Uppsaliensis*, Abstracts of Uppsala Dissertations from the Faculty of Social Sciences, 1973, 7. (a)

Gabrielsson, A. Similarity ratings and dimension analyses of auditory rhythm patterns. I. *Scandinavian Journal of Psychology*, 1973, **14**, 138–160. (b)

Garner, W. R. *The processing of information and structure*. Potomac, Maryland: Erlbaum, 1974.

Garner, W. R., & Gottwald, R. L. The perception and learning of temporal patterns. *Quarterly Journal of Experimental Psychology*, 1968, **20**, 97–109.

Gibson, E. J. *Principles of perceptual learning and development*. New York: Appleton, 1969.

Gibson, J. J. *The senses considered as perceptual systems*. Boston: Houghton-Mifflin, 1966.

Green, D. M. Temporal auditory acuity. *Psychological Review*, 1971, **78**, 540–551.

Greeno, J. G., & Simon, H. A. Processes for sequence production. *Psychological Review*, 1974, **81**, 187–197.

Guilford, J. P., & Nelson, H. M. The pitch of tones in melodies as compared with single tones. *Journal of Experimental Psychology*, 1937, **20**, 309–335.

Halperin, Y., Nachson, I., & Carmon, A. Shift of ear superiority in dichotic listening to temporally patterned nonverbal stimuli. *The Journal of the Acoustical Society of America*, 1973, **53**, 46–50.

Handel, S. Temporal segmentation of repeating auditory patterns. *Journal of Experimental Psychology*, 1973, **101**, 46–54.

Handel, S. Perceiving melodic and rhythmic auditory patterns. *Journal of Experimental Psychology*, 1974, **103**, 922–933.

Handel, S., & Yoder, D. The effects of intensity and interval rhythm on the perception of auditory and visual temporal patterns. *Quarterly Journal of Experimental Psychology*, 1975, **27**, 111–122.

Heise, G. A., & Miller, G. A. An experimental study of auditory patterns. *American Journal of Psychology*, 1951, **64**, 68–77.

Helmholtz, H. L. F. *On the sensations of tone as a physiological basis for the theory of music.* New York: Dover, 1954.

Jakobson, R., Fant, G., & Halle, M. *Preliminaries to speech analysis: The distinctive features and their correlates.* Cambridge, Massachusetts: MIT Press, 1969.

Jones, M. R. Cognitive representations of serial patterns. In B. H. Kantowitz (Ed.), *Human information processing: Tutorials in performance and cognition.* Hillsdale, New Jersey: Erlbaum, 1974.

Jones, M. R. Time, our lost dimension: Toward a new theory of perception, attention, and memory. *Psychological Review*, 1976, **83**(5), 323–355.

Kimura, D. Functional asymmetry of brain in dichotic listening. *Cortex*, 1967, **3**, 163–178.

Koffka, K. *Principles of Gestalt psychology.* New York: Harcourt, 1935.

Kubovy, M., Cutting, J. E., & McGuire, R. Hearing with the third ear: Dichotic perception of a melody without monaural familiarity cues. *Science*, 1974, **186**, 272–274.

Lashley, K. S. The problems of serial order in behavior. In L. A. Jeffress (Ed.), *Cerebral mechanisms in behavior.* New York: Wiley, 1951.

Liberman, A. M., Cooper, F. S., Shankweiler, D. P., & Studdert-Kennedy, M. Perception of the speech code. *Psychological Review*, 1967, **74**, 431–461.

Liberman, A. M., Delattre, P. C., & Cooper, F. S. The role of selected stimulus variables in the perception of unvoiced stop consonants. *American Journal of Psychology*, 1952, **65**, 497–516.

Mach, E. *The analysis of sensations.* Chicago: Open Court Publishing, 1914.

Martin, J. G. Rhythmic (hierarchical) versus serial structure in speech and other behavior. *Psychological Review*, 1972, **79**, 487–509.

Miller, G. A., & Heise, G. A. The trill threshold. *Journal of the Acoustical Society of America*, 1950, **22**, 637–638.

Miller, G. A., & Taylor, W. G. The perception of repeated bursts of noise. *The Journal of the Acoustical Society of America*, 1948, **20**, 171–182.

Peters, R. The measurement of temporal factors in auditory perception. In S. Singh (Ed.), *Measurement procedures in speech, hearing, and language.* Baltimore, Maryland: University Park Press, 1975.

Pinheiro, M. L., & Ptacek, P. H. Reversals in the perception of noise and tone patterns. *Journal of the Acoustical Society of America*, 1971, **49**, 1778–1782.

Preusser, D. The effect of structure and rate on the recognition and description of auditory temporal patterns. *Perception & Psychophysics*, 1972, **11**, 233–240.

Restle, F. Coding of nonsense vs. the detection of patterns. *Memory and Cognition*, 1973, **1**, 499–502.

Restle, F., & Brown, E. Organization of serial pattern learning. In G. H. Bower (Ed.), *The psychology of learning and motivation: Advances in research and theory* (Vol. 4). New York: Academic Press, 1970.

Richardson, E. G., & Meyer, E. *Technical aspects of sound.* Vol. III. *Recent developments in acoustics.* Amsterdam: Elsevier, 1962.

Royer, F. L., & Garner, W. R. Response uncertainty and perceptual difficulty of auditory temporal patterns. *Perception & Psychophysics*, 1966, **1**, 41–47.

Shepard, R. N. Circularity in judgments of relative pitch. *Journal of the Acoustical Society of America*, 1964, **36**, 2346–2353.

Shepard, R. N., Kilpatric, D. W., & Cunningham, J. P. The internal representation of numbers. *Cognitive Psychology*, 1975, **7**, 82–138.

Simon, H. A. Complexity and the representation of patterned sequences of symbols. *Psychological Review*, 1972, **79**, 369–382.

Simon, H. A., & Kotovsky, K. Human acquisition of concepts for sequential patterns. *Psychological Review*, 1963, **70**, 534–546.

Simon, H. A., & Sumner, R. K. Pattern in music. In B. Kleinmuntz (Ed.), *Formal representation of human judgment*. New York: Wiley, 1968.

Stevens, S. S., & Volkmann, J. The relation of pitch to frequency: A revised scale. *American Journal of Psychology*, 1940, **53**, 329–353.

Sturges, P. T., & Martin, J. G. Rhythmic structure in auditory temporal pattern perception and immediate memory. *Journal of Experimental Psychology*, 1974, **102**, 377–383.

Warren, R. M. Auditory temporal discrimination by trained listeners. *Cognitive Psychology*, 1974, **6**, 237–256.

Warren, R. M., Obusek, C. J., Farmer, R. M., & Warren, R. P. Auditory sequences: Confusions of patterns other than speech or music. *Science*, 1969, **164**, 586–587.

Winckel, F. *Music, sound and sensation*. New York: Dover, 1967.

Woodrow, H. S. A quantitative study of rhythm. *Archives of Psychology*, 1909, **18**(1).

Woodrow, H. Time perception. In S. S. Stevens (Ed.), *Handbook of experimental psychology*. New York: Wiley, 1951.

Chapter 8

HAPTICS*

JOHN M. KENNEDY

I. INTRODUCTION

By *haptics* (Revesz, 1950) is meant a possible mode of touching, contacting, and exploring in which the skin, the joints, and the muscles function together in obtaining information (Gibson, 1966; Kennedy, 1974; Miller, 1951). Today, haptics is still very much a conceptual enterprise, seeking to define and distinguish possible characteristics of *touch* (i.e., using the skin) or *contact* (a broader category, for it includes the use of tools) and *exploration* (i.e., being perceptual). Haptic touch is a hypothesized sensory system, conceived in frank opposition to another, equally hypothetical form of touch—passive cutaneous touch—in which the skin supposedly acts alone and gives punctate sensations localized in the skin. In haptics, the skin is in concert with muscles and joints, it is

* Assistance from the National Research Council of Canada is acknowledged.

said, providing a largely nonintrospectable percept, one determined by informative relations between stimuli, rather than individual punctate stimuli. Haptics is imagined to be active in obtaining information and giving an experience of an object, a distal pole in experience.

A fair treatment for haptics must acknowledge the intelligence with which its supposed properties have been predicted, but there will not be space here to track down the elusive allusions behind suspicious terms like *active* or *introspectable*. The most we can do is to understand and comment on the conjectures influencing modern expectations for haptics. Our coverage must be broad, for it will be necessary to examine a chain of events that connects object and percept: (*a*) what information is about (the perceiver's environment and body); (*b*) the medium for transmitting information to the body; (*c*) the body's equipment for extracting information and getting it to the brain, and (*d*) what perceptual and cognitive skills can do with haptically obtained information.

A. Background

A suspicion that passive touch and haptics are quite different was adumbrated even in the initial, late nineteenth-century experimental studies (Major, 1898). There were early studies on hand movement and kinesthetic guidance—for example, that of Woodworth (1899), who found that length judgments can be based on either duration of movement or position sense—on comparisons between touch and vision—Jastrow's (1886) argument that the handspan exaggerates small extents and underestimates larger extents, whereas the eye does the reverse (a view refuted by Churchill [1960]—and on joint versus muscle sensitivities—for example, Goldscheider's (1889) finding that position sensitivity depended on the joints, and not the muscles. Breadth is indicated in the young American Journal of Psychology's busyness with tactual afterimages, tactile illusions, reports on the skills of the blind, accuracy in and memory for lifted weights, etc.

Experimental psychology, recalling early experiments on touch and haptics, tends to envision acres of skin being prodded by von Frey hairs, and a rather mechanical use of psychophysics. This vision is too narrow, and it is unaware of the value and variety of the earlier work. It is true that the framework was often structuralist–introspective, but that was not the sole approach, nor was it unchallenged by its users (Zigler & Barrett, 1927). That framework was replaced by perception–cognition by the 1960s, and the 1970s seems to have information–processing as a main guide in research. The upshot has been oversimplified and excessive claims in every era, and the task here is to integrate the best from all extremes.

On the heels of the small studies and the structuralist experiments, there came a series of important essays. Katz (1925; see Krueger, 1970) offered the *World of Touch* as a companion to his volume on color. A phenomenologist, he took an interest in everyday techniques of manual exploration and modes of touch. Playing down the role of the skin, he noted that an expert physician can use the diagnostic technique of palpation even with his skin anesthetized (Katz, 1936). (Palpation involves prodding the body, noting the effort required, the depth achieved, the relations between surface and subsurface resistances, the condition of the patient's inspiration at the time, etc.). Katz was one of the first to propose that accurate touch is contingent upon active movement, and he emphasized the importance of vibration. He also noted that the same organ can express, perceive and execute; the hand serves different functions, and a new balance between the functions can be adopted at will.

Von Senden (1932, see also Valvo, 1971) culled reports from several centuries by surgeons, educators, and psychologists, describing the tactual world of blind subjects. Only his discussion of experiences after operations for cataract is well known, but von Senden himself gave equal prominence to pre- and postoperative experience. His conclusion was that blind subjects do not have a coherent integrated framework as part of their experience of space—shape, layout, and location are by-products of more fundamental senses, especially movement and duration. He was not alone in this conclusion: Both pedagogues and experimental psychologists have often concluded that tactual space and form is far from an immediate experience (unlike, say, smoothness or wetness).

Revesz (1950) made the term *haptics* well known. He brought a phenomenologist's systematic care to the entire range of touch and haptic experience, from skillful physical performance to self-perception of the body at rest. He went on to apply his terms and distinctions to artwork by blind people, notably the work of blind sculptors. Both conceptually and empirically he tried to establish haptics as a field of study parallelling optics and accoustics. He argued that constructions such as horizontal and vertical axes meant little to pure haptics, which is instead structured by directions of intended or instigated movements. Haptic geometry is only distantly related at best to optic projective geometry. However, he noted, if a subject tries to connect details and create an impression of the overall form then *visualization*, and optic principles will organize the haptically-derived information.

Parallels with accoustics should not be taken lightly. During a period in the 1930s there were adventures into the reception of speech by touch. One moderately successful way this can be done is to put the thumbs on the speaker's lips, with the fingers arrayed to touch the cheeks and throat. Another way is to apply a vibrator to the skin, perhaps constituting a kind of a cochlear model in which the place of the maximum vibration is informative (see Békésy, 1967). Skin vibrators are not good at direct replaying of speech sounds, for the skin is not normally sensitive to differences in frequency above 2–300 Hz, whereas speech mostly uses frequencies above that. Notable successes have been achieved with *slowed-down* speech signals (Keidel, 1974). The reawakened promise of this area of research has been well proclaimed by Kirman (1973).

Many of the vision-substitution systems (VSS) or hearing-substitution systems (HSS) use pure cutaneous touch, and will not be examined here. Two interesting developments do bear on haptics. One is a television system (TVSS) that controls a panel of vibrators placed usually on the subject's back. The vibrators can be set into action in groups, affording an "image" of any object before the camera (Bach-y-rita, 1972; White, Saunders, Scadden, Bach-y-rita, & Collins, 1970). A haptic factor enters when the subject is allowed manual contact with or control of the camera. The camera contact means that there is a haptic system of relations between the image on the back and the direction and focus of the camera.

The second development is a Sewell raised-line drawing kit (American Foundation for the Blind), which is attracting research attention in Holland (Bouma, 1974), Britain (Vincent, personal communication) and North America (Kennedy, Fox, & O'Grady, 1972).

The raised-line drawing is a convenient device for studying coding processes, representational stimuli, and spatial frameworks in haptics. To some extent, we understand what a line can depict in vision (Kennedy 1975), but what would a flat outline drawing mean to the blind? Would training be needed before outline illustrations could usefully join Braille text?

B. Summary

This brief overview finds haptics originally beginning with simple sensory tasks, overshadowed by physiological theory at times, and gradually moving to the modern position, in which imagination and technology are probing into practical but complex perceptual tasks. Some years ago, Gibson (1962) summarized haptics as a discipline throwing off the punctate studies, proclaiming activity as necessary for high accuracy, and pursuing the distal "real object" pole of experience. But even Gibson, like Revesz, doubted that haptics could find devices like flat pictures to be meaningful, perceptually. Now every Gibsonian claim can be tempered, and more recent research has made every traditional limit on haptics untenable or suspect.

Haptics is worthy of its advances. It is, in normal operation, the most conceptually sophisticated of all the senses. Its organ is, in everyday use, often simultaneously or successively expressive, executive, and perceptual. It can be active or passive. It can involve any combination of huge or small expanses of skin and a variety of muscles and joints in coordinated action. It can employ tools in each of its functions. It is reactive in two ways, one dealing with feedback (reafference) and the other involving one body part perceiving another. It can operate under varying loads. It is a respectable system indeed! Naturally then, it will be some time before any definitive statement of haptics can be written. The most that can be done in the short space of this chapter is to illuminate basic principles to be accounted for and highlight some key studies.

II. THE ENVIRONMENT

A. Physical Features

The environment for haptics is largely the distribution of resistant and thermal properties surrounding the body, including solid, or liquid, or gaseous volumes and surfaces. Electrical forces make an occasional cause for attention. Both inertia and the abiding pull of gravity normally act as the invariant bases for resistance. Touch also has the distinctive property of acting on itself more commonly, and with less need of external aids, than any other sense. Any of the body parts are able to contact some others, and correspondingly there is no one station point for touch, no clear distinction between a fixed point of reference and a separate environment. Instead, there is an area of contact and a direction from which contact is made.

At one extreme, there are slight forms, like mist, too insubstantial for a definite haptic perception of their bounds. At best, mist allows perception of a pervasive dampness. As density increases, there is an opportunity for pressures to become effective in two ways: first, as viscosity (Stevens, 1966), and, second, as a surface or abrupt change in density. In Meissner's demonstration, the student dips his finger into a bowl of mercury. Touch seems to be best actuated by abrupt changes of pressure, for the percept of the mercury is like a clear, firm ring (the surface) and uniform low pressure beneath the surface, instead of (veridically) continuous increase in pressure with depth (see Békésy, 1967, for extensive studies on comparable effects with patterns of vibration; Bower, 1974, for discussion).

Katz distinguished *surfaces*, *streams* (of air or liquid), and *films* (think of brushing cobwebs aside) as three distinctive modes of haptic experience, and of course each has a corollary in the environment. *Voluminous media* can be added too, for Katz noted that a kind of haptic transparency occurs when we feel, say, a rigid object through a soft cover.

At the opposite extreme from mist, the haptic range of activity is curtailed by dangers to tissues, where continuous pressure is too great, or change in pressure so rapid and intense that it constitutes a blow, or the temperature of the skin reaches freezing or searing point.

The limits of sensitivity (for the psychophysics, see Stevens, 1975) enclose a rich market for haptics. Quite simply, the possible variations in resistance are so myriad, so complex that they defy any standard physics of location and pressure, any ordinary-language categorizing schemes, and any extant mathematical models. Through touch we perceive viscosity, slipperiness, softness, textures of all kinds, as well as the elasticity of a material, the coarseness of a particular fiber, the cancerous lump deep inside the breast, the knotted muscles and torn tendons inside a patient's limb. Many of these characteristics and features can be reliably and quickly identified by the trained practitioner, but we cannot describe them yet in explicit physical terms. Haptics is the practical world of wool graders (Binns, 1937), or testers squeezing fruit to determine ripeness (Sheppard, 1955). It is not a world that theoretical physics comprehends yet.

Higher-order relationships, the place of a given variable in a complex of variables, are the targets for haptics. A classic illusion, dealing with the thermal environment, bears this out. A twisted pair of pipes, one flowing with warm water the other with cold, can give an overall impression of *heat* to a hand clasping them. Exchange of heat, rather than the individual sections taking and giving heat, is the percept.

Balanced treatments of the relationship between haptic activity and the haptic environment are rare. A model for such treatments has, fortunately, been provided. Taylor, Lederman, and Gibson (1973) describe texture, considering ridges, grooves, and the plateaus between them as elements. Just as explicitly, they construe the force, direction and feedback effects of movements, and the relevant skin configurations contact requires. This account may well provide a paradigm for attempts to understand particular haptic skills. It falls midway between the overall approach of the phenomenologists and the very narrow approach that concentrates solely on one component of the haptic system.

Haptics relates to pain, temperature, surface characters, and spatial location. Uttal (1973) points out these various characteristics may not go together in a haptic equivalent of the color pyramid. They do not seem to grade into one another, perceptually; we can add that neither is there a physical substrate, nor any scheme that grades temperature into surface.

Haptics may be a system that exists in parallel with several functions of the same organ (expression and execution), and may itself also have several parallel modes of functioning (detecting injury, thermal properties, orientation to gravity, and the layout of the environment's resistance). The modes, however, are not independent (e.g., lowering temperatures can make us more sensitive to pressure and roughness).

B. Social Environment

There is a social environment, as well as a physical one, that influences haptics. The characteristics of social touch put a strain on the methods of psychophysics. What are the dimensions of a friendly pat, as opposed to a brush-off? There are difficulties in principle, as well as in measurement. Social events exist in the context of intentions. No physicalistic criteria can specify intentions, and the apparently friendly pat can be deceitful, inadvertent, etc.

Social touch should not be dismissed as too difficult to study. There cannot be infinite social ambiguity, or communication would be impossible, and some social touches may be less falsifiable than others. A developmental approach may uncover many invariants. Alternatively, some social effects may occur even if the subject recognizes the possibility of fakery. Furthermore, most adults are as alert as any experimenter to the need to recognize intentions; how they normally construe contacts and try to disambiguate them is an important question in its own right. We should also note that meaning arises in the physical domain as well as the social domain, and if we can understand how something reveals, represents, acts as a sign in one domain, this will advance understanding in the other.

The contacts, hugs, and caresses between, say, parent and child in different cultures (and species) offer a theme linking perceptual and social psychology. These contacts may be a major influence on maturation of the autonomic system (Montagu, 1971), for the neonate of various species dies without these hugs, licks, and rubs, through failure of the autonomic system. Handling is important in gentling; grooming, in social development; and a brisk toweling is standard veterinarian practice for aiding infant development in many species. Montagu has described beneficial effects on early maturation of human infants due to warm, soft, highly tactile, sleeping–resting facilities. The infant monkey, of some species, even favors contact–comfort mothers over nourishment mothers (Harlow & Harlow, 1966).

We might accept that neonates and infants develop, autonomically, in proportion to the amount and variety of their haptic experience. However, in all probability, as social and intellectual awareness grows, the significance, rather than the physical quantity and type, of the haptic input must take precedence. One thing seems sure—meaning is more important to the mature haptic world than mass, length, or duration.

As a notable beginning to experimental social haptics, one study neatly presented the distinction between active and passive touch. It has been demonstrated that it is easier to be tickled than to tickle ourselves (Weiskrantz, Elliot, & Darlington, 1971)!

C. Scale

Temperature can refer to climate, weather, a body, or a tiny spot. Thus, the haptic environment has different scales, and the kinds of exploratory activity each scale normally exacts can be quite different. Revesz, Katz, and von Senden commented on factors bearing on many possible scales, and their schemas might be integrated as follows:

1. On a small scale, the *manipulative*, the most delicate of movements may be employed (e.g., rolling a tiny object between our fingers or exploring an irregularity on a tooth).
2. On the larger scale of *reaching*, whole limbs may cooperate (e.g., in spanning a bar to determine its length or making a large sweeping movement to test the smoothness of an expanse of surface).
3. On a still larger scale, the entire body posture may be employed, as in pacing out a room. This might be termed the *domestic* scale.
4. Finally, there is the *geographic* scale, which might be explored in terms of *duration* of walking, or running, or being carried.

Von Senden's evidence lead him to the surprising conclusion that each of these scales are important to blind people in terms of motion, time taken by motions, and second-order spatial characteristics like roughness or resistance. Even the domestic scale he construed as a set of linked habitual movements and postures. His conclusion was not entirely fanciful, for blind subjects do resort to counting paces and estimating durations of steady movements, and they often adhere to fixed, habitual paths domestically, for obvious reasons of safety. Kennedy and Fox (1977) note that even if von Senden's evidence is sound, it informs us what blind people often or usually do (performance), and not what they can do (competence). When clues like temperature, texture, etc. are made constant and only form varies, blind subjects are quite capable of comprehending form, and they recognize similar forms made of quite different materials. Also, the success that blind subjects have with maps indicates that they recognize similar layout relationships in domains of quite different sizes. This means, it should be noted, that haptic form perception is largely independent of the duration and kind of movement required, for a map is explored with fine finger movements, whereas the depicted environment affords walking.

As we consider maps, and the translation from one set of movements to another, we are beginning to deal with *tools* for haptics. Tools and representations are of course things in the environment, but they are functioning as *intermediaries* between the perceiver and the target object, and they may best be considered under the general rubric of the haptic media.

III. THE HAPTIC MEDIA

Touch is the sense of immediate contact, it is said, but this can be misleading. First, the actual receptors for touch are embedded in tissue inside the body, and at best the top layer of skin makes proper contact. Thus, cutaneous touch relies on the shearing and compression of tissue under the skin. Also, skin receptors cofunction with receptors at least as far from the fingertips as our wrists, elbows, and shoulders. Second, many body appendages (hairs, nails, teeth) act as built-in tools for touch (Gibson, 1966). Third, we frequently use artificial tools for haptic exploration, as in poking with a stick and testing materials with scissors or a fork. Lotze noted that we actually seem to sense the object or surface that interests us—not the complex, but, apparently informative movements of the tool. Analogously, we may barely sense Katz's "transparent" intervening material, which can be either *around the target*, as in the case of the tissues around a tumor the physician is trying to palpate, or *around the perceiver*, like the physician's surgical gloves.

A rigid tool can tell us about a soft surface and, vice versa, a soft tool can tell us about an unyielding surface. Consequently, the sensory patterns are an integration of effects, which the perceiver must break down into components in order to register what his body is doing, where, with what tool, and to what kind of object (Gibson, 1962). The components are interrelated, and an error or lack of adjustment to one component entails further errors about the others. Gregory and Ross (1967) explored the effects of adding a weighted cuff to the arm and changing the body component in a lifting-weights task. A 500-gm weight modified the difference limen by a very small amount (20%), and after wearing the cuff for 30 min the limen actually went down *below* the level for the unweighted arm. On removing the cuff, the limen went *above* the level for the unweighted arm for a short period. In sum, changing the arm weight up or down impairs discrimination, but most of the weight change is compensated or filtered out.

An increase in load can change shape perception too, and can even accentuate the critical information. Weber and Dallenbach (1929) had subjects explore a contour with a stylus. Increased load increased the apparent size of the form, sharpened its perceived angles, and enhanced its apparent curvatures. Similarly, increased speed of excursions can accentuate curvature, as motorcyclists know well!

Tools are usually designed to increase target variations to suprathreshold levels, which need little discussion here. But it is a cautionary fact that what initially seems like a decrease in intensity of variations can be a helpful device too. A traditional trick of carpenters is to feel for any bumps and irregularities on a smooth surface through a thin piece of paper. One might imagine the paper intermediary would decrease sensitivity to the target ridges. In fact, the paper seems to decrease adventitious noise and lower the level of distracting or inhibitory receptive activity, for it allows the target to become more prominent, not less so (Gordon & Cooper, 1975).

Tool use, in an executive manner, is understood to occur in species as different as birds and higher primates. Tool use in an exploratory, perceptual manner is less recognized and may well be much more restricted. Higher primates will poke at objects with sticks, but this may be a "what will it do?" reflex rather than one of "what does it feel like?" Observations on 12–14-month-old children (Kennedy, Mueller, & Moscow, in press) suggest that exploratory prodding with a tool occurs as early as this age. Children who were loath to touch a static foreign object, and who showed distress if brought too close to it, were willing to reach out with rods to touch it.

Soviet investigators, following a motor-copy approach (Zaparozhets, 1965; Pick, 1964) have been interested in both manual contact and stylus use. Form discrimination in kindergarten children is improved by restricting the access to the form to a stylus that can proceed around the perimeter of the form. The improvement may be a matter of attention, because the stylus could direct the child's attention to the perimeter, or it might be a matter of acquiring a motor copy, but whatever the explanation, the fact remains that requiring tool use did not degrade form perception even at this tender age (cf. Jones, in preparation).

The tool-use side of haptics is full of promise, for its cognitive implications are profound for any society with even the barest degree of technology.

Tool use in exploratory functions is undoubtedly just as important as tool use in executive functions, but little is known, ontogenetically or phylogenetically, because executive tool use has gathered the limelight and the distinction between the two tool uses is rarely made. When the phenomenon is clearly pointed out, it may be that exploratory tool use will attract research. The first step is simply to recognize the exploratory function, but in the second step, several different kinds of media must be distinguished.

One kind of medium involves relationships or associations by arbitrary fiat (e.g., Braille, or three-dimensional block letters for the blind, or a set of experimenter-ordained cutaneous patterns standing for alphanumeric characters (Geldard, 1961). A second kind involves mappings retaining form (or vibratory-order) relationships.

The second kind of medium can be subdivided: (a) Perception substitution systems, in which an electrical/mechanical device applies a pattern onto the skin, making a partial copy of the distal object akin to a retinal or cochlear signal. An example of this would be a television substitution system (Bach-y-rita, 1972); (b) Iconographic, or echoic systems, in which a physical representation of the distal object is generated in a display independent of the subject, akin to a picture or to a loudspeaker's actions. The subject himself then has to act (or be made to act) to encounter the display, just as one would orient to a picture or speaker system. An example of this would be a raised-line drawing; and (c) Haptic exploratory systems, in which a tool is deployed by the subject and its motions copy a feature of the distal object. The tool's actions are constrained by the subject's movements, the tool's structure, and the key features of the distal object. An example would be the use of a stylus.

The three subdivisions are conceptually distinct so far as perception as a system is concerned. The first has a parallel with a retinal image, the second with a physical pictorial image, and the third has no direct parallel in vision—the nearest parallel is an aiming device. The first two are now widely studied (Bliss, 1970; Geldard, 1974; Kennedy & Fox, 1977), whereas the third is relatively neglected.

In sum, haptics entails a natural medium, consisting of the superficial skin and its appendages. Adjuncts, giving mediated haptic information, range from sheets of material to elongated rods. The adjuncts can create purely cutaneous images and codes, or, as a first step, generate a physically independent display that, as a second step, is then explored haptically. Of course, since the two steps are discrete, they can be recursive, so that one subject could explore haptically (directly with his skin or with a tool) a pattern that was being generated directly onto another subject's skin. There is no limit to the number of recursions, which is important in "yoking" subjects to test the merits of various displays, the importance of self-generated or directed exploration, etc.

In a haptic mediating system, information is preserved if there is correspondence between the distal target and the final image or cutaneous pattern. The correspondence can be between any ordered set of elements, be they spatially, temporally, or intensively distinguished or ordered. One of the most intriguing questions is which correspondences in ordering are *immediate*, or *perceptual* (Bower, 1974), and which require the subject to deliberately interpret. Which correspondences give an impression of the distal object and which appear to the subject as a code he can use for understanding, but not perception? At one extreme, is the subject deploying a rod and claiming "I feel the texture of sandpaper at the far end of the rod" and, at the other extreme, is the subject understanding that a particular Braille configuration stands for an *R*?

Issues of correspondence arise at the level of *elements* as well as at the level of *ordering* of elements. For example, in vision we substitute lines in outline drawings for corners, edges, wires and cracks. Are comparable surrogate functions possible in touch? The most interesting case is the subject who has been blind from birth and has had no experience with line drawings. A handful of people with these characteristics has been tested, but the few give surprisingly clear results. They can usually recognize some raised-line outline drawings of familiar objects without training, indicate where other lines might be added in conformity to normal visual practice, detect anomalies of shape in the drawings, etc. (Kennedy & Fox, 1977; Vincent, personal communication). One unexpected finding in this line of research is that blind subjects understand line depiction of rounded objects. Curved objects offer a clear distinction between a visible front and a nonvisible back—the division being a neat *occluding bound*. No such sharp bound is present for touch, but nevertheless, blind subjects can understand outline surrogates for occluding bounds without training.

IV. PHYSIOLOGICAL RECEPTORS AND PATHWAYS

Are haptics and passive cutaneous touch somewhat distinct physiologically? Sifting the evidence to date reveals pros and cons, and the issue can best be addressed generally, beginning historically.

Ordinary experience gives the impression that active and passive touch are served by continuous sensitivity in the skin and degrees of muscle strain. Goldscheider's (1889) work on the joints was interesting and surprising, for their role was not obvious phenomenologically. Even more remarkable and challenging was Blix's announcement in 1884 that there were small spots of localized high sensitivity separated by areas of low sensitivity—cold, warm, pressure, and pain spots. Blix's discovery, coupled with the prevailing preoccupation with Muller's law of specific nerve energy, brought new views of touch perception and the hope for distinct nerve endings and organs under each spot. The hope grew to a grand theory. Von Frey said touch was dependent on Meissner's corpuscles, warmth on Ruffini's corpuscles, and cold on Krause's end organs. Analogously, pain might rely on free nerve endings, and (as a corollary to this approach) touch transmission to the brain might depend mostly on large-diameter nerve fibers, whereas warmth and cold might use mostly intermediate-size fibers.

The distinction between actively obtained stimulation and passive touch was drawn as early as the 1880s, and it was noted that the Muller–Blix–von Frey notions might not apply to active haptics. Also, there was and is evidence for rejecting the original specificity hypothesis. The cornea has only free nerve endings but it has, as von Frey noted as early as 1885, many sensitivities. Glabrous (smooth) skin has many endorgans and hairy skin does not, but they possess the same sensitivities. There is variability in the locus and type of spots from day to day. (The variability may be due to minor changes in membranes like Schwann cells, which act to group so-called free nerve endings into bundles (see Cauna [1968]). The endorgans are not distinct isolated types; they form a graded distribution, shading into one another and changing with age. Consequently, they may be the result of aging and minor tissue damage rather than a genetically determined perceptual system.

The hypothesis of nerve-diameter specificity seems unsound, too. Sphygmomanometer (blood-flow cutoff) studies find no consistent order of loss of sensitivities, although large fibers are disabled first by blood-flow loss (Sinclair, 1967).

The first serious alternative to the specificity approach was Nafe's (1934) theory that patterns of excitation, not individual nerve firings, are the basis of tactual experience. Pattern theorists were, at times, quite extreme, proposing no distinction between passive touch and haptics, and arguing there was no evidence for any receptor specificity (Weddell, 1955). More recent positions (Melzack & Wall, 1962; Sinclair, 1967) are as follows:

1. Nerve endings are not entirely specialized, but merely somewhat biased in favor of some adequate stimuli.
2. Central cells are dependent on patterns of firing arriving from the periphery, and the patterns are based on (a) the biases of receptor cells at the periphery; (b) adaptation and summation effects; (c) the structure of connections from the periphery, including excitation and inhibition relations.

To this general picture, it might be added that the central cells may well be primed by an efferent copy of a movement or signals from joints and muscles, or perhaps even the vestibular system and other aspects of proprioception (Sherrington, 1906). Inhibition, for example, can occur from widely separated components of the system. In rostral dominance (Critchley, 1953) a touch near the head is felt while a simultaneous touch farther from the head is suppressed. Muscle activity can effectively give impressions of movement in an otherwise anesthetized finger (Goodwin, McCloskey, & Matthews, 1972), but in a normal hand the activity has no perceptual results (Gelfan & Carter, 1967), presumably because the joints dominate the muscle messages (Howard & Anstis, 1974).

The case for specialization of joint receptors, at least, seems sound. Howard and Templeton (1966) note that some joint receptors are active at most joint positions, some are maximally active at large joint angles, others are most active at small joint angles, and yet others depend on movement with some firing during one direction of movement and opponents firing during the other direction of movement.

On the other hand, there is no clear evidence for joint receptors acting differently under active, self-initiated haptics, as opposed to a passive touch. And if the joints do entirely dominate muscle signals, then at least one possible active–passive distinction is not usable by the haptic system.

What special haptic properties might be present in the pathways from the receptors to the brain?

The primary pathways for the haptic system's projections onto the cortex are the medial lemniscus tract (MLT) and the spinothalamic tract (STT). The MLT ascends via the dorsal columns and spinocervical tracts of the spinal cord to the medulla, where fibers cross over in order to project left body areas to the right side of the brain and vice versa. The MLT takes its name from the brain tract it uses from the medulla to the thalamus—thence it projects to the post-central somatosensory cortex. The MLT brain tract affords one pathway to the cortex for the proprioceptive (muscle, joint, and tendon) receptors as well as cutaneous receptors, while an ancillary route leads some proprioceptive projections to the cerebellum, presumably to assist tonus and posture regulation and help synchronize movements. Most proprioceptive fibers accompany the MLT's route in the spinal cord, but some cross over within the spinal cord itself, and parallel the STT.

The main anatomical difference between the MLT and STT is that the STT synapses and crosses over in the spinal cord, rather than in the medulla. Both synapse a second time in the thalamus before their final projection onto the cortex. Functionally, their main difference may be that the MLT allows good resolution with rapid detection of touch and pressure, whereas the STT is slower, less fine in resolution, and assists with pain and temperature. But it is important to note that some proprioceptive fibers travel alongside each of the two pathways, and so it is difficult to parcel out functions into any simple dichotomy such as proprioceptive versus cutaneous pathways, or pressure versus pain pathways. Wall (1970), for example, has found discriminations of vibrations, weights, textures, and two points can all be made by patients and animals in which the dorsal columns (MLT) have been sectioned. Interestingly, Wall proposes that the dorsal columns (MLT) are involved with motor acts serving sensory exploratory functions, for he finds defects of movements in his animals (see also, Gilman & Denny-Brown, 1966). Wall proposes that the phylogenetically newer MLT might be concerned with new, unrecognized events, and its role decreases once familiarity has been achieved—a notion that is particularly interesting, since there is a close link with orienting and contacting movements, which become disturbed once the dorsal column is sectioned.

There are also tantalizing findings relating to possible brain specialization. Milner and Taylor (1972), studying cerebral commissuratomy effects, find that the (nonverbal) right hemisphere can retain haptic patterns (wire figures) for over 2 min, whereas the left hemisphere loses its form distinctions rapidly. Hermelin and O'Connor (1971) report impressively distinct abilities in the left and right hands of young Braille readers. It seems the left index finger can read Braille, whereas the right only acts as the leader, determining location without recognizing the print's characters. Pressed into service, the unpracticed middle fingers of both hands match the skills of the adjoining index finger. Thus, the left-hand fingers can read Braille, while the right cannot, for these subjects. The difference is so strong that the right hand cannot identify a single character, suggesting an important hemispheric specialization, with, again, the right hemisphere dealing with patterns. The difference between hands is less striking in adults, which points to an important developmental trend—for example, escaping initial training biases (Smith, 1933).

Flowers (1975) finds the dominant right hand to be the one most capable of continuously monitored movements, although both hands can be equally adept at ballistic movements when given the requisite practice. Flower's results implicate the left hemisphere in many aspects of haptics, for feedback control applies to slow movements (Roy & Marteniuk, 1974) and long movements (Klapp, 1975).

However, hand and hemispheric specialization is not all-or-nothing, and normally may involve considerable cooperation (cf. Milner & Taylor, 1972). A homely experiment mentioned by Kornhuber (1971) makes this point. If one tries to put one's finger on the tip of one's nose, with either hand, two components of the motion will be found: first, a quick ballistic movement and, second, a slow, final correction. Interestingly, the hands function comparably again if the task is slightly altered. An unusual way to do the task is to bring the *nail* side of the finger to the nose. Often there is now only one movement, the ballistic one, and the finger lands with a jolt, and even the thumb performs poorly at this task. Thus, both hands show both kinds of movements in some tasks, and both show only one kind of movement in other tasks.

At present, hypotheses about hemispheric specializations in haptics are simply speculative. There are many degrees of freedom in interpreting individual studies. And there are possible conflicts between results (e.g., it is strange that pattern perception and monitored movements, which are often two sides of one task, should be attributed to different hemispheres). These cautions will be reinforced shortly when examining perceptual effects of different haptic tasks (see also Nachson & Carman, 1975).

In sum, evidence bearing on physiological aspects of haptics is as yet suggestive rather than definitive, typically showing no consistent separation between receptors, pathways, and hemispheres that might define a complete haptic system. If haptics is a distinct mode of functioning, it will be necessary to examine perceptual effects, rather than anatomy, to bring it to the fore.

V. PERCEPTUAL AND COGNITIVE PROCESSES

The chain of events underlying perception reaches from the environment through media to the sensory receptors and their pathways to the brain. The end result is a percept, and to consider haptics as a possible sensory system we must envision the percept as a product of a living chain, in which at times quite different skills can come into action, different perceptual principles come to the fore, and the product can influence and be influenced by the neighboring senses, or cognitive functions like memory.

A. Haptic Skills

To be concrete, to get an idea of how changeable the chain can be, consider what grade-school children actually do in determining the length of a bar, haptically. Abravanell (1968) listed some observations:

> Holds bar in palm and fingers; holds bar in fingers; holds ends of bar; presses ends of bar; spans length of bar in one hand; rotates bar; slides fingers . . . along length of bar from ends to center; holds bar at ends, letting it rest in palms with fingers

cupped around sides; clutches bar in center, sometimes twisting it; holds bar in center with one hand, other hand at end; aligns bar with . . . starting point of measuring instrument; measures length of bar against hand; actively palpates bar; slides fingers . . . along entire length of bar [p. 24].

The degrees of freedom include acquiring successive or simultaneous impressions, being active or passive, systematic or not, using ballistic or continuously monitored movements, cutaneous or joint information. The movements, which could have been guided by the experimenter's choices and directions, rather than the child's, range from well-practiced to unfamiliar movements or postures. They can be based on a global feeling or as cognitive a skill as measurement in units.

At times it has been said that the degrees of freedom are best exercised in particular ways. But haptics is a flexible system here at least: The relative value and importance of a contribution to the system can vary enormously. The weighting of a contribution can be a matter of instructions and attention, and within each degree of freedom there can also be more intransigeant effects operating in opposite directions in different tasks. For example, consider the question: Is active perception always more accurate than a related passive process? There are a series of answers!

One well-known origin of this question is the effect produced by pushing on one's eye—the visible world suddenly seems "jumpy." Comparably, in haptics, one can compare (a) feeling a surface with the left index finger moved normally, to and fro; and (b) feeling the surface when the finger is moving in the same path but is being pushed and pulled by the right hand. In both cases (a) and (b) the surface is stable; it does not appear "jumpy" to the passively moved finger. Passive movement does not destroy perceived *stability*. (Jones, 1973, finds *length* of passive movement of the arm to be also readily recognized.)

Superior active form perception was found by Gibson (1962). Cookie-cutter forms explored by the fingertips were easily recognized; if the cookie cutter was externally moved (twisted while resting on the palm), it was less well recognized, and if it simply pressed on the skin it was poorly recognized. Austin and Sleight (1952), keeping the subject's contact restricted to fingertips, found alphabetic and geometric forms were best recognized under active movement.

Landrigan and Forsyth (1974) separated mental choice of movements from being passively moved by instructing some subjects precisely where to go on a grid chart. In a form-perception task, those who mentally regulated their own movements were much superior to those who were told where to move, even if the self-regulating subjects were being moved passively once they made their choice. Thus mental skills, not physical control, can be the key variable.

In addition, Magee and Kennedy (1976) obtained better recognition of complex meaningful haptic forms when the subject was passive, which suggests that the double load of both controlling movement and attending to the resulting impressions may be too severe at times.

In a second study, Magee and Kennedy separated information from *cutaneous impressions* from information from *movements*. Either the form was moved under the subject's stationary fingertip (the cutaneous condition), or the fingertip was made to trace out the appropriate shape on a blank surface (the passive-movement condition). The "cutaneous" subjects were rarely accurate, while the "passive-movement" subjects were at least as accurate as subjects who were moving (actively or passively) over surfaces with the forms actually there. Evidently, the cutaneous impressions simply guide the hand, but the actual form perception depends on registering the movements made by the hand; cutaneous impressions are not needed once they have served their guidance function.

One might think that a self-regulating, active subject has a special advantage over a passive subject, in that the self-regulator can select movements familiar to him. The key hypothesis is that well-practiced exploratory movements are a better basis for detecting the exterospecific signals. However, Davidson (1972) allows us to reject this general rule. His blind subjects used a distinctive five-finger grip and arm movement in trying to register the curvature of a bar. Also, they were superior to blindfolded subjects in the task. When the blindfolded subjects were told to adopt the blind subjects' grip they improved, and in a direct within-group comparison the new grip was better than the subjects' usual strategy (see also Davidson & Whitson, 1974).

Another reason for supposing active subjects might be better is that the active perceiver can triangulate, as it were, on the exterospecific component. By making several movements, he assures himself of interospecific variability, and the invariants across the activity specify the extero-specific component (Gibson, 1962, 1966). A well-known putative example is the hefting, or jiggling, shoppers do, all over the world, in testing the weight of produce. However, the jiggling does not, in fact, improve the judgment! Sekuler, Hartings, and Bauer (1974) find discrimination of weight improves with duration (from 50 to 500 msec), but this is quite independent of jiggling. (Sekuler *et al.* note that the jiggling in their study did not bring more muscles into action as duration increased. Jiggling might be effective over and above the duration effect if it entails more and more of the musculature being active [McCloskey, 1974] in the hefts but, of course, this means the jiggling, per se, is not the critical variable).

It may well be that sensitivity in a well-practiced subject is not enhanced by jiggling, but the triangulation (invariants) hypothesis should not be entirely rejected at this point. Triangulation may play an important role in tuning sensitivity and calibrating-scale factors, or helping the subject to adapt to new conditions. In vision, information across points of observation may play a key role in perceptual learning, but once the learning has occurred, monocular vision may be tuned to the patterns that the binocular vision indicated were the key ones to attend (cf. Kennedy, 1974, p. 45).

B. Perceptual Principles

Perceptual systems not only obtain information, but because of the way they function they suffer from illusions, and entail grouping effects precisely because they do not treat individual inputs completely independently. To illustrate haptics as a perceptual system, illusions, figure–ground, aftereffects and apparent movement will be considered briefly here.

1. ILLUSIONS

Over (1966, 1968) argues cogently that haptic illusions are extremely important in testing orthodox, vision-based theories about geometrical illusions. For example, if it were established that certain illusions only arise in vision and not in touch, this would increase confidence in explanations that rely on purely visual or optical phenomena. Examples include the Delboeuf and Halteres illusions (Hatwell, 1960), and the horizontal–vertical L illusion (Day & Avery, 1970).

Some illusions are stronger in vision than in touch, but do exist to some degree in both (e.g., continuous versus broken-line illusions [Tedford & Tudor, 1969], Muller–Lyer [Hatwell, 1960] and Poggendorf [Costa, 1937] illusions). The cross-modal parallels suggest that the same common grouping processes are at work, a suggestion that is reinforced by transfer of training from one modality to the other (e.g., on the Muller–Lyer, Rudel & Teuber, 1963).

There are also illusions that only exist in touch, such as the rotating-hourglass illusion (Jones, Touchstone, & Gettys, 1974; see also Cormack, 1973). A cylinder rotated end over end when held between thumb and forefinger tip develops an apparent hourglass shape, the gradually slimming waist of the hourglass being the region between the fingers. The explanation here is probably that the axis of the rotating rod gives continuous contact and pressure, and therefore suffers adaptation, giving an impression of less pressure and suggesting that the rod is shrinking in the middle.

Blindfolded subjects may not provide good tests of general versus visual perceptual theories of illusions, because they could be visualizing the haptic input. Support for this objection was obtained by Frisby and Davies (1971). Good visualizers provided strong correlations between their haptic and visual impressions of the Mueller–Lyer. Accordingly, one might turn to blind subjects for a firmer test of competing theories.

Blind subjects are known to have strong geometrical illusions, as with versions of horizontal–vertical and continuous–broken-line illusions (Bean, 1938; Hatwell, 1960; Revesz, 1934). Revesz's own work seems to deny his later contention that horizontal and vertical axes mean little to haptics. Indeed, the illusions may prove to be very useful tools for examining the dimensions, scales, and organization of haptic space. When that organization is understood, one should note, it may turn out that similar or compatible geometries often form the structure of both vision and haptics. In that case, the idea that haptic illusions would disprove visual theories would be frustrated. At best, we can hope to discover one large set of illusions restricted to haptics, another large set restricted to vision, and a third large set common to both. Then the properties of the sets may indicate some idiosyncratic geometries in the two senses, and a general geometry underlying both.

2. FIGURE–GROUND

Rubin's figure–ground phenomena are a good vantage point for examining both surface perception and perception of representations, for the impression they provide is one of a foreground and background relationship between extended surfaces, and yet the actual display may be only a line figure. In other words, the display is being coded as a representation of surfaces by the subject (Kennedy, 1974, Chap. 6).

The possible relevance of figure–ground to posture and haptics was noted quite early (Woodworth, 1938). To test the importance of coding in haptics, Kennedy and Campbell (1976) tested for transfer from a (flat) raised-line shape to actual objects providing fully three-dimensional foreground–background relationships. The subjects were tested on either (a) a cut-out object mounted on a backboard at a height of about ¼ in.; (b) a cut-out hole in a foreground board, with a depth in the hole of about ¼ in. The shapes of the original raised-line figure, cut-out object and cut-out hole were identical. Subjects recognized the relationship between the raised-line figure and the second display much more readily when the second display was the object. The results suggest subjects tend to code the raised-line figure as a foreground, circumscribed object against a background. Follow-up studies indicated that the subjects could reverse the figure–ground relationship perceived in the raised-line display (see also Kennedy & Fox, 1977, for reversible figure–ground relationships perceived by blind subjects).

3. AFTEREFFECTS

Kinaesthetic aftereffects, indicating principles of adaptation (Koehler & Dinnerstein, 1947) and normalization (Gibson & Backlund, 1963) are well known. They seem to provide excellent examples of the framework of haptic space, which it seems is only partially independent of the limb or mode of contact. Walker and Shea (1974) set a narrow bar on the subject's left (or right) and a wide bar on the subject's right (or left). The subject grasped the bars alternately, *always using only one hand*, moving his hand back and forth between the bars. Test bars, each of identical, intermediate width, were then substituted for the narrow and wide exposure bars. The test bars seemed to the subject to be of different sizes: smaller on the wide-bar side, larger on the narrow-bar side! Curiously, no intermanual transfer occurred. Thus, the aftereffect is restricted to the exposed hand, but also depends on position in space, an adaptation contingent on location in a spatial framework.

4. APPARENT MOVEMENT

As Kirman (1973) has it, phi is a bonus from haptic interactions, while masking (Levin & Benton, 1973) entails a loss from the same kind of interactions. Cutaneous apparent movement was recognized by early Gestalt psychology, particularly by Italian researchers (see Sherrick, 1968). It is of special importance to sensory-substitution systems because it helps different patterns, whose details would otherwise be entirely within the two-point threshold, to become clearly distinguishable (Bach-y-Rita, 1972; see also Katz, 1925).

Phi can occur across continuous skin or across empty spaces between digits or hands or limbs. Even when contiguous areas of skin are being stimulated, the apparent movement can be localized outside the plane of the skin, presumably in the manner that we can sense an object rush by us, as with the wind created by its passing. The phenomenon of localization beyond the skin is of special importance to theories about haptics, rather than passive cutaneous touch, because it has been argued that only active subjects can successfully achieve it consistently. That is, when subjects control the camera in TVSS, they may phenomenally localize the relevant distal object in space.

The hypothesis that localization needs active control is doubtful, as yet. First, it runs counter to everyday experience with the "wind of passage." Second, a subject in the TVSS *ducked* when the image on his back was zoomed, which is an appropriate response if he localized the distal object in front of him, and yet the control was not in his hands. Third, subjects may well learn as much if they are allowed simply to rest their hands on the camera so that, passively, they can get the key information, which is, surely, the orientation and maneuvers of the camera. Fourth, Guarniero (1974) has given a careful account of his own experiences as a blind subject in TVSS use, and repeatedly noted that localization in space relative to his body was phenomenologically a puzzle, although the relative location of two objects could be perceived clearly and readily after a matter of a few hours of practice.

C. Haptics, Intersensory Relations, and Memory

For centuries, it was often argued, against considerable opposition, that haptics must be the fundamental sense for calibrating the others. The notion has been embedded in motor theories of perception, from memory engram theories (Taylor, 1962) to copy theories like the Soviet one. It still pops up in theories of illusions (Tedford & Tudor, 1969) and theories of the evolution of the senses (Gregory, 1968).

The alternative is that vision, for example, develops in parallel to touch, or as the tutor of touch. Indeed, for all we know, it might have been that evolution had vision as the slave of taste—the tongue or its equivalent being the master sense! Protagonists of touch usually contend that vision produces percepts of (supposedly) nonvisual features like hardness, and thus must originally have been educated by touch. The counterargument is not difficult to find: In principle, complex visible events often indicate the supposedly nonvisual features quite precisely. In the case of hardness, we can readily tell which is harder when we see two objects collide.

Questions of evolution aside, it is now well known that vision often dominates touch in practice. Visual capture occurs when touch and vision are in conflict over the proportions or size of an object (Katz, 1925; Rock, 1966). Haptics seems much more amenable to change and modification than vision (Rock & Harris, 1967). Stance itself is often more dependent on vision than proprioception (Lee & Lishman, 1975).

Furthermore, when vision is ambiguous, touch has been found to be powerless to influence the rate of reversals, as Shopland and Gregory (1964) have shown with the Necker cube. This Necker cube demonstration would have been especially convincing if the first impression of the cube had not been influenced by previous haptic exposure to the cube, as it would seem that the visual reversal rate is largely independent of visual information too (Kennedy, 1974, p. 139).

Haptic touch can certainly modify other perceptions: for example, auditory localization (Willott, 1970) or, as noted above, visual perception of shape when children are encouraged to explore with a stylus. Accordingly, any simple notion of haptics as a fundamental sense or as a subordinate sense must be rejected.

Intersensory correspondences may be present in early infancy. Bryant (1974) has found that infants can recognize visual and haptic shape counterparts and show preference for an object that makes a sound over one that is silent. Also, the last decade has seen promising indications of haptic–visual correspondences in babies no more than a few weeks old (Bower, 1972). The indications have to be taken cautiously; Yonas (1975), for example, has found that responses like reaching, blinking at zooming objects, shielding the head with the arms, or leaning forward are not consistent in the infant of less than about 6 months of age, and may simply be controlled, in younger infants, by moving contours rather than full-fledged shape-in-space perception.

Some theories reject the notion of early, intersensory correspondences, and attribute later intersensory links to the intervention of language, which might act as a link. Certainly, it is obviously true that subjects can and do often aid themselves with language. Becker (1931) found that telling the veridical names for shapes to the subjects helped them learn to differentiate the shapes. Like Becker, Zigler and Barrett (1927) found that if differentiation went on without veridical verbal help, subjects often could tell items *apart*, but could not tell what the items *were*.

The linguistic-strategy hypothesis seems farfetched when used exclusively. Notably, it does not account for haptic–visual transfer in higher primates like chimpanzees, who can transfer from vision to haptics, choosing which of a pair of haptic objects matches one in a photograph (Davenport & Rogers, 1971).

Many studies in the last 15 years have examined cross-modal transfer in school-age children, and have often traced out increasing levels of performance both within modality and between modalities. One important difficulty, in interpreting the results is that improvement in a cross-modal task could be due more to increasing skill in one modality, rather than better cross-modal transfer (Bryant, 1974). Bearing this caution in mind, consider three popular hypotheses:

1. Any form of intersensory transfer involves loss of information.
2. Storing information in haptic memory is less efficient than storing in visual memory (Goodnow, 1971; Posner, 1967).
3. Absolute features are difficult to compare cross modally, while relational features are comparatively easy (Bryant, 1974).

The wealth of work in the cross-modal area, and the fuzziness of many of the concepts, precludes a simple summary. For example, while intramodal visual equivalence matches for shape properties are often superior to either haptic equivalence matches or intermodal matches, length and angle judgements are often essentially similar (Stanley, 1974).

Further, Posner (1973) recognizes that some studies do not fit his hypothesis of inefficient haptic storage. And Bryant does not always provide clear and consistent criteria for defining a feature as absolute or relational.

It seems likely that all three hypotheses are correct, but only if tasks are selected appropriately. Notice, for example, that the coding task can be varied while the physical stimuli remain unchanged. Sophisticated subjects may choose an absolute feature, like the number of angles in a shape task (a feature that is easy to recall) whereas unpracticed subjects may try to retain an overall-shape impression, and the haptic overall-shape impression may be much more codable and recallable by blind subjects than by the sighted (Davidson, Barnes, & Mullen, 1974; Shagan, 1970). Only when hypotheses are clearly stated in terms of particular codings and relations between senses will they have a chance of being valid. The appropriate type of hypothesis may be one like the following: When a dimension of sensitivity is well-differentiated in one sense, in comparison to another sense, the well-differentiated sense will be the better modality for storage. To date, no study directly addresses this kind of hypothesis. Some studies involving visual and haptic sensitivities show comparable levels of performance at zero delay before testing, whereas a short delay detracts more from haptic performance than visual performance (Rose, Blank, & Bridger, 1972). But the fact that initial levels of performance were equal does not mean that the task was sensitive enough to indicate the degrees of differentiation within the two senses.

Haptics is like a magnet in attracting different kinds of codings and skills. The average person, cajoled into an experimenter's box and mysteriously blindfolded, has the time, motive, and initiative to conjure up and try out strategy after strategy. This intelligence must be respected. But one strategy in particular may be deeply rooted, and has been acknowledged by most theorists (Pick, 1974), namely, the interweaving of peculiarly visual skills with haptically derived information. Some of the evidence suggesting this intimate linkage is as follows:

1. If a cylinder is rolled between finger and thumb, first with the arm outstretched, and then close to the head, the cylinder feels larger near the head (Bartley, 1953). Why should estimates of size depend, haptically, on proximity to the head? One possibility is that the head acts as a zero point for haptic axes, just as it does for the eye.

2. Let a U be traced on the forearm, with the open end toward the hand. When the forearm is outstretched the U will indeed be coded as a

U. But when the forearm is bent across the body, the U will be coded as a C (Pick, personal communication). It seems again that orientation is body and head dependent, rather than skin-region dependent.

3. One hand is palm down on a table. A finger is touched and the hand rotated, palm up. Now, in reporting which finger was touched, subjects often report the *place*, but not the finger, suggesting a visual coding, rather than proprioceptive coding (McKinney, 1964). Attneave and Benson (1969) report place rather than finger coding in a similar vibrator-location task, and also interpret the effect as visual coding.

4. Blind and sighted subjects respond similarly to perspective transformations of shape in letters (Pick & Pick, 1966) and raised line drawings of familiar objects (Kennedy, 1974). For example, both kinds of subjects treat an elliptical shape as a depiction of a circle, and a trapezium as a depiction of a rectangle.

There is a tricky issue of interpretation here. When should a spatial system be described as a visual system? One criterion is the presence of *perspective*, particularly perspective with the head and eyes as a zero point; thus the first and last points, above, are especially important. But, in the last analysis, it may be that all the sensory systems participate in a general or abstract amodal geometry, rather than a visually based visual-image geometry. That is, haptics may indeed use a perspective geometry, but it need not always be employed as a visual-image making system; the research on blind subjects suggests this possibility (see also Warren, 1973; Warren & Pick, 1970).

CONCLUSION

Is there a haptics? It is tempting to conclude that haptics does not exist. The idea that active perception is best has not proved to be loaded with presents: It fails as often as it works in tasks that entail high memory loads, and the emphasis is better placed at times on mental planning than actual physical control. Also, there is little physiological support for a coherent theory of haptics.

Yet, haptics is alive and well. First, the active-perception hypothesis is not a total failure. At certain times, it has been supported. Second, haptics was born in phenomenology. It rejected elementary attempts to tie perception to physiology. So haptics is untroubled for the moment by physiology's inability to give it a substrate. Third, because haptics is a set of perceptual skills (and incorporates constancy), we expect from the outset that it should weigh an item of information heavily one time and lightly the next, in tune with the purposes of the moment. (Thus, we study the task to realize how sensible perceivers may vary their strategies.) Fourth, haptics involves more than perceptual organs. It is a set of tasks in an environment, an overall function of a chain of events from object to perception. To focus on one link would be to miss the point (e.g., apparent objects being detached from the skin in phi, Katz's insights into practical haptics, and surrogate representations of real objects). Fifth, precisely because haptics is sandwiched between sensations and cognition, it partakes of both at times. To dismiss haptics because it shades off at the edges would be like denying the existence of white because there is gray.

In conclusion, haptics is a *discipline*. It studies the acquisition of knowledge via contact. It is not a *hypothesis* that can be rejected; it is a domain of enquiry that as yet provides us with mysteries and puzzles, but is a vigorous enterprise and likely to remain so.

References

Abravanel, E. The development of intersensory patterning with regard to selected spatial dimensions. *Monographs of the Society for Research in Child Development*, 1968, **33**, (2, Whole No. 118).

Attneave, F., & Benson, B. Spatial coding of tactual stimulation. *Journal of Experimental Psychology*, 1969, **81**, 216–222.

Austin, T. R., & Sleight, R. B. Accuracy of tactual discrimination of letters, numerals and geometric forms. *Psychological Bulletin*, 1952, **43**, 239–249.

Bach-y-rita, P. *Brain mechanisms in sensory substitution*. New York: Academic Press, 1972.

Bartley, S. H. The perception of size or distance based on tactile and kinaesthetic data. *Journal of Psychology*, 1953, **36**, 401–408.

Bean, C. H. The blind have optical illusions. *Journal of Experimental Psychology*, 1938, **22**, 283–289.

Becker, F. Tactual learning and transfer of geometric forms. *Clark University Thesis Abstracts*, 1931, **3**, 125–128.

Beckesy, G. von. *Sensory inhibition*. Princeton, New Jersey: Princeton Univ. Press, 1967.

Binns, H. Visual and tactual judgement as illustrated in a practical experiment. *British Journal of Psychology*, 1937, **27**, 404–410.

Bliss, J. C. A provisional bibliography on tactile displays. *Institute of Electrical Engineers Transactions on Man–Machine Systems*, 1970, MMS-11, 101–108.

Bouma, H. *Progress Report*. Institute for Perception Research, **9**, Eindhoven, Holland, 1974.

Bower, T. G. R. Object perception in infants. *Perception*, 1974, **1**, 15–30. (a)

Bower, T. G. R. The evolution of sensory systems. In R. B. MacLeod & H. Pick (Eds.), *Perception*. Ithaca, New York: Cornell Univ. Press, 1974. Pp. 141–152. (b)

Bryant, P. *Perception and understanding in young children*. London: Methuen, 1974.

Cauna, N. Light and electron microscopal structure of sensory end organs in human skin. In D. R. Kenshalo (Ed.), *The skin senses*. Springfield, Illinois: Thomas, 1968. Pp. 15–28.

Churchill, A. V. Tactual and visual interpolation. A cross-modal comparison. *Canadian Journal of Psychology*, 1960, **14**, 183–190.

Cormack, R. H. Haptic illusion: Apparent elongation of a disc rotated between the fingers. *Science*, 1973, **179**, 590–592.

Costa, A. L'illusion di Poggendorf al tatto. *Archivo Italiano Psicologica*, 1937. **15**, 363–369.

Critchley, M. Tactile thought with special reference to the blind. *Brain*, 1953, **76**, 19–35.

Davenport, R. K., & Rogers, C. M. Perception of photographs by apes. *Behavior*, 1971, **39**, 318–320.

Davidson, P. W. Haptic judgements of curvature by blind and sighted humans. *Journal of Experimental Psychology*, 1972, **93**, 43–55.

Davidson, P. W., Barnes, J. K., & Mullen, G. Differential effects of task memory demand on haptic matching of shape by blind and sighted humans. *Neuropsychologia*, 1974, **12**, 395–397.

Davidson, P. W., & Whitson, T. T. Haptic equivalence matching of curvature by blind and sighted humans. *Journal of Experimental Psychology*, 1974, **102**, 687–690.

Day, R. H., & Avery, G. C. Absence of the horizontal-vertical illusion in haptic space. *Journal of Experimental Psychology*, 1970, **83**, 172–173.

Flowers, K. Handedness and controlled movement. *British Journal of Psychology*, 1975, **66**, 39–52.

Frisby, J. P., & Davies, I. R. L. Is the haptic Mueller-Lyer a visual phenomenon? *Nature*, 1971, **231**, 463–465.

Geldard, F. A. Cutaneous channels of communication. In W. A. Rosenblith (Ed.) *Sensory communication*, Cambridge, Massachusetts: M.I.T. Press, 1961. Pp. 73–87.

Geldard, F. A. *Cutaneous communication systems and devices*. Austin, Texas: The Psychonomic Society, 1974.

Gelfan, S., & Carter, S. Muscle sense in man. *Experimental Neurology*, 1967, **18**, 469–473.

Gibson, J. J. Observations on active touch. *Psychological Review*, 1962, **69**, 477–491.

Gibson, J. J. *The senses considered as perceptual systems*. Boston: Houghton-Mifflin, 1966.

Gibson, J. J., & Backlund, F. A. An after-effect in haptic space perception. *Quarterly Journal of Experimental Psychology*, 1963, **15**, 145–154.

Gilman, S., & Denny-Brown, D. Disorders of movement and behavior following dorsal column lesions. *Brain*, 1966, **89**, 397–418.

Goodnow, J. Eye and hand: Differential memory and its effects on matching. *Neuropsychologia*, 1971, **9**, 89–95.

Goldscheider, A. Untersuchungen über den Muskelsinn, *Archiv Physiologische Liepzig*, 1889, **4**, 369–502.

Goodwin, G. M., McCloskey, D. I., & Matthews, P. B. C. Proprioceptive illusions induced by muscle vibration: Contributions by muscle spindles to perception. *Science*, 1972, **175**, 1382–1384.

Gordon, I. E., & Cooper, C. Improving one's touch. *Nature*, 1975, **256**, 203–204.

Gregory, R. L. The evolution of eyes and brains—a hen-and-egg problem. In S. J. Freedman (Ed.) *The neuropsychology of spatially oriented behavior*. Chicago: Dorsey Press, 1968.

Gregory, R. L., & Ross, H. E. Arm weight, adaptation and weight discrimination. *Perceptual and Motor Skills*, 1967, **24**, 1127.

Guarniero, G. Experience of tactile vision. *Perception*, 1974, **3**, 101–104.

Harlow, H. F., & Harlow, M. K. Learning to love. *American Scientist*, 1966, **54**, 244–272.

Hatwell, Y. Etude de quelques illusions geometriques tactiles chez les aveugles. *L'Année Psychologique*, 1960, **60**, 11–27.

Hermelin, B., & O'Connor, N. Functional asymmetry in the reading of Braille. *Neuropsychologia*, 1971, **9**, 431–435.

Howard, I. P., & Anstis, T. Muscular and joint-receptor components in postural persistence. *Journal of Experimental Psychology*, 1974, **103**, 167–170.

Howard, I. P., & Templeton, W. B. *Human spatial orientation*. New York: Wiley, 1966.

Jastrow, J. Perception of space by disparate senses. *Mind*, 1886, **11**, 539–554.

Jones, B. When are vision and kinaesthesis comparable? *British Journal of Psychology*, 1973, **64**, 587–591.

Jones, B. Effects in children of a brief period of guided tactual exploration on shape recognition (In preparation).

Jones, K. N., Touchstone, R. M., & Gettys, C. F. A tactile illusion: The rotating hourglass. *Perception & Psychophysics*, 1974, **15**, 335–338.

Katz, D. *Der aufbau der tastwelt*. *Zeitschrift fur Psychologie*, 1925, **11**, 1–270.

Katz, D. A sense of touch: The techniques of percussion, palpation and massage. *British Journal of Physical Medicine*, 1936, **2**, 35–41.

Keidel, W. D. The cochlear model in skin stimulation. In F. A. Geldard (Ed.) *Conference on cutaneous communication systems and devices*. Austin, Texas: Psychonomic Society, 1974. Pp. 27–32.

Kennedy, J. M. *A psychology of picture perception*. San Francisco: Jossey-Bass, 1974.

Kennedy, J. M. Drawing was discovered not invented. *New Scientist*, 1975, **67**, 523–525.

Kennedy, J. M., & Campbell, J. Figure-ground coding of raised-line tactile displays. Canadian Psychological Association conference, Toronto, 1976.

Kennedy, J. M., & Fox, N. Pictures to see and picture to touch. In D. Perkins & B. Leondar (Eds.) *The arts and cognition*. Baltimore: Johns Hopkins Univ. Press, 1977.

Kennedy, J. M., Fox, N., & O'Grady, K. Can haptic pictures help the blind to see? A study of drawings to be touched. *Harvard Education Association Bulletin*, 1972, **16**, 22–23.

Kennedy, J. M., Mueller, E., & Moscow, J. Infants finger painting. Project Zero technical reports, Harvard Univ., in press.

Kirman, J. H. Tactile communication of speech: A review and an analysis. *Psychological Bulletin*, 1973, **80**, 54–74.

Klapp, S. T. Feedback vs. motor programming in the control of aimed movements. *Journal of Experimental Psychology: Human Perception and Performance*, 1975, **1**, 147–153.

Koehler, W., & Dinnerstein, D. Figural after effects in kinaesthesis. In *Miscellanea Psychologica: Albert Michotte* Louvain, Belgium: Univ. of Louvain, 1947.

Kornhuber, H. H. Motor functions of cerebellum and basal ganglia. *Kybernetic*, 1971, **8**, 157–162.

Krueger, L. E., David Katz's Der Aufbau der Tastwelt (The world of touch): A synopsis. *Perception & Psychophysics*, 1970, **7**, 337–341.

Landrigan, D. T., & Forsyth, G. A. Regulation and production of movement effects in exploration-recognition performance. *Journal of Experimental Psychology*, 1974, **103**, 1124–1130.

Lee, D. N., & Lishman, J. R. Visual proprioceptive control of stance. *Journal of Human Movement Studies*, 1975, **1**, 87–95.

Levin, H. S., & Benton, A. L. A comparison of ipsilateral and contralateral effects of tactile masking. *American Journal of Psychology*, 1973, **86**, 435–444.

Major, D. R. Cutaneous perception of form. *American Journal of Psychology*, 1898, **10**, 143–147.

Magee, L. E., & Kennedy, J. M. Contact, Kinaesthesis and guidance in recognition of haptic pictures. Paper presented at the conference of the Canadian Psychological Association, Toronto, 1976.

McCloskey, D. I. Muscular and cutaneous mechanisms in the estimation of the weights of grasped objects. *Neuropsychologia*, 1974, **12**, 513–520.

McKinney, J. Hand schema in children. *Psychonomic Science*, 1964, **1**, 99–100.

Melzack, R., & Wall, P. D. On the nature of cutaneous sensory mechanisms. *Brain*, 1962, **85**, 331–352.

Miller, G. A. *Language and communication*. New York: McGraw-Hill, 1951.

Milner, B., & Taylor, L. Right hemisphere superiority in tactile pattern-recognition after cerebral commissurotomy: Evidence for non-verbal memory. *Neuropsychologia*, 1972, **10**, 1–15.

Montagu, A. *Touching: The human significance of the skin*. New York: Columbia, 1971.

Nachshon, I., & Carmon, A. Hand preference in sequential and spatial discrimination tasks. *Cortex*, 1975, **11**, 123–131.

Nafe, J. P. The pressure, pain and temperature senses. In C. Murchison (Ed.) *Handbook of general experimental psychology*. Worcester, Massachusetts: Clark Univ. Press, 1934.

Over, R. A comparison of haptic and visual judgements of some illusions. *American Journal of Psychology*, 1966, **79**, 590–595.

Over, R. Explanations of geometrical illusions. *Psychological Bulletin*, 1968, **70**, 545–562.

Pick, H. L. Perception in Soviet psychology. *Psychological Bulletin*, 1964, **62**, 21–35.

Pick, H. Visual coding of non-visual spatial information. In R. B. MacLeod & H. Pick (Eds.) *Perception*. Ithaca, New York: Cornell Univ. Press, 1974. Pp. 153–165.

Pick, A. D., & Pick, H. L. A developmental study of tactual discrimination in blind and sighted children and adults. *Psychonomic Science*, 1966, **6**, 367–368.

Posner, M. I. Characteristics of visual and kinaesthetic memory codes. *Journal of Experimental Psychology*, 1967, **75**, 103–107.

Posner, M. I. Coordination of internal codes. In W. G. Chase (Ed.), *Visual information processing*. New York: Academic Press, 1973. Pp. 35–73.

Revesz, G. System der optischen and haptischen raumaus-schungen. *Zeitschrift fur Psychologie*, 1934, **131**, 296–375.

Revesz, G. *Psychology and art of the blind*. Toronto: Longmans, 1950.

Rock, I. *The nature of perceptual adaptation*. New York: Basic Books, 1966.

Rock, I., & Harris, C. S. Vision and touch. *Scientific American*, 1967, **216**, 96–107.

Rose, S., Blank, M., & Bridger, W. Intermodal and intramodal retention of visual and tactual information in young children. *Developmental Psychology*, 1972, **6**, 482–486.

Roy, E. A., & Marteniuk, R. G. Mechanisms of control in motor performance: Closed loop vs. motor programming control. *Journal of Experimental Psychology*, 1974, **103**, 985–991.

Rudel, R. G., & Teuber, H. L. Decrement of visual and haptic Mueller-Lyer illusion on repeated trials: A study of cross-modal transfer. *Quarterly Journal of Experimental Psychology*, 1963, **15**, 125–131.

Sekuler, R. W., Hartings, M. F., & Bauer, J. A. Jiggling a lifted object does not aid judgement of its perceived weight. *American Journal of Psychology*, 1974, **87**, 255–259.

Senden, M. von. *Raum- und Gestalt-auffassung bei operierten Blind ge borenen vor und nach der Operation*. Leipzig: Barth, 1932. (Tr. P. Heath, *Space and sight*. London: Methuen, 1960)

Shagan, J. Kinaesthetic memory in blind and sighted individuals. Unpublished doctoral dissertation, George Washington Univ., 1970.

Sheppard, D. The sensory basis of the cheese-grader's skill. *Occupational Psychology*, 1955, **29**, 150–163.

Sherrick, C. E. Studies of apparent tactile movement in D. R. Kenshalo (Ed.), *The skin senses*. Springfield, Illinois: Thomas, 1968. Pp. 157–175.

Sherrick, C. E. The art of tactile communication. *American Psychologist*, 1975, **30**, 353–360.

Sherrington, C. S. *The integrative action of the nervous system*. London: Cambridge Univ. Press, 1906.

Shopland, C., & Gregory, R. L. The effect of touch on a visually ambiguous three-dimensional figure. *Quarterly Journal of Experimental Psychology*, 1964, **16**, 66–70.

Sinclair, D. C. *Cutaneous sensation*. London: Oxford Univ. Press, 1967.

Smith, J. M. The sensory function of the non-preferred hand. *Journal of Experimental Psychology*, 1933, **16**, 271–282.

Stanley, G. Adding and averaging angles: Comparison of haptic-visual and visual-visual information integration. *Acta Psychologica*, 1974, **38**, 331–336.

Stevens, S. S. Transfer functions of the skin and muscle senses. In A. N. S. de Reuck & J. Knight (Eds.) *Touch, heat and pain.* London: Churchill, 1966. Pp. 3–16.

Stevens, S. S. *Psychophysics.* New York: Wiley, 1975.

Taylor, J. G. *The behavioral basis of perception.* New Haven, Connecticut: Yale Univ. Press, 1962.

Taylor, M. M., Lederman, S. J., & Gibson, R. H. Tactual perception of texture. In E. C. Carterette & M. P. Friedman (Eds.), *Handbook of Perception.* Vol. 3. New York: Academic Press, 1973. Pp. 251–272.

Tedford, W. H., & Tudor, L. L. Tactual and visual illusions in the T-shaped figure. *Journal of Experimental Psychology*, 1969, **81**, 199–201.

Uttal, W. R. *The psychobiology of sensory coding.* New York: Harper, 1973.

Valvo, A. *Sight restoration after long term blindness: The problems and behaviour patterns of visual rehabilitation.* New York: American Foundation for the Blind, 1971.

Walker, J. T., & Shea, K. S. A tactual size after effect contingent on hand position. *Journal of Experimental Psychology*, 1974, **103**, 668–674.

Wall, P. D. The sensory and motor role of impulses travelling in the dorsal columns towards cerebral cortex. *Brain*, 1970, **93**, 505–524.

Warren, D. H. Early vs. late blindness: The role of early vision in spatial reference systems. Paper presented at the Society for Research in Child Development Conference, April 1973, Philadelphia.

Warren, D. H., & Pick, H. L. Intermodality relations in localization in blind and sighted people. *Perception and Psychophysics*, 1970, **8**, 430–432.

Weber, C. O., & Dallenbach, K. M. Properties of space in kinaesthetic fields of force. *American Journal of Psychology*, 1929, **41**, 95–105.

Weddell, G. Somesthesis and the chemical senses. *Annual Reviews of Psychology*, 1955, **6**, 119–136.

Weiskrantz, L., Elliott, J., & Darlington, C. Preliminary observations on tackling oneself. *Nature*, 1971, **230**, 598–599.

White, B. W., Saunders, F. A., Scadden, L., Bach-y-rita, P., & Collins, C. C. Seeing with the skin. *Perception & Psychophysics*, 1970, **7**, 23–27.

Willott, J. F. Perceptual judgments with discrepant information from audition and proprioception. *Perception & Psychophysics*, 1970, **14**, 577–580.

Woodworth, R. S. Accuracy of voluntary movement. *Psychological Review Monograph Supplements*, 1899, **3**, 13.

Woodworth, R. S. *Experimental psychology.* New York: Holt, 1938.

Yonas, A. Difficulties in establishing the perceptual bases for responses to stimuli in infants. Talk given at Scarborough College, Univ. of Toronto, November, 1975.

Zaparozhets, A. V. The development of perception in the preschool child. In P. H. Mussen (Ed.), European research in cognitive development. *Monographs of the Society for Research in Child Development*, 1965, **30**(2, Whole No. 100).

Zigler, M. J., & Barrett, R. A further contribution to the tactual perception of form. *Journal of Experimental Psychology*, 1927, **10**, 184–192.

Part III

Interacting Perceptual Systems

Chapter 9

MULTIMODAL PERCEPTION*

LAWRENCE E. MARKS

I. INTRODUCTION

"Multimodal perception—awfully specialized, isn't it? A small twig (or maybe a broken branch!) on the tree of perception?" Reactions like this are not uncommon. Given the way in which the topic of perception is often subdivided—into visual perception, auditory perception, tactile perception, etc.—multimodal perception occupies only the intersection of the subtopics and hence is left to play a minor role. Yet one can, I believe, take the opposing view that multimodal perception, the way sensory systems interrelate, plays a fundamental role, and that it is the rule, rather than the exception. Because all or most of our senses are continuously

* Preparation of this chapter was supported, in part, by Grant ES-00354 from the National Institutes of Health. The review of the literature for this chapter was completed in 1975.

active, as least during waking hours, one might even treat multimodal perception as coextensive with virtually all of perception.

Multimodal perception covers a wide variety of diverse subjects, only a few of which can be dealt with here. Because the present chapter deals primarily with questions about the perception of objects and space by different senses, I will take the opportunity first to give some notion of the scope of multimodal perception.

For one, there is the phenomenological observation that the qualities of experience of different senses can, in some aspects, bear similarities. Soft and loud sounds are analogous to dim and bright lights, to mild and strong pains. Such observations have led to the postulation of supramodal dimensions or attributes of sensation—attributes like quality, intensity, and duration that apply to all percepts (see, for example, Boring, 1933; Külpe, 1893). Stevens (1959) and others (e.g., Stevens, Mack, & Stevens, 1960; Stevens & Marks, 1965) have measured the notable consistency with which subjects are able to match the subjective intensities of percepts on different sense modalities.

A related subject is synesthesia, the curious phenomenon where percepts proper to one modality arouse images or take on sensory attributes proper to other modalities. Some individuals report, for example, that music or voices take on colors, tastes, or other nonauditory characteristics. Synesthesia consists in large measure of regular and consistent cross-modal translations among dimensions of sensory experience (Marks, 1975, 1978).

Another subject, and the one of primary concern here, is multimodal perception of objects and events—the ways in which our several sensory channels function in concert to enable us to apprehend the world. It requires only a moment's reflection to think of a broad variety of examples where the same properties of objects or events make themselves known through different sensory modalities.

A. Common Features of Sense Perception

A few of the prominent features of multimodal perception, and of the significant questions that need answers, can be seen in the following example. While driving along a highway I spotted a sign that read, "Toll 25¢—Exact Change Keep Left." Experience had taught me that the exact change lane was by far the fastest. Moreover, I had at least a vague knowledge of the contents of my pocket: several quarters, together with an assortment of smaller change. Unfortunately, the traffic was heavy, and I didn't want either to fumble with change or to look away from the road. So I reached into my pocket, sampled a few coins in succession with my fingers, and pulled out a quarter.

Under other circumstances, I might have behaved in a different fashion and relied on vision instead of touch. That is, I would have pulled out a handful of coins, inspected them visually, and selected the large, silver coin with the profile of George Washington or the figure of an American eagle. In the absence of such detailed information from vision, however, the selection was made by touch, essentially on the basis of the coin's perceived size.

Size is one of the properties of objects that is available as information to several sense departments, and when size is fully sufficient as a characteristic to distinguish one object from another, size alone may be adequate for accurate perceptual discrimination. The size of a quarter serves well to distinguish it from other American coins. Of course, I could have been fooled if, for example, I had recently traveled abroad and still had foreign coins in my pocket. Although an error of this sort might never be made with vision, where the fine details of pattern serve as clear identifying features, such an error might well occur by touch. Hence, one limitation on the equivalence of cross-modal perception stems from intrinsic differences in the capacities of different senses to discriminate small variations in the stimulus.

Several properties of objects and events in addition to size make themselves known to us by means of more than one sense modality. Shape and texture are two other examples. There is some heuristic value to looking at multimodal perception in terms of Aristotle's doctrine of common sensible attributes. According to Aristotle, there are two categories of sense perception that are essential to its nature, and which he termed *peculiar objects* and *common objects*. Later philosophers called these *secondary qualities* and *primary qualities*. Whereas each peculiar or secondary quality, like color, pitch, taste, and odor quality, can be apprehended only by one sense, the common, or primary, qualities (like size, shape, and number) were said by Aristotle to be "not the peculiar objects of any sense, but common to them all [*De anima*, 418a3]."

Aristotle was fortunate enough to live well before the British empiricist school of Locke, Berkeley, and Hume; instead of beginning the study of perception with the senses, as was the wont of many who followed, Aristotle realized that "In discussing any form of sense-perception we must begin with the sensible objects [*De anima* 418a1]." Hence we begin from a philosophical viewpoint much like naive realism; we might wish to say, as [Plato *Theaetetus*, 184d] did, that we perceive *through* our senses rather than *with* them.

Given this starting point, it is quite natural to ask about multimodal perception. One begins with objects and events in the environment and asks what environmental features present themselves through more than one modality, with what precision do different senses accomplish this perception, how is multimodal information assembled and integrated, and what happens when different senses disagree.

B. Topics in Multimodal Perception

One of the main questions in multimodal perception is that which asks what features or properties of the world make themselves known through different sense modalities (i.e., to what extent different senses can provide equivalent information). A second important question is how this is done (i.e., what perceptual mechanisms or cognitive devices serve to accomplish multimodal perception).

Perhaps the simplest, or at least the most direct, empirical problem is that of perceptual equivalence. Here the question concerns the degree of systematic correspondence of information transmitted by different senses; in other words, the linearity of the perceptual mapping between modalities. One goal is to elucidate the conditions, if any, under which one can identify sizes and shapes of objects as well by touch as by sight. A related topic is the extent that information gleaned through one sense can be transferred to another modality. After I learn to identify coins of a foreign currency by sight, will I immediately be able to discriminate the same coins by touch? Will I at least learn the tactile identifications more rapidly after the visual learning?

Finally, we may inquire as to what the perceptual result is when different senses present concurrent information. Do the senses combine the information that they process so that, for example, determining an object's spatial position is better when two senses are used than when either one is used alone? Or does one sense dominate and suppress the information from the other? In particular, what happens when the senses provide contradictory information? How does the perceptual apparatus placate the antagonistic sense data?

C. Perceptual Interactions

The senses are always or almost always active, and the environment makes available information to all modalities. It is important to distinguish between two situations in which a person receives concurrent, multimodal stimulation. In one, the information presented through two or more modalities is correlated and connected; in the other, the information is orthogonal and independent. There exists an extensive literature on the subject of sensory interactions, much of which deals with such matters as the effect of a visual stimulus on the perceptibility of a sound or the effect of an auditory stimulus on the perception of visual flicker. Very often, there is no obvious connection, either in the real world or in perception, between the two conjoined stimulus events. Only by a great and metaphorical stretch of the imagination could one speak of common or conflicting information between a flash of light and a pulse of tone that do not even arise from the same point in space. There is no good reason for the perceptual system to try to integrate two such events, and this is reflected in the experimental results, which are often inconclusive or contradictory. There may be some interactions of this type between sensory systems, but the effects, if real, seem to be small.

More sizable and, I believe, of greater theoretical import are the perceptual interactions that take place when the stimulation of different senses reflects mutually relevant information. A concrete example was provided by Kinney and Luria (1970), who studied the perception of size under water. Because the refractive index of water is greater than that of air, the visual image in two dimensions of an object viewed under water is larger than that of the same object viewed in air; in Kinney and Luria's experiment, the increase amounted to about 30%. Hence, visual size should be modified by water. Tactile size, however, should be unaffected. To a diver under water, then, there should be a discrepancy between the size of an object as it is seen and as it is felt. After certifying that there is no significant discrepancy between seen size and felt size in air, Kinney and Luria asked what happened to the perceived size of objects when they are seen and felt at the same time under water. The answer was that the objects were perceived to be as big as they looked, even though the subjects could see their hands as well as the disks. With conflicting information, visual size dominated tactual size.

I have been able to demonstrate this same phenomenon to myself in a paradigm similar to one employed by Rock and Victor (1964). While feeling two identically sized coins, one with each hand, I viewed one hand and coin through a magnifier. Not only did the magnified coin look larger than its twin, but it also felt larger to the touch.

D. Synthesis of Multimodal Information

Knowing what it is that the senses do jointly is a significant first step, but it is only the first step. How does the perceptual apparatus accomplish multimodal perception? What makes it possible to see and feel the same sizes and shapes, and what integrates the information from different senses into a (usually) unified perceptual event? Philosophers and psychologists used to speak of integration as the domain of the *synthetic faculty,* by which was often meant little or nothing more than that multimodal perception took place. Plato recorded how Socrates asked, in his typical manner, of Theaetetus, "But now, through what organ does that faculty work, which tells you what is common not only to these objects but to all things?" Theaetetus responded knowledgeably of common properties—existence, similarity, unity, number—that "there is no special organ for all these . . . the mind in itself is its own instrument for contemplating the common terms that apply to everything [*Theaetetus*, 186c]."

Several ways exist whereby "the mind in itself" might organize perceptual information derived from different modalities. One hypothesis is that some perceptual or cognitive mechanism serves to mediate between perceptions that arise from different sense departments and to interconnect the perceptions of common objects or events. The most obvious candidate for such a mediating process or device is language. In somewhat oversimplified terms, we might say that the property of *twoness* of a pair of objects or events is perceived in common through different senses because we call a pair of sounds, a pair of tastes, or sights, or smells by the same word *two*.

Alternatively, sensory information might be integrated and correlated through a process of translation that does not require language. Two objects might feel the same size as they look because information from one modality is translated into information of another. Tactile information might be transformed, for example, into visual images.

A third possibility is that there exist certain features of stimuli that are appreciated directly, even when sensed through different modalities. According to this hypothesis, no mediation is required, in that the suprasensory property is sufficient in itself to account for multimodal perception (e.g., Gibson, 1966).

II. MULTIMODAL PERCEPTION OF SIZE

Let us begin by looking at one of the simpler properties of objects that can be registered by more than one sense, namely their size. Size—the spatial extensiveness of an object in one, two, or three dimensions—is a fundamental feature of things in the world and of our perception of them. Not surprisingly, size is also a feature that different senses seem, in general, to be able to handle in a notably well-integrated fashion. Under normal circumstances, a meterstick, for instance, feels about as long as it looks.

A. Perception of Linear Extent

The simplest case to consider is the perception of length—spatial extensiveness in one dimension. A convenient and important property of the visual perception of length is that to a good first approximation, perceived linear extent is proportional to physical length; hence the psychophysical function that relates the perceptual dimension to its physical correlate is a linear one. Gustav Fechner postulated in 1860 his famous dictum that psychological magnitudes grow as the logarithm of corresponding physical magnitudes, but not long afterwards Ewald Hering (1876) pointed out the impropriety of such a formulation for the perception of linear extent. It is clear and apparent, wrote Hering, that perceived length is directly proportional to physical length itself, not to the logarithm of length. A line 50-cm long looks as if it is 10 times a line of 50 mm.

Modern psychophysical investigations confirm the correctness of Hering's proposal for several varieties of perceived linear extent. Probably the most extensively studied variety is visually perceived length. Stevens and Guirao (1963) and Teghtsoonian and Teghtsoonian (1965) employed the procedure of magnitude estimation, where the subjects' task was to judge how long the stimuli (lines, rods) appeared to be by assigning numbers in proportion to perceived length. Results of these studies demonstrate a very near proportionality between numerical judgments of length and corresponding physical length, as depicted by the solid line in Fig. 1. Other procedures have been employed to scale length, including the method of category rating, where the numerical endpoints of the response continuum are specified by the experimenter (e.g., Stevens & Guirao, 1963). Here, too, a linear relation obtained between visual perception of length and physical extent.

Now to the question of how length is perceived through modalities other than vision. The equivalence or nonequivalence of perception

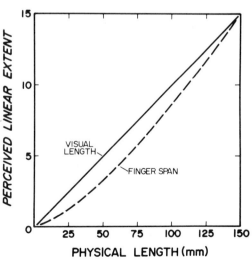

FIG. 1. Perception of linear extent by sight (solid line) and by proprioception (dashed curve). Apparent length is proportional to physical length, whereas apparent finger span is proportional to physical length raised to the 1.4 power.

through different sense modalities is intimately related to the psychophysical functions. As we just saw, a linear psychophysical function governs perception of visual length. It follows that if we perceive length through other modalities just as we do through vision, then the psychophysical relation between perceived and physical length must in every case be linear. To put it another way, suppose one scales length as perceived through some sense modality (not vision) and finds that perceived length bears a nonlinear relation to physical length; it then follows that there cannot possibly be an equivalence between perception of length through that modality and through vision.

The dashed line in Fig. 1 shows one type of nonlinear relation. Here, a given increment in physical length produces a small perceptual increase when added to a short length, but a large one when added to a greater length. The psychophysical function is positively accelerated, in contrast to the linear function found with visual length (solid line). Relatively short physical objects are perceived to be smaller than they are by sight, whereas long objects appear about equal by both modalities. The particular function shown by the dashed line does obtain for at least one type of perceived linear extent, namely finger span (the apparent thickness of objects held between thumb and forefinger). Stevens and Stone (1959) demonstrated this by the method of magnitude estimation, and their result was subsequently confirmed by Teghtsoonian and Teghtsoonian (1970). Hence it would seem that vision and finger span cannot provide equivalent information about linear extents.

Teghtsoonian and Teghtsoonian (1965) examined another type of felt length, namely length perceived proprioceptively by the two arms. They asked subjects to judge the lengths of rods that were felt by the index fingers of the two hands. Just as with visual length, this type of proprioceptive length was found to be directly proportional to physical length.

There is another step that must be taken in order to certify the equivalence of perception through different modalities. Though the perception of linear extent by both vision and two-hand proprioception is proportional to physical length, we still cannot know with certainty whether the two modes are equal to each other. Does a given length appear equal when perceived by the different modalities? The study by Teghtsoonian and Teghtsoonian (1965) described above suggested that two-hand proprioception and vision probably provided equivalent perceptions, but because the two modalities were studied separately, that question was not put to direct test. To answer the question, there must be a direct comparison of two or more senses. It is possible, for instance, to have two perceptual dimensions both proportional to their physical correlates, but not equal to each other. One sense might perceive the lengths of all objects to be some constant fraction of the lengths perceived by another sense.

One of the earliest studies to compare directly different senses was conducted by Jastrow (1886). Jastrow wanted to learn whether vision, kinesthesis, and finger-span proprioception all provided the same perception of length. His procedure called upon the subjects to match the linear extents perceived by different modalities, and the experiment was exceptionally well balanced in that Jastrow examined every possible pairwise comparison: all three cross-modal comparisons, plus the three intramodal comparisons. Moreover, matching was done in both directions (for example, both visual length to kinesthetic distance and kinesthetic distance to visual length).

When subjects matched visual length to finger span, all linear extents were perceived larger by eye than by hand, but the difference diminished as the physical length increased. This outcome is consistent with the corresponding curves shown in Fig. 1; Teghtsoonian and Teghtsoonian (1970) previously noted that Jastrow's data were consistent with a nonlinear relation between visual length and finger span. If apparent visual length grows proportionately to physical length, then apparent finger span must perforce grow disproportionately to physical thickness, and in particular must grow as an accelerated function like that shown in Fig. 1.

Jastrow also examined perception of distance through kinesthesis, which was accomplished by having subjects sweep their arms and judge the extent of movement. Unfortunately, the data obtained with kinesthesis were ambiguous: The comparison between kinesthetic extent and finger span suggested that perception of the linear extent of arm movement was proportional to physical distance, just like perception of length by vision; but the comparison between arm movement and vision failed to confirm the predicted collinearity. In other words, Jastrow's set of round-robin matches across the three sensory modalities failed to display transitivity.

Other investigations suggest, however, that the perception of distance by kinesthesis is very much like the perception of length by sight. Piéron (1922) examined the reproduction of length by active and passive movements of the arm and the recognition of length by sight. The results suggest an equivalence between arm movement and vision in the perception of linear extent. Perceived extent of arm movements was scaled by Ronco (1963), who employed a battery of procedures that included magnitude estimation and halving and doubling (where subjects produced arm movements that appeared half or twice as great as standard movements). Perception of kinesthetic distance was virtually proportional to physical distance of movement, as it must be if visual and kinesthetic extents are perceived as equivalent. A similar conclusion may be drawn from results of a study by Connolly and Jones (1970) in which subjects matched visual lengths and distances of arm movements.

There is another sensory mode for the perception of size that should be mentioned, namely active, or haptic, touch. The pen that one writes with has a length that is perceived not only by sight, but also by tactually exploring up and down the pen's contours. This sort of perception through active exploration, which combines information from the tactile, kinesthetic, and proprioceptive modalities, is frequently used and is undoubtedly important as a means of acquiring information about objects in the world. Abravanel (1971b) asked subjects to judge the total lengths of pairs of objects; in one experimental condition, both members of the pair were seen; in another, both were felt; in the third condition, one was seen and the other felt. The syntheses of length were virtually identical under the three conditions, thereby suggesting that vision and haptic touch can provide equivalent information about the length of objects.

The unidimensional size of an object is not only perceptible through several different senses, but moreover, as has been said, different senses (vision, haptic touch, kinesthesis) can give essentially equivalent perceptions of length, extent, or distance. This cross-modal equivalence should be distinguished from a related but separable question, namely the accuracy, reliability, or precision of cross-modal matching as compared to intramodal matching. Different senses may give equivalent perceptions of linear extent, in that there is no systematic discrepancy between the sizes perceived by them, but at the same time cross-modal matches are limited in their precision by the information-processing capacities of the individual senses. Abravanel (1968) has traced the manner in which precision in cross-modal matching of length improves through childhood.

Every sense department has a limited ability to discriminate differences in stimulation. Furthermore, different senses appear to vary in their ability to store and retrieve information. More than a century ago, Abbott (1864) called attention to the importance of modality differences in memory; he argued that information gained through each sense is stored in its own appropriate, modality-specific memory. Posner (1967) experimentally demonstrated the rapid fading of kinesthetic memory as compared to visual memory for length, and Marteniuk and Roy (1972) found poor codability of kinesthetic distance (limb movement), though better codability of proprioceptive location (limb position). Such differences among modality-specific codes and memories may play a significant role in cross-modal matching, particularly when the matching is done successively with a standard stimulus followed by comparison.

Jones and Connolly (1970) looked at the variability of intramodal and cross-modal matches of length, under several conditions of successive presentation. Intramodal visual and kinesthetic matches were equally precise, and both were more precise than cross-modal matches. Variability was greatest when the subjects had to execute a kinesthetic match to a remembered visual standard. It is possible that much of this excess variability comes about because the visual standard must be translated into a kinesthetic equivalent, which then fades rapidly from memory (Connolly & Jones, 1970).

To summarize, unidimensional size (length or distance) is basically the same when perceived by sight, by haptic touch, by kinesthesis (movement of the arm), and by some types of proprioception (between two arms or two hands). Curiously, though, there appears to be one mode of length perception not equivalent to the others: The apparent thickness of objects held between the thumb and forefinger of one hand deviates systematically from other forms of apparent linear extent. Nonequivalence between finger span and visual length is particularly surprising, considering the vast experience people have in simultaneously viewing objects and holding them in their hands. Despite the vast opportunity, there appears to be no learning of cross-modal equality.

B. Perception of Two-Dimensional Size

A few words should be said about the perception of size in two dimensions. Here too, as in the case of unidimensional size, different modalities often, but not always, give equivalent information. Kinney and Luria (1970) had subjects select, both by active touch and by vision, aluminum disks that appeared equal in size to the remembered size of standard American coins (penny, nickel, dime, quarter). The disks selected under the two conditions were virtually identical (and essentially equal to the actual sizes of the remembered coins). Sometimes, though, modalities of vision and touch are not equivalent. Anstis and Loizos (1967) compared the perception of small holes (diameters of about ⅛–½ in.) by sight and by touch. Holes of the same physical size appeared equal in size to the eye and to the tongue, but systematically larger to the eye and tongue than to the finger.

III. MULTIMODAL PERCEPTION OF SPACE

A. One Space, or Many?

The location of objects in space can be picked up through touch as well as through sight, and sometimes through hearing as well. One of the oldest realms of philosophical speculation and psychological experimentation concerns the interrelations among the representations of space by different modalities. From this work, several conceptualizations have emerged. The first states that there is but one psychological space: a single supramodal space to which the percepts of all modalities are referred, but that is not itself of any particular modality. Alternatively, there may be a single psychological space, but one that is modal in nature. The primary psychological representation might consist of a visual space that acts as a standard and into whose terms spatial representations from all other modalities are translated. A third possibility is that no one modality possesses a primary spatial representation. Instead, there may be several functionally equivalent spaces—one visual, another tactile–kinesthetic, still another auditory—amongst which there needs to be translation of information. Some mechanism, perhaps akin to a Maxwell's demon, would serve to gate the passage from one modality to another of appropriate features and properties of spatial relations.

The existence of a common, supramodal space is suggested by Auerbach and Sperling's (1974) study of the relation between visual and auditory direction. Subjects were required to discriminate the spatial location of one auditory stimulus from another, one visual stimulus from another, or a visual stimulus and an auditory one. Discriminability under these three conditions suggested little or no variability produced by a process of translation between auditory and visual space. Instead, it appeared that the locations of both auditory and visual stimuli were referred directly in perception to a single, common space. On the other hand, Warren's (1970) finding (viewing a patterned visual environment increases the precision of auditory localization of an unseen source) suggests that under some conditions, at least, auditory information maps into a visual representation.

Objects and events perceived through sight and touch may sometimes be represented in a common perceptual or cognitive space, but what about the representations of objects and events perceived through other senses? Spatial location can also be determined, for example, through proprioception (the feeling of position of one's body and limbs) and through kinesthesis (the feeling of body and limb movement). Berkeley (1709) proposed a famous, but unsupported, doctrine of the primacy of such a tactile–kinesthetic space. According to Berkeley's hypothesis, visual (and auditory) space is derived from touch through association, and hence is secondary to tactile space. If anything, however, the reverse is more likely true, with visual space being primary and tactile space being derived, as Abbott (1864) suggested. In infants, vision is more effective than touch in controlling object-oriented motor activity (Bower, Broughton, & Moore, 1970). Harris (1963, 1965) has interpreted the perceptual learning that results when visual images are displaced optically in terms of a modification of tactile–proprioceptive space through vision.

The latter interpretation of the relation between tactile and visual space is commensurate with Attneave and Benson's (1969) conclusion—to wit, that both tactile and visual information are referred to a single spatial representation, and that representation is fundamentally visual in nature. A casual observation that I have made is also consistent with this interpretation: If a person sits with his eyes closed and one hand outstretched, and I trace the lower-case letter *b* on his outstretched palm, he perceives the traced letter to be *b* if the palm is held to face inward (toward the person); but if the palm is held facing outward (away from the person), he perceives the letter to be *d*. Now, the pattern of tactile stimulation on the palm is identical in the two cases, but the tracing in visual space is different, and it corresponds to *b* in the former condition and to *d* in the latter.

One interpretation of this outcome is that the combination of tactile information (tracing on the hand) and proprioceptive information (position of arm and palm) goes into visual space. Another interpretation, which is perhaps more in line with Gibson's (1966) theory, is that the information is referred immediately to real space, not to a phenomenal space.

B. Resolution of Conflicting Information

Some important ideas may be gleaned from investigations of the way in which the perceptual system handles discrepant spatial information from different senses. The results of many studies are summarized by the timeworn phrase, *seeing is believing*. When senses are in conflict, the typical result is that vision emerges the victor. For instance, it is harder to displace the perceived spatial position of a sound when the sound source can be seen than when it cannot be seen (Witkin, Wapner, & Leventhal, 1952). Displacing the spatial location of an object visually was shown to have a marked effect on perceived auditory location, whereas acoustic displacement had little or no effect on visually perceived location (Pick, Warren, & Hay, 1969). Audition may bias vision, however, when the visual field is unstructured (Bertleson & Radeau, 1974).

Vision can also bias proprioception. If the visual image of a person's hand is displaced, he feels his hand to be where he sees it (Pick *et al.*, 1969). Though proprioceptive displacement also influences visually perceived position, the latter effect is notably smaller. Proprioception does rank above hearing in this hierarchy, for if proprioceptive and auditory cues are in conflict, felt position (proprioception) dominates (Pick *et al.*, 1969; Willott, (1973). For futher discussion of this, see Howard (1973).

Evidence from studies of intersensory conflict eludes any simple interpretation. Spatial information arrives with modality-specific labels, and disagreements lead to interactions in a hierarchy of dominance, with vision on top and hearing on the bottom. Every ventriloquist comprehends this hierarchy, at least implicitly.

Perhaps the nature of this hierarchical order should not be surprising. After all, vision is typically considered to be primarily a spatial sense. Indeed, it is considered to be the provider of spatial information *par excellence*. If vision is best at the job, why not rely on it the most? To be sure, when the visual image is displaced optically (by means of prisms), reliance on visually perceived position leads to perceptual errors. The prism-wearer reaches for the object as he sees it, and unless he also sees his hand to guide it, misses the object. But one can hardly blame the evolution of perceptual systems for failing to anticipate the experimental tricks of psychologists. For a related argument concerning intersensory integration, see Freides (1974).

IV. MULTIMODAL PERCEPTION OF FORM

The perception of shape, or figural form, is an exceedingly complex issue, much more complex than is the perception of size. Basically, we have two sensory means for obtaining information about objects' shapes: vision and haptic touch. The concern here is the degree of equivalence of shape information that is derived through vision and touch and the question of how information obtained from different sensory channels is correlated and combined.

A. Development of Cross-Modal Equivalence

When my children were about 2 years of age, one of their favorite toys was a plastic box together with a set of flat plastic shapes (square, disk, oval, triangle, and star), each of which could be inserted into the box. But each shape could be inserted only through the one appropriately shaped hole in the box. Besides being a source of considerable amusement, this toy also provided an excellent opportunity for the children to explore the different shapes and forms simultaneously by haptic touch and by vision. From casual observations of the children's behavior, it was clear that their haptic skills lagged well behind the visual.

This observation finds support in experimental studies, which generally note haptic form perception to be poorer than, or at least not better than, visual form perception. Rudel and Teuber (1964) examined the ability of children 3–5 years of age to make shape discriminations. When the standard stimuli and comparisons were presented in succession, 3-year-old children were unable to match even simple shapes perceived by touch alone either to their visual equivalents or to the same stimuli felt. Tactile-to-tactile matching and tactile-to-visual matching could be accomplished only when the standard and the comparison stimuli were presented simultaneously. The same result obtained when 4-year-old children attempted to match more complex shapes. One of the significant features of cross-modal identification of shapes is the greater difficulty involved in tactile as compared to visual perception. Indeed, when both visual and tactile information are potentially available, children seem to rely predominately on the visual information about shapes (Abravanel, 1972).

It is well established that children's capacity to match forms cross-modally increases with age (e.g., Birch & Lefford, 1963). Blank and Bridger (1964) inquired how well 3-, 4-, and 5-year-old children could pick out by sight which of two stimuli (such as cylinder and triangle) matched each of several standards held in the hand. Correct identifications increased with age, from 68% correct at age 3 to 95% correct at age 5. Even adults can display superior capacity to identify forms by sight as compared to touch. Abravanel (1971a) found intramodal visual matching of complex, unfamiliar forms to be superior to intramodal haptic matching, and the latter in turn to be slightly superior to cross-modal matching. An important variable here may be amount of practice, for Gibson (1962) has reported that young adults can achieve perfect cross-modal accuracy in form perception if they are given sufficient practice.

B. When Are Vision and Touch Equivalent?

A basic question we wish answered is, Under what circumstances do vision and touch provide equivalent information about the forms or shapes of objects? Gibson's (1962) result says that vision and touch can give equivalent information, but findings from other studies point out many circumstances, such as unfamiliarity with the materials or lack of practice, under which they do not. Several possible reasons emerge to explain why equivalence may fail to obtain.

For one, the ability to match accurately tactile and visual forms must ultimately be limited by the sensory capacity of the individual modalities. Significant factors that influence accuracy are the time allotted for exploration and manipulation of the stimuli and the demands that the task places on memory. Relevant here is Rudel and Teuber's (1964) finding that young children could not make intramodal haptic matches or cross-modal haptic-to-visual matches when the standard and comparison stimuli were presented successively, but could make these matches when multimodal perception was simultaneous. Rose, Blank, and Bridger (1972) compared intramodal and cross-modal matching of shapes in 4-year-old children under three conditions: simultaneous presentation, successive presentation, and presentation with a 15-sec delay. With simultaneous presentation of standard and comparison, intramodal and cross-modal matching was virtually perfect; but with separation in time between standard and comparison, performance deteriorated, particularly when at least one stimulus was haptic. These results suggest again that difficulty in storage or retrieval of haptic information in memory may be a major source of difficulty.

Coding and memory for haptic information also depends on the time available for exploration and manipulation of the forms. In the study by Abravanel (1971a) described earlier, for instance, the stimuli were available to the subjects for only 3 sec at a time. Davidson, Abbott, and Gershenfeld (1974) found that the time allotted to haptic touch had a large effect on the accuracy of cross-modal matching. When the presentation time of the standard stimulus, either visual or haptic, increased from 4 to 16 sec, the number of errors decreased markedly. When the exposure time of a haptic comparison stimulus was similarly increased, errors also decreased. Deficiency in cross-modal performance may result, therefore, at least in part from the lack of sufficient time to extract haptic information, or, when there is a visual standard, time to translate the representation from a visual to a haptic mode.

One hypothesis is that some type of learning is required for the coordination of information from different sense modalities. In order, for example, to perceive that a certain complex form felt with the hand is the same as another form seen with the eye, it might be necessary to have appropriate mediators or cues attached to critical features of the haptic and visual percepts. An obvious candidate for a mediator is language. Because rhesus monkeys failed to display any gains in a cross-modal transfer of training paradigm, Ettlinger (1960, 1961) concluded that the translation of information about shape from one modality to another required language. However, transfer of training is a different paradigm from cross-modal matching. Lobb (1970) conducted a carefully controlled study in which adult humans were trained either to make form discriminations by sight and then subsequently by touch, or to make the discriminations by touch and then by sight. Only the former condition led to transfer of training. Transfer of training between modalities appears to be more subtle or evanescent than the equivalence found by direct matching, even in humans.

In fact, tactile and visual equivalence has been demonstrated in nonverbal organisms: Both nonhuman primates (Davenport & Rogers, 1970) and human infants (Bryant, Jones, Claxton, & Perkins, 1972) seem capable of some cross-modal matching of objects. Hence verbal mediation may be useful, important, and perhaps even sufficient for cross-modal equivalence, but language does not appear to be necessary for equivalence (cf. von Wright, 1970).

Even if language is not always necessary for cross-modal transfer, undoubtedly language is sometimes employed to mediate translation of information from one modality to another. When language is not needed, or at least not used, cross-modal equivalence may reflect the ability of different senses to register directly the important features of stimulation. Gibson (1966) has argued that this sort of equivalence need not rely on associative learning, but rather that "there must be another simple type of perceptual development, the registering of the concurrent covariation from different organs. . . . Insofar as the linkage is invariant, the information is the same in all of them, that is, the systems are equivalent [p. 289]." Pick, Pick, and Thomas (1966) and Shaffer and Ellis (1974) have presented evidence that equivalences between visual and haptic perception of form can come about by means of direct registration of distinctive features.

Just as language is not required for the apprehension, through different modalities, of perceptual equivalence, neither is it necessary to perceive directly by different senses the critical stimulus properties. Both mechanisms are probably sufficient, but neither is necessary. The appropriateness of either depends on the complexity of the stimuli, the degree of familiarity, and so forth. One possibility is that early stages in the development of some types of cross-modal equivalence (e.g., the visual and tactile recognition of complex shapes) are marked by the use of mediators, but subsequently the mediators may become superfluous.

References

Abbott, T. K. *Sight and touch: An attempt to disprove the received (or Berkeleian) theory of vision.* London: Longman, Green, 1864.

Abravanel, E. The development of intersensory patterning with regard to selected spatial dimensions. *Monographs of the Society for Research in Child Development,* 1968, **33,** Whole No. 118.

Abravanel, E. Active detection of solid-shape information by touch and vision. *Perception & Psychophysics,* 1971, **10,** 358–360. (a)

Abravanel, E. The synthesis of length within and between perceptual systems. *Perception & Psychophysics,* 1971, **9,** 327–328. (b)

Abravanel, E. How children combine vision and touch when perceiving the shape of objects. *Perception & Psychophysics,* 1972, **12,** 171–175.

Anstis, S. M., & Loizos, C. M. Cross-modal judgments of small holes. *American Journal of Psychology,* 1967, **80,** 51–58.

Aristotle. *The works of Aristotle*. Oxford: Oxford Univ. Press (Clarendon), 1931.

Attneave, F., & Benson, B. Spatial coding of tactual stimulation. *Journal of Experimental Psychology,* 1969, **81,** 216–222.

Auerbach, C., & Sperling, P. A common auditory-visual space: Evidence for its reality. *Perception & Psychophysics,* 1974, **16,** 129–135.

Berkeley, G. *An essay towards a new theory of vision*. Dublin: Jeremy Pepyat, 1709.

Bertleson, P., & Radeau, M. The effect of structurization of the visual field on dominance in auditory-visual conflict. Paper presented at Fifteenth Annual Meeting of The Psychonomic Society, Boston 1974.

Birch, H. G., & Lefford, A. Intersensory development in children. *Monographs of the Society for Research in Child Development,* 1963, **28,** Whole No. 89.

Blank, M., & Bridger, W. H. Cross-modal transfer in nursery-school children. *Journal of Comparative & Physiological Psychology,* 1964, **58,** 277–282.

Boring, E. G. *The physical dimensions of consciousness*. New York: Appleton, 1933.

Bower, T. G. R., Broughton, J. M., & Moore, M. K. The coordination of visual and tactual input in infants. *Perception & Psychophysics,* 1970, **8,** 51–53.

Bryant, P. E., Jones, P., Claxton, V., & Perkins, G. M. Recognition of shapes across modalities by infants. *Nature,* 1972, **240,** 303–304.

Connolly, K., & Jones, B. A developmental study of afferent-reafferent integration. *British Journal of Psychology,* 1970, **61,** 259–266.

Davenport, R. K., & Rogers, C. M. Intermodal equivalence of stimuli in apes. *Science,* 1970, **168,** 279–280.

Davidson, P. W., Abbott, S., & Gershenfeld, J. Influence of exploration time on haptic and visual matching of complex shape. *Perception & Psychophysics,* 1974, **15,** 539–543.

Ettlinger, G. Cross-modal transfer of training in monkeys. *Behaviour,* 1960, **16,** 56–65.

Ettlinger, G. Learning in two sense-modalities. *Nature,* 1961, **191,** 398.

Fechner, G. T. *Elemente der Psychophysik*. Leipzig: Breitkopf und Härtel, 1860.

Freides, D. Human information processing and sensory modality: Cross-modal functions, information complexity, memory, and deficit. *Psychological Bulletin,* 1974, **81,** 284–310.

Gibson, J. J. Observations on active touch. *Psychological Review,* 1962, **69,** 477–491.

Gibson, J. J. *The senses considered as perceptual systems*. Boston: Houghton-Mifflin, 1966.

Harris, C. S. Adaptation to displaced vision: Visual, motor, or proprioceptive change? *Science,* 1963, **140,** 812–813.

Harris, C. S. Perceptual adaptation to inverted, reversed, and displaced vision. *Psychological Review,* 1965, **72,** 419–444.

Hering, E. Zur Lehre von der Beziehung zwichen Leib und Seele. I Mittheilung. Über Fechner's psychophysisches Gesetz. *Sitzungsberichte der Mathematisch-naturwissenschaftlichen Classe der Kaiserlichen Akademie der Wissenschaften,* Wien, 1876, **72,** 310–348.

Howard, I. P. The spatial senses. In E. C. Carterette & M. P. Friedman (Eds.), *Handbook of perception*. Vol. III, *Biology of perceptual systems*. New York: Academic Press, 1973. Pp. 291–315.

Jastrow, J. The perception of space by disparate senses. *Mind,* 1886, **11,** 539–554.

Jones, B., & Connolly, K. Memory effects in cross-modal matching. *British Journal of Psychology,* 1970, **61,** 267–270.

Kinney, J. A. S., & Luria, S. M. Conflicting visual and tactual-kinesthetic stimulation. *Perception & Psychophysics,* 1970, **8,** 189–192.

Külpe, O. *Grundriss der Psychologie*. Leipzig: Engelmann, 1893.

Lobb, H. Asymmetrical transfer of form discrimination across sensory modalities in human adults. *Journal of Experimental Psychology,* 1970, **86,** 350–354.

Marks, L. E. On colored-hearing synesthesia: Cross-modal translations of sensory dimensions. *Psychological Bulletin*, 1975, **82,** 303–331.

Marks, L. E. *The unity of the senses.* New York: Academic Press, 1978.

Marteniuk, R. G., & Roy, E. A. The codability of kinesthetic location and distance information. *Acta Psychologica*, 1972, **36,** 471–479.

Pick, A. D., Pick, H. L., Jr., & Thomas, M. L. Cross-modal transfer and improvement of form discrimination. *Journal of Experimental Child Psychology*, 1966, **3,** 279–288.

Pick, H. L., Jr., Warren, D. H., & Hay, J. C. Sensory conflict in judgments of spatial direction. *Perception & Psychophysics*, 1969, **6,** 203–205.

Piéron, Mme H. Contribution expérimentale à l'étude des phénomènes de transfert sensoriel: La vision et la kinésthesie dans la perception des longueurs. *L'Année Psychologique*, 1922, **23,** 76–124.

Plato. *The collected dialogues.* New York: Pantheon, 1961.

Posner, M. I. Characteristics of visual and kinesthetic memory codes. *Journal of Experimental Psychology*, 1967, **75,** 103–107.

Rock, I., & Victor, J. Vision and touch: An experimentally created conflict between the two senses. *Science*, 1964, **143,** 594–596.

Ronco, P. G. An experimental quantification of kinesthetic sensation: Extent of arm movement. *Journal of Psychology*, 1963, **55,** 227–238.

Rose, S. A., Blank, M. S., & Bridger, W. H. Intermodal and intramodal retention of visual and tactual information in young children. *Developmental Psychology*, 1972, **6,** 482–486.

Rudel, R. G., & Teuber, H.-L. Crossmodal transfer of shape discrimination by children. *Neuropsychologia*, 1964, **2,** 1–8.

Shaffer, R. W., & Ellis, H. C. An analysis of intersensory transfer of form. *Journal of Experimental Psychology*, 1974, **102,** 948–953.

Stevens, J. C., Mack, J. D., & Stevens, S. S. Growth of sensation on seven continua as measured by force of handgrip. *Journal of Experimental Psychology*, 1960, **59,** 60–67.

Stevens, J. C., & Marks, L. E. Cross-modality matching of brightness and loudness. *Proceedings of the National Academy of Sciences*, 1965, **54,** 407–411.

Stevens, S. S. Cross-modality validation of subjective scales for loudness, vibration, and electric shock. *Journal of Experimental Psychology*, 1959, **57,** 201–209.

Stevens, S. S., & Guirao, M. Subjective scaling of length and area and the matching of length to loudness and brightness. *Journal of Experimental Psychology*, 1963, **66,** 177–186.

Stevens, S. S., & Stone, G. Finger span: Ratio scale, category scale, and jnd scale. *Journal of Experimental Psychology*, 1959, **57,** 91–95.

Teghtsoonian, M., & Teghtsoonian, R. Seen and felt length. *Psychonomic Science*, 1965, **3,** 465–466.

Teghtsoonian, R., & Teghtsoonian, M. Two varieties of perceived length. *Perception & Psychophysics*, 1970, **8,** 389–392.

Warren, D. H. Intermodality interactions in spatial localization. *Cognitive Psychology*, 1970, **1,** 114–133.

Willott, J. F. Perceptual judgments with discrepant information from audition and proprioception. *Perception & Psychophysics*, 1973, **14,** 577–580.

Witkin, H. A., Wapner, S., & Leventhal, T. Sound localization with conflicting visual and auditory cues. *Journal of Experimental Psychology*, 1952, **43,** 58–67.

von Wright, J. J. Cross-modal transfer and sensory equivalence—a review. *Scandinavian Journal of Psychology*, 1970, **11,** 21–30.

Part IV

Perceptual Memory Codes

Chapter 10

SENSORY MEMORY SYSTEMS*

ROBERT G. CROWDER

One main function of a sensory memory system is to hold information in relatively raw form until some higher-order perceptual mechanism can integrate it sufficiently with other samples of information to trigger a learned category state. Such a memory system is necessary because the category states that result from perceptual processing are not ordinarily related to instantaneous states of the world, but rather to events lasting an appreciable time. More importantly, these category states are related in many cases to stimuli that must be defined as changes in energy over time. To perceive that a sentence is being spoken in the form of a question, with a rising intonation at the end, some perceptual analyzer must simultaneously have a record of the pitch used by the speaker within the sentence and also at its end. Passing to an example two logarithmic steps faster, we note that the perception of a stop consonant depends, in part, on changes in resonant frequency that occur during a period of about 40 msec. These

* Preparation of this chapter was supported, in part, by NIH Grant 1 RO 1 MH26623-01. Some of the material has been taken from *Principles of learning and memory,* by R. G. Crowder (Hillsdale, N. J.: Erlbaum, 1976). Reprinted by permission of the author and the publisher.

two examples show that the most natural uses of sensory memory in the service of perception occur in the auditory modality; however, if a Gibsonian (Gibson, 1950) perspective on perception is adopted, then the same points apply profoundly to the analysis of visual perception.

There are two other rational arguments for the existence of sensory memory in addition to the role of memory in perception of dynamic cues. Some authors (Liss, 1968; Massaro, 1970) have commented that since accurate perception can occur with impossibly brief stimulus exposures, there must be some trace outlasting the stimulus energy that supports perceptual analysis. Finally, even those who are most worried about the evidence for sensory memory (Holding, 1975, p. 40) are repelled by the consequences of assuming that neural events initiated by the stimulus are abruptly chopped off when the stimulus itself terminates. These considerations have apparently been adequate to convince most students that sensory memory exists; what controversies there are focus on the experimental operations used to demonstrate it.

I. CONCEPTUAL ISSUES IN DEMONSTRATING SENSORY MEMORY

One fundamental error in evaluating evidence for sensory memory is to assume that any memory process carrying the signature of one or another sensory modality is, therefore, necessarily a sensory memory. Instead, such a process may well be an instance of imagery in memory. One seldom fails to recognize the odor of a skunk even though many years sometimes pass between exposures; yet, by the criterion being applied here, such an authentically olfactory memory does not qualify as a sensory memory. For these and other logical points, we should continue to consider sensory memory in the abstract, before turning to the experimental evidence.

A. The Distinction of Sensory Memory from Memory Imagery

It is because of the separation of sensory memory from imagery that terms such as *preperceptual* and *precategorical* have been used for iconic and echoic memory (the sensory stores postulated for the visual and auditory sensory systems, respectively). Imagery can have a postcategorical locus. Failure to keep this distinction has led such investigators as Deutsch (1975, p. 110) and Holding (1975, p. 38) to complain about the inconsistencies of reported decay times for visual storage. In fact, modality-specific interference has been demonstrated in visual memory for periods well outside conventional estimates of iconic memory (Kroll, Parks, Parkinson, Bieber, & Johnson, 1970; Posner, Boies, Eichelman, & Taylor, 1969). However, at least one perfectly simple distinction separates the type of imagery studied by Posner *et al.* (1969) from iconic memory: Visual imagery can result from a mental transformation of information presented in another modality (say, auditory-to-visual recoding) whereas, of course, iconic memory must be initiated by genuine visual stimulation in the eye. Most of the long-lasting modality-specific memory effects that are cited as embarrassments for models of sensory storage are attributable to mediated encoding operations that capitalize on one or another sensory feature.

The opposition often posed between sensory memory and verbal memory is partly to blame for this confusion. Although Atkinson and Shiffrin (1968) were careful to allow short-term storage not only in the auditory–verbal–linguistic domain but also in a series of other (largely unspecified) coding domains, many subsequent writers have oversimplified their model to allow for only three memory stores—sensory storage, short-term verbal memory, and long-term memory. But if encoding can sometimes occur along sensory attributes (i.e., encoding into short- and long-term storage), it should not be surprising to find evidence for such encoding in conventional short- and long-term memory paradigms. To put it concretely, the subject is being portrayed here as deliberately encoding into memory the visual aspects of some stimulus he is looking at, such as the three circular features in the letter set QOG, for example. Such encoding would depend on the use of a limited-capacity attention system, just as does verbal encoding (Atkinson & Shiffrin, 1968; Waugh & Norman, 1965), and it would result in genuinely visual memory, but not iconic memory. The subject could conceivably effect the same encoding given auditory presentation of the same stimulus.

A theoretical context for this distinction can be found in the distinction proposed by Tulving (1972) between *semantic memory* and *episodic memory*, although Tulving (1975) would not be happy with the interrelation between the two that we are about to suggest. The semantic memory system records a person's enduring knowledge (his name, the multiplication tables, the critical features of a violet, the relation of the word *larceny* to the category *crime*, and so on). The episodic memory system, on the other hand, records information that is indexed by the spatial and temporal context in which it occurred. One view (Anderson & Bower, 1974) of the relation between these two systems (see also Crowder, 1976, Chap. 11) is that episodic memory is a marking process applied to the semantic memory system. Thus, if the word *larceny* occurs on a memory list, a tag is established at the permanent location of that word in semantic memory that gives information about the spatial and temporal context prevailing during the occurrence of *larceny* on the list. Although interest has mainly been directed at the marking of semantic-memory locations for verbal information, the semantic memory system must necessarily carry much modality-specific information, such as the facts that the letter *H* has a crossbar and that the word *grasshopper* is moderately long. This type of information, perhaps arranged into feature lists, has to be stored in memory and, since it has long been divorced from the temporal and spatial circumstances of its original acquisition, it must be in semantic memory.

To encode a stimulus categorically along sensory dimensions is to direct attention to nodes in semantic memory having to do with sensory features of an established category state. Obviously, once the node in question has been located it makes no difference through what sensory modality access originally occurred. The feature list for the letter *Q* includes a closed loop, whether the subject reached that list by seeing it or hearing it. True sensory memory, according to the distinction proposed here, does not participate at all in the semantic memory system or in the marking of events upon that system; it occurs at an earlier stage of information processing, before the different modalities have converged on the common, abstract categories.

Deutsch's elegant experimental analysis of memory for pitch (Deutsch, 1975) provides an excellent example of a nonverbal memory structure within the semantic memory system: In these studies a standard tone is played, followed by a series of six interference tones and a final comparison tone that must be judged as same or different in relation to the standard. The data from this technique have led Deutsch to a model that includes an organized, learned memory structure (tone height) upon which tonal experiences are recorded by their temporal contexts, just as experiences with a word on a list are recorded by their temporal context upon the stable, verbal, semantic memory structure. Because the relation between the interference tones and the standard-comparison pair remains the same in different regions of the (logarithmically organized) musical scale, Deutsch concludes that the corresponding memory structure is also logarithmically organized. This memory situation is unrelated to sensory storage, however, because if Deutsch is right it depends on a stable semantic-memory structure that the subject brings with him, rather than activity in the sensory system. An important clarification would be the testing of a subject with absolute pitch: The standard tone would be presented verbally and the rest normally, and if the same data pattern occurred under these circumstances as Deutsch has obtained with normal subjects, it would conclusively indicate that the memory of the standard tone used for comparison with the comparison tone is not at all a sensory memory.

B. A Developmental Illustration

Another conceptual (but not experimentally useful) guide to the proper definition of sensory memory and its distinction from other memory processes is a developmental illustration. Leaving aside any possible maturational sharpening of the sensory apparatus, it ought to be true that a newborn infant has the same sensory memory capabilities as an adult, even though the infant probably has no feature lists or category states with which to associate the products of his sensory analysis. The term *precategorical* can thus be understood in this *microgenetic* sense to refer to an infantile level of information processing. Infants should fail in Deutsch's experiments because they have no organized array of category states into which to sort their tonal experiences, even though they have the same echoic memory as Deutsch's subjects (and perhaps even the same overall memory capacity).*

It is time to clarify the terms *preperceptual* and *precategorical*, by way of summarizing the argument so far. Of course there is a sense in which the mere detection of stimulation constitutes a perceptual or categorical act, as does the identification of the sensory channel containing the information. For this reason, the terms *precategorical* and *preperceptual* are misleading because nobody has proposed a level of memory prior to such crude classifications and it is hard to imagine what such storage would be. The single point of separation between precategorical and postcategorical memory is the contact made by stimuli with learned classification systems carried in the semantic-memory system. Naturally, there are physical features sorted out before this point of contact but, by convention, we are defining categorization as this one level, which corresponds to the level of Morton's *logogen* system (Morton, 1970). The newborn has only precategorical memories to the extent he lacks category states beyond this same level.

The developmental analogy clarifies another logical property of sensory memory: Just as the child who learns category states to correspond to his

---

* The possibility of complex unlearned categorization at the sensory level (Hubel & Wiesel, 1968; Eimas & Corbit, 1973) is ignored in this formulation and incorporation of it lies beyond the scope of this discussion, but note that here, too, the developmental illustration is instructive (Bornstein, Kessen, & Weiskopf, 1976).

sensory experience does not forfeit the sensory experience itself thereby, the categorization of input by adults does not necessarily rob them of their sensory memories for the input. Sensory storage is logically prior to categorization, not necessarily chronologically prior to it. The categorical and precategorical memories may coexist: The persistence of the McCullough (1965) phenomenon, in vision, which we must surely assign to sensory memory, does not mean that the subject fails to classify the gratings as such when they are first displayed. In audition, the persistence of memory for the speaker's voice (Cole, Coltheart, & Allard, 1974) does not mean the subject failed to categorize what the speaker said.

C. Multiplicity of Memories

Given the several modalities, each with its own specialized memory systems, both precategorical and postcategorical, and the further separation of postcategorical memory into short- and long-term storage (all taking into account Tulving's distinction between episodic and semantic memory), it is natural to be concerned that information-flow diagrams would become cluttered with too many boxes. Holding (1975) says for example, that "it is clearly undesirable to entertain a proliferation of postulated stores [p. 38]." In actuality, this proliferation should alarm only those who place a structural, rather than a functional, interpretation on memory storage. If one does not insist that each memory store be a "place," then multiple stores should be no more disturbing than the corresponding multiplicity of information-processing operations. Whether physiological psychologists should ever find it convenient to propose neuroanatomical groupings corresponding to storage properties that are isolated experimentally by psychologists is beside the point, and usually, in practice, after the fact.

But regarding memory stores functionally, rather than structurally, has the further advantage of drawing the general problem of memory back to the general problem of information processing (see Craik & Lockhart, 1973). The functional approach holds that storage in a particular format or code is the property of persistence of whatever information-processing activity was necessary to initially get the information into that code. This thought is not only reassuring in its implication that we do not need two armies of psychologists, one for information processing and the other for memory (retrieval is another story), but also prepares us for the possibility that even within a sensory memory system there may be considerable functional variation. We should thus not be surprised if different readout and decay parameters show up within a modality, since the processing operations might vary considerably themselves.

II. EVIDENCE FOR ICONIC AND ECHOIC STORAGE

The sources of evidence demonstrating sensory storage in vision (iconic storage) and audition (echoic storage) are much more controversial than is the issue of whether such memory exists. Much of the controversy is motivated by the false assumption that each mode has but a single sensory memory system with fixed properties whose parameters are the targets of experimental competition. As it happens, the evidence from both vision and audition can be organized around four major headings with entries from most of the possibilities filled. There is no a priori reason that this should have been the case, but it suggests a methodological organization for this review, rather than an organization featuring the separate modalities.

There are two reasons that this review concentrates on echoic and iconic storage to the exclusion of the minor modalities. First, it is through visual and auditory perception that humans receive language messages exclusively and, second, the research so far available on such modalities as olfaction (Engen & Rose, 1973), kinesthesis (Laabs, 1974; Pepper & Herman, 1970) and touch (Watkins & Watkins, 1973), for example, simply do not provide a basis for the crucial distinction, identified in Section I,1, between sensory memory and modality-specific imagery.

A. Repetition Methods

Demonstration of sensory memory by the repetition methods consists of exposing the subject to the same stimulus energy repeatedly and varying the interval of time between successive repetitions. The behavior observed is the ability to detect that repetition is occurring and the dependence of this detection on the cycle time of the stimulus. The proper control condition for such experiments would be a condition without repetition, but no experiments have included this precaution so far. The logic for visual and auditory experiments diverges somewhat beyond these gross descriptive points.

1. VISION

Haber and Standing (1969) repeatedly exposed a pattern of letter shapes at varying rates, asking subjects whether the perception was phenomenologically continuous or intermittent. When the time between onsets of the pattern was longer than about 300 msec (or slightly longer with dark pre- and postexposure background fields) there were reports of perceptual discontinuities, but at shorter cycle times the pattern appeared continuous. Furthermore, it made little difference, over a range of from 4 to about

200 msec, how long that pattern lasted as against a blank interstimulus interval; what counted was the time between successive onsets. Haber and Standing (1969) also showed that the results were similar if the stimulus pattern were alternated between the two eyes rather than being presented to a single eye.

Haber and Standing's (1969) "direct" measurement of iconic memory thus points to a storage time of about .25 sec, with the representation being set up in the first handful of milliseconds. Of course, the basic method in their study is entirely subjective and this subjectivity would invalidate their experimental-blinking technique as a primary demonstration method. However, the temporal parameters isolated by them are not subjective in the same sense, and since these parameters agree so neatly with those obtained in primary demonstrations (Sperling, 1960), we may welcome the study as a piece of converging evidence.

2. AUDITION

a. NOISE. Guttman and Julesz (1963) played for their subjects a repeating segment of random (white) noise produced such that there were not abrupt transitions between the end of one segment and the beginning of the next. Again the subjects' subjective reports were the basic datum, in conjunction with the dependence of these reports on cycle time. The results showed that with 50-msec segments repeated at rates of about 20 Hz or faster, the subjects simply perceived a low tone. Between about 4 and 20 Hz the report was of a "motorboating" sound, with the fact of repetition effortlessly apparent. Between 1 and 4 Hz there was a "swooshing" sound; still slower repetition rates were seldom detected, and only through considerable effort.

Again we are left with a highly subjective response measure that is difficult to evaluate alone, although Huggins (1975a, p. 154) has noted that the transitions in these reports as a function of cycle times correspond well with well-known sensitivity properties of the auditory system. It is perplexing that no reports of replication and refinement of the Guttman and Julesz technique have been published in the intervening years, despite its status as a classic demonstration (Neisser, 1967). Of particular importance is the issue of what relevance the use of random noise is to the outcome. Huggins (1975a) has noted that it could be some parameter from the signal that underlies the percept of reptition rather than the "raw signal itself [p. 154]." It is the staggering possibility that people do, in fact, carry the raw signal from cycle to cycle that makes the demonstration dramatic; however, the cue might instead be an overall amplitude contour or overall frequency contour. What if the experiment were replicated with a single 1000-Hz tone with amplitude-modulated cycles in the same ranges tested by Guttman and Julesz? It would probably be equally indicative of echoic memory if these conditions yielded reports of "motorboating," "whooshing," and so on, as obtained in the study with noise, but the result would seem less startling.*

b. SPEECH. Another application of the repetition method was reported by A. Treisman (1964), who asked her subjects to listen to coherent verbal messages, one in each ear. The two messages were actually identical, one being lagged by a variable period of time relative to the other. The task was to shadow the message in one of the ears. Treisman's assumption was the common one that shadowing was fully demanding of attention, so that any memory for the unattended ear must be based completely on precategorical sensory memory. There were two independent variables, the time lag separating the two channels' receipt of the same information and whether it was the leading or the lagging message that had to be shadowed. The behavior of interest was how detection of repetition depended on these two factors.

When the first occurrence of the message was in the ignored channel the lag had to be reduced to about 1.5 sec in order for the subject to notice the repetition; however, when the first occurrence of the message was in the attended ear, repetition was detected at lags as long as 4.5 sec. It is the discrepancy between these two figures that makes the experiment a convincing one. When the attended channel leads, information in it has been subject to full categorical analysis and the memory representation should be more persistent than when the ignored message leads, in which case there would be only precategorical information to support recognition of identity after a delay. Thus, the Treisman (1964) study supports a time duration for echoic memory of about 1 or 2 sec, given the crucial assumption that there is no categorization of the ostensibly ignored message.

B. Continuation Methods

The repetition and continuation methods have much in common. In both cases, information from the same source must be compared against itself, so to speak, with variation in the interval separating the information to be compared. In the repetition methods, however, the information is locally identical, as well as being from the same source, whereas in the continuation methods a nonrepeating stream of stimulation is segmented

* With Michael Kubovy and James Cutting, the author has observed that an intensity covariate of the Guttman–Julesz type of stimuli is compelling, informally: It was easy to see the VU meter of the tape recorder bobbing in a distinctive rhythmic pattern during playback of tapes constructed in their manner, the cycle of the bobbing corresponding to the known cycle time of the noise loop.

with variation in the gap between segments. There are only two major applications of this technique, both of which are in audition. Informally, though, there is merit in the view that the continuity of perception observed in reading or watching movies, bridging as it does the blackouts separating patterned stimulation, is a consequence of iconic storage that would fall under this heading.

1. AUDITION

a. TEMPORALLY SEGMENTED SPEECH. Huggins (1975a,b) has performed several experiments with subjects' being asked to shadow speech that had been *temporally segmented*—that is, interrupted with periods of silence inserted into the stream (no loss of information in the speech message itself). One finding of Huggins was that 63-msec segments of running speech could be shadowed at 55% accuracy when segments were separated from one another by silent intervals of from 125 to 500 msec; within this range of separations performance did not vary as a function of separation. This result suggests some inherent limit on isolated speech segments lasting 63 msec. When the silent gaps were further reduced, however, there was a sharp improvement in shadowing up to intervals as short as 60 msec (of silence between segments), at which point a performance ceiling obscured what further improvements in intelligibility there may have been. Huggins (1975a) calls this improvement in the shadowing of 63-msec speech fragments, which occurs between silent intervals of 125 and 60 msec, the *gap-bridging* result, and he associates it theoretically with echoic memory. If two speech segments, each too short to be understood (at better than 55% scores) individually, can reside together in echoic memory, then some higher-order processing system can draw information from both segments pertinent to a single category state. If the first segment has already departed from echoic memory before the second is registered there, however, this possibility does not exist. As Huggins observes, a visual analog to this process is found in the integration of movie frames.

A subsequent study (Huggins, 1975b) shows that the gap-bridging result is dependent more upon real time than on the information content carried per unit time in the speech signal. This result comes from the orthogonal manipulation of silent-interval duration and the automatic compression–slowing of the speech signal. Whether the speech rate was fast or slow, the changes in performance resulting from shortening of the silent interval between adjacent speech segments were evident between about 50 and 200 msec. A related study on the perception of dichotic pulse trains (nonspeech) also showed conspicuous performance differences between about 50 and 100 msec.

Thus, Huggins' work can be interpreted as showing echoic memory serving in just the functional role anticipated in the first sentences of this chapter; that is, holding individually uninterpretable packages of information in unprocessed form until a higher-order analysis system can assign the totality to some category state. The order of magnitude suggested by Huggins' work is 100 msec, but any closer estimate would be reckless on the basis of these studies, since shadowing is only an imperfect reflection of intelligibility, dependent on such factors as the difficulty of the passage being shadowed (Wingfield & Wheale, 1975). Since inflection points in his data are often located at the ceiling or floor, all we can be sure of is that gap bridging occurs on the order of tenths of a second, rather than hundredths of a second.

b. MEMORY FOR SPATIAL CHORDS. Another application of the completion method has been reported recently by Kubovy and Howard (1976). The basic stimuli in their study were chords of six simultaneous pure tones taken from adjacent positions of the diatonic scale. Each chord lasted 300 msec. In dichotic presentation, interaural time disparities of six different values were introduced for the six tones in such a way that the tones distributed themselves across apparent auditory space (that is, from left to right "inside the head"). We may now consider two successive spatial chords of this type in which the perceived locations of five of the six tones remain the same in both, but that of the sixth tone is shifted toward what seems like the left or the right. If there is a memory record of where each tone had been located in the first chord, the tone that is shifted may stand out against the background of the others. Of course, without such a memory record the subject will simply hear the two chords with none standing in relief. It was this logic that Kubovy and Howard exploited to test the duration of echoic memory.

Depending upon the order in which any of the six tones was played by shifting its position in one chord relative to the prior chord, Kubovy and Howard constructed sequences of 18–20 chords in which either an ascending or a descending diatonic scale was presented. The subject's task was to decide which scale had occurred on each trial. The sequence of tones in the pattern began at some randomly chosen location in the scale and then cycled for the remainder of the 18 or 20 chords. The six tones were assigned different "home" locations on each trial in order to prevent long-term memory from accumulating concerning these positions. (The buildup of such learning during a trial is a logically important but, in practical terms, unlikely possibility.) The main independent variable was the duration of a silent interval separating each chord from its neighbors. The logic was that figure–ground separation, and hence the perception of a scale, would depend on two successive chords' falling simultaneously within echoic memory. With widely separated chords this should be less likely than with closely spaced chords, just as in the gap-bridging logic of Huggins.

Kubovy and Howard tested six highly practiced subjects with pause durations of from 150 to about 10,000 msec. Their report was a preliminary communication not intended as a definitive parametric study, but five of the six subjects tested gave decay times of around 2 or 3 sec. (For these subjects, performance declined to half in about 1 sec.) A sixth subject was still performing perfectly at a pause duration of 9500 msec, an anomaly for which the authors have no insight except for a small demonstration that, despite his possession of absolute pitch, he was not employing a verbal code. The decay times in the Kubovy–Howard study are an order of magnitude slower than in the Huggins study, but this difference is not disturbing in view of the tremendously higher information content of the signal in the latter than in the former.

C. Sampling Methods

In order to establish the persistence of sensory information, sampling methods capitalize on giving the subject too much information for immediate categorization in the time allotted and then cuing the subject to report only a selected portion of the input. The cue must direct attention to a subset of the stimuli defined by some sensory dimension, rather than by a postcategorical dimension. Further, it is anticipated that as the occurrence of the cue is delayed beyond offset of the stimulus, the subject will be increasingly unable to select the cued information because of decay in the sensory store. This logic was first worked out by Sperling (1960) for iconic storage.

1. VISION

a. SPERLING'S METHOD. Sperling's (1960) work departed from the observation that over a range of exposure durations (15–500 msec) and a range of information loads (4–12 letters presented simultaneously) people seem able to report only about 4.5 letters in a controlled tachistoscopic experiment. His main objective was to test the validity of subjects' comments that just after the flash nearly the whole display seemed available but then faded before they could read off more than 4 or 5 letters. The crucial experimental operation was to present a cue—after stimulus offset, but presumably during the time before fading of the visual trace of the letters—indicating which portion of the display should be reported (for example, high, medium, or low tones, which would correspond to the top, middle, or lower of three rows of letters). The information within any of the cued subsets of the stimulus was well within the limit of about 4.5

letters. On the assumption that the subject would have performed equally well whichever the subset chosen for partial report, Sperling took the proportional accuracy on the cued subset and multiplied it by the number of potential subsets in order to estimate the total availability of information in iconic memory. By varying the delay between stimulus offset and cuing, Sperling hoped to get such capacity estimates early and late in the life of the icon.

In one of Sperling's (1960) experiments, three rows of 4 letters each were exposed for 50 msec. In the *whole report condition,* the subjects were simply asked to report all they could of the 12-letter display, which turned out to be around 4.5 letters. In the *partial report* condition, one of three tones, as explained, occurred at intervals of 0–1 sec after display offset. The results showed that if the partial-report cue occurred immediately on display offset there was a total capacity estimate of between 9 and 10 letters; however, within 500 msec or so, performance had declined to the level of whole report (that is, about 1.5 letters per row).

Averbach and Coriell (1961) published a similar experiment that converged with the conclusions of Sperling, even though quite different procedures were used. In the Averbach–Coriell study, only one letter from a 2 × 8 display was cued. Proportional accuracy on this single item was compared with proportional correctness in a whole report condition. Furthermore, the sampling cue was visual rather than auditory: A bar marker appeared just over or under the position that had been occupied in the display by the to-be-reported letter. The capacity estimates turned in by Averbach and Coriell with immediate cuing were about 12 letters; when the cue was delayed to about 200 msec or longer, however, performance on the cued letter declined to an asymptotic level of around 30%.

b. Is SPERLING'S EFFECT DUE TO A TRULY VISUAL PROCESS? The Sperling and Averbach and Coriell demonstrations show that there is a large-capacity memory system available immediately after stimulus termination and that this memory system can be used to transcend the limits of a 4.5-letter memory span. But this inference is not, technically, conclusive on the genuinely visual nature of the extra capacity. Two further findings of Sperling (1960) help to tie his method to iconic storage. Detailed critiques of these and other points may be found in Dick (1974) and Coltheart (1975).

The inherently visual nature of the performance advantage for partial report in Sperling's study was supported by one of his other experiments (Sperling, 1960), in which the major variable was whether the pre- and postexposure background fields were light, as in his main experiment, or dark. He found that with the dark background the performance advantage of partial report over whole report lasted to somewhere between 2 and 5 sec, rather than to only about 500 msec, as with the light background. Dick (1974) and Coltheart (1975) have observed that this result is a powerful refutation of such alternative mechanisms for the partial report advantage as selective rehearsal, output interference, and cue guessing (Holding, 1975).

The second important demonstration offered by Sperling (1960) in favor of an iconic interpretation of the partial-report superiority was a companion experiment in which the poststimulus cue demanded a postcategorical selection (letters versus digits) rather than a precategorical selection (top row versus bottom row). If the iconic store is organized only by sensory dimensions the subject should not be able to read out selectively one conceptual class versus another, because in order to know which characters to report, one must first have identified them by the very process that limits memory span to 4.5 items. Indeed, Sperling found that when a high or low tone cued report of letters versus digits from a mixed display, partial report was proportionally no better than whole report. More recent comparisons by von Wright (1972) amplify Sperling's operations, but completely sustain his conclusions.

2. AUDITION

There have been two strategies in auditory research for keeping some information in raw form at the time of its reception in order to set up the possibility of sampling a precategorical memory later. The first is to provide such a dense rush of information that the subject cannot categorize it on arrival (Sperling's approach), and the second is to require the subject to ignore some of the input by directing his attention elsewhere.

a. AUDITORY ANALOGS TO SPERLING'S STUDY. Moray, Bates, and Barnett (1965) were the first investigators to realize an auditory analog to Sperling's spatial-report technique. Their subjects received, through stereo headphones, four spatially separated messages of one or more characters each. Just as this presentation episode ended, a light signaled which of the four channels to report, through a spatial code. The results of these cued-report trials were compared with a condition in which the subjects were responsible for all four channels. As in Sperling's demonstration, estimates of total capacity based on the partial-report cuing condition exceeded those based on the whole-report condition. However, Moray *et al.* used but a single delay between stimulus presentation and partial-report cue, leaving open the possibility that partial report would have been better at *any* cue delay. The reduced output interference of the partial-report condition might account for such a consistent advantage, and the experiment might thus have nothing to do with echoic memory. In Sperling's experiment, the partial-report advantage disappeared after delays of something less than 1 sec, even though output interference would have been expected to operate independently of cue delay.

Darwin, Turvey, and Crowder (1972) performed an experiment very similar to that of Moray *et al.*, with two additions. First, they sampled a range of delays between the multichannel message and the cue for partial report. This operation showed that the advantage of partial report over whole report did indeed decline to 0 after about 4 sec. Second, Darwin *et al.* compared the partial report based on channels in auditory space with partial report based on a conceptual distinction—letters versus digits. Unfortunately, this control experiment was not conclusively negative, as Sperling's had been in the visual modality, for there remained a small and transient advantage of the partial report condition. The authors observed that this partial-report advantage for a postcategorical dimension was very small compared to the advantage for channel cuing. However, the association between the cue itself and its assigned significance would be much easier for the spatial cuing (left cue–left channel) than for the categorical cuing (left cue–digits only). The increased processing time demanded by the cue in the control experiment could extend performance further out along a decay function. This confounding weakens the impact of the Darwin *et al.* study (although Massaro, 1975, p. 430, is worried about a confounding in the opposite direction). Massaro (1975, pp. 429–430) has pointed out that, in absolute terms, without taking whole report into account, recall from spatial categories is not better than recall from conceptual categories in the Darwin *et al.* experiments. This curiosity has prompted further research (Massaro, 1976) but it is irrelevant to the matter of echoic storage because that capacity must be derived from the comparison of whole and partial report.

Fortunately, M. Treisman and Rostron (1972) and Rostron (1974) have provided further evidence on the application of Sperling's logic to echoic memory. The subjects in their experiment heard six tones over three widely separated loudspeakers. These tones were presented in two volleys of three tones each. Each tone lasted 100 msec, and there was no pause between the two volleys. After a delay of 0–1.6 sec, a probe tone was presented for a recognition response. Performance showed a sharp decline with delays of 0–1.6 sec, whether scored by a d' measure or by a corrected measure of items available. The latter gave an estimate of 3.5 items available in the immediate cuing condition. Treisman and Rostron compare this figure with a typical score of 2.6 items from a whole-report *recall* experiment with their materials. If one wished to accept this comparison between recognition and recall, therefore, a case can be made for surplus capacity along the lines of Sperling's argument. A further report using essentially the same method (Rostron, 1974) extended the delays between stimulus offset and partial-report cue to intervals of 1.9, 3, and 5 sec. Rostron's reasoning was that these longer delays could be used instead of a whole-report condition to estimate the asymptotic level of memory span. The results obtained by Rostron depended on which performance measure was consulted. With the d' index, scores still declined briskly between 3 and 5 sec; however, with the corrected raw-score measure, performance declined only slightly after 1 sec. If the latter measure can be accepted as showing a valid estimate of whole report, the Rostron study may be correspondingly accepted as a replication of the Sperling study in audition.

b. SAMPLING IGNORED MESSAGES. Subjects in a study by Eriksen and Johnson (1964) were asked to select a novel they found absorbing and bring it to the experimental session, where their main task would be simply to read it. At irregular intervals during the 2-hr session (28 times in all) a faint tone was sounded. The interest was in whether the subject could detect this tone. To measure this detection, the experimenter turned off the reading light at intervals of from 0 to about 10 sec after the occurrence of a stimulus tone. Subjects were to report, on such occasions, whether they had heard a tone during the 10–15 sec prior to the interruption. There were also catch trials, in which reading was interrupted without relation to stimulus tone. Although the rate of false alarms on catch trials was about 20%, queries immediately after the occurrence of a tone produced an accuracy rate of about 60%. This declined, but only to 50%, when the query was delayed by up to 10 sec. It is the decay in accuracy rate that supports an echoic-memory interpretation of Eriksen and Johnson's experiment. In a companion experiment, they showed that when the subject was under instructions to report immediately any tone he heard, spontaneous detections under uninterrupted reading conditions occurred far below the rates of accuracy for even the longest delay intervals in the main experiment.

The ballpark estimate of 10 sec that may be inferred from the Eriksen and Johnson study is substantially larger than those supported by other demonstrations. But this discrepancy is not bothersome when we recall that in their experiment a detection response was required, rather than a recognition or identification response. Furthermore, the signal was a steady tone, rather than some more complex auditory event. It is quite possible that information necessary for a more complex response would have been lost well before 10 sec in their experimental setting.

Two experiments have employed the sampling technique with a subject shadowing one of two dichotic messages and ignoring (ostensibly) the other. The assumption is that shadowing is so demanding that no categorization can occur through the ignored channel and, therefore, any subsequent memory for it must be a raw sensory trace. Norman (1969) had subjects shadow monosyllabic words in one channel at a rate of two words per second. From time to time, lists of six two-digit numbers occurred in the other channel at a rate of one two-digit number per second. At the end of such a number list, the experimenter interrupted the shadowing and tested for recognition of the numbers. The results showed excellent recognition of the last two pairs of digits, but essentially no memory for those occurring more than 2 sec back. Glucksberg and Cowan (1970) altered Norman's procedure by presenting continuous messages through both channels, the one to be ignored as well as the one to be shadowed. Into the ignored stream of words they spliced single digits at irregular intervals. The shadowing task was interrupted from time to time in order to ask the subject whether he had recently heard any digits in the ignored channel and, if so, which. The delay separating occurrence of the query and occurrence of the critical digit was the independent variable. The results showed a systematic decay in accuracy as this delay was extended to several seconds. Almost more convincing than this decay alone was the observation that subjects seldom reported that there had *been* a digit in the ignored channel without also knowing correctly which one. This observation is consistent with the assumption that subjects were categorizing the digits at the time of the query, rather than at the time of their occurrence, otherwise there would have been the errors of omission and commission typical of verbal short-term memory. It is this possibility of spontaneous categorization that controls the credibility of all studies using the sampling method. More detailed critiques of these studies may be found in Massaro (1970) and Crowder (1975a).

D. Masking Methods

The technique of *backward masking* has been used in both vision and audition to support models of sensory processing and sensory memory. In backward-masking experiments, some target event is presented and then followed, after some variable time interval, by a masking stimulus. The destructive effects of the mask upon the target are observed as a function of the delay between the two. When the mask reduces performance on the target it must, of course, be true that the two interacted at some point. But some investigators (particularly Crowder & Morton, 1969; and Massaro, 1970) have gone beyond this conservative observation to claim that the fact of masking establishes that the target was held in the form of a sensory trace. The logic behind this inference is more indirect than that behind the other demonstrations that we have been considering. Similarly indirect is the logic by which the decay time of sensory memory can be inferred from the time after which the mask no longer affects performance on the target. When the mask comes too late to affect performance on the target, it could be because the target has already decayed, or alternatively, it could be because all useful information has by then been extracted from a still robust trace. There are other logical points that will assist our evaluation of the evidence based on masking.

1. POSSIBLE MASKING MECHANISMS

Crowder (1975b) has distinguished four logically separable types of interaction that can occur in backward masking (see also Breitmeyer & Ganz, 1976; Massaro, 1975; Turvey, 1973; Weisstein, 1968). Masking by *erasure* occurs when the mask displaces the target in some fixed-capacity storage location. Buffer memories of digital computers often operate this way, as do models of short-term memory based on the computer analogy (Atkinson & Shiffrin, 1968; Waugh & Norman, 1965). Masking by *integration* occurs when the target and mask are received together by some higher-order processor; performance suffers because the gestalt formed by the target and mask has a more reduced signal-to-noise ratio than that of the target alone.

There are two varieties of masking by *interruption,* which may be distinguished by the terms *attentional interruption* and *nonattentional interruption*. In the former there is a stage of information processing dependent on an attentional resource with limited capacity. Before the work of this limited resource upon the target is complete, the mask arrives and diverts attention to itself. The target is thus deprived of its full share of readout by the attention mechanism. In nonattentional interruption there is unlimited capacity on the receiving end of the readout process, but the activity of each stimulus event is inhibited by the activity of any other event in the same temporal region. Each event begins feeding information into a central processing system of unlimited capacity directly on occurrence. But each event also exerts a sort of lateral inhibitory influence on its neighbors' output of information. When a mask follows a target, it degrades readout of the target, not by diverting attention to itself, but by inhibiting what the target can supply to central processing. The two attentional theories make identical predictions for a simple masking situation, but they differ in their expectations for the *disinhibition* experiment, in which the mask is followed by a subsequent mask, with the consequence of restoring performance on the target to better than it would have been with but a single mask. There should be no disinhibition according to attentional interruption, because diversion of attention from the first to the second mask would not affect the original target. However, according to the nonattentional interruption model, the second mask ought to inhibit whatever the first mask was doing; since the first mask was itself inhibiting the target, performance would improve if the target were released from this inhibition. Nonattentional interruption fits with neural models of lateral inhibition (see Breitmeyer & Ganz, 1976; Deutsch, 1975).

2. BACKWARD MASKING IN VISION

Investigators of backward masking in vision have not insisted that it serve as a primary demonstration technique for iconic storage, and therefore we need not review the large literature on it (but see Breitmeyer & Ganz, 1976; Kahneman, 1968; Lefton, 1973; Turvey, 1973). Much of this literature has dealt with the opposition of integration masking and interruption masking (without a clear distinction between the attentional and nonattentional versions of the latter). The assumption by those advocating an interruption model has been that masking occurs during the readout of information from the icon into the categorical system (Haber, 1969; Sperling, 1963), while advocates of integration have generally avoided the concept of iconic storage in their account of masking (Eriksen, 1966), likening the effect of the mask to a photographic double exposure early in the peripheral visual system.

There is now good evidence (Turvey, 1973) that visual backward masking occurs at two levels, corresponding to relatively peripheral and relatively central stages of information processing. This two-factor interpretation supports both the integration and the interruption models with three main arguments: First, in peripheral masking, a target display can be masked by any bright stimulus, even a uniform flash of light. In central masking, however, there must be some similarity of detail between target and mask. Second, in peripheral masking, the inhibitory effect of the mask is determined by a multiplicative rule relating target energy (brightness and duration) and the interstimulus interval separating target offset to mask onset. In central masking, however, it is the interval separating the two *onsets* that determines masking, rather than energy factors. Third, both forward and backward masking occur peripherally, while only backward masking occurs centrally. Finally, the justification for using the terms peripheral and central for these distinctions is the fact that they line up neatly with the differences between monoptic masking (target and mask to the same eye) and dichoptic masking (mask to the contralateral eye). Thus, the peripheral masking operation seems to obey the integration model, while the central masking operation seems to be a case of interruption. These abrupt conclusions should be tempered by a reading of the papers by Breitmeyer and Ganz (1976) and Turvey (1973), for they show that the state of affairs is in fact a more subtle blending of these operations than this sketch has allowed.

It is not certain what implications the central–peripheral masking distinction may have for the locus of iconic memory. Turvey (1973, p. 46) associates peripheral (integration) masking with the input to iconic storage and central (interruption) masking with the readout from iconic storage to short-term memory. Such a view appears to place the icon itself in a relatively central position. Dick (1974, p. 584) has argued that the existence of dichoptic masking demonstrates that the icon could not be retinal, but must be cortical. However, the evidence adequate to locate the site of masking is not logically adequate to locate the icon (Crowder, 1976, p. 43; Sakitt, in press): A peripheral icon (e.g., retinal) could forward information to some central locus (e.g., cortical) where the interaction between target and mask would take place.

a. A RETINAL LOCUS FOR THE ICON? A series of studies by Sakitt (1975, 1976) has provided a dramatic bit of evidence for a retinally located icon, an assignment that would draw the modern studies of iconic memory back to the classical work on positive retinal afterimages. Sakitt's argument depends on the testing of a subject with a missing cone system but intact rods (a rod monochromat), and there are three parts to this argument. First, Sakitt showed that although this subject had a grossly disturbed visual system in general, she was completely normal as a subject in the standard Sperling partial-report paradigm. Second, the phenomenon of rod saturation was used by Sakitt to show that the same subject could obtain an icon-like image that must have been, on logical grounds, based entirely on rod vision at the level of the photoreceptors on the retina. White stimuli were presented against a less bright white background at such an intensity that the subject reported seeing nothing with her eyes open. However, when she subsequently closed her eyes, the subject saw the letters outlined on a darker background; this visual experience must have resulted from rod photoreceptors saturated at different intensities by the original stimulus. Third, Sakitt showed that the subjective duration of the icon had the same spectral sensitivity as did the rod system, both for the special subject and for normals.

Although students of iconic memory are probably unhappy with identification of the icon with retinal processes, the only evidence seriously at odds with this identification is a recent report by Treisman, Russell, and Green (1975). These authors presented evidence that information about motion is subject to the same pattern of decaying partial-report superiority that Sperling originally observed with static information. Sakitt (1976) has commented on the weakness of this effect and on its possible attribution to output interference; however, more information on the iconic storage of movement is a matter of urgent theoretical priority.

3. BACKWARD MASKING IN AUDITION

There are two research programs using the masking method to find out about echoic memory, one using tonal stimuli and the other using verbal stimuli; in other respects the two efforts are quite similar.

a. RECOGNITION MASKING OF TONES. Massaro (1970) studied the effects of a masking tone on the absolute identification of a prior target tone. In one of his experiments, there were two possible 20 msec targets, 870 or 770 Hz. These were designated as *high* and *low*, and the subject's main task was to identify which had occurred on a given trial. Following practice in identifying the two tones without mask, the main experiment was an examination of performance as a function of the delay between target and a 20-msec, 820-Hz masking tone; these delays ranged from 0 to 500 msec. Massaro (1970) observed that recognition of the target was only slightly better than chance when 40 msec or less intervened between target and mask, but with longer delays performance improved, gradually reaching asymptote at about 250 msec. Massaro maintained that these findings were sufficient to infer the existence of echoic memory. The logic was that 20-msec tones were too short to be identified on the spot and that, therefore, there must have been some trace outlasting the actual presentation in order for performance to be improving with increasing delays before the mask. The fact that this improvement occurred during the silent intertone interval is also consistent with the action of the masking tone in terminating processing of the target. Massaro has maintained (1972, p. 129) that the point of asymptotic performance permits estimation of the decay time of echoic memory.

It is possible that some of the masking observed in this situation is caused by subjects' imperfect ability to resolve the times of occurrence of the target and mask, rather than by interference by the mask with echoic memory (see Crowder, 1975a). However, this alternative explanation is considerably less likely in other studies by Massaro than in the original demonstration. For example, in one experiment (Massaro, 1975, Experiment IV) the masking stimuli were not 20 msec in duration, like the targets, but were 100 msec long, which would render their temporal resolution easy. Another argument against the concept of temporal resolution is the lack of symmetry between forward and backward masking (Massaro, 1973), a result we shall have a closer look at below. In recent studies, Massaro (1975) has extended his basic procedure to a two-interval, forced-choice method and to a same-different technique. That the masking results do not depend on the use of tonal stimuli is shown by comparable experiments (Massaro, 1974) using sustained vowel sounds and consonant-vowel syllables.

b. DECAY OF ECHOIC STORAGE IN TONAL MASKING? An apparent major discrepancy between Massaro's work on tonal masking and that of Crowder and Morton (1969) on masking by the suffix of verbal materials (see below) is that Massaro has proposed a time decay within 250 msec for the tonal system, whereas Crowder and Morton have proposed a figure of 1 or 2 sec. In fact, there is no valid evidence favoring either estimate, and therefore the two programs are not in conflict. As we stated earlier, delaying a mask might either permit decay of the target's sensory trace or it might permit readout from that trace to the degree that subsequent masking would have no behavioral consequence. Massaro seems recently (Massaro, 1974, p. 200) to have accepted both decay and readout processing during the silent intertone interval, but such a dual-factor model overdetermines performance, since only one of the two mechanisms is really necessary. Crowder (1969) has made the same error.

Striking confirmation that the asymptotic performance Massaro finds at 250-msec intertone delays is a reflection of time necessary to read out the stimulus trace, rather than a concomitant echoic decay, comes from experiments (Massaro, 1972, 1974) in which the comparison is between a conventional masking paradigm and a paradigm in which the target tone is left on during the interval before the occurrence of the mask. Thus, in this new situation we are comparing cases with exactly the same period separating target and mask onsets: in one case there is the (presumed) echoic trace surviving during the delay, and in the other case the target tone itself is occurring during the delay. The consistent finding has been that the same growth function relates performance to delay in the two situations, with the same asymptote. Thus, the asymptote in the conventional masking studies of Massaro represents the time required to perceive the target, and not the effective life of echoic memory. The echoic trace probably does decay, but 2 sec or 2 min are equally as plausible as estimates of 200 msec.

c. THE LOCUS OF TONAL MASKING. Massaro has performed some of the experimental operations necessary to identify the masking in his paradigm with regard to the peripheral–central distinction and with regard to the four types of masking identified earlier in this section. Massaro and Kahn (1973) showed, for example, that a "masking" light had no effect on performance, even though the task insured that the subject perceived the light (see Crowder & Morton, 1969, Experiment II). This result rules out an extremely centralized form of interruption (attentional) hypothesis, in which a single attentional channel would be distracted by the mask from the target. But as we saw earlier, setting up a central locus for the masking effect does not guarantee a similarly central locus for the putative sensory store.

The rejection of a global attentional interruption model by Massaro and Kahn (1973) does not discount, however, the possibility that interruption occurs within the auditory analysis system. Indeed, Massaro (1975, pp. 446–457) has gone on to oppose versions of the integration and interruption model (although his interruption hypothesis contains much of what we are calling the *erasure mechanism*.) Like Turvey (1973), Massaro has been able to isolate two underlying masking operations. The best evidence for distinguishing them is the comparison of forward and backward masking (Massaro, 1973). Using the familiar paradigm, he simply ran some trials on which the mask came earlier than the target, at varying delays, with the subject being aware of which of the two stimuli was which. At intertone intervals of 80 msec or less there was both forward and backward masking, with the former less severe than the latter. But whereas there was no forward masking with delays greater than 80 msec, backward masking was observed out to delays of 480 msec, the longest delay tested. When the mask came first there was no possibility that it would interrupt processing of the target, so its action probably came from some type of summation with the target, or auditory double-exposure. But outside the range of 80 msec there was considerable backward masking that could not be assigned to integration. Experiments on choice between erasure and the two forms of interruption have not been conducted. If disinhibition were found to occur in Massaro's paradigm, however, it would rule out all possibilities except nonattentional interruption.

d. THE SUFFIX EFFECT. Crowder and Morton associated the operation of a stimulus suffix with echoic memory (Crowder & Morton, 1969). In the suffix experiment, a list of eight or nine items is read aloud for the subject to recall immediately in order. In the control condition, there is either silence following the last item or some innocuous cue such as a buzzer. In the experimental condition, however, there is an extra word, the suffix, presented after the last item in the memory list in time with the prevailing rate of presentation for the list as a whole. The subject is fully informed that the suffix will be occurring, what the suffix word will be, and that he need not recall it. In some studies the word *recall* has been used on the understanding with the subject that it will be his cue to recall the list. Any word at all, however, has the same effect (Crowder, 1972; Morton, Crowder, & Prussin, 1971). Whereas the buzzer and the suffix have exactly the same informational value, they lead to quite different performance: With the nonverbal cue, there are both large primacy and large recency effects in performance, whereas recency is eliminated or reduced with the verbal suffix. That is, performance over the initial and interior positions is unaffected by the suffix, but there is a large increase in errors at the end of the list for the suffix condition.

Crowder and Morton associated the suffix effect with a form of echoic memory. Their assumption was that ordinarily there is an extra source of information concerning the last item (or items) when the list has been presented aurally. They conceived of this extra information, echoic memory, as residing in a storage mode that would be highly susceptible to interference from subsequent input. Since the system is logically prior to categorization, it would not matter whether the subsequent input were relevant memory information or a redundant suffix, insofar as its effect on echoic memory for the previous item. It now appears that the system's capacity corresponds roughly to one item in an immediate memory experiment, although the mere question of how to measure this capacity raises problems that are far from being resolved (Watkins & Watkins, 1973).

It should be stressed that the main component of performance in the immediate memory situation is conventional, postcategorical, short-term memory. The contribution of echoic storage is parallel and supplementary. It is parallel because information about the last item is assumed to be stored simultaneously in short-term verbal storage and also in the echoic store. It is supplementary information because the subject is believed to use the echoic information to adjust any discrepancies between it and the short-term memory information. It is erroneous to consider the last item as being *in* echoic memory at the time the suffix occurs. It is identified immediately, just as are all the other items. Unlike these earlier items, however, the last item has dual representation, which places it at an advantage (the recency effect). In the experimental paradigm being considered, there is considerable time delay between the presentation and the recall of this last item, since recall is constrained to begin with the first item in the list. Although the suffix effect occurs whether or not this is the case (Roediger & Crowder, 1976), the explanation of how echoic information assists performance over so long a time span remains unexplained.

It is possible that echoic information spans the delay between presentation and recall of the last item in raw form. The more likely model, however, postulates a stage of covert rehearsal of the last few items prior to the start of overt recall. For example, the subject could review the last three items well within a second of the termination of presentation, comparing his memory of them in verbal form with whatever echoic traces remain of the last sounds he heard. Thus, when public recall begins, performance is all strictly based on conventional short-term memory. The suffix, when it occurs, would deprive the subject of the echoic trace just as he is on the verge of comparing it against the verbal memory of the last few items.

A number of experiments have been conducted with the suffix effect (see summaries in Crowder, 1972, 1976, chap. 3). By and large these have produced data that are consistent with the echoic-memory model presented above, but are not, by themselves, conclusive in forcing that interpretation. Several of these results parallel those obtained with tonal masking. First, the size of the suffix effect is reduced when a temporal delay is posed between presentation of the last memory item and the suffix, just as tonal masking diminishes with increasing intertone intervals (Massaro, 1970). Second, the suffix effect is independent of the meaning of the word used as the suffix, just as the tonal masking result seems to be independent of the similarity in Herz between the target and masking tones (Massaro, 1970). Third, gross physical differences between the memory list and the suffix (such as voice quality, location in auditory space, and switching to nonspeech sounds) do, however, reduce or eliminate the effect, just as the tonal masking result seems not to occur with a mask of white noise (Loeb & Holding, 1975). Fourth, no suffix effect is obtained when the memory list is presented visually and the suffix aloud, just as Massaro and Kahn (1973) failed to observe cross-modality masking. As we shall see presently, the presence of both integration and interruption processes is also a feature of both paradigms.

e. ECHOIC MEMORY, SPEECH, AND THE MODALITY EFFECT. A strength of the Crowder–Morton explanation for the suffix effect over other explanations that cover the basic suffix experiment equally well (Kahneman, 1973) is that the Crowder–Morton theory accommodates a second experimental finding, the modality effect, whereas the alternatives do not. When visual and auditory presentation are compared for the same immediate memory lists, the two give quite comparable results, except for the last few items, for which auditory presentation holds an advantage (Crowder, 1972). The modality effect shows roughly the same pattern of data as the suffix effect (one function with both primacy and recency and another with primacy but little recency) and Crowder and Morton assigned both to echoic memory. In the auditory-control condition of the suffix experiment and of the modality experiment, the large recency effect was assumed to reflect echoic information. This echoic information could be removed either by presenting a suffix to interfere with it or by using visual presentation, where no echoic traces would be set up in the first place. Alternative explanations of the suffix must acknowledge the similarity at the empirical level between the modality and suffix comparisons as a coincidence and must remain silent as to the cause of the former.

The theoretical unity of the suffix and modality experiments, and the echoic-memory interpretation for each, have been greatly supported by evidence that each occurs as a function of the type of speech sound being remembered (Crowder, 1971). The basic finding was that when subjects were asked to remember a series of items distinguished only by place of articulation (e.g., the list *bah, bah, gah, dah, gah, gah, dah*) there was neither a recency effect in the control condition nor a selective effect of the suffix upon performance at the end of the list. With the same stimuli there was no modality effect either—visual and auditory presentation led to equal performance. However, when vowel sounds were substituted on a one-to-one basis for the stop consonants (for example, *gah, gah, gee, goo, gee, gee, goo*), both the suffix effect and the modality effect returned in their familiar forms (details of this research program may be found in Crowder, 1971, 1973a,b, 1975a; and Darwin & Baddeley, 1974). Although the dependence of the suffix and modality effects upon the speech units being employed as stimuli must remain a complete mystery to alternative accounts of the suffix effect (Crowder, 1975a), it is readily understandable from the viewpoint of an echoic memory system intimately tied to the perception of speech (Darwin & Baddeley, 1974).

f. MASKING MECHANISMS IN THE SUFFIX EFFECT. Since the term *backward masking* is just a shorthand expression for an experimental result, rather than an explanation of that result, we may consider the suffix experiment in terms of masking models, the echoic trace for the last list item serving as target and the suffix word serving as the mask. Crowder (1975b) has initiated experiments designed to clarify the suffix effects in terms of the mechanisms identified earlier in this section—erasure, integration, attentional, interruption, and nonattentional interruption. In one of these studies, there was a comparison between conditions with either a single suffix word or three suffix words, the latter presented in a continuation of the presentation rhythm. The finding was a larger performance impairment by the suffix when there was a single suffix word than when there were multiple ones. This result rules out the erasure hypothesis, for if the first suffix masks the target information by obliterating it from memory there is no way for a subsequent event of any kind to restore it.

A strong version of the integration hypothesis, which states that the suffix effect is due entirely to a process of overwriting (the suffix and last item "sounding together" at some central auditory stage), was eliminated by a second experiment, which showed that a suffix presented at the same time as the last memory item had a smaller effect than a suffix that was delayed somewhat. By an integration hypothesis, when the combination of the signal and noise is built in experimentally, as in the simultaneous condition, performance should be worst of all. A weak version of the integration hypothesis states that *some* of the interference of the suffix with performance comes from simple combinational masking, and this weak position is impossible to deny: What if a 125 dB SPL suffix were presented along with the last memory item?

Only the nonattentional-interruption hypothesis can be tolerated by all the data (e.g., multiple suffixes having a weaker effect than single ones and the weaker effect of a simultaneous suffix than a delayed one). Attentional interruption will not suffice to explain the disinhibition result, because the effect of a second mask in diverting attention away from the first mask should be of no use to the target. Nonattentional interruption is consistent with disinhibition, however. Erasure is ruled out by disinhibition as well. Integration, as we have seen, may occur, but it cannot account for the entire masking observed.

It may be noted that the overall function relating performance to the timing of the suffix relative to the last memory item is U-shaped. Memory for the last item is good when there is no delay (simultaneous suffix) and good again when several seconds of delay intervene, but poor when the suffix occurs at some intermediate delay.* This nonmonotonic masking function occurs in visual masking (Averbach & Coriell, 1961; Turvey, 1973) has also been observed in the auditory masking of tones (Massaro, 1970, 1975, Fig. 2). The favored explanation of these functions is a mixture of integration and interruption: When the target and mask arrive together they are treated as a perceptual unit, and whatever masking occurs does so as a direct result of lowered signal-to-noise ratio. Then, as the mask is delayed, the interruption process sets in and continues for delays up to the point that the target can be processed fully before arrival of the mask, where masking may still occur, but without empirical consequence.

III. COMMENTARY

Although the organization of this chapter has stressed the communality of evidence for iconic and echoic memory, it is appropriate, in conclusion, to comment on the differences. In the visual work, the Sperling partial-report sampling technique has been the most thoroughly explored area of evidence, with the much larger literature on visual masking serving in only a supplementary role. In the auditory work, however, it has been only the masking method that has produced substantial programs of

---

* In subsequent unpublished research I have shown that the maximum interference point of the function relating suffix effect to suffix delay is independent of the presentation rate. This excludes the otherwise plausible hypothesis that the U-shaped function simply comes from the rhythm of presentation.

research (on tonal masking and the suffix effect). Since the masking method is inherently weak support for sensory storage—as it accomplishes the destruction of information and not the manifestation of it—this leaves the visual evidence in a healthier state. Although the studies described as auditory applications of the sampling, repetition, and continuation methods are promising starts, none of these has, unfortunately, been the basis of a sustained effort, at least in public sources.

The other striking contrast between the evidential bases of iconic and echoic storage is the rather wide agreement that the former lasts for approximately ¼ sec in contrast to the complete lack of concensus about decay time in the case of the latter. Although the disparity of decay estimates in the auditory case may make some observers nervous, it is probably the consequence of the wide variety of stimulus information that has been studied in the auditory experiments. We have seen auditory methods involving faint tones, tones varying in pitch, white noise, and simple melodies, as well as verbal inputs, whereas the visual studies use almost exclusively alphanumeric characters drawn against a plain background. If the view of sensory storage as a persistence of sensory information processing is accepted, then it is no longer surprising that such diverse auditory stimuli as those listed above have produced diverse estimates of storage time. The next step is, of course, to show that there is a sensible relation between stimulus complexity and decay time within the same experimental paradigm, rather than across paradigms.

References

Anderson, J. R., & Bower, G. H. A propositional theory of recognition memory. *Memory & Cognition,* 1974, **2,** 406–412.

Atkinson, R. C., & Shiffrin, R. M. Human memory: A proposed system and its control processes. In K. W. Spence & J. T. Spence (Eds.), *The psychology of learning and motivation* (Vol. 2). New York: Academic Press, 1968.

Averbach, E., & Coriell, A. S. Short-term memory in vision. *Bell System Technical Journal,* 1961, **40,** 309–328.

Bornstein, M. H., Kessen, W., & Weiskopf, S. Color vision and hue categorization in young human infants. *Journal of Experimental Psychology: Human Perception & Performance,* 1976, **2,** 115–129.

Breitmeyer, B. G., & Ganz, L. Implications of sustained and transient channels for theories of visual pattern masking, saccadic suppression, and information processing, *Psychological Review,* 1976, **83,** 1–36.

Cole, R. A., Coltheart, M., & Allard, F. Memory of a speaker's voice: Reaction time to same- or different-voiced letters. *Quarterly Journal of Experimental Psychology,* 1974, **26,** 1–7.

Coltheart, M. Iconic memory: A reply to Professor Holding. *Memory & Cognition,* 1975, **3,** 42–48.

Craik, F. I. M., & Lockhart, R. S. Levels of processing: A framework for memory research. *Journal of Verbal Learning and Verbal Behavior,* 1973, **12,** 599–706.

Crowder, R. G. Improved recall for digits with delayed recall cues. *Journal of Experimental Psychology*, 1969, **82**, 258–260.

Crowder, R. G. The sounds of vowels and consonants in immediate memory. *Journal of Verbal Learning and Verbal Behavior*, 1971, **10**, 587–596.

Crowder, R. G. Visual and auditory memory. In J. F. Kavanagh & I. M. Mattingly (Eds.), *Language by ear and by eye*. Cambridge, Massachusetts: MIT Press, 1972.

Crowder, R. G. Representation of speech sounds in precategorical acoustic storage. *Journal of Experimental Psychology*, 1973, **98**, 14–24. (a)

Crowder, R. G., Precategorical acoustic storage for vowels of short and long duration, *Perception & Psychophysics*, 1973, **13**, 502–506. (b)

Crowder, R. G. Inferential problems in echoic memory. In P. M. A. Rabbitt & S. Dornic (Eds.), *Attention & performance*. Vol. V. New York: Academic Press, 1975. (a)

Crowder, R. G. Mechanisms of masking in the stimulus suffix effect. Paper presented at the 16th Annual Meeting of the Psychonomic Society, Denver, Colorado, November, 1975. (b)

Crowder, R. G. *Principles of learning & memory*. Hillsdale, New Jersey: Erlbaum, 1976.

Crowder, R. G., & Morton, J. Precategorical acoustic storage (PAS), *Perception & Psychophysics*, 1969, **5**, 365–373.

Darwin, C. J., & Baddeley, A. D. Acoustic memory and the perception of speech. *Cognitive Psychology*, 1974, **6**, 41–60.

Darwin, C. J., Turvey, M. T., & Crowder, R. G. An auditory analogue of the Sperling partial report procedure: Evidence for brief auditory storage. *Cognitive Psychology*, 1972, **3**, 255–267.

Deutsch, D. The organization of short-term memory for a single acoustic attribute. In D. Deutsch & J. A. Deutsch (Eds.), *Short-term memory*. New York: Academic Press, 1975.

Dick, A. O. Iconic memory and its relation to perceptual processing and other memory mechanisms. *Perception & Psychophysics*, 1974, **16**, 575–594.

Eimas, P. D., & Corbit, J. D. Selective adaptation of linguistic feature detectors. *Cognitive Psychology*, 1973, **4**, 99–109.

Engen, T., & Rose, B. M. Long-term memory of odors with and without verbal descriptions. *Journal of Experimental Psychology*, 1973, **99**, 222–225.

Eriksen, C. W. Temporal luminence summation effects in backward and forward masking. *Perception & Psychophysics*, 1966, **1**, 87–92.

Eriksen, C. W., & Johnson, H. J. Storage and decay characteristics of nonattended stimuli. *Journal of Experimental Psychology*, 1964, **68**, 28–36.

Gibson, J. J. *The perception of the visual world*. Boston: Houghton-Mifflin, 1950.

Glucksberg, S., & Cowan, G. N. Memory for nonattended auditory material. *Cognitive Psychology*, 1970, **1**, 149–156.

Guttman, N., & Julesz, B. Lower limits of auditory periodicity analysis. *Journal of the Acoustical Society of America*, 1963, **35**, 610.

Haber, R. N. Information-processing analyses of visual perception. In R. N. Haber (Ed.), *Information-processing approaches to visual perception*. New York: Holt, 1969.

Haber, R. N., & Standing, L. Direct measures of short-term visual storage. *Quarterly Journal of Experimental Psychology*, 1969, **21**, 43–54.

Holding, D. H. Sensory storage reconsidered. *Memory & Cognition*, 1975, **3**, 31–41.

Hubel, D. H., & Wiesel, T. N. Receptive fields and functional architecture of monkey striate cortex. *Journal of Physiology*, 1968, **195**, 215–243.

Huggins, A. W. F. Temporally segmented speech. *Perception & Psychophysics*, 1975, **18**, 149–157. (a)

Huggins, A. W. F. Temporally segmented speech and "echoic" storage. Paper presented at

Symposium on Dynamic Aspects of Speech Perception, Eindhoven, Netherlands, August 1975. (b)

Kahneman, D. Method, findings, and theory in studies of visual masking. *Psychological Bulletin*, 1968, **70**, 404–426.

Kahneman, D. *Attention and effort*. Englewood Cliffs, New Jersey: Prentice-Hall, 1973.

Kroll, N. E. A., Parks, T., Parkinson, S. R., Bieber, S. L., & Johnson, A. L. Short-term memory while shadowing: Recall of visually and aurally presented words. *Journal of Experimental Psychology*, 1970, **85**, 220–224.

Kubovy, M., & Howard, F. P. The persistence of a pitch-segregating echoic memory. *Journal of Experimental Psychology, Human Perception and Performance*, 1976, **2**, 531–537.

Laabs, G. J. The effect of interpolated motor activity on the short-term retention of movement distance and end location. *Journal of Motor Behavior*, 1974, **6**, 279–288.

Lefton, L. A. Metacontrast: A review. *Perception & Psychophysics*, 1973, **13**, 161–171.

Liss, P. Does backward masking by visual noise stop stimulus processing? *Perception & Psychophysics*, 1968, **4**, 328–330.

Loeb, M., & Holding, D. H. Backward interference by tones or noise in pitch perception as a function of practice. *Perception & Psychophysics*, 1975, **18**, 205–208.

Massaro, D. W. Preperceptual auditory images. *Journal of Experimental Psychology*, 1970, **85**, 411–417.

Massaro, D. W. Stimulus information versus processing time in auditory pattern recognition. *Perception & Psychophysics*, 1972, **12**, 50–56.

Massaro, D. W. A comparison of forward versus backward recognition masking. *Journal of Experimental Psychology*, 1973, **100**, 434–436.

Massaro, D. W. Perceptual units in speech recognition. *Journal of Experimental Psychology*, 1974, **102**, 199–208.

Massaro, D. W. *Experimental psychology and information processing*. Chicago: Rand McNally, 1975.

Massaro, D. W. Perceptual processing in dichotic listening. *Journal of Experimental Psychology: Human Learning & Memory*, 1976, **2**, 331–339.

Massaro, D. W., & Kahn, B. J. Effects of central processing on auditory recognition. *Journal of Experimental Psychology*, 1973, **97**, 51–58.

McCullough, C. Color adaptation of edge detectors in the human visual system. *Science*, 1965, **149**, 1115–1116.

Moray, N., Bates, A., & Barnett, T. Experiments on the four-eared man. *Journal of the Acoustical Society of America*, 1965, **38**, 196–201.

Morton, J. A functional model for memory. In D. A. Norman (Ed.), *Models of memory*. New York: Academic Press, 1970.

Morton, J., Crowder, R. G., & Prussin, H. A. Experiments with the stimulus suffix effect. *Journal of Experimental Psychology Monograph*, 1971, **91**, 169–190.

Neisser, U. *Cognitive psychology*, New York: Appleton, 1967.

Norman, D. A. Memory while shadowing. *Quarterly Journal of Experimental Psychology*, 1969, **21**, 85–93.

Pepper, R. L., & Herman, L. M. Decay and interference in the short-term retention of a discrete motor act. *Journal of Experimental Psychology Monograph*, 1970, **83**, 1–18.

Posner, M. I., Boies, S. J., Eichelman, W. H., & Taylor, R. L. Retention of visual and name codes of single letters. *Journal of Experimental Psychology Monograph*, 1969, **79**, pt. 2.

Roediger, H. L., III, & Crowder, R. G. Recall instructions and the suffix effect. *American Journal of Psychology*, 1976, **88**, 115–125.

Rostron, A. B. Brief auditory storage: Some further observations. *Acta Psychologica*, 1974, **38**, 471–482.

Sakitt, B. Locus of short-term visual storage. *Science,* 1975, **190,** 1318–1319.

Sakitt, B. Iconic memory. *Psychological Review*, 1976, **83,** 257–276.

Sperling, G. The information available in brief visual presentations. *Psychological Monographs,* 1960, **74,** 1–29.

Sperling, G. A model for visual memory tasks. *Human Factors,* 1963, **5,** 19–31.

Treisman, A. M. Monitoring and storage of irrelevant messages in selective attention. *Journal of Verbal Learning and Verbal Behavior,* 1964, **3,** 449–459.

Treisman, A. M., Russell, R., & Green, J. Brief visual storage of shape and movement. In P. M. A. Rabbitt & S. Dornic (Eds.), *Attention and performance.* Vol. V. New York: Academic Press, 1975.

Treisman, M., & Rostron, A. B. Brief auditory storage: A modification of Sperling's paradigm applied to audition. *Acta Psychologica,* 1972, **36,** 161–170.

Tulving, E. Episodic and semantic memory. In E. Tulving & W. Donaldson (Eds.), *Organization of memory.* New York: Academic Press, 1972.

Tulving, E. Ecphoric processes in recall and recognition. In J. Brown (Ed.), *Recall and recognition.* New York: Wiley, 1975.

Turvey, M. T. On peripheral and central processes in vision. *Psychological Review,* 1973, **80,** 1–52.

Weisstein, N. A. A Rashevsky-Landahl neural net: Simulation of metacontrast. *Psychological Review,* 1968, **75,** 494–522.

Watkins, M. J., & Watkins, O. C. The postcategorical status of the modality effect in serial recall. *Journal of Experimental Psychology,* 1973, **99,** 226–230.

Watkins, M. J., & Watkins, O. C. A tactile suffix effect. *Memory and Cognition,* 1974, **2,** 176–180.

Waugh, N. C., & Norman, D. A. Primary memory. *Psychological Review,* 1965, **72,** 89–104.

Wingfield, A., & Wheale, J. L. Word rate an intelligibility of alternated speech. *Perception & Psychophysics,* 1975, **18,** 317–320.

von Wright, J. M. On the problem of selection in iconic memory. *Scandinavian Journal of Psychology,* 1972, **13,** 159–171.

Chapter 11

THE RELATIONSHIP BETWEEN VERBAL AND PERCEPTUAL CODES*

ALLAN PAIVIO

I. INTRODUCTION

Much of our perceptual behavior consists of translating nonverbal perceptual information into language and vice versa. Children just beginning to speak delight in pointing to objects or to pictures and naming them. Older individuals habitually describe scenes, activities, faces, sounds, and every manner of nonverbal perceptual experience. Conversely, given name or description, they can point to the object or select a relevant picture from an array. This form of translation is so commonplace and effortless that the average person finds it difficult to see that there is any worthwhile theoretical problem to be answered. We are puzzled by illusions, negative afterimages, and hallucinations, but picking out grandmother from a group photograph when asked to do so is a banal fact that arouses little interest. This relative emphasis has been shared by

* The author's research reported in this chapter was supported by grants from the National Research Council of Canada (A0087) and the University of Western Ontario Research Fund.

perceptual psychologists as well. A glance at textbooks dating before 1970 shows that much more attention has been devoted to the examination and explanation of illusions than to comparably detailed treatment of the perception–language problem. The situation has changed rapidly in recent years, however, and this chapter aims to capture the flavor of these developments. It is concerned in particular with the nature of the mental representations or codes that are involved in the perceptual processing of both language and concrete objects and events, as well as the relation between the two.

With some notable exceptions (e.g., Gibson, 1966, p. 277 ff.), perceptual theorists have generally found it necessary to postulate some kind of memory substrate in order to account for perceptual identification. The underlying representations have been variously characterized as images, schemata, hypotheses, templates, prototypes, cell assemblies, neuronal models, holograms, and structural descriptions. Such concepts refer to long-term memory representations of perceptual objects and linguistic patterns. The hypothetical representations may be viewed as relatively concrete and static or as highly abstract and dynamic entities, but all share the idea that object identification involves the so-called *Höffding step* (e.g., see Neisser, 1967, p. 50)—that is, some kind of comparison process between the stimulus pattern and the underlying memory representation.

The same general assumptions apply to the relation between perceptual and linguistic processes, but the conceptual problems are magnified because now one must consider the representational substrate for the relationship, as well as the two classes of perceptual events. How should we conceptualize this complex problem? Must one postulate separate *kinds* of representations for verbal and nonverbal phenomena, or will a common representational code suffice if it is abstract enough? In either case, how are we to explain the ability to relate the two classes of events, as when we name a picture or select a picture corresponding to a name? If two modality-specific representations are assumed, are they relatively independent or are they interdependent? If the latter, which modality is the leading or dominant form of representation?

All theories that bear on such questions must assume that words and things are differentiated at some level of perceptual processing, since people do not confuse objects with their names. Whether such differences are maintained in long-term memory is a matter of controversy, however, as is the nature of the memory substrate. At least four logical possibilities have been proposed. One view is that the "deep" memory coding is primarily linguistic. Another is that nonverbal perceptual processes are somehow predominant even in memory. A third view is that the verbal–

nonverbal distinction is maintained in long-term memory. Finally, many contemporary theorists assume that the memory substrate is neither wordlike nor thinglike, but abstract and amodal. Each of these views will be discussed, along with illustrative observations.

II. LINGUISTIC DOMINANCE

The favored theory at one time held that perception was guided or dominated by verbal coding. According to this view, objects and events were identified when categorized by the perceiver. The categories were linguistic, or at least followed the lines of linguistic divisions. Linguistic determinism as proposed by Whorf (1956) was the prototype of this theoretical approach, and variants of it have been expressed by Bruner (1957), Haber (1966), and Glanzer and Clark (1963), among others. These theories shared the general assumption that perception of an object involved an initial sensory and perceptual analysis in which the object was distinguished from its background and then quickly translated into a linguistic or language-like representation. Whorf assumed that perception itself was determined by the linguistic categories, so that speakers of different languages perceived the world in the way in which their language categorized it. Later theorists (e.g., Haber, 1966) were more inclined to emphasize the role of verbal coding in the translation of the percept into memory. The evidence seems to favor the latter interpretation. For example, Brown and Lenneberg (1954) showed that measures of verbal codability of colors were more strongly related to recognition accuracy for the colors after longer delays between the presentation of target stimuli and later recognition tests. Ellis (1972) subsequently suggested that the verbal labels have their effect on memory primarily at the encoding or attentional stage. That is, they direct the subject's attention to distinctive features of the stimulus, thereby affecting what is remembered. This could be taken as evidence for a weak form of the Whorfian hypothesis, in which verbal coding is viewed as having a selective effect on an early stage of perceptual processing, such as the subjects's looking strategies (cf. Erdelyi, 1974). However, strong linguistic determinism has generally been abandoned in favor of other theoretical alternatives.

III. PERCEPTUAL DOMINANCE

One recent development involves essentially a volte-face with respect to the Whorfian hypothesis. This reversal is most apparent in research by

Berlin and Kay (1969) and E. Rosch (1975c). Berlin and Kay found that the speakers of 20 different languages showed substantial agreement in their choice of the best examples of colors corresponding to basic color names in their language. Berlin and Kay referred to these salient regions in the color space as color-name focal points. Rosch went on to show that eight chromatic focal colors were psychologically salient, even for the Dani people of West Irian, who have essentially a two-term color language. In a recognition experiment, she found that the Dani recognized focal colors better than nonfocal ones, despite the fact that the focal colors were not more codable than in-between colors for the Dani. Rosch then showed experimentally that the Dani learned new color names in a paired-associate task more easily when the names were paired with focal colors, according to Berlin and Kay's best-example clusters, than when they were paired with nonfocal colors. Thus, the data supported the conclusion that the perceptually salient focal colors functioned as natural prototypes for the acquisition of color names.

The generalization was further strengthened by experiments in which Rosch used geometric forms, facial expressions of emotion, and a series of semantic categories as perceptual stimuli. The evidence suggested that some forms, expressions, and category exemplars were better perceptual representations of the categories than other exemplars. Thus, Rosch's research demonstrated just the opposite of linguistic determinism, namely, that it is the human perceptual system that determines linguistic categories rather than the other way around. It seems appropriate to refer to this view as perceptual dominance or determinism.

The perceptual-dominance hypothesis and the evidence related to it suggest that the representations involved in perceptual processing are in some strong sense iconic or analogical in nature. That is, the representational activity aroused by words (e.g., category exemplars) is isomorphic with the activity aroused directly by perceptual objects. Such representations are explicitly assumed in the next approach, which also draws a distinction between verbal and nonverbal representations.

IV. DUAL CODING THEORY

A number of psychologists have proposed distinct memory substrates for language and for visual–spatial information (e.g., Brooks, 1968; Posner, 1973; Posner, Boies, Eichelman, & Taylor, 1969; Tversky, 1969; Wallach & Averbach, 1955). I have presented similar views along with specific assumptions concerning distinctions and interrelations between the two systems (e.g., Paivio, 1971, 1972, 1975a, 1977). The theory assumes that cognitive behavior is mediated by two independent but richly interconnected symbolic systems that are specialized for encoding, organizing, transforming, storing, and retrieving information. One (the image system) is specialized for dealing with perceptual information concerning nonverbal objects and events. The other (the *verbal system*) is specialized for dealing with linguistic information. The systems differ in the nature of the representational units, the way the units are organized into higher-order structures, and the way the structures can be reorganized or transformed. I will elaborate on this statement, emphasizing those features that are most relevant to the theme of the chapter. Among other things, the accent is on visual perception and its memory substrate, although the theory and research encompass other sensory modalities as well (Conlin & Paivio, 1975; Paivio & Okovita, 1971; Paivio, Philipchalk, & Rowe, 1975).

The functional representations of the image system are assumed to be perceptual isomorphs or analogs. This implies that perceptual distinctions along such continuous dimensions as size, color, and shape are also represented in a relatively fine-grained fashion in perceptual memory. The statement is an inference based on behavioral isomorphism between patterns of reactions to perceptual information and reactions to analogous memory representations that are activated by verbal or other cues when the perceptual events are absent (e.g., Paivio, 1975b). Thus, imaginal representations presumably are involved in the receptive processing of perceptual images (scenes or pictures) as well as the generation of consciously experienced imagery and its overt expression in drawings and other forms. Note that this statement distinguishes between image as a representational unit of the system and image as experience. For present purposes, I will sometimes use the neologism *imagen* (short for *image generator*) as a convenient label for the underlying representation, paralleling Morton's (1969) use of the term *logogen* to describe the hypothetical word generator in his word recognition model. The new term has no new theoretical implications. It simply makes explicit the logical distinction between a functional unit and its expressions in consciousness or behavior.

The representational units of the verbal system (the term *logogen* will serve as a succinct label) are assumed to be discrete entities corresponding to the functional units of language. They are only arbitrarily related to perceptual information. Thus, they are not perceptual analogs except in the sense that the representational structures must bear a lawful relation to the sequential patterns of linguistic stimuli and responses. The verbal system, per se, does not "contain" the perceptual or semantic information that corresponds to our knowledge of the world. Instead, such information must be retrieved from the nonverbal representational system.

How are the two systems related? Dual-coding theory assumes that they are functionally independent but interconnected. Independence implies that perceptual and cognitive activity can go in one or other system alone, or that both systems could be active concurrently. Thus, one can observe and take account of the objects and events in a social situation while carrying on a conversation that may be entirely unrelated to that situation. The same freedom does not apply *within* symbolic modalities, however, since one can not read a verbal message efficiently while carrying on a conversation on an unrelated topic. At the same time, the two representational systems must be substantially interconnected, since we can name things, draw pictures in response to names, and mentally translate into nonverbal images, or vice versa. The functional interconnections must be enormous in number, but nonetheless incomplete, for we know many things that we find difficult to describe. Conversely, we know many linguistic concepts that have no direct nonverbal perceptual counterparts.

A dual coding interpretation of such functional relations includes the idea of processing levels or stages. The first is the initial (temporary) sensory registration of stimulus information commonly referred to as *iconic storage* (e.g., Neisser, 1967), which is irrelevant here. Next is the representational level, where the stimulus activates a corresponding symbolic representation in long-term memory—words activate logogens and nonverbal objects or pictures arouse imagens. Next is the *referential* level, which refers to interconnections between verbal and nonverbal representations that enable an object to be named and thereby evoke some referential image in a probabilistic fashion that is determined by the situational context and the individual's past experiences with members of a conceptual class. Finally, the *associative* level refers to associative connections between different verbal representations, as reflected in word associations, for example, or analogous associations between images.

The entire scheme is illustrated in a simplified way in Fig. 1 using the concepts *dog*, *cat*, and *animal*. The verbal representations are depicted as discrete entities connected in a kind of network (for a plausible model, see Kiss, 1975), whereas the nonverbal representations are perceptual analogs organized into perceptual nested sets. Referential links exist between systems for the concepts *dog* and *cat*. The broken-lined connection for the general concept of animal implies that a direct connection could be formed; alternatively, the word *animal* might activate an imagen only indirectly, via its verbal associations with the *cat* or *dog* logogen.

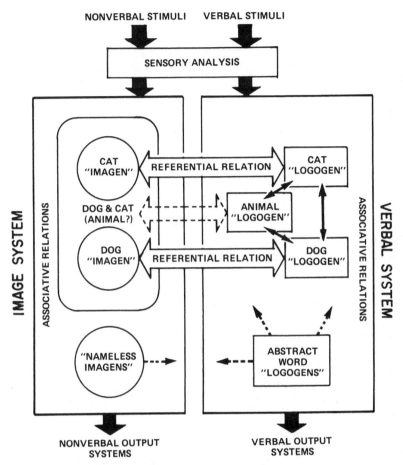

FIG. 1. A simplified schematization of a dual-coding model, showing the representational units and interconnections (the dotted lines represent potential interconnections) between nonverbal (image) and verbal symbolic systems.

The figure also illustrates the idea that each system includes representations that have no direct referential connection, such as verbal representations corresponding to function words and highly abstract language. Thus, the interconnections between systems are assumed to be most direct between representations corresponding to specific concrete words and the objects to which they refer, and increasingly indirect as the words become more abstract. Imagery ratings, imagery reaction times to words, and labeling reaction times to pictures are operational indicators of the availability of such interconnections (Paivio, 1971, Chap. 3).

The depicted model includes no representations for control processes, sensory analyzers, motor-output systems, and the like. Such processes obviously would need to be considered in any complete model of perceptual and linguistic processing. Nonetheless, the model specifies functional distinctions and relations between the two hypothetical systems so as to have clear, testable implications. It implies, for example, that perceptual recognition should depend primarily on the availability of a representation corresponding directly to the target stimulus. It should not depend on referential or associative connections to other representations, because their activation would depend on prior arousal of the target (for alternative possibilities, however, see Erdelyi, 1974). These implications have been supported by the results of visual (Paivio & O'Neill, 1970) and auditory (O'Neill, 1971) word-recognition experiments in which the potential for different levels of processing was manipulated by varying relevant word attributes. The model also has obvious implications for reaction-time tasks. These will be discussed following consideration of another view of the relationship between verbal and perceptual codes.

V. COMMON-CODE THEORIES

The fourth class of theory assumes that verbal and perceptual information are ultimately represented in a common symbolic format in long-term memory. Osgood's (1957) three-level theory of neural processing is a neobehavioristic version of such a model. According to Osgood, words (linguistic signs) and pictures (perceptual signs) are processed separately at the *projection* and *sensory integration* levels, but their common meaning is represented in the same form at the *representational* level. This representation consists of a "simultaneous distinctive bundle of fractional responses" or $r_m - s_m$ components. The theory was applied to the analysis of word recognition by Osgood and Hoosain (1974), who explained the salience of the word in perceptual recognition in terms of "the convergence of feedback from central mediational process with feedforward from peripheral sensory processes upon the integration of word-form percepts [p. 168]." Imagery would be similarly explained as a dependent event that is recreated through feedback from the more central meaning system to the perceptual integration system (Osgood, 1973, p. 286–287).

Other theorists assume that perceptual and linguistic events are represented cognitively as structural descriptions expressed in a propositional language (e.g., Anderson & Bower, 1973; Chase & Clark, 1972; Norman & Rumelhart, 1975). Propositions are abstract statements about relations between structural entities. "*A* is above *B*" is a proposition. It is conceptualized as two labeled nodes (representing *A* and *B*) connected by a labeled relation. It would be part of a network of nodes and relations in which the components are themselves defined in terms of propositional descriptions. Thus, knowledge is represented much as in a dictionary, where words are defined in terms of words whose verbal definitions are to be found elsewhere in the dictionary. The main point in the present context is that verbal and nonverbal perceptual events become amodal, or "neutralized," at this representational level. Moreover, these models generally assume that translations between perceptual and linguistic information are mediated by the abstract descriptions. The latter function as a kind of *interlingua* that permits communication between the two kinds of stimulus events. Figure 2 shows a simplified version of such a model.

As in the case of Osgood's theory, the descriptive model allows for modality distinctions at an initial stage of perceptual analysis on the input side, and of motor programs (e.g., speaking, writing, drawing) on the output side, but conceptual knowledge in long-term memory is amodal. Thus, any task that requires a translation of nonverbal to verbal information, such as picture naming, would first involve a decomposition of the input information into an abstract description. A picture of a dog and the word *dog* would be judged as conceptually identical because both access the same description. This has a number of implications that differ from

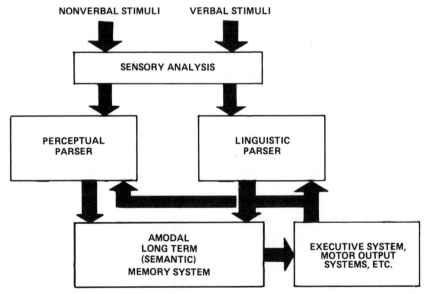

FIG. 2. A simplified schematization of a common-coding model. Verbal and nonverbal representations are interconnected only via the common (amodal) representational system.

those of dual coding. For example, pictures and their names should not be independent in memory tasks, and conceptual knowledge concerning the attributes of things should be accessed equally quickly with pictures or words as stimuli, allowing for any time difference in the perceptual analysis of the two classes of stimuli. Relevant evidence will be reviewed later in this chapter.

A final observation, before turning to the data, is that weaker forms of the above theories can be easily constructed simply by combining the assumptions of different models. For example, one can imagine a multiple-coding theory that includes distinct but interconnected long-term memory representations for perceptual and verbal information at one level (dual coding) and abstract representations common to both systems at another level. The difference between this and the propositional models is the specific assumption that verbal and nonverbal representational systems are relatively directly connected, as well as having pathways to the abstract semantic level. Thus, direct translations between codes or indirect translations via the semantic system would be optional processing strategies that depended on task demands.

VI. EMPIRICAL EVIDENCE

The following is a selective review of studies most directly relevant to the previously discussed theories, particularly as they apply to tasks that emphasize perceptual variables and processes. Some findings indicate that at least two distinct coding systems mediate perceptual performance involving nonverbal and verbal stimuli. Others suggest that some kind of common code may be involved as well.

A. General Evidence for Distinct Representations

A variety of research findings support the general idea of distinct verbal and nonverbal systems. Neuropsychological evidence indicates that certain verbal and nonverbal skills are localized in different hemispheres (e.g., Kimura, 1973). Studies of individual differences show that verbal and nonverbal abilities are factorially independent (e.g., Forisha, 1975; Guilford, 1967; Paivio, 1971, Chap. 14; Paivio & Ernest, 1971). Various memory studies also suggest that verbal and nonverbal symbols (e.g., names and pictures) for the same concept are mnemonically independent, in that the two forms of representation can have additive effects on recall or can be independently forgotten (see Paivio, 1975a).

Other studies point to qualitative distinctions in the symbolic representations of nonverbal and verbal information. Brooks (1968) and others (e.g., Byrne, 1974) have demonstrated modality-specific interference between visual perception and visual imagery. For example, reading interferes more than listening with memory for messages that describe spatial information. Earlier, Perky (1910) showed that visual imagery interferes with visual perception, and this was confirmed by Segal (1971), using signal detection methods. Segal and Fusella (1970) specifically demonstrated that visual imagery interferes more with visual than auditory perception (and vice versa for auditory imagery). Thus, we have evidence for distinct verbal and nonverbal symbolic modalities (Brooks) as well as sensory distinctions within the nonverbal system (Segal).

Roger Shepard and his collaborators provided some of the most precise evidence for modality-specific perceptual representations. They did so by demonstrating a high degree of qualitative and quantitative isomorphism between mental representations and observable events, rather than by contrasts with verbal representations. Reaction time and multidimensional scaling procedures made it reasonable to infer that shapes of mental maps were analogous to physical maps, that mental paper folding proceeded in a manner comparable to actual paper folding, and that mental images of letters or numerals could be rotated much as if one were rotating an actual form at some specifiable speed (for detailed discussions of the findings, see Cooper & Shepard, 1973, Cooper & Shepard, Chap. 3, this volume). Many of these studies involved variants of the comparison task reviewed in the following section.

B. Evidence from Comparison Reaction-Time Studies

The most systematic information on perceptual and verbal codes has come from reaction-time studies in which subjects were required to determine whether or not a given stimulus was the same as another. The match could be based on physical identity or on some shared attribute, such as a common label. The latter was particularly relevant, because the information had to be accessed or generated from long-term memory, and appropriate manipulations would have permitted inferences about the nature of the common code. The inferential power of the paradigm was demonstrated by Posner and his colleagues. Posner and Mitchell (1967) required their subjects to indicate whether pairs of letters were the same or different. Instructions defined *same* in terms of physical identity (e.g., *AA* or *aa*), name identity (e.g., *Aa*), or rule identity (e.g., both vowels). The results showed that *same* responses were fastest for physical matches and slowest for rule matches. The differences in reaction times provide suggestive evidence concerning the time needed to access representations at different levels. For example, the difference between physical and name match may reflect the time required to "look up" the common label after the visual code has been aroused for the different letters.

Posner *et al.* (1969) subsequently showed that subjects could also generate effective visual codes. They reasoned that when a subject was presented the first letter auditorily and the second visually, and knew in advance whether the second would be capital or small, he might be able to generate the appropriate visual information. If so, he should show as efficient matching for audiovisual as for visual identity pairs, and both should be superior to visual name-identity matches. This is precisely what happened with practiced subjects: Given an interstimulus interval of approximately .75–1 sec, they matched a new visual letter as rapidly when the first letter was auditory as when it was visual.

Taken together, the data from the various experiments by Posner and his collaborators provide strong evidence for at least two kinds of representations: one containing information corresponding rather directly to visual–spatial patterns and the other, to language. Rule matches might reflect some more abstract code, but the data could also be explained in terms of verbal processes if we simply assume that it takes longer to access a more general label, such as *vowel*, than a more specific name.

Similar paradigms have been used extensively in picture–word comparison experiments. These have yielded evidence for verbal–nonverbal dual coding, as well as for a common code. Rosenfeld (1967) measured *same–different* comparison times between successive stimuli, which were either figures or their labels (e.g., three red triangles). In a given session, the second stimulus was always either verbal or pictorial, whereas the first stimulus could be either. All four combinations were used, with or without a delay between successive stimuli. The delay condition is most relevant here because it permits time for the first stimulus to be encoded into a form suitable for comparison with the second. Rosenfeld tested three hypotheses concerning the nature of the representation involved in comparison. The common-abstract-entity theory states that both types of stimuli are encoded into the abstract form, so it predicts no difference in comparison time for the different combinations of pictures and words. If the representation is more like pictures than words, or more directly accessible for pictures, the prediction is that comparisons would be faster when the second stimulus is a picture rather than a word; the reverse prediction follows if the representation is more accessible for words than pictures. Rosenfeld's results supported the figural hypothesis: For picture- and word-target stimuli, respectively, it was faster to make the comparison with pictures (656 and 675 msec) than with words (828 and 811 msec). The decision was also faster if the successive stimuli were of the same type but the differences were small. The order of conditions was picture–picture, word–picture, word–word, and picture–word, in increasing order of reaction times. This could be taken as support for functional dominance of the image code.

Paivio and Begg (1974) used the same combination of picture–word conditions in a variant of the matching task. The subjects in three experiments searched through an array of 25 pictures or words for a target item that had been presented as a picture or a word. In two experiments, the pictures were line drawings of familiar objects and the words were their printed labels. The search times in both experiments were consistently faster when the array items were pictures than when they were words, regardless of target mode. Search was also faster with pictures than with words as targets when the search array also consisted of pictures, but target mode had no consistent effect with word arrays. These results are consistent with either dual coding or a strong imagery theory. That is, subjects may have translated both pictures and words into a picture-like representation in order to make the comparison.

Dual-coding theory predicted a different pattern of results in the third experiment, which involved photographs of the faces of famous people and their printed names as stimuli. The reasoning was as follows. Faces, like names, may require foveal fixation for specific identification, so that the array effect (picture superiority) obtained in the previous experiments should not occur with faces as stimuli. However, the face-face comparison should still be faster than the name–face comparison because of encoding variability in the images generated to the names. Such variability was not expected in the case of verbal coding of face targets in the face–name condition. The results were completely consistent with predictions: the name–face condition was significantly slower than the remaining conditions, which did not differ from each other. Taken together, the results of all three experiments suggested that items that are cognitively represented both verbally and as nonverbal images can be searched and compared in either mode, depending on task demands. The mode actually used depends on the expected mode of the comparison stimulus. In the search experiments such expectations were determined by the contextual information provided by the mode of the search array as a whole. In other experiments, such as the Posner et al. (1969) study of visual-code generation, described above, the expectations were controlled by the mode of the comparison stimuli encountered on previous trials. Such a procedure was also used by Tversky (1969) in a comparison study involving names and schematic faces, with results consistent with dual coding.

Seymour (1975) conducted a series of picture–word comparison experiments designed to provide evidence on the nature of the representational data base for such comparisons. Some of his results are clearly consistent with a form of dual coding. For example, comparisons in which the two stimulus displays are presented simultaneously showed much slower comparison times for sentence–picture than for picture–picture combinations. This difference was virtually eliminated under the successive condition, when subjects presumably had time to translate descriptions into a code that was functionally equivalent to the form of the subsequent picture. These findings essentially confirm those of Rosenfeld and Posner *et al*. However, other aspects of the data seemed to be inconsistent with dual coding. For instance, the magnitude of the *same–different* effect differed for the two conditions: *Yes* reaction times (RTs) were generally faster than *no* RTs, as is usual in such experiments, but the difference was much greater for description–picture than for picture–picture conditions. From this, Seymour argued that the figural codes generated by pictures and by descriptions might not be strictly equivalent bases for verification of a test picture. This is not a strong argument against dual coding, however, since there is no reason to assume strict equivalence under the two conditions. Recall, for example, that Paivio and Begg (1974) explicitly predicted faster face–face than name–face comparisons because of greater variability in the images generated to names (cf. Denis, 1975; Snodgrass, Wasser, & Funkelstein, 1974).

Another difficulty for dual coding is the occurrence of semantic-confusion effects in picture–word comparison tasks. These are not explainable as phonological confusions between verbal labels or confusions of images based on visual similarity. For example, subjects take longer to indicate that simultaneously displayed pairs are not the same when they share membership of a functional class (e.g., a glove and a picture of a hat) than when they are unrelated. These and other findings led Seymour to favor "Clark and Chase's (1972) notion of a single abstract (propositional) code which incorporates facilities for description of physical properties and locative relations [p. 283]." He also found it necessary, however, to allow "that such descriptions may be constructed more rapidly for pictures than for verbal input [p. 283]," which amounts to a concession that word–picture comparisons involve a modality specific component.

Rosch (1975a, b) has obtained some of the most convincing evidence that names and their concrete referents are linked by modality-specific cognitive representations. In addition, however, she found support for common abstract representations of some kind. She used a modified form of comparison task, introduced by Beller (1971), in which the comparison stimuli are preceded by a priming stimulus that may or may not be related to the comparison stimuli. Beller showed subjects a prime that was one of a pair of letters to be matched. Such priming shortened reaction time for both physical and name matches, and physical matches were facilitated even when the prime was presented acoustically.

Rosch reasoned that a prime can facilitate a response only if it contains some of the information needed for the response. Thus, priming effects should tell us something about the nature of the information contained in mental representations generated by color names. She presented either the name of a basic color category as a priming stimulus or the word *blank* to subjects in advance of a pair of colors. The colors were either good members or poor members of basic color categories, according to the Berlin and Kay (1969) research discussed earlier. Several experiments showed that *same* responses to physically identical colors were facilitated by prime presented 2 sec in advance of a color pair when the colors were good members of the category, but priming inhibited identity responses to poor members of the categories. Rosch concluded that the cognitive representation of color categories contains information used in encoding physical color stimuli and that the representation reflects the prototype structure of color categories. Moreover, the representations appear to be at the level of a concrete physical code in that they must contain some of the information contained in actual perception of color stimuli. In brief, they are highly modality-specific or image-like.

Rosch (1975a) applied the same technique to the study of cognitive representations generated by superordinate category names, such as *furniture, fruit,* and *vehicle.* These were used as primes for comparisons involving specific members of categories (e.g., *chair, apple, car*). The instances were presented either as words or as pictures. Moreover the examples were selected to be high, medium, or low in their rated goodness as examples of the categories. The logic in this case was that if the mental code generated by a semantic category name is like a representation of a prototype of the best example of the category, or in some other way includes information about the internal structure of the category, *same* pairs of good examples should be more strongly facilitated by the prime than *same* pairs of poor examples. This result occurred in three experiments: Category priming facilitated responses to physically identical good members and hindered responses to physically identical poor members of the category. Thus, as in the color–label experiment, cognitive representations of categories appeared to be more similar to the good examples than the poor examples. However, it was not clear that the mental representations were highly concrete, inasmuch as subjects were asked to respond *same* if the two items of a pair belonged to the same category. A further experiment accordingly required subjects to give an identity response only if the stimuli were physically identical. The results in this case showed no effect of priming, suggesting that perception was affected by an abstract representation of the meaning of the category name.

Two further experiments were concerned with the question of whether the representation of words and pictures was derived from a common meaning, or from dual codes specific to the modality of the stimulus. The results were partly consistent with both interpretations. A common portion was suggested by the fact that, within 2 sec, subjects could generate a representation of the meaning of the category name that was equally representative of a pair of words or pictures under conditions in which the subject was uncertain of the type of stimulus that was to appear. However, the results also revealed a modality-specific component: When the time intervals between the prime and the stimulus were reduced below 2 sec, generation of representations for both pictures and words under conditions of uncertainty required a longer time interval than generation of a representation for either words or pictures alone under conditions of certainty. Thus, Rosch concluded that there was a "depth meaning of superordinate categories not specifically coded in terms of words or pictures, but that the depth meaning is translated into a format in preparation for actual perception which differs slightly for words and pictures [p. 226]." Additionally, less time was required to prepare for pictures than for words, and comparison times in all experiments were generally faster for pictures than for words, suggesting that pictures may be closer to the nature of the underlying representation than are words. Rosch's experiments provide evidence for separate modality-specific representations corresponding to pictures and words, as well as a more abstract representation that captures the common generic meaning of both, but at the same time does not seem to be completely amodal.

C. Tests of Dual-Coding Theory

The final series of studies to be considered were designed to test specific assumptions of the dual-coding model described earlier. A comparison reaction-time study by Moyer (1973) provided the paradigm for the series. It has long been known that the reaction time to choose between two stimuli that differ on some attribute such as size varies inversely with the magnitude of the perceptual differences. For example, the greater the difference in the lengths of two lines, the more quickly people can decide which is longer. Moyer extended this generalization to comparisons of the sizes of animals presented only as names. The animal names had been previously ranked according to the relative sizes of the animals themselves. The experimental subjects were visually presented the names of two animals, such as *frog–wolf*, and were required to throw a switch under the name of the larger animal. The interesting result was that the reaction time for the decision increased systematically as the difference in animal size became smaller. Moyer concluded that subjects somehow compare the animals names by making an internal psychophysical judgment, after first converting the names to analog representations that preserve animal size. Smaller size differences between animals are represented as smaller differences between the internal analog, with resulting decreases in discriminability and increased reaction times.

We extended Moyer's symbolic distance paradigm in a variety of ways (Paivio, 1975c). One experiment showed that size comparisons were just as fast and showed the inverse relation to memory-size differences when comparisons were made across conceptual categories. That is, it took longer to indicate the larger member of a pair such as *cat–toaster* than a pair such as *mouse–toaster*. These findings indicate that the comparisons are based on analog representations containing rather fine-grained size information. The comparability of comparisons within conceptual categories (animal–animal) and between categories (animal–object) is also interesting because it is inconsistent with most network models of semantic memory. For example, models of the type used by Collins and Quillian (1969) would predict faster reaction times for comparisons *within* categories than those *between* categories.

Other experiments involved comparisons of pictures and words in the same task. A clear prediction from dual-coding theory is that size comparisons would be faster with pictures than with words, even when the pictures contain no perceptual size information. This follows from the assumption that pictures have more direct access to the image system, where the relative size information is presumably stored. Models which assume that such knowledge is represented in a conceptual system common to both pictures and words would predict no difference. Consistent with dual coding, reaction times in several experiments were faster for comparisons involving pictures than words. Moreover, both pictures and words show the usual symbolic-distance effect (Paivio, 1975b).

An even more interesting picture–word difference occurred when picture-size information conflicted with long-term-memory information. Subjects were shown a pair of pictures or words, so that the two represented objects differed in real-life (memory) size. Sometimes the two were also shown with one member of the pair physically larger than the other and in such a way that the relation was either congruent or incongruent with real-life size. For example, the *mouse–toaster* pair would be presented so that the mouse was smaller than the toaster in the congruent case and larger than the toaster in the incongruent case. The object names were treated similarly by varying the relative size of the printed words. Predictions followed from the reasoning that the pictures accessed the image system relatively directly, so that perceptual and memory information concerning objects would conflict when the two were incongruent. The conflict was not expected with analogous manipulations involving printed words, since the words would have to be read before the corresponding conceptual representations were activated in the image system; accordingly, print size should be irrelevant. Again, common-coding theories that assume conceptual representations to be amodal do not predict such effects. The interactions predicted by dual coding were fully confirmed: The Stroop-type conflict occurred with pictures, but not with words. These results provide strong support for the idea that size information is represented in a nonverbal visual memory system that is continuous with the system that processes perceptual information more directly.

The conclusion was further strengthened by other experiments in which subjects were required to make relative-distance judgments of pairs of pictured objects. This task is particularly interesting in the present context because it is a classical perceptual task, in the sense that subjects judge the appearance of pictured objects (that is, which one *looks* farther away). By contrast, the size-comparison task requires judgments concerning *memory*-size differences rather than the appearance of objects as pictured. Nonetheless, in both cases the judgments must take account of the same memory information. This is so in the case of distance judgments because the pictures contain no perspective or other distance cues, and the judgments accordingly must be based on the relative-size information contained in the pictures together with remembered size. Thus, when the objects are shown about equal in size, the function relating reaction times to size difference should be the same for distance and size comparisons. The two tasks should differ only in that the reaction times should be longer on the average for distance than for size comparisons, as the former involves a more complex judgment. Both predictions were confirmed (Paivio, 1978).

Another prediction is that the Stroop-type conflict demonstrated for size comparisons should be reversed when subjects judge relative distance. Reaction times should be relatively fast in the incongruent case, because the larger object, being pictured smaller than its partner, should clearly look farther away. The relative distance judgment should be more uncertain and reaction times slower in the congruent condition, where the conceptually larger object is also pictured as relatively large. These predictions, too, were clearly confirmed (Paivio, 1975c, Exp. 3), demonstrating once more the continuity between perception and perceptual memory, and indicating as well that the same memory representations can be used for different ends, depending on task demands.

Dual-coding theory predicts yet another pattern of results when picture pairs and word pairs are compared on attributes that are presumably represented directly in the verbal system, rather than the image system. The pronounceability of object names is an obvious example. The information in this case should be accessed more directly when the items are presented as printed words than when they are presented as pictures. This is an obvious prediction, because it is already known that it takes longer to name pictures than to read words (e.g., Fraisse, 1968), but it is important in this context in order to establish a direct contrast with the findings for size comparisons. In addition, it provides a control for possible artifacts, such as reaction times being affected by the bizarreness of pictured objects that appear abnormally small or large relative to their partners. Such artifacts would be ruled out if physical size differences in the pictured objects and printed words, whether congruent or incongruent with real-life size, had no effect on pronounceability comparisons times. The actual results were completely as expected: Pronounceability comparisons were faster with words than pictures, and pictured or printed size had no effect.

The results of the different experiments strongly favor dual-coding theory over amodal coding models as they are presently formulated. This conclusion must be reconciled, however, with the earlier suggestion that certain findings from comparison reaction-time studies seem to require some kind of common coding system as an explanatory device.

VII. CONCLUSIONS

The following conclusions are justified by the data. First, there is substantial support for dual coding, not simply at a relatively superficial stage of perceptual processing, but at the level of long-term memory for linguistic and nonlinguistic events. Second, some data provide support for a relatively abstract code common to both verbal and nonverbal information. Paradoxically, however, the common code does not appear to be completely amodal. The findings suggest instead that even categorical semantic information is in some sense more picturelike than wordlike. R. Anderson and McGaw (1973) concluded similarly on the basis of recall data that people use images of highly probable exemplars to represent the meaning of general terms. Thus the effective representation of *animal* is more likely to look like *dog* than *squirrel*. Additionally, Seymour (1975) found it necessary to assume that the propositional representations are accessed more quickly with pictures than with words as stimuli, suggesting at least a processing bias in favor of picture-like representations.

The above generalization is consistent also with some recent views of abstract semantic memory. Clark, Carpenter, and Just (1973) assumed that pictures and descriptions were both encoded as propositions. Nonetheless, they repeatedly distinguished between linguistic and perceptual coding as though different kinds of propositional structures were involved. Moreover, they concluded that the perceptual representations were dominant, in the sense that translations between pictures and descriptions were biased by certain preferred codings for the perceptual stimuli. Thus, "there are similarities between linguistic and perceptual representations that may have arisen from a basic conceptual organization of space . . . which . . . is molded in the main by constraints on our perceptual apparatus, [and] appears to be directly reflected in the linguistic properties of spatial terms . . . and how we process them [p. 377]." J. Anderson and Bower (1973, p. 187), while proposing an abstract representational format for perceptual and linguistic stimuli in their model of human associative memory, also adopted a "sensationalistic bias" that assumes elementary features of the system to be ultimately derived from perceptual experience with things.

How can the evidence and the different views be reconciled in a single theory of verbal and perceptual codes? Multiple coding apparently needs to be incorporated into the model. It could retain the idea of verbal and nonverbal representational systems, which are orthogonal to sensory systems (cf. Paivio, 1972), and add an abstract representational system for more general information common to both systems. The entire model could be interpreted in neuropsychological terms as a hierarchically organized neuronal structure, such as Hebb's (e.g., 1968) lower-order and higher-order cell assemblies, which retain perceptual information even at the higher levels. Thus we might assume that the common representations for general categories like *furniture* and *birds* grow out of representations for specific instances, particularly those that are most prototypical of the series in Rosch's sense. These general perceptual representations would function as the referential base for general terms. These referents would be accessible more quickly from pictorial than from verbal stimuli, because the representations are in fact outgrowths of specific imaginal representations.

Such a model could accomodate a verbal or lexical system organized after the fashion suggested by recent associative network models (e.g., Kiss, 1975; Collins & Loftus, 1975). After all, there is plenty of evidence that associative relations between linguistic units can have a powerful effect on language performance, although some of this is probably confounded by effects resulting from associative experiences involving the referents of the words (e.g., *tables* and *chairs*) rather than between the words alone. It remains to be determined just how much "cognitive work" can go on entirely within such a verbal network, independently of its connections with perceptual representations.

References

Anderson, J. R., & Bower, G. H. *Human associative memory*. New York: Holt, 1973.

Anderson, R. C., & McGaw, B. On the representation of meaning of general terms. *Journal of Experimental Psychology*, 1973, **101**, 301–306.

Beller, H. K. Priming: Effects of advance information on matching. *Journal of Experimental Psychology*, 1971, **87**, 176–182.

Berlin, B., & Kay, P. *Basic color terms*. Los Angeles: Univ. of California Press, 1969.

Brooks, L. R. Spatial and verbal components of the act of recall. *Canadian Journal of Psychology*, 1968, **22**, 349–368.

Brown, R. W., & Lenneberg, E. H. A study in language and cognition. *Journal of Abnormal and Social Psychology*, 1954, **49**, 454–462.

Bruner, J. S. Neural mechanisms in perception. *Psychological Review*, 1957, **64**, 340–358.

Byrne, B. Item concreteness vs spatial organization as predictors of visual imagery. *Memory & Cognition*, 1974, **2**, 53–59.

Chase, W. G., & Clark, H. H. Mental operations in the comparison of sentences and pictures. In L. Gregg (Ed.), *Cognition in learning and memory*. New York: Wiley, 1972.

Clark, H. H., Carpenter, P. A., & Just, M. A. On the meeting of semantics and perception. In W. G. Chase (Ed.), *Visual information processing*. New York: Academic Press, 1973.

Collins, A. M., & Loftus, E. F. A spreading-activation theory of semantic processing. *Psychological Review*, 1975, **82**, 407–428.

Collins, A. M., & Quillian, M. R. Retrieval time from semantic memory. *Journal of Verbal Learning and Verbal Behavior*, 1969, **8**, 240–247.

Conlin, D., & Paivio, A. The associative learning of the deaf: The effects of word imagery and signability. *Memory & Cognition*, 1975, **3**, 335–340.

Cooper, L. A., & Shepard, R. N. Chronometric studies of the rotation of mental images. In W. G. Chase (Ed.), *Visual information processing*. New York: Academic, 1973.

Denis, M. *Représentation imagée et activité de memorisation*. Monographies françaises de psychologie XXXII. Paris: Centre National de la Recherche Scientifique, 1975.

Ellis, H. C. Verbal processes in the encoding of visual pattern information: An approach to language, perception, and memory. In M. E. Meyer (Ed.), *Third Western symposium on learning: Cognitive learning*. Bellingham: Western Washington State College, 1972.

Erdelyi, M. H. A new look at the new look: Perceptual defense and vigilance. *Psychological Review*, 1974, **81**, 1–25.

Forisha, B. D. Mental imagery verbal processes: A developmental study. *Developmental Psychology*, 1975, **11**, 259–267.

Fraisse, P. Motor and verbal reaction times to words and drawings. *Psychonomic Science*, 1968, **12**, 235–236.

Gibson, J. J. *The senses considered as perceptual systems*. Boston: Houghton-Mifflin, 1966.

Glanzer, M., & Clark, W. H. The verbal loop hypothesis: Binary numbers. *Journal of Verbal Learning and Verbal Behavior*, 1963, **2**, 301–309.

Guilford, J. P. *The nature of human intelligence*. New York: McGraw-Hill, 1967.

Haber, R. N. Nature of the effect of set on perception. *Psychological Review*, 1966, **73**, 335–351.

Hebb, D. O. Concerning imagery. *Psychological Review*, 1968, **75**, 466–477.

Kimura, D. The asymmetry of the human brain. *Scientific American*, 1973, **228**, 70–78.

Kiss, G. R. An associative thesaurus of English: Structural analysis of a large relevance network. In A. Kennedy & A. Wilkes (Eds.), *Studies in long term memory*. New York: Wiley, 1975.

Morton, J. Interaction of information in word recognition. *Psychological Review*, 1969, **76**, 165–178.

Moyer, R. S. Comparing objects in memory: evidence suggesting an internal psychophysics. *Perception & Psychophysics*, 1973, **13**, 180–184.

Neisser, U. *Cognitive psychology*. New York: Appleton, 1967.

Norman, D. A., & Rumelhart, D. E. *Explorations in cognition*. San Francisco: Freeman, 1975.

O'Neill, B. Word attributes in dichotic recognition and memory. Unpublished doctoral dissertation, Univ. of Western Ontario, 1971.

Osgood, C. E. Motivational dynamics of language behavior. In M. R. Jones (Ed.), *Nebraska symposium on motivation*. Lincoln: Univ. of Nebraska Press, 1957.

Osgood, C. E. The discussion of Dr. Paivio's paper. In F. J. McGuigan & R. A. Schoonover (Eds.), *The psychophysiology of thinking*. New York: Academic Press, 1973. Pp. 285–287.

Osgood, C. E., & Hoosain, R. Salience of the word as a unit in the perception of language. *Perception & Psychophysics*, 1974, **15**, 168–192.

Paivio, A. *Imagery and verbal processes*. New York: Holt, 1971.

Paivio, A. Symbolic and sensory modalities of memory. In M. E. Meyer (Ed.), *The third Western symposium on learning: Cognitive learning*. Bellingham: Western Washington State College, 1972.

Paivio, A. Coding distinctions and repetition effects in memory. In G. H. Bower (Ed.), *The psychology of learning and motivation* (Vol. 9). New York: Academic, 1975. (a)

Paivio, A. Neomentalism. *Canadian Journal of Psychology*, 1975, **29**, 263–291. (b)

Paivio, A. Perceptual comparisons through the mind's eye. *Memory & Cognition*, 1975, **3**, 635–647. (c)

Paivio, A. Images, propositions, and knowledge. In J. M. Nicholas (Ed.), *Images, perception, and knowledge*. The Western Ontario Series in the Philosophy of Science. Dordrecht: Reidel, 1977.

Paivio, A. A dual coding approach to perception and cognition. In H. I. Pick, Jr. & E. Saltzman (Eds.), *Modes of perceiving and processing information*. Hillsdale, New Jersey: Lawrence Erlbaum Associates, 1978.

Paivio, A., & Begg, I. Pictures and words in visual search. *Memory & Cognition*, 1974, **2**, 515–521.

Paivio, A., & Ernest, C. Imagery ability and visual perception of verbal and nonverbal stimuli. *Perception & Psychophysics*, 1971, **10**, 429–432.

Paivio, A., & Okovita, H. W. Word imagery modalities and associative learning in blind and sighted subjects. *Journal of Verbal Learning and Verbal Behavior*, 1971, **10**, 506–510.

Paivio, A., & O'Neill, B. J. Visual recognition thresholds and dimensions of word meaning. *Perception & Psychophysics*, 1970, **8**, 273–275.

Paivio, A., Philipchalk, R., & Rowe, E. J. Free and serial recall of pictures, sounds, and words. *Memory & Cognition*, 1975, **3**, 586–590.

Perky, C. W. An experimental study of imagination. *American Journal of Psychology*, 1910, **21**, 422–452.

Posner, M. I. Coordination of internal codes. In W. G. Chase (Ed.), *Visual information processing*. New York: Academic Press, 1973.

Posner, M. I., Boies, S. J., Eichelman, W. H., & Taylor, R. L. Retention of visual and name codes of single letters. *Journal of Experimental Psychology Monograph*, 1969, **79**, (1, Pt. 2).

Posner, M. I., & Mitchell, R. F. Chronometric analysis of classification. *Psychological Review*, 1967, **74**, 392–409.

Rosch, E. Cognitive representations of semantic categories. *Journal of Experimental Psychology: General*, 1975, **104**, 192–233. (a)

Rosch, E. The nature of mental codes for color categories. *Journal of Experimental Psychology: Human Perception and Performance*, 1975, **1**, 303–322. (b)

Rosch, E. Universals and cultural specifics in human categorization. In R. Brislin, S. Bochner, & W. Conner (Eds.), *Cross-cultural perspectives on learning*. New York: Halstead Press, 1975. (c)

Rosenfeld, J. B. Information processing: encoding and decoding. Unpublished doctoral dissertation, Indiana Univ., 1967.

Segal, S. J. Processing of the stimulus in imagery and perception. In S. Segal (Ed.), *Imagery: Current cognitive approaches*. New York: Academic Press, 1971.

Segal, S. J., & Fusella, V. Influence of imaged pictures and sounds on detection of visual and auditory signals. *Journal of Experimental Psychology*, 1970, **83**, 458–464.

Seymour, P. H. K. Semantic equivalence of verbal and pictorial displays. In A. Kennedy & A. Wilkes (Eds.), *Studies in long term memory*. New York: Wiley, 1975.

Snodgrass, J. G., Wasser, B., Finkelstein, M., & Goldberg, L. B. On the fate of visual and verbal memory codes for pictures and words: Evidence for a dual coding mechanism in recogntion memory. *Journal of Verbal Learning and Verbal Behavior*, 1974, **13**, 27–37.

Tversky, B. Pictorial and verbal encoding in a short-term memory task. *Perception & Psychophysics*, 1969, **6**, 225–233.

Wallach, H., & Averbach, E. On memory modalities. *American Journal of Psychology*, 1955, **68**, 249–257.

Whorf, B. L. *Language, thought, and reality*. Cambridge, Massachusetts: Technology Press, 1956.

AUTHOR INDEX

Numbers in italics refer to the pages on which the complete references are listed.

SUBJECT INDEX

A

Accent, perception of rhythm and, 236–237
Accent-structure hypothesis, 272–273
Acceptance angle, 7
  calculation of, 7
Accoustics, haptic, 291–292
Adaptation, to light
  lamina and, 48
  photon noise and, 13
Aftereffects, kinesthetic, 309
Age
  cross-modal matching and 335
  rate of mental rotation and, 135
  temporal field and, 205
Alphabet, pattern, 259
  dimensionality of, 260–265
Alpha rhythm, perception of succession
  and, 211
Ambiguity, spatial transformation and, 106
  direction of rotation and, 153
  in object identification, 132
Ames balloon demonstration, 158
Angular orientation, recognition of, by bees,
  36–37
Ant
  eye of, specialized region for detection of
    polarized light in, 45
  resolution of visual patterns in, 51
  sun-compass response in, 29
Anticipation, synchronization and, 245
Aphasia, perception of succession and,
  213–214
Apprehension, capacity of, 206
Art, rhythmical structures in, 242–243
Assembly, mental, 140–141
Assimilation, in pattern perception, 267
Associationism, pattern perception and,
  266–267
Attention
  perception of succession and, 213
  verbal labels and, 377

B

Audition, *see also* Memory, echoic
  coordination with vision, 89
  in infants, 90–91
  information transmitted by, 219–220
  perception of duration in, 219, 220, 221
Auditory patterns, *see* Pattern perception;
    Rhythm perception
Auditory space, 332
Auditory streaming, 283–284
Autocorrelation, in motion perception,
  56–58
Autonomic nervous system, development
  of, touch and, 295–296

B

Bee
  ability to discriminate intensities, 18
  angle vision of, 76
  pattern recognition in, 36–43
  sun-compass response in, 29
Bending, perception of, 168
Biological clock, in perception of duration,
  231–232
Blindness
  echolocation devices in, 95–97
  environmental scales and, 296
  mental rotation in, 135
  recognition of raised-line drawings in, 300
Bloch's law, 224
Blur circle, 6, 10, 11
Branch patterns, attraction of stick insects
  to, 30
Brightness, of colors, 193–194

C

Cabbage butterfly, *see Pieris*
Carcinus, optomotor memory in, 50
Cat, spatial frequency perception in, 68
Change
  character of, 203

HANDBOOK OF PERCEPTION

EDITORS: *Edward C. Carterette and Morton P. Friedman*

Department of Psychology
University of California, Los Angeles
Los Angeles, California

Volume I: Historical and Philosophical Roots of Perception. 1974

Volume II: Psychophysical Judgment and Measurement. 1974

Volume III: Biology of Perceptual Systems. 1973

Volume IV: Hearing. 1978

Volume V: Seeing. 1975

Volume VIA: Tasting and Smelling. 1978

Volume VIB: Feeling and Hurting. 1978

Volume VII: Language and Speech. 1976

Volume VIII: Perceptual Coding. 1978

Volume IX: Perceptual Processing. 1978

Volume X: Perceptual Ecology. 1978

· · · · ·

CONTENTS OF OTHER VOLUMES